# SMALL FINDS AND ANCIENT SOCIAL PRACTICES IN THE NORTH-WEST PROVINCES OF THE ROMAN EMPIRE

# SMALL FINDS AND ANCIENT SOCIAL PRACTICES IN THE NORTH-WEST PROVINCES OF THE ROMAN EMPIRE

*Edited by*

STEFANIE HOSS & ALISSA WHITMORE

OXBOW | books

Oxford & Philadelphia

Published in the United Kingdom in 2016 by
OXBOW BOOKS
10 Hythe Bridge Street, Oxford OX1 2EW

and in the United States by
OXBOW BOOKS
1950 Lawrence Road, Havertown, PA 19083

Paperback Edition: ISBN 978-1-78570-256-3
Digital Edition: ISBN 978-1-78570-257-0 (epub)

A CIP record for this book is available from the British Library

Printed in Southampton by Hobbs the Printers Ltd

For a complete list of Oxbow titles, please contact:

UNITED KINGDOM
Oxbow Books
Telephone (01865) 241249, Fax (01865) 794449
Email: oxbow@oxbowbooks.com
www.oxbowbooks.com

UNITED STATES OF AMERICA
Oxbow Books
Telephone (800) 791-9354, Fax (610) 853-9146
Email: queries@casemateacademic.com
www.casemateacademic.com/oxbow

Oxbow Books is part of the Casemate Group

*Front cover:* Gladiator glass © The Vindolanda Trust; York *gorgoneion* (no. 7) © York Museums Trust, Yorkshire Museum; "R"-shaped brooch from from the harbor of Forum Hadriani, © Restaura.nl.

# Contents

# Introduction: Small finds and ancient social practices

## Stefanie Hoss and Alissa Whitmore

During the last 40 years, archaeological scholarship has become much more interested in the social activities that make up the experience of daily life in the Roman Empire. Whereas the built environment provides the setting for much of Roman daily life and can structure it by providing various facilities and constraints (Grahame 2000; Gardner 2007, 97–122), social practices can best be identified archaeologically by small finds. While architecture may indicate the intended purpose of a given space, finds convey its actual use and moreover can reveal the functions of spaces that are not architecturally framed. Variations in finds and artefact assemblages furthermore can also reflect differences in the origins, gender, wealth and standing of their owners and users, revealing important information about the social structure of a given society. As the complete body of scholarship on small finds, identity and social practices is too large to be adequately summarized here, this introduction aims to highlight research and key issues that were central to the formation of this volume.

## Archaeology, small finds and identity

Roman archaeology has long used artefacts to examine variations in ancient societies, but it has often concentrated on specific, isolated aspects of identity. Early scholarship often concentrated on social status and ethnic origin as the main features of identity in archaeological analyses. While small finds are still regularly used to reflect upon the lives and activities of the upper and lower classes (Pitts 2007, 696–697), scholars have moved beyond typical associations of gold and luxury objects with the wealthy, and more modest objects for the rest, and now grapple with the complex meanings that objects held and the differences in ancient life that they reflected and maintained. Baird's (2015) reanalysis of a Campanian slave's gold bracelet

'love gift', for instance, focuses on the archaeological and social contexts of the find to tease apart the multiple meanings, including disempowerment and subjugation, that the bracelet may have held for the woman who wore it. Branching out from wealth, other small finds studies have focused on additional social categories, most notably soldier and civilian status (Gardner 2007; Allison 2013).

Another large area of small finds studies and Roman social realities is ethnicity in its various forms (for a summary of this, see Eckardt 2014, 4–10). Within Roman provincial archaeology, ethnicity has long been governed by the dichotomy of 'Roman' versus 'indigenous', with the latter often being used as an envelope term encompassing both people living in a region before the advent of the Romans and those that came into this region after the Roman conquests as auxiliaries, traders or settlers.

Various scholars have illustrated ethnically diverse practices through small finds. Eckardt and Crummy (2008) have illustrated changes in grooming among local populations after the Roman introduction of toilet sets (bronze tweezers, nail cleaner and ear scoop) into Britain. Jewellery worn or interred as grave goods can also indicate ethnic identity, though caution and an awareness of circulation patterns is needed for such analyses (Cool 2010). Food habits have also provided a window onto the ethnic backgrounds of soldiers and others living in the provinces. Among auxiliaries, the preference for specific cooking pots was an important proof for the presence of ethnic units from Africa and Gaul in Britain (Cool 2006, 39–41; Swann 2009). Evidence for the Italic origin of a group living in the Northwestern provinces is often seen in the finds of imported Mediterranean delicacies such as olives, dates, grapes and fishy condiments like *garum,* or in cooking techniques such as the use of *mortaria* (Cool 2006, 42–43, 119–128).

But as ever, time and place play an important role here: food and drink habits can change and while olives may be an important indicator of *Romanitas* in 1st century Britain, the case is quite different in 3rd century Southern Gaul. This simple truth can also be observed in the realm of objects not connected to food and drink, where fashions and cultural assimilation lead to the use of *bricolage* – the wholesale appropriation of objects and practices from other cultures – and hybridisation – the mixing and matching of elements from different cultures into one entity to create a new style. Examples of *bricolage* include the incorporation of such items of dress as the Aucissa brooch from Italy or the ring belt buckle from the Sassanid empire into the dress of provincial Roman soldiers (Hoss 2015a; 2015b). Hybridisation is among other things visible in various brooch forms, including plate brooches in the form of a letter, like the example on the cover of this book depicting the letter R (perhaps an abbreviation for ROMA[1]): while writing was introduced to the provinces north of the Alps by the Romans, the use of letters as a brooch form and the spring mechanism closing the brooch are both characteristic for the provinces (Hoss 2015b, 144).

Gender has been a recurring theme in recent years, as scholars have sought to use small finds to gender various spaces and activities (Nevett 1999; Allison 2006a). The location of women within Roman military forts and barracks (van Driel Murray 1994; Allason-Jones 1999; Allison 2006b; 2013) is likely among the most intriguing and controversial of these small finds studies. As this area of research has developed, important critiques have been raised in two key areas which are worthy of consideration regardless of the identities or activities under study: the first concerns the methodologies for associating artefacts with people and activities and the second revolves around the archaeological contexts in which finds have been recovered.

## Methodologies for associating finds with activities and people

A key concern when interpreting the social function of artefacts is reconstructing how and by whom objects were used in the past. While the historical and iconographic records can offer some of these details, these sources only offer a small window onto the past, and one that is limited by the interests and bias of the ancient authors and artists which was rarely centred upon daily life, the lower classes, women, or life in the provinces.

In associating artefacts with activities, one of the biggest challenges is the distinct probability that many objects in antiquity were used for different tasks in different ways, and thus, a one-to-one correspondence between objects and activities may not be characteristic of the ancient world (Allison 2013, 42–45). This reality complicates the use of small finds to situate activities in ancient spaces. It is also distinctly possible that our preconceived functional artefact categories are too simplistic, an issue that seems readily apparent when thinking about the division between medical and toilet instruments. Laudable efforts have been made to typologically categorise tweezers into surgical and toilet categories based upon length and features of the jaws (Jackson 1986, 137–138). The discovery of surgical tweezers in four houses in Pompeii's Insula of the Menander, however, where they are found in domestic assemblages accompanied by inkwells, gaming counters, beads and lamps, may indicate that this functional division of tweezers into toilet and surgical categories was not recognised by the Romans (Allison 2009, 25–27).

While acknowledging the multifunctionality of objects is an important first step, the best way to deal with this in our analyses and interpretations of the past is still unclear. One approach has been to inclusively group artefacts into multiple categories which reflect all of their potential functional interpretations, based upon information provided in ancient texts and conclusions drawn from other archaeological contexts and small finds scholarship (Allison's 'fuzzy categories', 2013, 44–45, 65–108). By using Geographic Information Systems (GIS) programs to plot and manipulate finds categories, Allison has been able to plausibly situate various activities in Roman military spaces while accounting for the potential multipurpose use of many objects (Allison 2013, 281–343).

## Connecting artefacts and social identities

As one of the most common ways that societies organise themselves, gender is a frequently studied aspect of Roman identity, with small finds, especially dress accessories, playing a large role in these studies. While much of the discussion below deals with scholarship on gender, it is equally relevant and applicable to any facet of social identity.

Much research has been devoted to the subject of gender in Roman archaeology, specifically to problematizing and fine tuning previous, often less methodologically and theoretically rigorous, approaches to the study of gender in the past. Modern scholarship acknowledges that gender, or any other social category, cannot be studied in isolation, since one's identity is the sum of numerous, overlapping and intersecting social characteristics (Meskell 2007; Gardner 2007, 229–239; Geller 2009, 69–71; Cool 2010; Eckardt 2014, esp. 1–27).

A related critique of earlier scholarship is that undoubtedly, gender and other aspects of identity varied between Rome and the provinces and changed over time. The majority of our textual evidence on gender roles, for instance, stems from the capital. Given the geographic and temporal breadth of the empire, as well as the vast array of cultures that it contained, it seems improbable that gender ideologies and roles, especially the dress accessories which are so often used to examine gender and identity archaeologically, would be shared over time and space (Allason-Jones 1995; Carroll 2012, 288–299). It is therefore critical to take into account regional differences in how objects were used, and the many recent studies of Roman identities and dress accessories that focus on specific regions provide excellent resources for such an endeavour (Rothe 2009; 2013a; 2013b; Ivleva 2011; 2012; Carroll 2012; 2013; 2015).

As these and other critiques illustrate, strict associations between objects and a given social category are overly simplistic, but at the same time, small finds present a rich resource for scholars, since objects are used in the everyday performance of social identities (e.g. Gardner 2007, 203–206). This tension can be seen in a number of studies which both acknowledge the pitfalls of gendering objects, oftentimes by illustrating counterexamples for traditional gendered associations, and also attempt to isolate objects which can be more exclusively linked with one gender or another (van Driel Murray 1994; Allason-Jones 1995; Gardner 2007, 80, 230–231; Allison 2015).

This leaves scholars in a difficult position. If a counter-example for virtually every gender and object association can be produced, does this mean that the Romans had no "exclusive" gendered artefacts? And if we cannot definitely assign gender to objects and spaces, how can we study gender archaeologically? Such questions have been raised by archaeologists working in other cultures and time periods, and one of the most relevant critiques is that strict associations between objects and genders ignores the fluidity that gender may have had in the past (Conkey 1991; Dobres 1995; Crass 2001; Arnold 2002; Hollimon 2006; Geller 2009, 67–68). This concern is equally valid for classical scholars, since, in addition to changes in gender roles over time, the Romans may have recognized fluid and alternative genders including the *cinaedi, tribades* and eunuchs (cf. Monserrat 2000; Cool 2002, 41–42, Clarke 2005; Williams 2010; Conde Feitosa 2013; Eckardt 2014, 116; Rowlands 2014).

While the critiques of gender associations and artefacts should be taken into account, scholarship that doesn't link objects with specific identities is often severely limited in the conclusions that it can draw regarding social life in the past. An alternative approach is to use multiple sources and data sets, including ancient texts, iconography and grave goods found with anthropologically sexed skeletons, to create associations between artefacts and identities. Incorporating multiple sources can help to offset the biases and issues inherent in data sets, as well as potentially reveal patterns across different sources, which may be indicative of associations between objects and identities that would have been recognized by the Romans (c.f. Costin 1996; Hill

1998; Brumfiel 2006). Tailoring this to the Roman world, the previously mentioned studies of ethnicities, *bricolage* and hybridisation illustrate the need to consider the geographic and temporal contexts of artefacts and to recall that societies, their practices and the use and appearance of objects change over time. Accordingly, when creating links between objects, social practices and identities, local sources and datasets that are contemporary with the area under study should be favoured whenever possible, so that a more precise understanding of the gender norms at a given time and place can be obtained.

## Context, artefacts and behaviour

Another important critique regarding the use of finds to reconstruct social practices involves the identification and interpretation of artefact deposition and site formation processes. While this subject will be discussed in greater detail elsewhere (see Whitmore, this volume), it bears mention here as well, as context is one of the most important components of archaeological interpretation and can significantly impact our reconstructions of ancient social life.

The analysis and interpretation of the distributions of small finds in ancient spaces and buildings holds the potential to allow archaeologists to populate ancient spaces with people and activities and better understand how built structures were used. Such an approach, however, requires close attention to archaeological contexts and an understanding of how specific archaeological sites were formed, as only objects found in occupation or primary rubbish deposits can be used to reconstruct daily activities in a given space (c.f. Schiffer 1985). While Pompeii and other rapidly abandoned sites seemed to offer the promise of abundant occupation contexts, more nuanced approaches in recent years have illustrated the need to be even more critical in our interpretations of finds and contexts, both at Pompeii (e.g. Allison 1992; Dicus 2014) and in the provinces (e.g. Hodgson 2014).

Put simply, if the artefacts in any built space were introduced through means other than occupation – for instance, as part of a levelling layer or post-abandonment dump – these objects cannot be used to reconstruct the 'normal' use of these spaces. We cannot force the artefacts to tell the story that we want, but instead, must carefully interpret them, because regardless of their findspots, artefacts can reveal ancient behaviours. Objects recovered in construction and demolition contexts offer insights into Roman construction, recycling and waste management practices, while materials in squatting contexts reveal the activities of the homeless, a social group that is typically difficult to see in other archaeological contexts (c.f. Ault 2005; for more discussion and citations, see Whitmore, this volume).

## Social practices

Central to this volume is the assertion that ancient behaviour and activities leave physical patterns that are detectable in the archaeological record. A major difficulty in the use of finds in archaeology is the manner in which objects can be connected to activities or social practices. The main tools to achieve this are various archaeological theories of practice, many of which came into use parallel with the heightened interest in daily life from the 1980s onwards. Most of the theories used subsequently owe much to sociology and anthropology, but also other thinkers such as Marx, Heidegger and Wittgenstein (Gardner 2007, 39–51; 2008, 100). While there are many differences in the way specific theories approach matters like intention, reciprocal influences between humans and objects, and the relationships between practices and social structures, a common denominator is the focus on what people do, and how this shapes both the objects they use and the manner in which these objects become part of the archaeological record. It is not the aim of this introduction to summarize the numerous theories on the ways in which humans use objects and are influenced by them, as this field has grown very large in the last forty years and competent summaries are available elsewhere (Knappett 2014, 4700–4708; Beaudry & Hicks 2010; Taylor 2008). But as studies in this volume aim to use finds in order to research ancient behaviours and identities, it seems important to offer a definition of social practice.

A simple explanation is that ancient social practice is what people *did*. Social practices are people's habitual behaviours that are both informed and produced by individual human agency and wider social structures, as well as the means through which agency and social organisation are maintained (Gardner 2007, 19–20, 35–61; 2008, 96). Keeping in mind this dynamic relationship between social structure (which includes norms and the ways in which societies organise and rank their members) and social agents (individuals), we favour a balance between the determinism of an individual completely shaped by and forced to conform to his or her society and the individual governed by a wholly free will. While most individuals will inevitably fall slightly to the left or right of the perfect centre line between these two extremes, the main body of any population will be clustering around it.

Social practices then are actions taken by individuals conditioned by social norms, but with the ability to change these norms. From the wide palette of social practices, those that use objects and are habitual have the best chance of being recognizable through archaeology, as they leave patterns in architecture, urban layouts and the distributions of small finds, which scholars can analyse and interpret for information on ancient peoples and their societies (c.f. Gardner 2007, 63–122). It is the remains of such practices that are the focus of this volume.

## Discussion of the volume

The present volume originated in a session of the same name at the Theoretical Roman Archaeology Conference in Reading in 2014 and has been enhanced by additional TRAC/RAC conference papers and chapters solicited from other small finds scholars, many of them young and upcoming. Our goal for this session, as well as the present volume, is to highlight the unique information that critical approaches to small finds and artefacts can provide about life in the past. Contributors were encouraged to reflect upon the impacts that context and site formation processes have on artefact interpretation and to be as explicit as possible when linking finds with activities and social groups. A secondary intent was to showcase original research on activities that are underrepresented in current scholarship. Consequently, several papers focus on spaces or activities for which little information exists in texts or iconography. Other chapters integrate small finds and other types of ancient sources and in many cases juxtapose the different conclusions suggested by various types of evidence.

Uniting these papers is a focus on the material remains– most often, small finds, but also pottery, textiles, tiles and pigments – of social life in the Roman provinces. Geographically, chapters concentrate on the Northwest provinces, primarily Britannia and the *Germaniae*, but many integrate evidence from all over the empire. Three wider themes are also present in this volume: the body and identity, religion and the social use of space. Our first four papers focus on how clothing, accessories and make-up were used in the presentation of self and the projection of social identity. Burandt offers a typology of Roman hobnailed shoes, relating different types of shoes to people of varying social statuses, while Köstner explores the evidence for Roman socks and the various ways in which they were worn. Michel provides a comprehensive look at the archaeological evidence for the use of make-up by Roman women throughout the empire. Hoss analyses iconographic evidence to prove that plate brooches, objects commonly associated with women in modern scholarship, were also part of high status military wear.

The next set of chapters focuses on religion in the Northwest provinces. Vejby's paper explores the functions of objects commonly recovered in Roman votive deposits from Brittany and the Roman (re)use of Neolithic megaliths in their religious practices. Birkle analyses an assemblage of unique votive plaques found in Weissenburg, Bavaria, which depict Roman deities with mixed, incongruous physical attributes, including the titular Mars with breasts. Durham examines Romano-British bronze figurines of deities, which offer insights into local religious practices as well as the spread of Eastern religions into Britain. Parker's contribution uses jet *gorgoneia* pendants to explore the embodiment of protective magic in Roman Britain.

Transitioning between religion and social spaces, Klenner's chapter analyses ceramic assemblages to examine eating and drinking habits in Roman *mithraea*, a religious space and practice upon which ancient texts remain largely silent, as would be expected for a mystery religion. Whitmore examines archaeological site formation processes to evaluate the possible origins and meanings of cloth working instruments recovered in Roman bathhouses. Lastly, Birley's contribution uses artefact distributions to dismantle the alleged spatial and social boundary between Vindolanda's military fort and *vicus* and argue for their integration into a single community.

This book consists of the contributions of many different people, all of whom we owe a debt of gratitude. First and foremost the authors, who trusted us with the publication (and sometimes translation) of their papers and were patient with our editorial suggestions. We are very grateful to Restaura NL, the Vindolanda Trust, and the York Museums Trust for allowing us to use their object photos on our cover. Large thanks are also due to our editors at Oxbow, who were not put out by the changes that this volume underwent nor by the unavoidable delays that characterize finishing a book. And lastly, we would like to thank our friends and relations, who shared us for much too long with this book, were understanding and supportive when things got sticky, and duly celebratory when it was finished.

We hope that the contents of this book will stimulate discussion among small find specialists, spark interest in small finds for non-specialists and generally contribute to the knowledge about social life in the Roman world.

Stefanie Hoss and Alissa Whitmore
Cologne and Des Moines, October 2015

## *Note*

1    The brooch is from recent excavations in Forum Hadriani, now Voorburg near The Hague/NL (Hoss 2014, fig. II-5.8). Image provided courtesy of Restaura.nl.

## Bibliography

Allason-Jones, L. (1995) 'Sexing' small finds. In P. Rush (ed.) *Theoretical Roman Archaeology: Second Conference Proceedings*, 22–32. Aldershot, Avebury.

Allason-Jones, L. (1999) Women and the Roman army in Britain. In A. Goldsworthy & I. Haynes (eds) *The Roman Army as a Community*, 41–51. Journal of Roman Archaeology Supplementary Series 34. Portsmouth, Journal of Roman Archaeology.

Allison, P. M. (1992) Artefact assemblages: not the 'Pompeii Premise.' In E. Herring, R. Whitehouse & J. Wilkins (eds) *Papers of the Fourth Conference of Italian Archaeology 3: new developments in Italian archaeology*, 49–56. London, Accordia Research Centre.

Allison, P. M. (2006a) Engendering Roman Spaces. In E. C. Robertson, J. D. Seibert, D. C. Fernandez & M. U. Zender (eds) *Space and Spatial Analysis in Archaeology*, 343–354. Calgary, University of Calgary Press.

Allison, P. M. (2006b) Mapping for gender. Interpreting artefact distribution inside 1st and 2nd century AD forts in Roman Germany. *Archaeological Dialogues* 13(1), 1–20.

Allison, P. M. (2009) Understanding Pompeian Households Practices through their Material Culture. *FACTA* 3, 11–33.

Allison, P. M. (2013) *People and Spaces in Roman Military Bases*. Cambridge, Cambridge University Press.

Allison, P. M. (2015) Characterizing Roman artifacts to investigate gendered practices in contexts without sexed bodies. *American Journal of Archaeology* 119(1), 103–123.

Arnold, B. (2002) Sein und Werden: gender as process in mortuary ritual. In S. M. Nelson & M. Rosen-Ayalon (eds) *In Pursuit of Gender: worldwide archaeological approaches*, 239–256. Walnut Creek, Altamira Press.

Ault, B. A. (2005) Housing the poor and homeless in Ancient Greece. In B. A. Ault & L. C. Nevett (eds) *Ancient Greek Houses and Households: chronological, regional, and social diversity*, 140–159. Philadelphia, University of Pennsylvania Press.

Baird, J. A. (2015) On reading the material culture of ancient sexual labor. *HELIOS* 42(1), 163–175.

Beaudry, M. C. & Hicks, D. (2010) *The Oxford Handbook of Material Culture Studies*. Oxford, Oxford University Press.

Brumfiel, E. M. (2006) Methods in feminist and gender archaeology: a feeling for difference – and likeness. In S. M. Nelson (ed.) *Handbook of Gender in Archaeology*, 31–58. New York, Altamira Press.

Carroll, M. (2012) The insignia of women: dress, gender and identity on the Roman funerary monument of Regina from Arbeia. *Archaeological Journal* 169, 281–311.

Carroll, M. (2013) Ethnische Tracht und römische Kleidung am Niederrhein. In A. Wieczorek, R. Schulz & M. Tellenbach (eds) *Die Macht der Toga – Mode im römischen Weltreich*, 223–228. Exhibition Roemer und Pelizaeusmuseum Hildesheim. Regensburg, Schnell & Steiner.

Carroll, M. (2015) Projecting self-perception on the Roman frontiers: The evidence of dress and funerary portraits. In D. J. Breeze, R. H. Jones & I. A. Oltean (eds) *Understanding Roman Frontiers. Papers Offered to Professor Bill Hanson on the Occasion of his Retirement*, 154–166. Edinburgh, John Donald.

Clarke, J. (2005) Representations of the Cinaedus in Roman art: evidence of "gay" subculture? *Journal of Homosexuality* 49(3), 271–298.

Conde Feitosa, L. (2013) *The Archaeology of Gender, Love and Sexuality in Pompeii*. British Archaeological Report S2533. Oxford, Archaeopress.

Conkey, M. W. (1991) Contexts of action, contexts for power: material culture and gender in the Magdalenian. In J. M. Gero & M. W. Conkey (eds) *Engendering Archaeology: Women and Prehistory*, 57–92. Oxford, Blackwell.

Cool, H. E. M. (2002) An overview of the small finds from Catterick. In P. R. Wilson, *Cataractonium: Roman Catterick and its Hinterland. Excavations and Research, 1958–1997. Part II*, 24–43. York, English Heritage & Council for British Archaeology.

Cool, H. E. M. (2006) *Eating and Drinking in Roman Britain.* Cambridge, Cambridge University Press.

Cool, H. E. M. (2010) Finding the foreigners. In H. Eckardt (ed.) *Roman Diasporas*, 27–44. Journal of Roman Archaeology Supplementary Series 78. Portsmouth, Journal of Roman Archaeology.

Costin, C. L. (1996) Exploring the relationship between gender and craft in complex societies: methodological and theoretical issues of gender attribution. In R. P. Wright (ed.) *Gender and Archaeology*, 111–140. Philadelphia, University of Pennsylvania Press.

Crass, B. A. (2001) Gender and mortuary analysis: what can grave goods really tell us? In B. Arnold & N. L. Wicker (eds) *Gender and the Archaeology of Death*, 105–118. Walnut Creek, Altamira Press.

Dicus, K. (2014) Resurrecting refuse at Pompeii: the use-value of urban refuse and its implications for interpreting archaeological assemblages. In H. Platts, J. Pearce, C. Barron, J. Lundock & J. Yoo (eds) *TRAC 2013: Proceedings of the 23rd Theoretical Roman Archaeology Conference*, 65–78. Oxford, Oxbow Books.

Dobres, M. A. (1995) Beyond gender attribution: some methodological issues for engendering the past. In J. Balme & W. Beck (eds) *Gendered Archaeology*, 51–66. Canberra, Australian National University.

Eckardt, H. & Crummy, N. (2008) *Styling the Body in Late Iron Age and Roman Britain. A Contextual Approach to Toilet Instruments*. Montagnac, Editions Margeuil.

Eckardt, H. (2014) *Objects and Identities in Roman Britain and the North-Western Provinces*. Oxford, Oxford University Press.

Gardner, A. (2007) *An Archaeology of Identity: Soldiers and Society in Late Roman Britain*. Walnut Creek, Left Coast Press.

Gardner, A. (2008) Agency. In R. A. Bentely, H. D. G. Maschner & C. Chippindale (eds) *Handbook of Archaeological Theory*, 95–108. Lanham, Altamira.

Geller, P. L. (2009) Identity and difference: complicating gender in archaeology. *Annual Review of Anthropology* 38, 65–81.

Grahame, M. (2000) *Reading Space: Social Interaction and Identity in the Houses of Roman Pompeii*. British Archaeological Report S886. Oxford, Archaeopress.

Hill, E. (1998) Gender-informed archaeology: the priority of definition, the use of analogy, and the multivariate approach. *Journal of Archaeological Method and Theory* 5(1), 99–128.

Hodgson, N. (2014) The accommodation of soldiers' wives in Roman fort barracks – on Hadrian's Wall and beyond. In R. Collins & F. McIntosh (eds) *Life in the Limes: Studies of the People and Objects of the Roman Frontiers*, 18–28. Oxford, Oxbow Books.

Hollimon, S. E. (2006) The archaeology of nonbinary genders in Native North American Societies. In S. M. Nelson (ed.) *Handbook of Gender in Archaeology*, 435–450. New York, Altamira Press.

Hoss, S. (2014) Metal. In M. J. Driessen, E. Besselsen (eds), *Voorburg-Arentsburg: Een Romeinse havenstad tussen Rijn en Maas*, Themata 7, 613–677. Amsterdam, University of Amsterdam Press.

Hoss, S. (2015a) The origin of the ring buckle belt and the Persian wars of the 3rd century. In L. Vagalinski & N. Sharankov (eds) *Limes XXII*. (Bulletin of the National Archaeological Institute 42, 2015), 319–326. Sofia, NIAM-BAS.

Hoss, S. (2015b) Frontier finds – military fashions. In D. J. Breeze, R. H. Jones & I. A. Olteanu (eds) *Understanding Roman Frontiers. Papers Offered to Professor Bill Hanson on the Occasion of his Retirement*, 135–153. Edinburgh, John Donald.

Ivleva, T. (2011) Brooches tell tales: British-made brooches in Germania Inferior and Superior as indicators of the presence of British emigrants. In K. Huijben, S. J. A. G. van de Liefvoort & T. J. S. M. van der Weyden (eds) *SOJA Bundel 2010, Radboud Universiteit Nijmegen*, 51–56. Nijmegen, Boxpress.

Ivleva, T. (2012) Britons Abroad: the Mobility of Britons and the Circulation of British-made objects in the Roman Empire. Unpublished PhD thesis, Leiden University (NL).

Jackson, R. (1986) A set of Roman medical instruments from Italy. *Britannia* 17, 119–167.

Knappett, C. (2014) Materiality in archaeological theory. In C. Smith (ed.) *Encyclopedia of Global Archaeology*, 4700–4708. New York, Springer.

Meskell, L. (2007) Archaeologies of Identity. In T. Insoll (ed.) *The Archaeology of Identities: A Reader*, 23–43. New York, Routledge.

Monserrat, D. (2000) Reading gender in the Roman world. In J. Huskinson (ed.) *Experiencing Rome: Culture, Identity, and Power in the Roman Empire*, 153–181. New York, Routledge.

Nevett, L. (1999) *House and Society in the Ancient Greek World*. Cambridge, Cambridge University Press.

Pitts, M. (2007) The Emperor's New Clothes? The utility of identity in Roman archaeology. *American Journal of Archaeology* 111, 693–713.

Rothe, U. (2009) *Dress and Cultural Identity in the Rhine-Moselle Region of the Roman Empire*. British Archaeological Report S2038. Oxford, Archaeopress.

Rothe, U. (2013a) Die norisch-pannonische Tracht: gab es sie wirklich? In G. Grabherr, B. Kainarth & T. Schierl (eds) *Relations Abroad? Brooches and Other Elements of Dress as Sources for Reconstructing Interregional Movement and Group Boundaries from the Punic Wars to the Decline of the Western Empire*, 33–48. IKARUS Band 8. Innsbruck, Innsbruck University Press.

Rothe, U. (2013b) Whose fashion? Men, women and Roman culture as reflected in dress in the cities of the Roman north-west. In E. Hemelrijk & G. Woolf (eds) *Women and the Roman City in the Latin West*, 243–268. Mnemosyne Supplements, History and Archaeology of Classical Antiquity (360). Leiden, Brill.

Rowlands, R. M. (2014) Eunuchs and Sex: Beyond Sexual Dichotomy in the Roman World. Unpublished PhD thesis, University of Missouri-Columbia.

Schiffer, M. (1985) Is there a "Pompeii Premise" in archaeology? *Journal of Anthropological Research* 41(1), 18–41.

Swann, V. (2009) *Ethnicity, conquest and recruitment*. Journal of Roman Archaeology Supplementary Series 72. Portsmouth, JRA.

Taylor, T. (2008) Materiality. In R. A. Bentely, H. D. G. Maschner & C. Chippindale (eds) *Handbook of Archaeological Theory*, 297–320. Lanham, Altamira.

Van Driel Murray, C. (1994) A question of gender in a military context. *Helinium* 34(2), 342–362.

Williams, C. A. (2010) *Roman Homosexuality*. Oxford, Oxford University Press.

# Part 1

# Small finds, the body and identity

# Iron footed – hobnail patterns under Roman shoes and their functional meaning

## Boris Burandt

*Keywords*: Roman; Shoes; Hobnails; Shoe nails; Hobnail patterns; Leather; Ancient Fashion; Ancient Workspace

*In Roman antiquity, there was a close connection between the form of a shoe and the pattern for the hobnails on its sole. While this seems obvious at first glance, this paper is nevertheless the first study to investigate the connection between imperial Roman hobnail patterns and the basic shoe-forms they appear on. In addition, the connection between the form of the shoe, the hobnail pattern and their use will be examined, as the intended use of a shoe had a strong influence on its shape and especially on the construction of its sole. Heavy working boots giving extra traction on difficult terrain can thus easily be distinguished from comfy slippers meant for an easy stroll. As a consequence, the preserved hobnails of a Roman shoe sole can give us a lot of information about the whole shoe, even when the leather of the shoe is lost.*

## Introduction

It has been common knowledge in archaeology for many years that the soles of Roman shoes during the Imperial period were nailed and several authors have already published on the nailing patterns of Roman shoes (see below). But these studies have so far been focused on the finds from a single site and defined their respective types on this fairly small dataset. Also interesting is the fact that these typologies have been exclusively based on the arrangement of the nails on the sole itself, disregarding the rest of the shoe. Accordingly, previous studies on this topic deal with the chronological or regional aspects of hobnail patterns. This is certainly also due to the fact that shoe soles with nailing patterns have survived the ages in larger numbers than the leather of the upper part (either upper or the vamp). So a new analysis of Roman hobnail patterns combined with the preserved parts of the leather of Roman shoes can offer new insights.

## Typology

There seems to exist a logical connection between certain hobnail patterns, different shapes of shoes and the actual use of these shoes in ancient daily routine. The following typology should make it possible to not only name the practical application field of a shoe, but also to offer a cautious hypothesis on the shoe's original shape, even when the leather of the upper is missing. This also applies to the numerous Roman footprints preserved on bricks, in cement or otherwise. The present article is limited to finds of the 1st–3rd century AD in the North-Western provinces of the Roman empire, mainly Britain and the two *Germaniae*.

Typologies of Roman hobnail patterns were developed by three authors: C. van Driel-Murray (1983, 20–22), T. G. Padley (1989, 2–5) and Q. Mould (1997, 331–335). The finds from Bonn (DE) were the basis for the classification by van Driel-Murray. Her typology is mainly based on the circumferential row of nails next to the edge of the sole

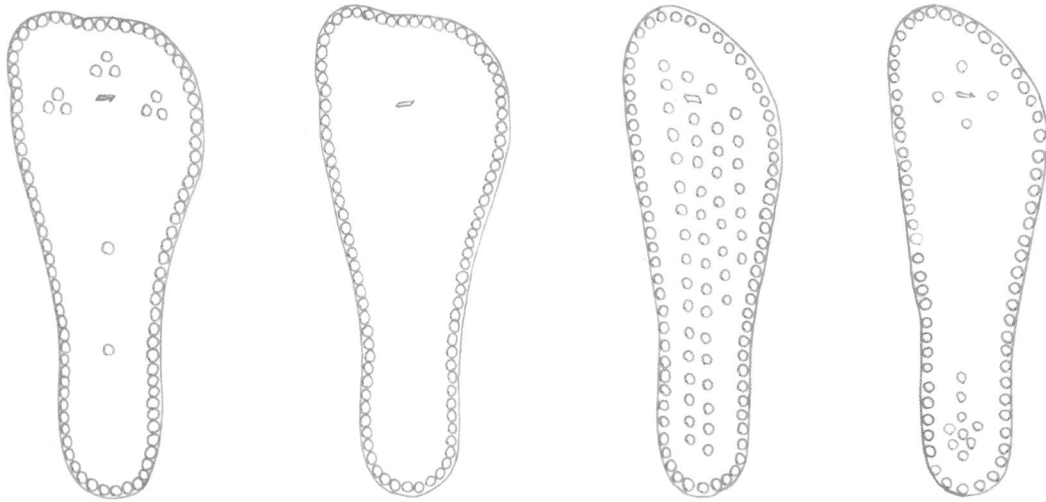

*Hobnail pattern A*

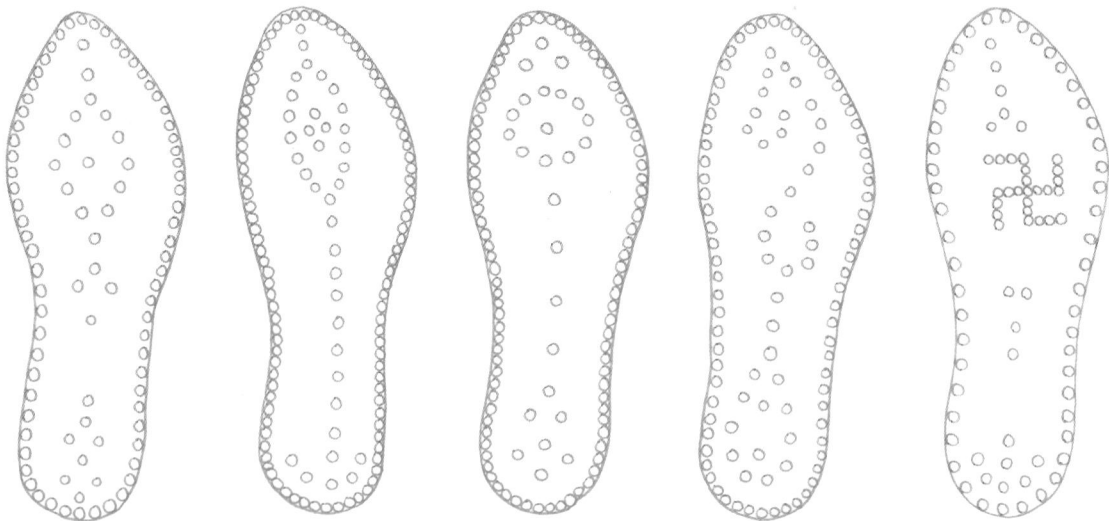

*Hobnail pattern B*

and distinguishes three variants, namely soles with one continuous row of nails, soles with two parallel rows of nails and soles with a continuous outer row and a second inner row of nails which is interrupted under the instep. However, the inner structure of the nail pattern, such as decorative motifs or more nails scattered across the middle, is ignored here. Padley's typology was formulated on the basis of the Roman shoes of Carlisle, and largely coincides with these categories. Mould's typology was developed for the finds from Birdoswald and is more concerned with the inner structure of the nailing pattern than with the outer row of nails. Mould distinguishes shoe soles with a decorative pattern into three categories: soles with a relatively small number of nails (type A), soles with an extensive, but loose nailing pattern (type B) and soles with an extensive and close nailing pattern (type C). Looking at the finds from different parts of the Roman Empire, Mould's typology seems to be the most convincing solution, as it not only includes shoes from military contexts, but also from civilian ones. Hence, the

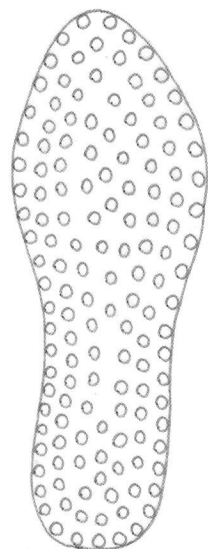

*Hobnail pattern C*          *Hobnail pattern D*

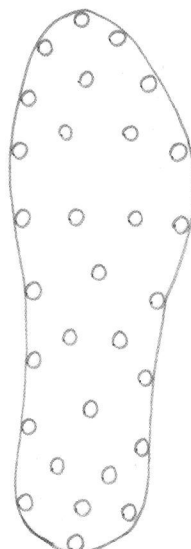

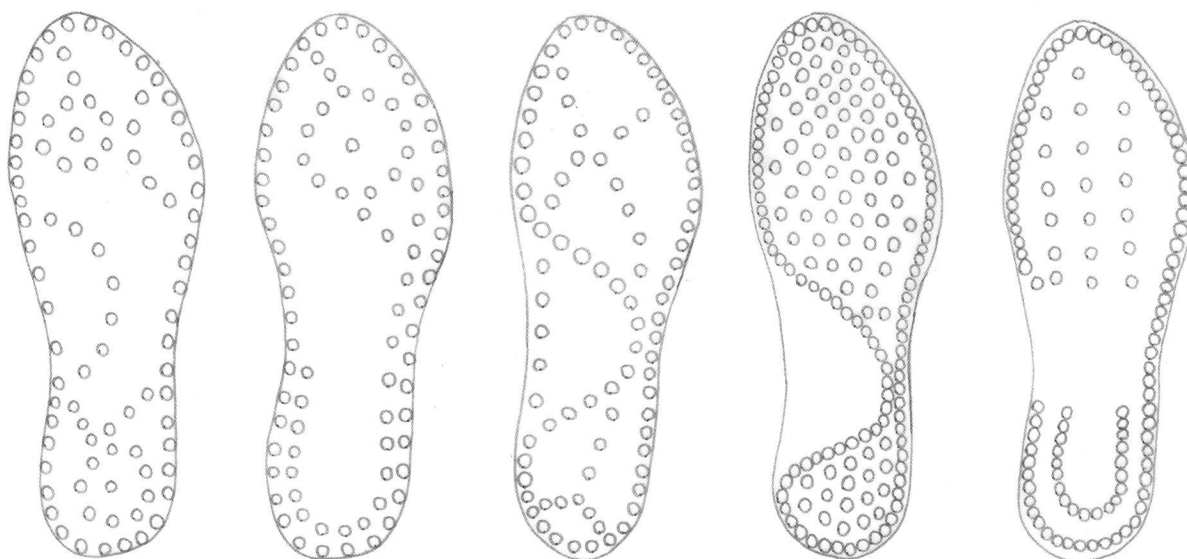

*Hobnail pattern E*

Fig. 2.1: Typology of Roman hobnail patterns (drawing: B. A. Burandt)

basic principle of Mould's categorisation will be borrowed for this article, but because of the greater amount of material considered here and a different research focus, certain modifications are necessary.

In addition to the finds from the Bonnerberg in Bonn (DE), Carlisle and Birdoswald (both UK), which formed the basis of the aforementioned articles, the finds from Mainz (DE), Valkenburg (NL), Zugmantel, Kleiner Feldberg and the Saalburg (all DE) will be included in this study. Based on

these finds, I would like to distinguish five basic categories of hobnail patterns (Fig. 2.1), used for five different basic shapes of footwear (Fig. 2.2).

## Hobnail patterns

*Pattern A:* A single, more or less continuous row of nails, which runs along the outer edge of the sole, with very little or no internal nailing.

*Pattern B:*   A single, more or less continuous row of
          nails, which accompanies the outer edge of
          the sole, with decorative internal nailing with
          a relatively small number of nails.
*Pattern C:*   A large number of nails scattered over the whole
          sole area.
*Pattern D:*   A small number of nails scattered over the
          whole sole area.
*Pattern E:*   A large number of nails, but with a clear
          emphasis on the ball and the heel.

## *Shoe forms*

*Form I:*    Sandals (*solae*) – essentially just a leather sole
          with toe straps.
*Form II:*   Closed shoes (*carbatinae*) – an ankle-high,
          mostly closed leather shoe with attached sole.
*Form III:*  Open shoes (*carbatinae?*) – an ankle-high
          leather shoe with an open construction, in
          which the leather is cut away as much as
          possible. It is similar to the military *caliga*, but
          ends at the ankle.
*Form IV:*   Closed boots (*calcei*) – a leather boot with a
          mostly or completely closed structure, reaching
          over the ankle.
*Form V:*    Open boots (*cailgae*) – a leather boot of open
          structure and reaching over the ankle, with the
          leather cut away in large parts of the vamp (the
          upper part of the shoe that sits over the instep)
          for ventilation and to reduce friction.

Purely logical considerations suggest that persons doing heavy work in rough terrain would have to rely on shoes with maximum slip resistance and traction. These groups include soldiers, but also waggoners, farmers or men pulling barges and other ships along the rivers. All of them would have insisted on shoes with a relatively dense nailing pattern, offering enough grip even in wet conditions and on poor soil.

For the more sedentary artisans forming the majority of the Roman population, and for the urban upper classes, these aspects were less important, as they mostly remained in their houses or workshops or used the well-maintained roads in or between Roman settlements – instead of walking for long stretches through rough country. The nailing of their shoes served mainly to protect the leather, for which a significantly lower number of nails is required. It seems that aspects of fashion also played a greater role here, which explains the more decorative hobnail patterns on these shoes. No hobnails are needed for the open sandals (shoe form I) of the Imperial period. Their very open design does not guarantee a secure grip for the wearer's foot anyway, so any nails on this form are presumably just a protection for the leather of the sole.

## The finds

If we look at the finds after these basic considerations, it quickly becomes obvious that the nailing patterns preserved on Roman shoes and as prints on other materials fit these requirements. Among the finds from the camps and *vici* of places like Zugmantel, Kleiner Feldberg and Saalburg presented by A. L. Busch (1965, 158–210), there is a wide spectrum of Roman footwear, from children's shoes to slippers or heavy soldiers' boots, all dating to the 2nd or 3rd century AD. Due to the soil conditions at these sites, a large number of shoes were preserved with their uppers, vamps and soles more or less intact, so that it is possible to detect the combination of certain hobnail patterns with specific forms of shoes.

Cat. Nos 123–126 and 129–132 (Busch 1965, tab. 6: unless stated otherwise cat. nos in text refer to Busch 1965) must have been designed as sandals, recognisable by the hole for the toe straps. The toe strap of cat. no. 122 is completely preserved (Busch 1965, tab. 6). Among the finds, the shoes cat. nos 122–124, 126 and 130 undoubtedly show evidence of having been nailed (Busch 1965, tab. 6). While the nails themselves became a victim of corrosion, the holes and imprints of the nail heads are clearly visible on the soles. In four instances, the nailing is limited to a single row of nails, which runs along the edge of the sole. The only exception is No. 123 (Busch 1965, tab. 6), which has three nails located just behind the hole for the toe strap, forming a trefoil and providing a minimal internal pattern. This nail pattern is consistent with category A, confirming the hypothesis that a loose-fitting sandal hardly requires any nails. The finds of Roman *solae* from Birdoswald presented by Q. Mould (1997, 337, fig. 245) and the sandals from Mainz compiled by J. Goepfrich (1986, 50, fig. 48) indicate the same. Some of them have three or four trefoils of hobnails next to the hole for the straps. On some of the Mainz finds, a nail pattern in the form of an arrow or a lozenge under the ball of the foot can be observed, and a single find of a *sola* has four parallel rows of nails over the entire surface of the sole. Because these last three variations are singular discoveries, they can be regarded as exceptions. The majority of the sandals at this site also have soles with only one row of nails running along the edge of the sole. This proves that the practical requirements for sandals are small: The sole has to provide a minimum of traction and is mainly designed to protect the feet from street filth and sharp stones.

All those shoes presented by Busch that can be called *carbatinae* (Busch 1965, tab. 6, cat. nos 210–222, 282) show a nailing pattern with a single, continuous row of nails along the edge and a decorative element on the sole. The element is formed by a central row of nails following the sole's longitudinal axis and swelling to a lozenge-like motif under the ball of the foot. Inside this lozenge either a single nail or the trefoil already known from the *solae*

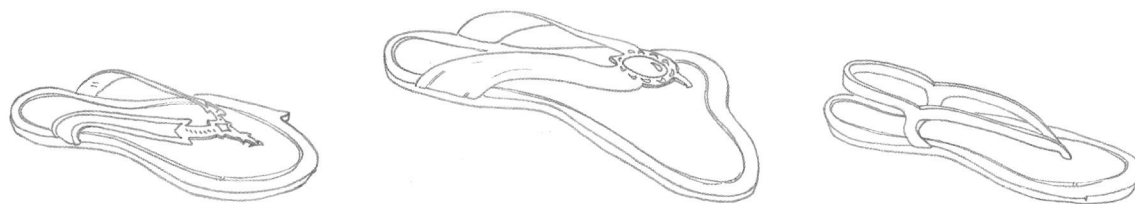

*Shoe form I*

*Shoe form II*

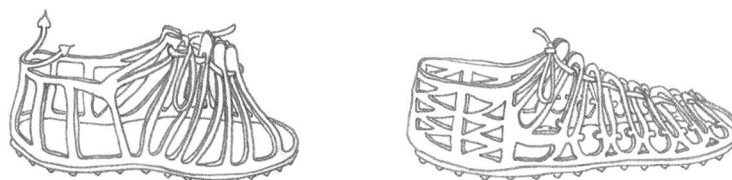

*Shoe form III*

*Shoe form IV*

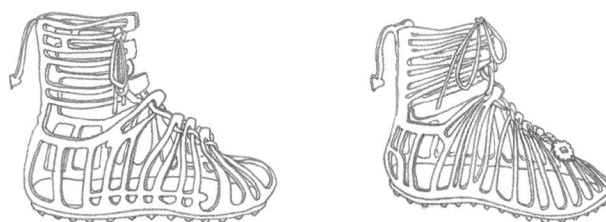

*Shoe form V*

*Fig. 2.2: Typology of Roman shoes (drawing: B. A. Burandt)*

can be observed, making this ornamental element resemble
an eye and so adding an apotropaic symbol to the shoe.
This pattern, which only uses a relatively small number of
nails (about 75–85 per sole), can therefore be assigned to
category B. It protects the sole against abrasion along its
entire length, gives the wearer a minimum level of grip and
at the same time fulfils a decorative function. The preserved
leather uppers of those soles all belong to the shoe form II,
as they seem to be relatively closed.

Two shoes excavated in Birdoswald, which also are
closed *carbatinae*, show a nailing pattern with significantly
more nails (Mould 1997, 330, fig. 239, cat. nos 7–8.), fitting
the hobnail pattern E. In addition to the row of nails that
runs along the edge, there are two interlocking rows of nails
forming an oval shape at the heel and the ball of the foot.
Although a large part of the heel of cat. no. 8 is missing,
the sole of cat. no. 7 has 130 nails and the sole of cat. no.
8 has 71 nails. We can thus cautiously reconstruct a total
number of about 150 and 100 nails respectively for these
shoes, which is well above the figures for hobnail patterns
of *carbatinae* from the Taunus area.

If one does not want to explain this inconsistency with the
famous exception that proves the rule, it could be explained
with a wearer whose work demanded more traction from a
shoe. But the short height of the upper and the decorative
design of the vamp speak against this theory. So it seems
to be indeed a regional feature that should not be taken as
the norm.

No *carbatinae* of shoe form II with a preserved nailing
pattern have been published from Mainz and Valkenburg.
However, there are two *carbatinae* from Mainz which
belong to shoe form III (Goepfrich 1986, 31, fig. 37, cat.
nos 27–28), because they have an open construction of the
vamp and an upper that ends below the ankle. Both clearly
show the holes of the nailing pattern with a continuous
row of nails along the edge of the sole and more widely
spaced nails distributed in a wide arc over the area under
the heel and ball of the foot. The area under the instep
remained free of nails. The pattern corresponds to category
E. As already indicated briefly in the definition of the shoe
forms, the upper and vamp of those finds are very close
to the military *caligae*, but in contrast to them, they end
below the ankle.

One of the reliefs of the 2nd century AD 'Negotiator'
pillar from Neumagen on the Moselle shows a man
towing or hauling a barge transporting wine barrels
(Goepfrich 1986, 19, fig. 23). Here, one can clearly see
a shoe whose construction perfectly matches that of the
finds from Mainz. This type of shoe can therefore be
assumed to have been used by civilians, who had to do
hard physical labour on rough country and relied on good
traction. This confirms the theory formulated above on
the relationship between the shoe's nailing pattern, its
use and the owner's work.

There are several examples of nailed shoes of the
form IV from Mainz, Zugmantel and the Saalburg dating
to the 1st to the early 3rd century AD, with the patterns
belonging almost exclusively to category B. The patterns
are composed of a continuous row of nails along the edge
of the sole with a central line over the whole length of the
sole. Under the ball of the foot is a decorative motif, which
forms a 'S' in most cases, but can also be replaced by
three trefoils, a lozenge or a swastika. The only exception
to this pattern is a boot dating to the 1st century AD from
Mainz, whose hobnail pattern corresponds to category E.
This might be an indication of a change in fashion from
the 1st–2nd century AD.

While the closed boots of the Early Imperial period have
a nailing pattern identical to that of military boots (discussed
below), in the 2nd century the pattern has significantly
less nails.

Four military *caligae* – open boots of shoe form V – with
a recognisable hobnail pattern were excavated in Valkenburg
(Groenman-van Waateringe 1967, 130–146, cat. nos 4, 18,
30, 90) and 11 in Mainz (Goepfrich 1986, 26–30, fig. 35 a.
36, cat. nos 1–3, 814, 20), all displaying hobnail pattern E.
It is significant that all soles show nailing under both the
heel and ball of the foot, but not under the instep. Here, the
ball and heel are clearly supported, comparable to modern
sports shoes, where the heel and ball of the foot is also
specially supported, while the instep is left unprotected.
The consequent use of these patterns in the military context
indicates that it must have been a perfect solution, offering
adequate support for soldiers. The motifs used on the heels
and balls of the foot know a great variation, with nailed
circles with central single nail occurring just like crosses,
Y-symbols, parallel lines or a dense mass of nails with no
apparent order.

There are some sporadic finds of soles that are completely
nailed, with nail bordering nail (category C) in the
archaeological material of the North-Western provinces. One
find of that kind was excavated in Vechten (Groenman-van
Waateringe 1967, 139, fig. 51), but it is an exceptional find
that is difficult to relate to a specific type of shoe. The high
number of nails used and the find location suggest a use in
the military context, and consequently a *caliga* as shoe form.

The situation is similar with hobnail category D: Finds
with nailing patterns of this type come from Birdoswald
(Mould 1997, 335, fig. 243). They seem to be a phenomenon
of the late 3rd century and Late Antiquity and could be a
result of the increasing shortage of materials in the Roman
Empire during this period. Apparently they show the attempt
to save iron without limiting the practical utility of the shoe.
On the basis of the occurrence of this pattern and the military
use of the locality, this category may have belonged to the
military sector as well. Due to the typological development
of shoes in the Roman army, a closed boot of form IV could
be reconstructed here.

## Conclusion

As I have shown, the following can be said: a nailed sole found isolated from its upper and vamp or an imprint of a hobnailed sole in another material can still impart some information about the type of shoe it used to belong to and the kind of work performed by its former wearer. While one has to be cautious with this approach, it seems possible to relate hobnail patters with shoe forms.

Thus the hobnail pattern A corresponds with shoe form I, that is, *solae* in the broadest sense. Category B indicates shoe form IV, but shoe form II appears with this pattern as well. Categories C and D are exceptionally rare in the find material. However, category C is most likely connected with shoe form V and category D with shoe form IV. Category E can be found in connection with shoes of form III and V.

In addition, it can be stated that closed *carbatinae* of form II are the hardest to determine, as they show a high variance in their hobnail patterns. In many cases they were carried out completely without attached sole and nailing. However, they also are the chronological least sensitive shoe shape of the Roman period, being worn by civilians of very different professions and very different ranks, which might explain why they have a higher variance of hobnail patterns.

The different demands of life in the Roman provinces for soldiers, barge haulers, artisans and upper class *equites* determined the demands that were made of their footwear, which in turn determined hobnail patterns. This tangible relationship between the practical use of the shoe and its hobnail pattern is significant for all shoe forms presented here.

## Bibliography

Busch, A. L. (1965) Die roemischen Schuh- und Lederfunde der Kastelle Saalburg, Zugmantel und Kleiner Feldberg. *Saalburg Jahrbuch* 22, 158–210.

Forrer, R. (1942) *Archaeologisches zur Geschichte des Schuhes aller Zeiten*. Schönenwerd, Publications of the Bally-Schoemuseum.

Groenman-van Waateringe, W. (1967) *Romeins lederwerk uit Valkenburg Z.H.* Groningen, Wolters.

Göpfrich, J. (1986) Roemische Lederfunde aus Mainz. *Saalburg Jahrbuch* 42, 5–67.

Lau, O. (1967) *Schuster und Schusterhandwerk in der griechisch-roemischen Literatur und Kunst*. Bonn/Essen, Vela-Rohde KG.

Marschalleck, K. H. (1959) *Roemisches Schuhwerk an Rhein- und Scheldemuendung, mit einer Zusammenstellung provinzialroemischer Schuh- und anderer Lederfunde*, 249–273. Amersfoort, Berichten van de Rijksdienst voor het oudheidkundig bodemonderzoek (ROB) 9.

Mould, Q. (1997) Leather. In T. Wilmott (ed.) *Birdoswald, Excavations of a Roman Fort on Hadrian's Wall and its Successor Settlements: 1987–1992*, 326–341. London, English Heritage.

Padley, T. G. (1989) The leather shoes from Castle Street, Carlisle. *Archaeological Leather Group Newsletter* 6, 2–5.

Rhodes, M. (1980) Leather footwear. In D. M. Jones (ed.), *Excavations at Billingsgate Buildings 'Triangle' Lower Thames Street 1974*, 99–128. London, Middlesex Archaeological Society Special Paper 4.

van Driel-Murray, C. & Gechter, M. (1984) Funde aus der fabrica der legio I Minervia am Bonner Berg. *Beitraege zur Archaeologie des Rheinlandes* 4, 1–83.

von Massow, W. (1932) *Roemische Grabmaeler des Mosellandes und der angrenzenden Gebiete II. Die Grabmaeler von Neumagen*. Berlin/Leipzig, de Gruyter.

# 3

# Wearing socks in sandals: The height of Roman fashion?

## Barbara Köstner

*Keywords:* Roman; textiles; clothing; sock; footwear; nålbinding; textile techniques

*Roman socks are mentioned in ancient literature and letters and shown in various depictions and we even have some original textiles. The depictions and the textiles show two types of socks: Socks for closed shoes and boots, with no division of the toe, and another group with split toes to fit soleae, thong sandals.*

*Socks for closed shoes found in the North-Western provinces of the Roman Empire were sewn from cloth, but only few examples survive.*

*Evidence of Romans wearing socks in sandals in the North-Western provinces can be found in the depictions of men and women wearing socks in soleae from 2nd–3rd centuries AD. These show technical features like rolled hems and an overall herringbone pattern that lead to the conclusion that these socks were made in the nålbinding technique, like the textile originals that survived in dry conditions of the deserts of Egypt and the Near East.*

*Socks in soleae were worn by men, women and children. Sources and depictions point towards wearers with a higher social status; wealthy civilians or soldiers and their families. Servants, however, are shown wearing socks in their soleae as well. Socks with soleae in the North-West Provinces seem to be a fashion phenomenon restricted mainly to the 2nd–3rd centuries AD.*

## Introduction

'I ask you, father, if you agree, to send me from there some low-sided boots (*caligae*) and a pair of felt socks (*udones*)' (P.Mich. 8/468, 23–25, translation Trapp 2003, 55). These are the words of Claudius Terentianus, a Roman soldier stationed in Alexandria asking his father in Karanis for new garments in the early 2nd century AD.

This reference to socks[1] may astonish the modern reader, as most of us think of Romans in a Mediterranean cliché of barefooted sandal-wearers, and socks may be one of the last things we would expect when thinking about Roman dress.

This misconception may be due in part to our modern interpretation of 'fashion sins', but the main reason for the widespread unawareness of Roman socks is closely connected to the fact that they are rarely mentioned in Roman literature or depicted in Roman art as well as in the fragility of the material: archaeological textiles survive only under exceptional conditions. While in the North-Western Provinces, waterlogged sites like bogs, rivers and very humid soil are the main sites where textiles were preserved, the dry deserts of Egypt and the Near East had the conditions that conserved a large number of textile remnants. Unfortunately, most socks found in Egypt were unearthed during the big rush for artefacts in the late 19th and early 20th centuries, which meant that they were ripped out of their archaeological context and brought or sold to textile collections all over the world. Luckily, some examples derive from excavations of newer date and therefore are able to help with more precise dating.

After socks had been mentioned several times in general publications on Roman textiles and clothing (i.e. Roche-Bernard 1993, 11–13; Croom 2000, 59, 63, 97 and 109; Knötzele 2007, 41, 66–67), the awareness of the existence of socks in Roman times rose in the past decade, and several depictions of socks were identified among new finds, at least in Britain (Fitzpatrick 2004, 201; Worrell 2005, 452–453). A broad investigation on the [14]C-dating of socks from Roman Egypt, now stored in European museums, was carried out as part of the EU-Project *DressID – Textiles and Identities in the Roman Empire* and shed new light on the dating of these garments (De Moor *et al.* forthcoming).

If one takes a close look at socks in Roman times, an astonishing amount of original finds of socks and depictions of Romans wearing them emerge. But so far, socks have only been published scattered in collection's catalogues and with a marked lack of systematic typology. While most publications concentrate on the form and textile production technique of single socks (De Moor *et al.* 2008) or a small group of technically similar objects in one collection (Burnham 1972), a general overview on socks is yet a lacuna. This paper aims to give a first overview on Roman socks in general and their makers and wearers, considering questions of design, technique and origin as well as social status, age and gender of wearers. In order to answer these questions, the information from written sources, depictions in diverse forms of Roman art and textile originals are combined.

In written sources, a kind of cloth-boot, called '*soccus*', is referred to as sock, too (for different sources see Croom 2000, 63, 97, 109). Knötzele (2007, 60–61) sees them as kind of slippers, which seems quite logical, as they are listed among other types of shoes and after *soleae* in the Edict on Maximum Prices in 301 AD (Ed. Diocl. IX,18). This article will focus on "*udones*" as socks.

## Form follows function

The private letter of Terentianus has a pendant from the northern frontier of the Roman Empire. At Vindolanda, a fragment of a writing tablet was found in the boggy earth of the former Roman fort. 'I have sent you […] pairs of socks (*udones*) from Sattua, two pairs of sandals (*soleae*) and two pairs of underpants […]' (Tab. Vindol. II.346), reports the writer of this note. It was probably a family member who sent these items to a soldier, stationed at Vindolanda in the early 2nd century AD, most probably from period 4 of the fort, dated to AD 104–120 (Bowman & Thomas 1994, 17, 375).

The sources mentioning *udones* refer to *caligae* (openwork boots, see also chapter by Burandt in this volume) as well as to *soleae* (sandals).

It is most likely that *udones* were worn with both kinds of shoes. But as we have no precise description, we unfortunately do not know the exact form of *udones* or what kind of shoes they were made for. *Caligae*, the hobnailed boots typical for soldiers, required no special form of socks, and neither did other openwork or closed shoes and boots, while *soleae* required a special form of sock.

There is a range of possibilities of cushioning and warming your feet in closed shoes and boots: Textile insoles seemed to be quite common in the northern Roman provinces, as three surviving examples prove: they were found in Basel (18.5 cm long, green felt made of hare's wool, see Wild 1970, 20), Vindolanda (16.5 cm long, fitting the size of the child's sock found nearby, made of woollen diamond twill, see Wild 1993, 83) and Grewelthorpe (26 cm long, made of tabby-woven wool, see Turner *et al.* 1991, 197). Another possibility would be simple stripes of cloth, wrapped around the foot and leg, called *tibialia* and reported as worn even by Augustus in winter (Suetonius, *De vita caesarum: Augustus* 82, 1). Puttees, shown for example at the Elternpaarpfeiler from Neumagen (Von Massow 1932, Tab. 33), were also discussed as possible form of socks (Croom 2000, 57), while proper socks with a closed tip existed as well, as shown below.

*Soleae*, the true sandals of the Roman world, had a thong between the big toe and its neighbour and therefore required socks with a split toe to fit perfectly. Hence the form of the shoes determined the design of the socks and there are different forms of socks for different forms of shoes.

## Material

The two letters cited above unfortunately do not mention the form or material of the *udones* sent. In his translation of the letter of Terentianus (P.Mich. 8/468, 25), Trapp (2003, 55) suggests 'felt socks' as translation for 'udones'. As there is no specification of material mentioned in the text, 'felt socks' seems to be a suggestion based on older translations of the term. An indication of the material for socks is given by Martial, who mentions luxurious socks as possible gifts in his *Apophoreta*, dating around AD 84: '*Udones cilicii*: These are not formed of wool, but of the beards of the fetid goat. You may bury your feet in this hairy cavern.' (Martialis XIV, 140/141). We can conclude from this that wool – probably mostly sheep's wool – was the common material for socks, while special socks made from luxurious fibres like the 'beards' of goats existed as well.

## Socks with a closed tip for boots and shoes

Socks with a closed tip are very hard to distinguish in depictions and reliefs, because the shoes mostly cover the whole foot. Sometimes a small line above the top end of a shoe or boot may indicate socks worn in the shoe, but this is only a hint as the sock itself is not clearly visible or shoe and sock cannot be separated (i.e. see Von Massow 1932, Taf. 36, 185 a1, female servant on the right). These details may have been more visible when the relief was still painted in vibrant colours. Luckily some textile specimens survived in England and France that give an idea of Roman socks with a closed tip.

At Les Matres-de-Veyre, several inhumations from the 2nd century AD were discovered in the years 1851–1922, which – due to extraordinary good preservation

*Fig. 3.1: Sewn Stockings from Les Martres-de-Veyre, Ville de Clermont-Ferrand, Collections du Musée Bargoin (© F. Giffard, Ville de Clermont-Ferrand)*

circumstances – still contained woollen clothing, leather shoes and other items like spinning tools, vessels and food (Audollent 1923). Among the textiles were two pairs of socks: A pair of knee-length stockings and a pair of ankle-high socks (Figs 3.1 and 3.2). Both the stockings and the socks were sewn from flat pieces of cloth. The stockings

from the burial of a young woman (Audollent 1923, no. 48) were made from two pieces, one for the leg including the heel (50 cm high) and one for the rest of the foot (20 cm long). They join at the ankle; the main seam is running from the toes along the sole and up the back of the lower leg (Audollent 1923, 318). The fabric used is a brown

*Fig. 3.2: Sewn socks from Les Martres-de-Veyre, Ville de Clermont-Ferrand, Collections du Musée Bargoin (© A. Jourde, Ville de Clermont-Ferrand)*

2/2-twill, probably natural coloured wool, counting 9–10 Z-spun single threads per cm in warp and weft (Desrosiers & Lorquin 1998, 63). The stockings have a fringed upper end and a few centimetres below an area where the weft is missing, probably used as a tunnel for a drawstring. On one of the stockings there is an embroidered mark, reading 'PRI' (Audollent 1923, 318). The lady owning them wore these socks in closed shoes.

A pair of ankle-high socks from the same burial ground (Audollent 1923, no. 49) resembles modern cloth boots, but the woollen fabric they were made of is finer than that of the knee-length stockings described above. They are also sewn from two pieces, this time one for the sole (23 cm long) and one for covering the foot (12 cm high), sewn at the side and including strips of cloth at the ankle to close the sock snugly (Audollent 1923, 318–319). They are made from 2/2 twill as well, this time in a light brownish tone, probably undyed, the fabric counting *c*. 16 Z-spun threads in warp and weft (Desrosiers & Lorquin 1998, 63). The context of the find is unknown.

Much smaller than these (16 cm long), but made in the same design as the low socks from Les Martres-de-Veyre, is a child's sock from Vindolanda (England). It was found

in a layer dated to the third period of the wooden fort in AD 97–102/103 and was made from two pieces of medium-weighted diamond twill. It shows traces of wear (Wild 1993, 83, Inv. No. T/316).

A possible part of another stocking of a similar design to the stockings with the hem running under the foot from Les Martres-de-Veyre was found in 1850 in Grewelthorpe (England) along with an adult male bog body, dated to late 1st–3rd century AD and assumed to be of Roman origin. This fragment of a stocking resembles the foot part of the stockings from Les Martres-de-Veyre and was reported to be of yellow colour when found. It was made of a tabby in half-basket-weave (Turner *et al.* 1991).

Despite the small group of fragments, we can make a first attempt to classify sewn socks with closed tips according to their sewing pattern:

*Type 1:* Stockings built of two pieces, one for the foot and one for the leg, with a seam under the sole, running from the toes directly to the heel (stockings from Les Martres-de-Veyre, fragment from Grewelthorpe).

*Type 2:* Ankle-high socks, made of two pieces: one for the sole and one for the upper foot. The seam is running around the sole (Les Martres-de-Veyre socks, Vindolanda sock).

All the socks with a closed tip could have been worn very well with all kinds of boots and shoes, even openwork boots like *caligae* or *carbatinae* (for these forms see Burandt, this volume). They can even be worn in sandals without a thong or in slippers, which were used in the Roman Provinces in the 2nd century AD and later (Knötzele 60–61).

A third group of socks can be added, but these are worked in a different technique called *nålbinding*, where a single needle and short lengths of yarn are employed (see below for detailed explanation). Only a few nålbinding socks with closed tip exist, and all were found in Egypt. A white sock from Antinoupolis, now kept in Dublin (National Museum of Ireland, Inv. No. 1914:205) is one of very few examples made for adults. From the same location comes a colourful striped child's bootee, now kept in Oxford (Ashmolean Museum, Pritchard 2013, 50). A pair of multi-coloured children's socks from Fag-el-Gamous (Griggs *et al.* 1993, 230) is very well preserved and shows a colourful striped pattern too and some tassels to fix the socks at the ankle. All of these socks have up to now been dated vaguely as 'Coptic' which generally speaking means the 4th–6th centuries AD. It is remarkable that most nålbinding socks with closed tips were socks for babies or toddlers. It seems logical that those small feet, just learning to walk, would need socks that are easy to slip on and off.

## Socks for *Soleae*

*Soleae* are light thong sandals that were introduced to the North-Western provinces of the Roman Empire with the Roman dress culture. Although they were at first regarded as sandals for women, *soleae* soon became a common outdoor shoe for both men and women by the 2nd century AD (van Driel-Murray 2001; Knötzele 2007, 56). *Soleae* are much like modern flip-flops, consisting of a hard leather sole with a strap between the big toe and its neighbour. The strap was divided on the back of the foot and was then fixed to the side of the sole or bound behind the ankle. Because of the thong, *soleae* require a special form of sock with a separation between the big toe and its neighbour. These socks with single big toes can be worn with Roman thong footwear very comfortably as was proved in practical tests with copies carried out by the author.

Depictions of women wearing *soleae* and socks can be found on the funeral reliefs of the 2nd–3rd century AD from the Moselle region. One fragment of a funerary stele from Neumagen (Germany), the so-called *Avituspfeiler*, now located in the RLM Trier (Fig. 3.3), shows a woman, sitting in a basket-chair opposite her attendant (Von Massow 1932, 166, Tab. 26, 185 a1). The seated woman, most likely the head of the household, wears *soleae,* and with them, socks. The surface of the stone is picked on the socks to

indicate their woolly structure and hairy surface. Perhaps these are the luxurious furry socks Martial was referring to as 'Cilician socks'? In any case, the socks had a rolled hem at the ankle and split toes to fit the feet perfectly while wearing *soleae*. The same type of sock is also seen at another part of the same monument, where the seated mistress, the *ornatrix* and another female servant are all shown wearing thick socks with rolled hems in *soleae* (Von Massow 1932, 166, Tab. 38,185 a 12).

The colours these socks could have are shown on a painted shroud from Antinoupolis (Egypt) from the late 2nd century AD, now at the Metropolitan Museum of Art (Rogers Fund 1909, Accession No. 09.181.8.) (Fig. 3.4). A woman, wearing an elaborated dress with a fringed tunic and a lot of jewellery, wears bright red socks with her ornamented *soleae*. The separation of the big toe is clearly visible; the other toes are indicated under the snugly fitting surface of the socks. Thin red cords with tassels at her heels tie the sock to the ankle.

Men wearing socks appear in Roman art, too: A bronze statue from Roman London (Southwark, Tabard Square) shows a foot wearing a Mediterranean-type sandal, but lacks the depiction of individually visible toes. This may suggest that the depicted person is wearing socks (Fitzpatrick 2004, 301).

Socks are also well represented on a group of copper alloy knife or razor handles found in various parts of Britain and reported to the Portable Antiquities Scheme.[2] The handles have a length of 22–45 mm and are shaped in the form of a three-dimensional leg and foot, wearing a sandal (*solea*) and a sock reaching over the ankle. On five badly preserved pieces, only the rolled hems of the socks (like the one of the Neumagen relief) and the straps of the sandals are visible (PAS-IDs: GLO-443DF8, NCL-33E168, SOM-0DE1F2, SUR-E8CBD2, SWYOR-B98CF4). The surface of four better preserved pieces show elaborate herringbone pattern incisions all over the foot, with the pattern direction starting at the toes, running to the heel and covering the calf (PAS-IDs: CAM-DDFE12, NCL-920745, SOMDOR-4F6FB3, WAW-4A9746). One piece, found at Piercebridge in the river Tees near Darlington, shows the very detailed pattern of the sock (Fig. 3.5, PAS-ID: NCL-920745, Worrell 2005, 452–453). The pieces are not dated or stratified as they were stray finds, but one example from Misterton (Somerset) is datable via the extraordinary form of the *solea*: The triangular sole of ID SOM-0DE1F2 is the exaggerated form of a design in men's *soleae* that developed in the second half of the 3rd century AD and seems to proceed into the early 4th century (van Driel Murray 2001, 194–195). The herringbone pattern of the socks depicted on the handles points towards two possible materials: either the sock was made of self-patterned cloth with a herringbone twill or with the nålbinding technique, where the textile is built up by sewing loops with a single needle (see below). The rolled

*Fig. 3.3: Seated woman wearing socks with a separate big toe in solea, Funerary Stele from Neumagen (© Rheinisches Landesmuseum Trier, Photo Th. Zühmer)*

hems of these depictions, as well as the one appearing on the Neumagen relief make the latter (nålbinding) much more likely, as the hem of such socks naturally rolls up on itself.

No original find of these *soleae*-socks is known from the North-Western provinces of the Roman Empire. But several woollen socks with split toes were found during excavations in Egypt and are now kept in several European and North American collections. Among the best-preserved is a pair of polychrome children's socks now kept in Antwerp (Katoen Natie Inv. 721-01 a, b, see De Moor *et al.* 2008, 72–75 and 130–131), unfortunately with no known origin (Fig. 3.6). A pair of bright red adult's socks from Oxyrynchus is now kept in the Victoria and Albert Museum, London (Inv. 2085&A-1900) (Fig. 3.7).

Dorothy Burnham described the technique of these so-called 'Coptic socks' as 'Coptic knitting' in 1972. Although socks in this technique appear to be knitted at first glance, the technique used for them is quite different. It is usually called nålbinding (with different spelling, described by Burnham 1972 as *naalebinding*, Hansen 1990 as *nålebinding*, Claßen-Büttner 2012 as *nalbinding*). Nålbinding socks are made by a single needle looping

technique worked with a single, rather thick needle and short threads. This is in contrast to knitting, where two needles and a ball of 'infinite' yarn are employed. Other terms for this technique are 'needle-netting' (Shefer & Granger Taylor 1994, 221), 'single needle-netting' or 'cross-knit looping' (De Moor *et al.* 2008, 72–74). Sometimes this technique is still referred to as 'knitted' (Croom 2000, 59 and 61), which is technically misleading, like other terms such as 'knitted in Cross-Eastern Stitch' (Pfister & Bellinger 1945, 4 and 54–56), 'Coptic knitting' (Burnham 1972) or 'single-needle-knitting', since nålbinding is more like sewing than like knitting. (Fig. 3.8). Textiles produced in this way are very flexible and therefore perfect for snugly fitting socks.

Most of the socks are worked with split toes and cover the ankle. They all show a rolled hem at the ankle, which is due to the technique. Some socks have a split front part at the ankle and cord at the right and left side of the split, which were used to bind the socks at the back of the ankle. Welts at the joint of the foot- and heel-part are a technical feature and a decoration at the same time, and sometimes used a second time just for decoration at the shaft (i.e. white adult's sock, London, British Museum EA53912). Self-patterning occurs as well: Some examples show a ripped pattern at the ankle opening (fragment of an adult's sock worked in green wool, Bolton Museum and Art Gallery, Inv. 96.1914.30, see Pritchard 2013, 50, fig. 18), made by reversing the normal stitch to purl stitch.

Most of the socks were found in Egypt during excavations in the late 19th and early 20th centuries and have only fairly vague contexts like 'Coptic burial ground'. Consequently, many were dated to 4th–6th centuries AD (Cardon *et al.* 2011, 49, with further references). But recently some examples have been [14]C-dated, resulting in much earlier dates: The children's socks from Antwerp have been dated to AD 70–340 (Van Strydonck *et al.* 2004, 233, fig. 1), the white adult's sock from British Museum to AD 100–350, the child's sock to AD 200–400 (British Museum EA 53913, both: Pritchard 2013, 50). A pair of children's socks from Brussels was dated AD 240–400 (Royal Museums of Art History, Brussels ACO Tx 2497, Pritchard 2014, 47, all dates with 95.4% probability). Further results of ongoing research may also set the dates of some other socks into earlier periods (De Moor *et al.* forthcoming).

If one takes a close look at the excavated material from Roman sites in Egypt and the surrounding countries, early examples of socks in nålbinding are found at the main dated sites with textile preservation, too: fragments of a small sock made from linen (the only one from linen known yet) were found in Masada, dated to the late 1st century AD (Shefer & Granger Taylor 1994, 221–223, No. 109(Z)), an almost complete sock was excavated at Mons Claudianus, dated to the mid–late 2nd century AD (Bender-Jørgensen 1991, 91–92). The excavations at Dura-Europos revealed two ribbed fragments with horizontal coloured bands, which

Fig. 3.5: Knife or razor handle in form of a three-dimensional leg and foot wearing a sandal and a sock with herringbone-pattern (© Portable Antiquities Scheme/ Trustees of the British Museum)

Fig. 3.6: Children's socks in nålbinding-technique, now in Antwerp, Katoen Natie 721-01 a, b (© photo Hugo Maertens)

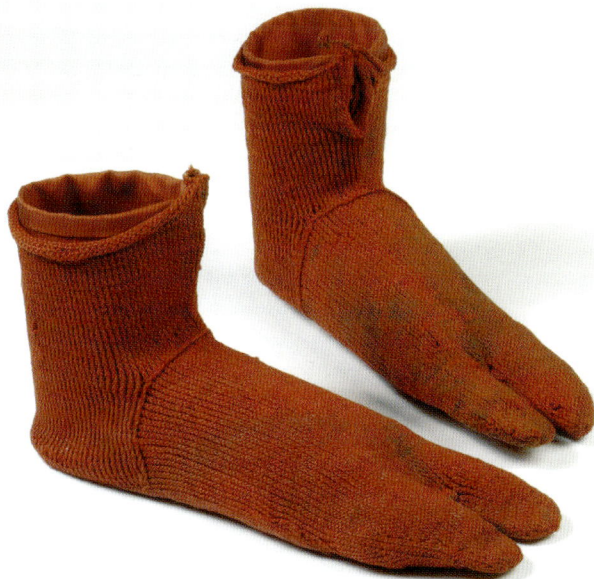

Fig. 3.7: Adult's socks in nålbinding-technique, now in London, Victoria and Albert Museum (© Victoria and Albert Museum, London)

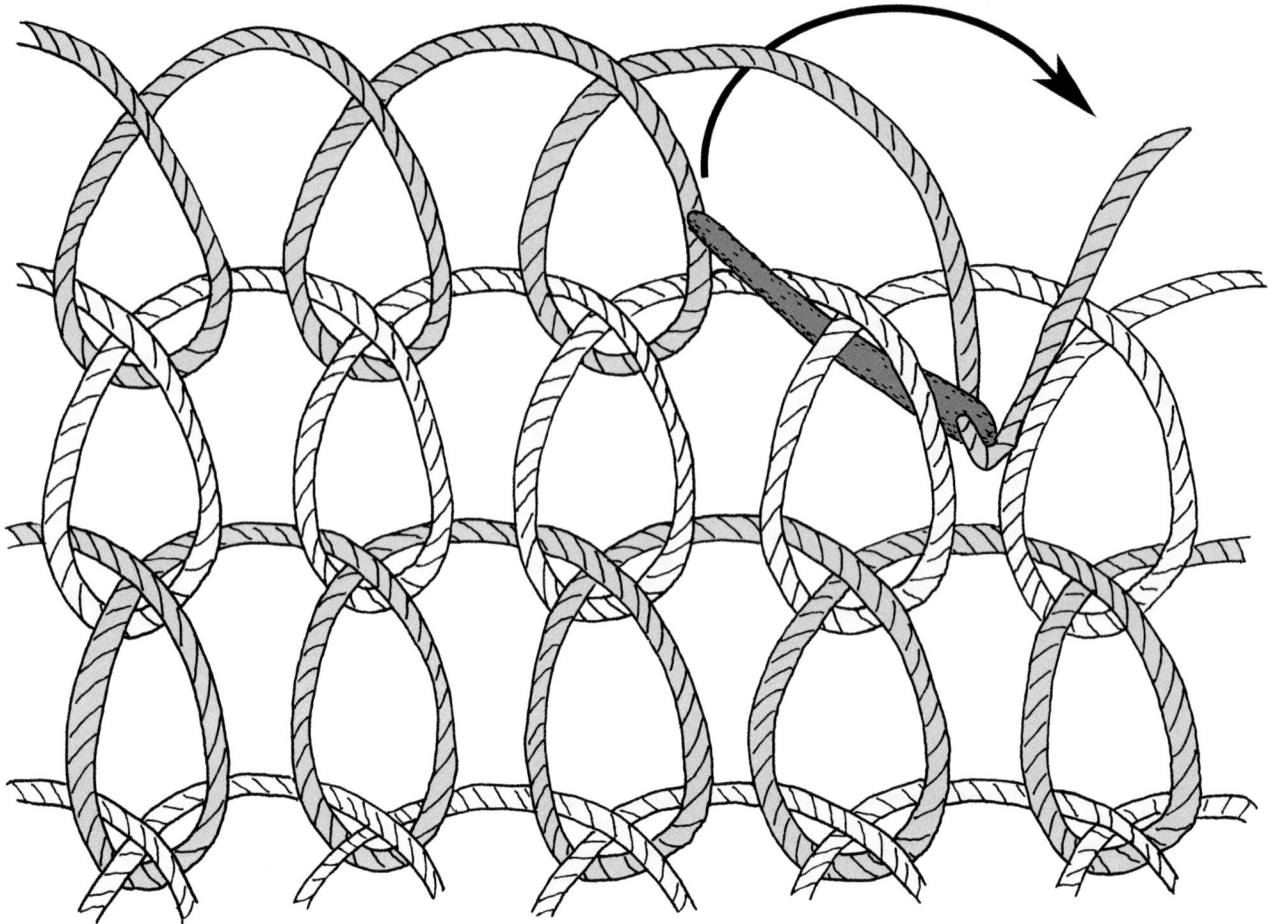

Fig. 3.8: Nålbinding, scheme of the Tarim or Coptic stitch, worked with a single needle and a short length of yarn (© Barbara Köstner)

may well have been the shafts of socks (Pfister & Bellinger 1945, 4 and 55–56, no. 266). They must have been produced before the destruction of the city in the mid-3rd century AD.

We can thus conclude that nålbinding-socks for *soleae* were worn from the 1st century AD onwards, with the largest amount of socks found dating to the 3rd–4th century AD. They were worked in the so-called Coptic- or Tarim-Stitch and made of plied wool, except the one plied linen example from Masada. While the main amount of nålbinding-socks from Roman and late-Roman times is worked in the Tarim-Stitch in a more or less standardised way, some adult's nålbinding-socks from Egypt differ in the employed stitch, colouring and layout. One fragmented sock is now kept in Vienna (MAK Wien, Inv. T 564–1883, 6th century AD), a polychrome pair in Florence (Museo Egizio, Inv. 12920, 4th-6th century AD). For both of these examples, a more complex stitch was used. More examples of 'Coptic socks' in complex stitches are now kept at the Basel Museum der Kulturen (Böttcher 2004). Only further research will show

if these examples can be regarded as additional group of nålbinding-socks of the same period.

From the rubbish dump of a small Roman fortress at Dios near the Red Sea comes a singular find of a sewn sock for *soleae* (Dios.4635.1, Inv. 646). It is made from woollen cloth in half-basket-weave (9.5–10 paired warp ends/cm, golden-brown, 32 reddish-brown threads/cm in the weft) and is tailored from four pieces (one for the sole, three for the upper part). It had a tongue for an extra-flexible fit. The sock can be dated by the occupation period of the fortress, AD 115–245 (Cardon *et al.* 2011, 47–49). It is quite possible that other sewn socks for *soleae* existed.

## Production

Textiles are goods that could be traded easily over long distances, but of course they could be produced locally as well. The fabric of the sewn socks with closed tip suggests its source, but only scientific testing would prove the provenance. While the socks from Les Martres-de-Veyre are made in a 2/2-twill, the sock from Vindolanda is made in diamond twill. Both fabric techniques fit very well into the local textile production tradition, and it is thus likely that the socks were made regionally and did not travel a long distance from producer to consumer. The half-basket-weave used for the Grewelthorpe and the Dios socks was used in the whole Roman Empire and cannot be tied to a single region. The nålbinding-socks were mostly made from 3- or 4-ply wool, the single threads spun in S-direction as well as in Z-direction, so no regional technique can be traced using the spin direction. It is most likely that they were produced locally as well. The pattern of the stitches on the socks is always a little different, so it seems possible to link it to a 'home-production', which would also ensure a perfect fit.

The woman named 'Sattua' mentioned in the Vindolanda writing tablet was probably the woman producing the socks sent to the soldier (Bowman & Thomas 1994, 336). She may have been the owner of a specialised workshop or just a skilled family member. Or she may not have made the socks, but purchased them and sent them to her family member – unfortunately it is not mentioned whether she was a relative or not.

The mark 'PRI' on the stockings from Les Martres-de-Veyre probably refers to the weaver (Desrosiers & Lorquin 1998, 63), seamstress or owner of the stockings. Evidence of professional sock-sewers is given in Diocletian's Edict on Maximum Prices, where the cutting and sewing of cloth for socks (*udones*) is listed as part of the work of a *bracarius* (Ed. Diocl. VII, 49).

As we have seen, the form of the shoes worn determined the form of the socks to wear with them. The majority of the socks worn in the North-Western Provinces would have had closed tips, corresponding to closed shoes and boots as the main footwear. But the depictions at Neumagen and the bronze foot and knife-handles from Britain show that socks for *soleae* in nålbinding-technique were known and worn by men and women in the North-Western provinces as well. As there are no surviving examples of socks for *soleae* from the North-Western provinces, we cannot sample them to find out where the *soleae*-socks worn in this region were made. They may have been imported from Egypt, but equally well they may have been made locally. Needles that could be used to make them are found at nearly every Roman site.

## Gender, age and status of people wearing socks

Unfortunately the contexts of the early finds of nålbinding-socks from burial grounds in Egypt are unknown, so we are lacking all the information about the gender or status of the former owners.

But we know that men, women and children wore socks: Men wearing socks are attested through written (Vindolanda writing tablet, letter from Alexandria) and pictorial sources (bronze knife-handles from Britain with *solea*-socks) and textile finds (Grewelthorpe man with sewn sock type 1). Women do not appear in the written sources, but are more frequent in pictorial representations: the Neumagen reliefs show several women wearing socks with *soleae*. Shrouds from Egypt depicting the deceased in their full glory in some cases depict red socks in the *soleae* (Metropolitan Museum of Art, Rogers Fund, 1909, Accession No. 09.181.8 and Paris, Musée du Louvre, AF 6440). Archaeologically recovered socks found in funerary context with women appear only at Les Martres-de-Veyre (sewn stockings type 1).

Socks for children are known through one depiction of Harpocrates wearing socks with closed tip, most probably made by nålbinding (from Karanis, Egypt, wall painting depicting Isis suckling Harpocatres, 3rd century AD, see Rowlandson 1998, 51, no. 11). A sewn sock of type 2 in a size only suited to children is known from Vindolanda. Small nålbinding-socks from Egypt, that could only have fitted children's feet, demonstrate the use of socks by children, even if these socks are rarely connected to an archaeological context.

While *soleae*-socks for adults were monochrome (white, brown, red, green, with only very few exceptions like the sock at Lyon, MT 29249), socks for children were often striped with multi-coloured bands.

Artistic depictions mainly show people of higher status wearing socks, like the women shown in Figures 3.3 and 3.4, but this may be due to the fact that wealthy people could afford to be depicted. On the other hand, there may have been differences in the quality of *soleae*-socks. Some of them are very thin, like the red adult's socks kept at the Victoria and Albert Museum or the ones shown on the shroud from Antinoupolis. These most likely were more expensive than the thicker socks. In addition to wealthy civilians, we know that soldiers wore socks, as proven by the letters from Vindolanda and Alexandria. The owner of the sewn *solea*-sock from the Dios fortress dump was also quite likely a soldier, and the sewn children's sock from Vindolanda is proof that their families also wore socks. Soldiers had a very good income and could well afford socks. The Neumagen reliefs demonstrate, however, that not only wealthy people wore socks, as they also depict servants wearing socks with their *soleae*. And another fact points towards people of a lower social status wearing socks, too: Mended socks were found as well. One original from Egypt is heavily mended with rectangular patches that were worked in nålbinding directly into the original structure of the sock (London, Victoria and Albert Museum, inv. 1243–1904; Kendrick 1920, 88, cat. no.

594). The parts that needed mending were those exposed to friction while walking: the sole, mainly at the ball of the foot, the heel and where the straps of the sandal were lashed. It is obvious that the sock was worn very often by someone who did quite a lot of walking. Experiments proved that nålbinding socks wear out quite fast when walking around in *soleae*. Fine socks made of thin yarn would be especially vulnerable. Mended socks seem to point towards poorer people as owners rather than to the upper classes. One example of a *soleae*-sock even has been repaired with another sock, by sewing the second sock under the sole of the old one to fix holes (Musée des tissus, Lyon, MT 29249).

## General dating

Socks with closed tips are found in the North-Western provinces as early as *c.* AD 100 AD but they were perhaps already worn earlier – with textile evidence being so scarce, we may just be missing the finds.

In Egypt and surrounding countries, *soleae* were worn as daily footwear in pre-Roman times already, and socks for *soleae* can accordingly be dated earlier than in the North-West. In Roman contexts, the Masada sock proves they are known as early as the late 1st century AD.

*Soleae* became common in the North-Western provinces by the 2nd century AD. The depictions of people wearing socks in *soleae* in the region appear in the 2nd century as well and continue to at least the second half of the 3rd century or even to the early 4th as seen at the Misterton knife-handle. This matches the general dating of the use of *soleae* in the North-Western Provinces. So in Roman times, wearing socks in sandals may be regarded as fashionable as wearing *soleae* itself.

## Summary

The quite comprehensible need for warm feet and socks as a means to get them can be traced all over the Roman Empire – from Egypt via Rome to the North-Western provinces. Socks are mentioned in literature and letters and shown in various depictions and we even have some original textiles. The depictions and the textiles show two types of socks: Socks for closed shoes and boots with no division of the toe, and another group of socks with split toes to fit *soleae*, thong sandals.

Socks for closed shoes like *caligae* or *carbatinae* or for sandals without a thong can be arranged in three groups: 1) Stockings sewn from cloth with a seam running under the sole, 2) Socks sewn from cloth with a circumferential seam running around the sole and 3) nålbinding socks in Tarim stitch with closed tip. Groups 1 and 2 were found in the North-Western provinces of the Roman Empire, while Group 3 is a form of sock found only in Roman Egypt up to now.

Further evidence of socks in the North-Western provinces of the Roman Empire can be found in the depictions of men and women wearing socks in *soleae* from 2nd–3rd centuries AD. As *soleae* are similar to flip-flops, they require a sock with split toes. Examples of those socks survived only in dry conditions of the deserts of Egypt and the Near East. These socks were made from wool in the nålbinding technique (so-called Tarim or Coptic Stich), which is an easy, but slow technique to make perfectly fitting and flexible socks. Socks for adults were mostly monochrome, while socks for children were striped in bright colours. The depicted examples of socks with split toes from the North-Western provinces show technical features like rolled hems and an overall herringbone pattern that lead to the conclusion that these socks were made in the nålbinding technique, too.

Socks in *soleae* were worn by men, women and children. Sources and depictions most often suggest that these individuals had a higher social status, such as wealthy civilians or soldiers and their families, but servants are shown wearing socks in their sandals as well. While *soleae* were the common shoe in Egypt and the Near East for centuries and therefore finds of socks for *soleae* are quite frequent, wearing socks in *soleae* in the North-West Provinces may be regarded as a fashion phenomenon restricted mainly to the 2nd–3rd centuries AD.

So, take a close look at the feet of Roman statues, reliefs, paintings and figurines! There may be socks where you previously did not expect to see them.

## Ancient sources

P.Mich. = Michigan Papyri: Trapp, M. (2003). *Greek and Latin Letters: An Anthology with Translation.* Cambridge: Cambridge University Press.

Suetonius = G. Suetonis Tranquillus, De vita caesarum: Rolfe, J. C. (1914), *Suetonius: Lives of the Caesars, Volume 1.* Loeb Classical Library 31. Cambridge MA: Harvard University Press.

Martialis = M. Valerius Martialis, Epigrammata: Barié, P. & Schindler, W. (2013, ed. and trans.). *M. Valerius Martialis, Epigramme*: lateinisch-deutsch. Berlin: Akademie-Verlag.

Tab. Vindol. = Vindolanda Writing Tablets: Bowmann, A. K. & Thomas, J. D. (1994). *Vindolanda: The Latin Writing Tablets. Volume II.* London: British Museum Press.

Ed. Diocl. = Edictum de pretiis rerum venalium: Lauffer, S. (1971, ed.), *Diokletians Preisedikt.* Berlin: de Gruyter.

## *Notes*

1   'Socks' as described in this article are to be understood as garments that cover the whole foot and the ankle, at most extending to the knee.
2   My sincere thanks go to Philippa Walton, Oxford, who drew my attention towards the other handles in this shape besides the Piercebridge example.

## Bibliography

Audollent, A. (1923) Les Tombes gallo-romains à inhumation des Martres-de-Veyre (Puy-de-Dôme). *Mémoires préséntes par divers savants à l'Academie des Inscriptions et Belles-Lettres 13*, Paris, 275–328 and pls VII–XI.

Bender-Jørgensen, L. (1991) Textiles from Mons Claudianus. A preliminary report. *Acta Hyperborea* 3, 83–95.

Böttcher, G. (2004) Koptische Nadelbindungstextilien im Museum der Kulturen Basel. *Experimentelle Archäologie in Europa. Bilanz*, 211–214.

Bowmann, A. K. & Thomas, J. D. (1994). *Vindolanda: The Latin Writing Tablets. Volume II*. London, British Museum Press.

Burnham, D. K. (1972) Coptic knitting: an ancient technique. *Textile History* 3, 116–124.

Cardon, D., Cuvigny, H. & Nadal, D. (2011) De pied en cap – A shoe from Dios and a hat from Domitinè/Kainè Latomia, in the Eastern Desert of Egypt. In A. De Moor & C. Fluck (eds) *Dress Accessories of the 1st millennium AD from Egypt*, 44–53. Tielt, Lannoo.

Croom, A. T. (2000). *Roman Clothing and Fashion*. Stroud, Tempus.

Claßen-Büttner, U. (2012) *Nadelbinden – was ist denn das? Geschichte und Technik einer fast vergessenen Handarbeit.* Books on Demand GmbH, Norderstedt.

De Moor, A., Verhecken-Lammens, C. & Verhecken, A. (2008). *3500 Years of Textile Art*. Tielt, Lannoo.

De Moor, A., Van Strydonck, M., Boudin, M. & Fluck, C. (forthcoming) Radiocarbon dating of late Roman woollen socks from Egypt. In A. De Moor, C. Fluck & P. Linscheid (eds) *Proceedings of the 8th Conference of the Research Group Textiles from the Nile Valley*. Tielt, Lannoo.

Desrosiers, S. & Lorquin, A. (1998) Gallo-Roman period archaeological textiles found in France. In L. Bender-Jørgensen & C. Rinaldo (eds) *Textiles in European Archaeology, Report from the 6th NESAT Symposium*, 53–72. Göteborg, Göteborg University, Dept. of Archaeology.

Fitzpatrick, A. P. (2004) Roman Britain in 2003 – Greater London. *Britannia* 35, 298–303.

Griggs, C. W., Kuchar, M. C., Woodward, S. R., Rowe, M. J., Evans, R. P., Kanawati, N., Iskander, N. (1993) Evidences of a Christian population in the Egyptian Fayum and genetic and textile studies of the Akhmim noble mummies. *Brigham Young University Studies* 33(2), 215–243.

Hansen, E. H. (1990) Nalebinding: definition and description. In P. Walton & J. P. Wild (eds) *Textiles in Northern Archaeology. NESAT III*, 21–27. London, Archetype Publications.

Kendrick, A. F. (1920) *Catalogue of Textiles From Burying-Grounds in Egypt*, Vol II, London, Victoria and Albert Museum.

Knötzele, P. (2007): *Römische Schuhe. Luxus an den Füßen.* Schriften des Limesmuseums Aalen 59. Esslingen, Archäologisches Landesmuseum Baden-Württemberg.

Pritchard, F. (2013) A survey of of textiles in the UK from the 1913–14 Egypt Exploration Fund Season at Antinoupolis. In A. De Moor, C. Fluck & P. Linscheid (eds) *Drawing the Threads Together. Textiles and Footwear of the 1st millennium AD from Egypt*, 34–55. Tielt, Lannoo.

Pfister, R. & Bellinger, L. (1945) The textiles. In M. I. Rostovtzeff, A. R. Bellinger, F. E. Brown, N. P. Toll & C. B. Welles (eds) *The Excavations at Dura-Europos. Final Report IV, Part II*. New Haven, Yale University Press.

Roche-Bernard, G. (1993) *Costumes et textiles en Gaule romaine*. Paris, Editions Errance.

Rowlandson, J. (1998): *Women and Society in Greek and Roman Egypt. A Sourcebook*. Cambridge, Cambridge University Press.

Shefer, A. & Granger-Taylor, H. (1994) Textiles from Masada. A preliminary selection. In J. Aviram, G. Foerster & E. Netzer (eds) *Masada IV. The Yigael Yadin Excavations 1963–65. Final Reports*, 149–282. Jerusalem, Israel Exploration Society and Hebrew University of Jerusalem.

Turner, R. C., Rhodes, M. & Wild, J. P. (1991) The Roman body found on Grewelthorpe Moor in 1850: a reappraisal. *Britannia* 22, 191–201.

Wild, J. P. (1970) *Textile Manufacture in the Northern Roman Provinces*. Cambridge, Cambridge University Press.

Wild, J. P. (1993) The textiles, in van Driel Murray, C., Wild, J. P., Seaward, M., Hillam, J., *Vindolanda III. The ealy wooden forts. Preliminary reports on the leather, textiles, environmental Eidence and Dendrochronology*, 76–90. Bardon Mill, Roman Army Museum Publications.

van Driel-Murray, C. (2001) Vindolanda and the dating of Roman footwear. *Britannia* 32, 185–197.

Van Strydonck, M., De Moor, A. & Bénazeth, D. (2004) 14C dating compared to art historical dating of Roman and Coptic textiles from Egypt. *Radiocarbon* 46(1), 231–244.

Von Massow, W. (1932) *Die Grabdenkmäler von Neumagen*. Berlin/Leipzig: Walter de Gruyter.

Worrell, S. (2005) Roman Britain in 2004 – finds reported under the Portable Antiquities Scheme. *Britannia* 36, 447–472.

# 4

# Laying it on thick – makeup in the Roman Empire

## Gisela Michel

*Keywords*: Beauty ideal; eyeliner; makeup; mummy portrait; pigments; Severan; gold sandwich glass; toilet implements

*Our knowledge about the ingredients and the use of makeup is mainly based upon literary sources and finds of toilet implements such as mixing palettes, spatulas and spoon-probes as well as special containers for pigments and makeup preparations. Further information is provided by the analysis of makeup residues, with additional evidence from iconographic evidence. Among the mummy portraits and the gold sandwich glasses are examples of women depicted with black-rimmed eyelids. This striking emphasis on the eyes reflects an oriental influence, which became a fashion in the wider Roman Empire in the Severan period.*

## Preliminary remarks

Makeup is usually put on for aesthetic reasons. In accordance with the beauty criteria of one's culture, some areas of the face are highlighted by touches of colour, which also appears to change their contours and proportions. The aim is always to approach the ideal of beauty – which is often closely linked with a high social status (Burhenne 1998, 8–9; Olson 2008, 63–64, 99) – but the manner in which it is reached can cover the whole range from slight enhancement to extreme exaggeration. Either using or consciously refraining from the use of makeup is thus not only a matter of personal taste, but also determined by social norms which also govern hairstyle, clothing, jewellery, accessories or other insignia of social rank. Makeup underlines a person's membership to a particular social group, which can be defined by gender, age, social or marital status, or occupation. Makeup can also include medical (e.g. Egyptian eye makeup) or religious functions (e.g. in oriental cults).

Our knowledge of makeup in the Roman Empire is mainly based on the written sources, which have repeatedly been the subject of research (Wilner 1931; Dubourdieu & Lemirre 2002, 89–114; Froschauer & Harrauer 2004, 43–59; Saiko 2005; Stewart 2007; Olson 2008; 2009; Bardiès-Fonty *et al.* 2009, 35–40). As further repetition

would be tedious, a brief summary (see below) will suffice here. Among the archaeological finds, toilet utensils and cosmetics vessels have also been presented, occasionally in very detailed publications (Riha 1986; Goethert 1989; Virgili 1989, 73–84; Froschauer & Harrauer 2004; Bardiès-Fonty *et al.* 2009; Eckhard & Crummy 2008, 39–41), but some additional notes can be made. Thanks to the progress in methods of scientific analysis, the recovery of makeup residues has come more strongly to the fore in recent years (Kour 1981; Paszthory 1992, 7–10; Froschauer & Harrauer 2004; Evershed *et al.* 2004; Bardiès-Fonty *et al.* 2009, 41–44, 126–127; Olson 2009, 294–299; Bridger & Ruthenberg 2015) and some of these will be used as illustration here.

However, little attention has so far been lavished on the representations depicting the use of makeup (Froschauer & Harrauer 2004, 3, 122, colour fig. 2; Stewart 2007, 32 fig. 14). This is not surprising, as iconographic evidence of makeup use is actually quite rare. While rare, these sources can provide significant insights and this paper will focus on them. A study on 'painted' – or rather 'made-up' – faces in representations of people can naturally only be based on paintings and mosaics, as these are the only sources depicting faces in enough detail and colour. Funerary reliefs and statues retaining well-preserved traces of colour are very rare. Roman mummy masks shall be excluded because they have been produced for the use in a death cult dominated by Egyptian traditions and therefore ultimately reflect Egyptian makeup norms. In contrast to these masks, the so-called mummy portraits painted on wood or linen were originally created to be used in a domestic context according to Roman traditions, as can be seen in individual finds of panels still preserved with their frame (see G. Gschwantler in Seipel 1999, 37–53, fig. 8) and of intact *tondi* (Parlasca & Seemann 1999, 43, fig. 43). They were only used as mummy portraits in a secondary use and were trimmed to fit the mummies.

## Beauty ideals and makeup as mirrored in the written sources

According to the written sources, makeup was used in Roman culture primarily in the service of increasing female attractiveness. In addition, there were religious and professional reasons to use makeup, for instance by the followers of oriental cults or by prostitutes and actors. Men wearing makeup were contemptuously derided as unmanly. Juvenal expresses this attitude very plainly when he describes in minute detail how one of the followers of a Thracian cult draws a line along the inner eye with the help of a kohl stick (Juvenal, *Saturae* II, 93–95). Of course he is not giving us makeup-tips, his detailed description of this (in his view) exaggeratedly effeminate behaviour serves to the reader's amusement.

Despite the fact that makeup was seen as typically female, most Roman writers – like their Greek predecessors – criticise its use very harshly (Saiko 2005, 67–84, 253–334). Using makeup is regarded as deception, simulating non-existent, or no longer existing, beauty. On a naturally beautiful face, makeup is regarded as unfortunate because it is unnecessary. The criticism of the Church fathers was particularly severe, concluding that, by using makeup, a woman revealed not only a superficial character with a penchant for loose morals but also ultimately presumed to correct God's creation. The only exception of this chorus of disapproval is Ovid, who advises his female readers to skilfully (!) use makeup to highlight their good points and detract from their bad (Ovid, *Ars amatoria* III, 199–209; but in regard to men he also disparages makeup, see *Ars amatoria* I, 509). In his view, makeup is part of the *cultus*, the art of looking good (for *cultus* as used by Ovid, see Dubourdieu & Lemirre 2002, 94, 108, 111; Saiko 2005, 190–197; Stewart 2007, 118; Olson 2008, 7–9, 109–110). The negative image evoked by the male authors gives the impression that nearly all women of that period regularly used too much makeup. This is certainly exaggerated and related to the fact that the authors primarily wrote about

upper class women, who had the leisure to use makeup on a regular basis. Most women likely limited makeup to special occasions.

Roman authors frequently name a pale skin colour as an important criterion of beauty (Wilner 1931; Dubourdieu & Lemirre 2002, 89–114; Froschauer & Harrauer 2004, 43–59; Saiko 2005; Stewart 2007; Olson 2008; 2009; Bardiès-Fonty *et al.* 2009, 35–40). Very tanned skin was frowned upon equally for women and men, as it was the mark of the majority of the population, which had to work outside in all weathers. While wealthy women shunned the sun, a light tan was an asset in the appearance of the well-kept man, as it demonstrated that he kept his body in form through exercise (according to Ovid, *Ars amatoria* III, 503; see Dubourdieu & Lemirre 2002, 90–91; Saiko 2005, 266). Women also emphasised their fair complexion with white makeup. After applying foundation, rouge was put on and the lips were coloured. It was important to distinguish 'aristocratic paleness' from a sickly sallow complexion (Ovid, *Ars amatoria* III, 199–200; see Dubourdieu & Lemirre 2002, 92–93; Saiko 2005, 180, 190–193, 215–218). It is quite likely that a considerable part of the female population of the period suffered from anaemia with its resulting sallow complexion as a result of early and frequent pregnancies in combination with malnutrition. Another cause of an unhealthy complexion was infectious disease. Martial therefore recommends that someone seeking to get rid of an irritating lover should not only use white makeup on the face, but also on the lips (Martial X, 22, 2–3).

A clear gaze was another indicator of a healthy appearance. Big eyes with strong eyebrows that ideally almost met over the bridge of the nose were regarded as a sign of beauty (Wilner 1931, 27–28; Dubourdieu & Lemirre 2002, 92–93, 101; Saiko 2005, 136, 255–257, 310; Olson 2008, 62–63). One therefore accented the eyelashes and eyebrows with dark make-up or – if necessary – glued on them artificially. In addition, one could emphasise the eyes with malachite green or saffron yellow (for saffron as eye shadow, see Ovid, *Ars amatoria* III, 204; Dubourdieu & Lemirre 2002, 106). Roman women probably also used blue eye shadow, as it was customary in the Orient and has been proven for Classical Greece (see Paszthory 1992; eye shadow from lapis lazuli, see Seipel 2001, 80, 87 (no. 7f) Greece: Bardiès-Fonty *et al.* 2009, 128).

The exact composition of makeup is not mentioned by the ancient written sources, but they tell us the natural and artificial dyes that were used for makeup, including harmful substances (Wilner 1931; Goethert 1989; Dubourdieu & Lemirre 2002, 89–114; Froschauer & Harrauer 2004, 43–59; Saiko 2005; Stewart 2007; Olson 2008; 2009; Bardiès-Fonty *et al.* 2009, 35–40). Although the Romans knew about the toxicity of pigments from copper, lead and mercury, advising that they be used in a diluted form, they seem to have underestimated their effects (Olson 2009, 308–309; see also Pliny, *Naturalis Historia* XXXIII, 122 on workers wearing transparent masks from animal bladders during the preparation of cinnabar). With the exception of Galen, who warns against the over-use (!) of these colorants, the ancient authors do not address the health risks of these makeup preparations; their criticism is limited to moral aspects (see Bardiès-Fonty *et al.* 2009, 42; Stewart 2007, 40, 43, 61–62). On the contrary, many authors even welcomed the toxic and therefore anti-inflammatory effects, especially in eyeliner and eye shadows. The effectiveness of some of these substances has recently been scientifically confirmed (see Kour 1981; Pászthory 1992; Froschauer & Harrauer 2004). Because of its excellent concealing effects and because it easily covered up wrinkles, *cerussa* or *psimythium* (white lead) was preferred in foundations to other white pigments that have been found more often in the archaeological record, such as chalk, kaolin and plaster (Bardiès-Fonty *et al.* 2009, 42–44). Red lead (burnt white lead) and cinnabar (mercury sulfide) were particularly popular as rouge, but harmless pigments based on red iron oxide, ochre and madder have also been recovered archaeologically (Bardiès-Fonty *et al.* 2009, 43, 126–127; Bridger & Ruthenberg 2015, 51).

While toilet utensils are often a combination of elaborate design and precious materials, functioning as status symbols in addition to their practical use, this is not necessarily true for the ingredients of the makeup concoctions. They range from luxury items like saffron or *purpurissum* to lamp-black, which could be had for free and which, according to the chemical analysis of the residue in kohl-containers, was the main ingredient in eye makeup (Froschauer & Harrauer 2004, 1–17, 61–109).

## Makeup preparations and makeup utensils: some examples

The archaeological finds primarily originate from graves, while those from settlement contexts are rare, with most coming from the Vesuvius area. Residues of cosmetic preparations are only preserved in exceptional circumstances: Among the grave goods of a 3rd century AD inhumation grave of a woman excavated in Frankfurt-Praunheim were a mixing palette, a spatula, a spoon-probe and a wooden box, lined with bronze sheeting and internal divisions, closed with a sliding lid (Woelcke & Jassoy 1931; Fasold 2006, 137, grave 1, T 273). On the inside, fragments of red and white makeup sticks were found, probably produced with the help of hollow plant stems (see Forbes, 20; Paszthory 1992, 10). During their chemical analysis, they were found to contain remarkably high amounts of both zinc and lead. A similar box from a grave in Xanten also contained a stick, which was composed of malachite, iron oxide, animal and/or plant ashes and some chalk in a base of fat and/or wax (Brückner 1960). As the box and a stone palette have been

detected by laymen, who gave the finds to the Rheinisches Landesmuseum Bonn (G) in 1959, no documentation of this grave exists.

Residues of makeup have also been discovered in Callas (dép. Var/F.). While excavating the foundations of a small building that had been refashioned into a chapel in the 11th century, a Roman bronze mirror box decorated with a coin of Nero was recovered (for mirror boxes see Lloyd-Morgan 1977). The tightly closed box still contained the well-preserved remains of a compact powder of pinkish-violet colour. During the chemical analysis, the powder was found to contain finely pulverized lime, beeswax and an organic dye, probably dyer's bugloss, which has roots with a red colorant (France-Lanord 1961). Another container created quite a media stir after its discovery in 2003 during the excavation of a temple complex in the London Southwark neighbourhood. The tin canister, still completely intact, was filled with a foundation. Chemical analysis proved that it was a compound from heated animal fat, with a filler of vegetable starch and tin oxide as a whitening pigment (Evershed *et al.* 2004; Stewart 2007, 36–38).

The products named above were probably produced commercially and purchased by the users. It was, however, more common to prepare the makeup at home as needed. For this purpose one used square stone mixing palettes as well as spatulas and spoon-probes. The handling of these implements is neither described nor depicted anywhere and has been concluded solely from their shape and the find contexts. Within graves, these objects are often found lying close together arranged as a set (Goethert 1989; Froschauer & Harrauer 2004, 4–5; Bridger & Ruthenberg 2015). They were also used for medicinal purposes, as is suggested by their inclusion into the grave goods of doctor's graves.

Remains of powdered pigments have mainly been found in pyxides (Froschauer & Harrauer 2004, 7; Bardiès-Fonty *et al.* 2009, 130–131, 188–189) and boxes with internal subdivisions and sliding lids (Bridger & Ruthenberg 2015). However, this does not mean that all finds of such containers can be interpreted as compacts or makeup boxes, as other uses are possible, such as the storage of medicinal substances, coins or jewellery. The compartments of a bronze box from the hoard of Mers-les-Bains (dép. Somme/F) were filled with coins and rings (Bardiès-Fonty *et al.* 2009, 123, no. 45).

Another kind of container for makeup pigments were vials of ultra-thin glass, as can be seen by residues of powdery substances occasionally still present. The forms used include small *balsamaria* in the shape of a small *amphora* without handles (Isings 9a). Some of these *amphoriskoi* were discovered still containing traces of a pink powder in tombs of the 1st century AD in Wederath-Belgium (Wederath no. 1026, see Goethert 1989, 280–281) and in Argenton-sur-Creuse (dép. Ingres/F, see Bardiès-Fonty *et al.* 2009, 132–133).

Similar vessels appear on a fresco of the same period, which originally belonged to a chamber grave in Morlupo (prov. Roma/I) (Naumann-Steckner 1999, 28–29): four *amphoriskoi* of a dark pink glass in addition to a spatula and two spoons probes are presented in a transparent cylindrical glass bowl.

Some glass vials were especially designed to function as a container for makeup powder. Two kinds of bottles are known, one fashioned in the form of a stylised dove (Isings 11) and another as a glass ball (Isings 10) with a short neck (Bardiès-Fonty *et al.* 2009, 132–134; Hinz 1984, 315–317, 359; Höricht 1986, 51, T XVII.106 (E 1961), 54). They were used only once, because in order to open them one had to break the tail of the dove and the short neck of the ball; the resulting (small) opening facilitated the extraction of small amounts of the powder. According to the find contexts respectively the analysis of the cremated remains, it seems that these vessels, which are attested for the 1st century AD, are limited to graves of women and girls.

## Painted faces

Pictorial representations of women engaged in the application of makeup have not been discovered so far.[1] The well known toilet-scenes show the (un)dressing, anointing or hairstyling of the mistress or depict her checking her look in the mirror (Guerrier 1978, 117–122; Freigang 1997; Ziegler 2000, 87–95; Schade 2003, 133–135). The number of known depictions with these scenes makes it unlikely that the omission of scenes depicting the use of makeup is due to the vagaries of preservation. It seems more likely that no lady wished to advertise that she had to resort to the use of makeup. According to Ovid, using makeup – as well as dental care and the use of beauty masks – should take place behind closed doors, because these areas of beauty care, while essential, might seem unattractive or repulsive to the observer. He urges the ladies to remember that beauty secrets only are fully effective when they remain secrets (Ovid, *Ars amatoria* III, 209–234; see Wilner 1931, 37; Olson 2009, 304).

Among the mummy portraits are examples of women shown with a remarkably pale, youthful smooth skin and rosy cheeks (Doxiades 1995, 68, fig. 55; Parlasca & Seemann 1999, 112–113 (no. 13), 277, 279 (no. 181); Borg 1996, cat. nos T 8.2, T 16.1, T 26.1, T 70.1; Bierbrier & Walker 1997, 112–113 (no. 108), 277, 279 (no. 181)). These portraits give us a good idea of the Roman ideal of a perfect complexion. However, whether the women in these pictures actually owed this complexion to nature or were discreetly made up, cannot be known. In some cases the faces maybe slightly embellished by the painter. Strong idealisation indeed can be excluded because there are images of men and women with grey hair and deep wrinkles.

While foundation and rouge is difficult to detect, it is possible to distinguish eye make up, provided the lower eyelid is also emphasised. Paintings in a naturalistic style are to be preferred, since with stylised portraits, it can be difficult to distinguish whether a thick black line is supposed to mean eyeliner or was used as a simplified manner of depicting the line of lashes (contrary to Froschauer & Harrauer 2004, 3, 7, which does not make this distinction). The best examples of course are portrait groups with both males and females, as they allow distinguishing between made-up and non made-up faces.

The earliest known evidence is probably the mummy portrait of a woman in Hildesheim wearing a fashionable hairstyle of the Trajanic period, whose eyelids are clearly edged with black colour (Borg 1996, 35, no. T 69.2). The same can be seen in a portrait now in Richmond, which shows a woman with the hairstyle of Plotina, Trajan's wife. That she is depicted with eye makeup is obvious when comparing her portrait to the mummy portrait of a young man in Copenhagen. As both panels are identical in style they doubtless have been executed in the same workshop (Borg 1996, no. 18, 1–2). Another case is a mummy portrait of a woman from Er-Rubayat in Egypt, now in Vienna, whose lower inner eyelid is traced with black makeup (Froschauer & Harrauer 2004, 3, 122, colour fig. 2). She wears a Hadrianic hairstyle consisting of plaits arranged like a turban. Further examples dating to the 2nd century AD are a well-preserved portrait mummy of a girl in Berlin (Parlasca & Seemann 1999, 168, no. 67) and the portrait of Klaudiane in Dijon (Aubert & Cortopassi 1998, 56, no. 18). The final example from the 2nd century is the late Antonine portrait of an elderly woman with a simple hairstyle with central parting, also from Er-Rubayat (Parlasca & Seemann 1999, 193, no. 96). Here, the black-rimmed eyelids contrast with the unadorned eyebrows.

The amount of evidence increases in the Severan period. The well-known Septimius Severus *tondo* in Berlin (Fig. 4.1), painted before the *damnatio memoriae* of Geta in AD 212 (Neugebauer 1936; Soechting 1972, who dates the picture to around AD 200; Rondot 2013, 33), presents Julia Domna with both the upper and the lower lid highlighted by a black line. This can be clearly seen although the panel's surface is slightly rubbed at the right eye. In contrast to the empress, Septimius Severus and Caracalla are depicted only with a black line on the upper eye lid to indicate the lashes.

The same large, oval, black rimmed eyes appear on a severely damaged portrait of a woman kept in London (Bierbrier & Walker 1997, 74–75, no. 52). In addition, the loosely coiffed, curled hair as well as the slight smile indicate that the empress Julia Domna served as a fashion model here. At least three mummy portraits from Antinoopolis depict sumptuously dressed and adorned women with Severan hairstyles and blackened eyelids (Bierbrier & Walker 1997, 160–192; Parlasca & Seemann

Fig. 4.1: Tondo of Septimius Severus with Julia Domna, Caracalla and Geta, Antikensammlung Berlin 31329 (copyright: bpk/ Antikensammlung, SMB/Johannes Laurentius)

Fig. 4.2: Ficoroni-medallion, Metropolitan Museum, New York 17.190.109 (copyright: Metropolitan Museum, New York)

1999, 301–302, nos 200–201). A mummy portrait of a young girl in Stanford has inner eyelids that also seem painted (Borg 1996, 66, no. T 40.2). Her wavy hair, which is loosely gathered and leaves the ears free, is typical of Late Severan fashions, just as the trim of her dress and her necklace. Another example can be seen on the portrait mummy of a woman from Saqqara, Egypt, which is in Dresden today (Doxiades 1995, 19, figs 11–12). On the crown of her head a loose coil of hair is visible pinned with golden hairpins, such as it was worn by empresses between AD 241 and 268, and both her eyes and her eyebrows are strongly emphasised by black make-up.

Since the Late Severan period, depictions on gold sandwich glass complement the mummy portraits. One famous example in this group is the group portrait on the bottom shard of a gold sandwich glass that today is inserted in the Desiderius Cross (Schade 2003, 29, no. T 6.3; Stewart 2007, 32; Kovacs 2014, 237, no. T 145.1). Both depicted women wear their hair in a low bun with uncovered ears, while the teenage boy's short haircut according to Bergmann (1977, 26–29) is reminiscent of Alexander Severus. The upper and lower eyelids of the older of the two women are outlined in black, while the younger, possibly her daughter, is not made up. Another fragment of a gold sandwich glass in the Vatican with the picture of a couple has been found inserted in the slab of the tomb of Bassa in the Panfilo-catacomb in Rome (Pillinger 1984, 83–86, no. T 106–107, figs 237–241, colour fig. 31; Kovacs 2014, 237, no. T 145.59). The heavily made-

up eyelids of the woman contrast with the eyes of her husband, whose style of hair and beard resembles that of the emperor Gallienus.

The most recent example is the Ficoroni-medallion (Fig. 4.2), picturing a woman and (probably) her son (Pillinger 1984, 35–36, fig. 78). Her hairstyle, consisting of a wide braid at the crown of her head combined with ringlets framing her face speaks for a date around the last quarter of the 3rd century AD (Schade 2003, 26–27). The contrast between the eyes of the young man and the woman illustrate that she wears eyeliner.

In contrast to Froschauer, who refers to the portrait of a bearded officer (Froschauer & Harrauer 2004, 3–8), the author is of the opinion that there is no clear evidence for adult men wearing makeup among the mummy portraits. As the persons depicted represent the wealthier classes of Egypt, who – despite their Egyptian surroundings – were oriented towards Rome in terms of clothing, jewellery, hair and general habits, men with makeup are not to be expected. Indeed, there are several mummy portraits of boys with eyeliner clad in white tunics and mantles. But these are characterised as members of Hellenized Egyptian cults by a hairstyle similar to the so called Horus sidelock which had been the children's hairstyle in Egypt since the Pharaonic period (Borg 1996, no. T 42.1; Bierbrier & Walker 1997, 113–114, no. 109; Parlasca & Seemann 1999, 158–159, no. 57 or 214, no. 121). On reaching the age of puberty this particular hairstyle was abandoned.

## Conclusions

That Roman women used makeup, including foundation, rouge, lipstick, eye shadow and eyeliner is well attested by Roman authors and by grave goods. In pictorial sources, i.e. mummy portraits and gold sandwich glass, it is only possible to recognise made-up faces by their strongly black-rimmed eyelids.

Enhancing the eyes is typically an oriental taste rather than a Roman one, as the latter usually tends to moderation. In Egypt, using eye makeup had a long tradition, going back into the Neolithic period. Black or green eyeliner was commonly used by both sexes as well as children and was neither limited to the cultic sphere nor functioned as a status symbol, but was part of daily body care, even for the working man, as it was supposed to protect against the intense sunlight and prevent infections (Pászthory 1992, 7–9; Fletcher 1995, 106–107; Manniche 1999, 135–137; Fletcher 2005, 9–10). Therefore the examples of heavily painted eyes among the mummy portraits of the 2nd century may be the result of a local, that is an Egyptian, influence. At least the author could not discover any other examples among the limited number of Roman portraits preserved on mosaics and wall paintings in houses and tombs from outside Egypt so far.

For the Severan period it can be noticed that the number of examples slightly increases. Moreover there is first evidence for the preference of heavy eye makeup out of Egypt because for the gold sandwich glasses Roman origin is presumed (see Pillinger 1984, 33–35; Nüsse 2008, 223; Kovacs 2014, 236–240). This phenomenon can be explained by the Syrian origin of Julia Domna and her successors as the use of eyeliner was not restricted to Egypt but widespread in the oriental world (see Dayagi-Mendels 1989; Paszthory 1992, 14; Jacob 2011). In fact, the Berlin *tondo* is the only surviving example showing the empress with made-up eyes. But imperial women always acted as trendsetters, whether they wanted to or not. Female portraiture of the Severan period closely imitates the voluminous hairstyle, the earrings and necklaces composed of big pearls, the clothes with richly embroidered borders and even the slight smile. Therefore it is plausible that the preference for strongly black-rimmed eyelids also goes back to the Severan women and became more widespread in the Roman Empire in this time (for further examples in Severan art illustrating the Syrian respectively African background of Julia Domna and Septimius Severus, see Kleiner 1992, 351–353).

Perhaps this fashion was even adopted by women in the Germanic provinces, as suggested by a find from a grave in Hürth-Hermülheim near Cologne. In 1987, the intact burial of an elderly woman in a sarcophagus from the second half of the 3rd century AD was discovered (Wentscher & Schleifring 1988, 4; Gottschalk 2007, 268, fig. 16; Gottschalk 2008, 118–119; 2014, 122–123, fig. 102).

Among the toilet articles that had been placed at her feet, a narrow glass bottle was especially remarkable, because it still contained a bone pin with a shaft coloured black, probably by kohl.

## *Note*

1  In contrast, some depictions from the Pharaonic period in Egypt demonstrate the application of rouge and eye make-up, see Fletcher (1995, 106–108); Manniche (1999, 138–140).

## Bibliography

Aubert, M.-F. & Cortopassi, R. (1998) *Portraits de l'Egypte romaine*. Paris, La Réunion des Musées Nationaux.

Bardiès-Fonty, I., Bimbenet-Privat, M. & Walter, P. (2009) *Le bain et le miroir. Soins du corps et cosmétiques de l'Antiquité à la Renaissance*. Paris, Gallimard.

Bergmann, M. (1997) *Studien zum römischen Porträt des 3. Jahrhunderts n. Chr.* Bonn, R. Habelt.

Bierbrier, M. & Walker, S. (1997) *Ancient Faces. Mummy Portraits from Roman Egypt.* London, British Museum Press.

Borg, B. (1996) *Mumienporträts. Chronologie und kultureller Kontext.* Mainz, P. von Zabern.

Bridger, C. & Ruthenberg, K. (2015) Schminke für eine Römerin. In P. Henrich, C. Miks, J. Obmann & M. Wieland (eds) *Non solum ... sed etiam. Festschrift für Thomas Fischer zum 65. Geburtstag*, 47–52. Rahden/Westfalen.

Brückner, A. (1960) Erwerbungsbericht 1959, II Römische Abteilung. *Bonner Jahrbücher* 160, 429.

Burhenne, V. (1998) *Make up! Aus der Geschichte der dekorativen Kosmetik.* Münster, Westfälisches Museumsamt.

Dayagi-Mendels, M. (1989) *Perfumes and Cosmetics in the Ancient World.* Jerusalem, Israel Museum.

Doxiades, E. (1995) *The Mysterious Fayum Portraits.* London, Abrams.

Dubourdieu, A. & Lemirre, E. (2002) Le maquillage à Rome. In P. Moreau (ed.) *Corps romains*, 89–114. Grenoble, Millon.

Eckhard, H. & Crummy, E. (2008) *Styling the Body in Late Iron Age and Roman Britain.* Montagnac, Monographies Instrumentum 36.

Evershed, R. P., Berstan, R., Copley, M. S., Mottram, H. R., Grew, F., Barham, E., Brown, G. & Charmant, A. J. H. (2004) Formulation of a Roman cosmetic. *Nature* 432, 35–36.

Fasold, P. (2006), *Die Bestattungsplätze des römischen Militärlagers und Civitas-Hauptortes Nida (Frankfurt am Main-Heddernheim und -Praunheim).* Frankfurt, Schriften des archäologischen Museums Frankfurt 20.

Fletcher, J. (1995) *Kosmetik und Körperpflege.* In G. Vogelsang-Eastwood (ed.) *Die Kleider des Pharaos*, 103–111. Hannover, Kestner-Museum/Amsterdam, Batavian Lion.

Fletcher, J. (2005) The decorated body in ancient Egypt. In L. Cleland, M. Harlow & L. Llewellyn-Jones (eds) *The Clothed Body in the Ancient World*, 3–13. Oxford, Oxbow Books.

Forbes, J. R. (1955) *Studies in Ancient Technology III.* Leiden, Brill.

France-Lanord, A. (1961) Boîte à miroir et à fard trouvée à Callas (Var). *Gallia* 19, 254–259.

Freigang, Y. (1997) Die Grabmäler der gallo-römischen Kultur im Moselland. *Jahrbuch Römisch Germanisches Zentralmuseum* 44, 326–327.

Froschauer, H. & Harrauer, H. (2004) *... und will schön sein. Schmuck und Kosmetik im spätantiken Ägypten.* Wien, Phoibos.

Goethert, K. (1989) Zur Köper- und Schönheitspflege in frührömischer Zeit. In A. Haffner, A. Abegg (eds) *Gräber – Spiegel des Lebens*, 275–288. Mainz: P. von Zabern.

Gottschalk, R. (2007) Zur spätrömischen Grabkultur im Kölner Umland. Zwei Bestattungsareale in Hürth-Hermülheim. Erster Teil: Die Gräber und ihre Befunde. *Bonner Jahrbücher* 207, 211–298.

Gottschalk R. (2008) Zur spätrömischen Grabkultur im Kölner Umland. Zwei Bestattungsareale in Hürth-Hermülheim. Zweiter Teil: Die Funde und ihre Deutung. *Bonner Jahrbücher* 208, 91–160.

Gottschalk, R. (2014) *Römer und Franken in Hürth.* Hürther Beiträge zur Geschichte. Bonn, Kultur und Regionalkunde Band 93.

Guerrier, J. (1978) Les origines de la scène de la toilette en Gaule romaine d'après un bas-relief du Musée de Sens. *Revue Archéologique de l'Est* 29, 117–122.

Hinz, H. (1984) Römische Gräber in Xanten. Grabungen 1962–1965. *Rheinische Ausgrabungen* 23, 301–370.

Höricht, L. A. S. (1986) *I vetri romani di Ercolano.* Rome, L'Erma di Bretschneider.

Isings, C. (1957) *Roman Glass from Dated Finds.* Archaeologica Traiectina 2. Groningen-Djakarta, J. B. Wolters.

Jacob, R. (2011) *Kosmetik im antiken Palästina.* Alter Orient und Altes Testament 389. Münster, Ugarit-Verlag.

Kour, A. (1981) *Mineralische Kosmetika im Altertum.* Experimentelle Untersuchungen über ihre antimykotische und antibakterielle Wirkung. Unpublished PhD thesis, University of Düsseldorf.

Kovacs, M. (2014) *Kaiser, Senatoren und Gelehrte.* Wiesbaden, Reichert.

Kleiner, D. A. E. E. (1992) *Roman Sculpture.* New Haven, Yale University Press.

Lloyd-Morgan, G. (1977) *The Typology and Chronology of Roman Mirrors in Italy and the North-western Provinces, with Special Reference to the Collections in the Netherlands.* Unpublished PhD thesis, University of Birmingham (download through http://ethos.bl.uk/OrderDetails.do?uin=uk.bl.ethos.554259)

Manniche, L. (1999) *Egyptian Luxuries. Fragrance, Aromatherapy, and Cosmetics in Pharaonic Times.* Cairo, American University in Cairo Press.

Naumann-Steckner, F. (1999) Glasgefäße in der römischen Wandmalerei. In M. J. Klein (ed.) *Römische Glaskunst und Wandmalerei*, 25–33. Mainz, P. von Zabern.

Neugebauer, K. A. (1936) Die Familie des Septimius Severus. *Die Antike* 12, 156–172.

Nüsse, H.-J. (2008) Römische Goldgläser. *Prähistorische Zeitschrift* 83, 222–256.

Parlasca K. & Seemann, H. (1999) *Augenblicke. Mumienporträts und ägyptische Grabkunst aus römischer Zeit.* Katalog Ausstellung Frankfurt. München, Klinkhardt & Biermann.

Olson, K. (2008) *Dress and the Roman Woman.* New York, Routledge.

Olson, K. (2009) Cosmetics in Roman Antiquity: substance, remedy, poison. *Classical World* 102, 291–310.

Paszthory, E. (1992) *Salben, Schminken und Parfüme im Altertum.* Mainz, P. von Zabern.

Pillinger, R. (1984) *Studien zu römischen Zwischengoldgläsern.* Wien, Verlag der Österreichischen Akademie der Wissenschaften.

Riha, E. (1986) *Römisches Toilettgerät und medizinische Instrumente aus Augst und Kaiseraugst.* Basel, Forschungen in Augst 6.

Rondot, V. (2013) *Derniers visages des dieux d'Egypte.* Paris, Presses de l'université Paris-Sorbonne.

Saiko, M. (2005) *Cura dabit faciem.* Kosmetik im Altertum. Trier, Bochumer Altertumswissenschaftliches Colloquium Bd 66.

Schade, K. (2003) *Frauen in der Spätantike – Status und Repräsentation.* Mainz, P. von Zabern.

Seipel, W. (ed.) (1999) *Bilder aus dem Wüstensand.* Wien, Kunsthistorisches Museum.

Seipel, W. (ed.) (2001) *7000 persische Kunst.* Vienna, Kunsthistorisches Museum.

Soechting, D. (1972) *Die Porträts des Septimius Severus.* Bonn, R. Habelt.

Stewart, S. (2007) *Cosmetics and Perfumes in the Roman World.* Stroud, Tempus.

Virgili, P. (1989) *Acconciature e maquillage.* Vita e costumi die Romani antichi 7. Rome, Quasar.

Wentscher, J. & Schleifring, J. (1988) Aus Hürth-Hermülheim. Zwei Sarkophage aus römischer Zeit. *Das Rheinische Landesmuseum Bonn, Berichte aus der Arbeit des Museums* Heft 3, 1–5

Wilner, O. L. (1931) Roman beauty culture. *Classical Journal* 27, 26–38

Woelcke, K. & Jassoy, A. (1931) Ein bronzenes Schminkkästchen aus einem römischen Skelettgrab von Frankfurt a. M.-Praunheim *Germania* 15, 36–40.

Ziegler D. (2000) *Frauenfrisuren der römischen Antike: Abbild und Realität.* Berlin, Weissensee.

# 5

# Of brooches and men

## *Stefanie Hoss*

*Keywords:* relief; brooches; gender; dress; soldiers; military; Roman

*Archaeologists have long assumed that all plate brooches were part of female dress. In this paper, the depictions of men in various materials are used to examine the use of disk brooches by men during the Roman period. The main bodies of evidence are tombstone reliefs and historical reliefs depicting soldiers as well as coins, busts and statues of emperors in paludamentum. These sources demonstrate the widespread use of plate brooches in military dress. This proves that in order to correctly associate ancient objects with social behaviour and, ultimately, with identity, it is crucial to make full use of all available sources in order to minimize the danger of misunderstanding the evidence.*

*The possible types of brooches worn on the depictions described are different to those commonly found in excavations of Roman military installations. This may indicate that different brooches were used for different circumstances, separating everyday wear from dress for special occasions. It confirms that certain brooch types were used in specific, socially significant ways as social markers.*

## Introduction

In antiquity, brooches were used to hold garments together and generally worn in the area of the upper torso, a highly visible position. As dress accessories, brooches were part of the complex area of personal attire inextricably linked in all cultures to self-representation, fashion and regionality.

The importance of garments and their accessories in defining and expressing identities within the Roman Empire has recently been re-emphasised by Rothe (2009, 5) and Swift (2011, 206–209). Among the many dress accessories, Ivleva (2012, 43–44) names brooches as the 'most useful for exploring the projection and 'social performance' of cultural and other identities', as brooches are both more varied than other accessories and often strongly regional in their distribution. She defines brooches as a tool to communicate different facets of one's identity, among them origin, status, gender and age. Allison also uses brooches as an example of gendered items (2015, 108–110).

Brooches seem to have developed in Europe during the Bronze Age and remained common north of the Alps until long after the Roman period (Beck *et al.* 2000, 7–100). In contrast to this, brooches had already become rare in the Mediterranean during the Iron Age, showing a preference to keep one's garments loosely wrapped about the person, not fixed with a brooch. In Italy proper – that is with the exception of Gallia Cisalpina – brooches went out of fashion for both sexes after about 500 BC (Böhme-Schönberger 2000, 101–102). Brooches were thus not employed in truly 'Roman' dress of either women or men. However, a number of reliefs demonstrate that there was an important exception to this rule (see below).

Generally, brooches can be classed into three broad form groups:

- *bow brooches*, which usually have a long and narrow body that is frequently arched and offers a large space between body and pin;

- *plate brooches*, with a flat and wide body and usually a smaller space between body and pin; and
- *penannular brooches* in the shape of a ring (these are disregarded in this study, as they are not pictured on men).

According to both the representations (on reliefs, mosaics and wall paintings) and the finds excavated from graves, women demonstrate a high variation of brooch use. At different times during the Roman period and/or in different regions within the Empire, different models of brooches were used to fix undertunics, overtunics and cloaks (Riha 1994, 19). At other times and/or in other regions, women do not seem to have used any brooches at all. These various different and quite distinctive styles of wearing brooches indicate that women used brooches as markers of cultural (but not necessarily ethnic) identities. The evidence suggests that quite often, women used brooches with a larger space between the pin and body to fix a cloak or a thick overtunic while brooches with a smaller space were being used for an undertunic or as decoration (Böhme-Schönberger 1997, 33).

Men, however, as pictorial evidence proves, could either wear no brooch at all or could use a single brooch to fasten their cloak on the right shoulder (Croom 2010, 56). This has been taken to mean that men only wore brooches with a comparatively large amount of space between the pin and the body (i.e. bow brooches), in order to be able to scrunch enough folds of the heavy cloth of the cloak in there (Riha 1994, 20).

This short overview of the archaeological theories on the different uses of plate and bow brooches has several ramifications: All brooches with a narrow space between body and pin – that is, all plate brooches – are usually interpreted as women's brooches by archaeologists. Bow brooches on the other hand are often supposed to have been predominately male. But if bow brooches were used for cloaks because of the larger amount of space between pin and body, women would have worn them for the same purpose (see above).

However, the assumption that plate brooches were used by women only is refuted by representations of males in various art forms, such as reliefs, sculpture and others: the vast majority of funerary reliefs depicting men wearing a cloak show round plate brooches (disk brooches, see Fig. 5.1). Similar brooches are also depicted on the portraits of princes and emperors of the imperial family. In order to better understand this phenomenon, it is necessary to look more closely at the evidence.

**Brooch depictions**

*Funerary reliefs*

Portrayals of common people on (funerary) reliefs form an important part of the evidence in the research on dress and its accessories. As Rothe (2009, 22–27) has shown, the representativeness of this evidence is mainly limited by three factors, namely (a) the small proportion of reliefs that have survived to modern times, (b) the relatively small proportion of the population that could afford to commission such a monument and (c) the question of whether the garments represent the dress actually worn by the depicted person. The first two are difficult to gauge and are further complicated by the disparities in monument commissioning and survival in the various regions of the Roman Empire during different periods.

As to (c), Rothe (2009, 24–27) states that the garments worn on 'portraits' are carefully chosen to make various social statements about the depicted person, while the garments worn on scenes depicting everyday life may have come much closer to ancient reality. One problem of the 'portraits' is the aspirational use of status-indicating garments. As Rothe cautions, we cannot be sure that all men depicted in *toga* were indeed legally Roman citizens, and in a similar manner we cannot be sure that everybody depicted in a soldier's dress indeed was a soldier. Dress was highly status-related in the Roman Empire (Rothe 2009, 9) and usurpation of status widespread, despite heavy penalties

### Disk brooches vs bow brooches on soldier's tombstones (n = 159)

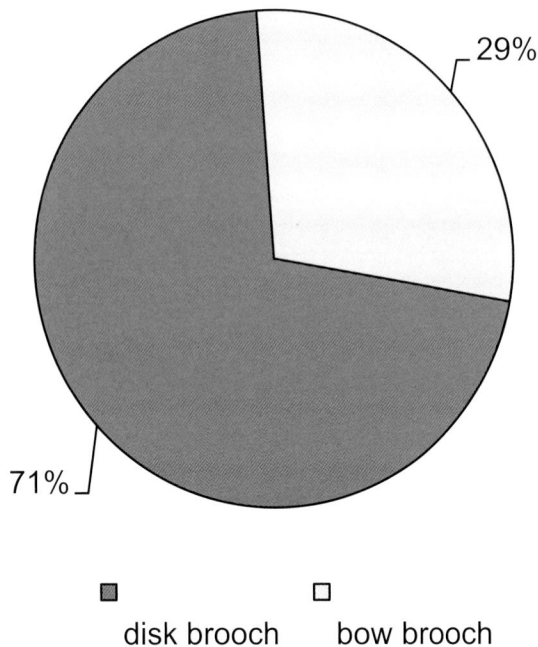

*Fig. 5.1: Relation of depictions of disk brooches versus bow brooches worn by males on tombstone reliefs*

(Reinhold 1971, 276–278). Accordingly, it seems logical that usurpation of status would also occur through the manner of dress on the 'portrait' depictions on tombstones. However, mass usurpation of a particular status ('citizen' or 'soldier') on funerary monuments seems extremely improbable. It therefore appears likely that the majority of tombstones depicted people portrayed with garments they could plausibly have worn – although they may never have done so in real life. The uncertainty around aspirational dress can thus be corrected by using as large a sample of depictions as possible.

Although some research has been done on the representation of the brooches on specific reliefs or specific brooches on various reliefs (Rothe 2013), the funerary reliefs have not yet been examined in a systematic fashion with relation to the brooches depicted on them. Such a study has only lately been made practical or possible by the large-scale publishing of these reliefs online, especially in the Lupa database (www.ubi-erat-lupa.org) and – in lesser numbers – in the Arachne database (http://arachne.dainst.org). The reliefs published in these databases will be cited here with their Lupa or Arachne number only, as this can be used to find them in the relevant database, where all the pertinent information about them is stored.

Unfortunately many reliefs – especially those from the northernmost provinces of the Empire – are of a quality of workmanship or preservation that allows no statements on the presence or absence of a brooch. In other cases, brooches are only suggested by the folds of the garments held together, a manner of representation that is also unhelpful for our inquiry. From those published reliefs that were available to me, 159 reliefs were detailed enough to be able to state at least the general brooch group (bow or plate brooch) with reasonable certainty. This is a large enough basis for the study to ensure that the result is marred as little as possible by the accidents of survival. We will now look at the reliefs in chronological order.

As mentioned above, in Italy (excepting Cisalpine Gaul), brooches were not part of the Roman male dress. The exceptions to this rule are Roman commanders (see below) and Roman soldiers, who are depicted on reliefs with cloaks fastened with brooches from the mid-1st century BC onwards. The first of these reliefs is the tombstone of Minucius Lorarius, found in Padua (I) and generally dated to the last quarter of the 1st century BC (Lupa 14644; Pflug 1989, no. 191, 232; Fig. 5.2). Minucius wears a cloak fastened in the region of the sternum with a bow brooch. The placement of the brooch on the breast instead of the right shoulder is unusual and was probably motivated by a wish to make it more visible. The brooch itself is represented with a head composed of three small globules probably representing a hinge with the needle, strong ridges along

*Fig. 5.2: Tombstone of Minucius Lorarius (Padua, I), dated to 42 BC (Lupa 14644, drawing B. A. Burandt)*

the back of the triangular bow and ending in a distinct foot-knob. It is very similar in appearance to the Alesia brooch, a form that according to Feugère (1985, 299–311) originates in Gallia Cisalpina, Gallia Narbonensis and Lugdunensis and is common in the military camps of Augustan period (Fischer 2012, 136). The tombstone depicts a subtype with a single foot-knob, which is especially common in Gallia Cisalpina, to which the Roman city of *Patavium*, modern Padua, belonged (Feugère 1985, 302–306).

From its origin in Northern Italy, the habit of setting up tombstones depicting the deceased soldier in his military dress spread with the army to wherever soldiers were stationed in the Roman Empire. In some regions, civilians took up the manner of honouring a deceased with a tombstone carrying his or her 'portrait' in relief fairly quickly as well. Consequently, it is not always possible to discern the tombstone of a soldier from that of a civilian if the inscription is missing and if there are no visual props in the relief that can be understood as proof of the deceased having been a soldier. The most important of those visual props are depictions of the deceased wearing a soldier's belt or holding a sword or other weapons or armour such as a helmet or shield (on some reliefs the weapons and armour are held by a servant).

Unfortunately, there is a rather large gap between the earliest reliefs depicting soldiers from Northern Italy and the next chronological group from the Rhineland, which is Julio-Claudian in date (AD 14–54), and thus almost a century younger. Because at that time, most soldiers were depicted wearing armour and no cloak, only two (published) stones from this period show brooches: One of them is a bust of a legionary from Mainz (Lupa 15798), another is the famous stone of the auxiliary Annaius Daverzus (Boppert 1992, 14, 49). Both wear bow brooches, whose type cannot be closer determined. The brooch of Annaius is worn with the head up, contrary to common usage, where the head is worn down.

The next three tombstones date into the Flavian period, one with a bow brooch and two with disk brooches. The bow brooch depicted on the tombstone of Vivianus found in Solymár near Budapest (Lupa 3059) could belong to a number of 1st century types with tapering bodies. While he is dressed like a soldier in tunic and mantle, he carries no weapons or other definitive indicators of this status and the inscription does not mention any army service. The disk brooch pictured on the tombstone of an unknown man from Thessaloniki is a flat disk (Lagogianni-Georgkarakos 1998, no. 99, 86, pl. 43), but the disk brooch shown on the stone of the soldier Ti. Exomnius Mansuetus (Lupa 3338) clearly has an elevated middle part.

Disk brooches were also worn by soldiers on horse, as the tombstones of Insus in Lancaster and of an unknown soldier found in Ribchester prove (Bull 2007, figs on pp. 24, 31, 32). Insus, whose stone is dated to between AD 75 and 120

wears a 'rosette brooch', i.e. a disk brooch with an outer ring resembling petals (Fig. 5.3). This is the oldest depiction of such a brooch on a tombstone. The undated tombstone from Ribchester closely resembling the Insus stone was erected for an unknown horseman. Here, the brooch is a simple disk brooch with a small, elevated middle. Both horsemen wear their brooches in the region of the sternum, probably to make them more visible as they turn sideways, towards the viewer, on their horses.

A relief dating to the Traianic period and depicting a (civilian or military) horseman found in Kalamotos near Thessaloniki just depicts a flat disk on his right shoulder (Lagogianni-Georgkarakos 1998, no. 65, 65, pl. 31), while a contemporaneous tombstone of a horseman from Budapest shows a large disk fibula with an elevated middle part on the right shoulder (Lupa 2978). As he also carries a sword in his right hand and a second relief shows his horse and *calo*, it is clear that he is a soldier. The same type of brooch is depicted on two Hadrianic stones, one commemorating a legionary from Vinkovci (HR, Lupa 3593) and the other a naval soldier from Athens (von Mook 1998, 30–31, cat. no. 249, pl. 37b).

While most reliefs depicting soldiers show the *sagum*, a thick rectangular piece of cloth that was the proverbial soldier's cloak (Speidel 2009, 243), from the mid-1st century AD onwards, many reliefs instead show the *paenula*, a poncho-like sleeveless cloak (often with a hood) that was usually closed with toggles at the front and seems to have gone out of fashion by the late 2nd/early 3rd century AD. Other capes also in fashion in the North-Western provinces in the 2nd century AD were the Gallic and the Treveran capes: The Gallic cape was a knee-length and basically cone-shaped garment with a V-shaped neckline and a hood. The Treveran cape, while having a similar shape and hood, was only waist-length (Rothe 2009, 42–43). These three outer garments made the wearing of a brooch unnecessary, which explains the scarcity of brooch depictions from this period.

The only tombstone dating to the Antonine period depicting a brooch (Lupa 770) shows a man wearing a bow brooch of an unidentifiable type. He has no weapons and the inscription is not preserved, so it is unknown if he was a soldier or not. Probably dating to the 2nd century is a torso from Budapest (Lupa 4518) wearing a muscle cuirass, a narrow *balteus* running from the right shoulder to the left hip and a cloak pinned on the right shoulder with a disk brooch.

The majority of tombstones depicting men with brooches are dated into the 3rd century AD, with 41 of them depicting bow brooches. Of these, eleven of the reliefs are not clear enough to identify the type of brooch (see Appendix, Table 5.1). Other tombstones show bow brooches that can be identified with more clarity. Three of these seem to be knee brooches (Lupa

*Fig. 5.3: Tombstone of the cavalryman Insus (Lancester, GB), dated AD 7–-120 (drawing B. A. Burandt)*

3513, 14871 and Noelke 1986, 213–225, fig. 1, 2), while four others clearly represent early crossbow brooches (*Armbrustfibel*, Lupa 6140, 8817, 14013, 14157). From the 23 reliefs depicting late crossbow or 'onion-headed' brooches (*Zwiebelknopffibel*), four are clearly dated into the 3rd century and the rest belong to the 4th century (Appendix, Table 5.2). Of the latter, eight are not reliefs but graffiti. The brooches are represented in a manner similar to other two-dimensional representations, such as on mosaics like the Great Hunt Mosaic in the Villa at Piazza Armerina (see Carandini *el al.* 1982, figs 17, 126, 130) or wall paintings such as the one in a 4th century AD tomb at Silistra (BUL, Croom 2010, fig. 14,2), with the main identification marks being the strongly arched bow and the upstanding foot. All of the reliefs and the mosaic mentioned depict soldiers, which is unsurprising, considering that the brooch types named have been strongly connected with high ranks serving in the army (Paul 2011, 30–32).

The largest group of men wearing any brooches on 3rd century tombstones (105 reliefs, Appendix, Table 5.3) wears disk brooches. Most of those depicted are clearly soldiers (82), while a minority of reliefs (25) carry no proof of the deceased having been a soldier in the depiction itself or the inscription (if present).

A different form of tomb relief are *sarcophagoi* depicting either a battle or a hunting scene and generally dating to the 2nd–4th centuries AD. They were commissioned by/for members of the Roman upper classes, who were also officers. The *sarcophagoi* with battle scenes are interpreted as having belonged to the highest echelons of this officer class (Faust 2012, 207–212). Most of them show at least the central person on the scene wearing a round brooch, often domed and in some cases topped by a bead or inscribed with a rosette (Appendix, Table 5.4).

Additions to these reliefs are some paintings commissioned by private individuals. The largest group is formed by 19 mummy portraits and dated into the second half of the 2nd century AD (see Paetz gen. Schieck 2010, 95–96). Nine of these show young men wearing a white tunic with a narrow *balteus* over it, decorated with round (bronze) mounts. The *balteus* assists in carrying the sword, hinted at by a white globular knob representing the ivory pommel in the lower corner of the painting. On their left shoulder lies a bunched dark blue *sagum*, with a silver or gold bow brooch riding on top (see for instance Parlasca &

Seeman 1999, 185, cat. no. 86; Borg 1996, 32). The brooch is executed fairly carelessly, giving a vague impression rather than an exact type.

Ten other mummy portraits represent young men wearing a white tunic with a *sagum* on top, pinned with an oval brooch consisting of a round (red) gemstone, surrounded by an edge decorated with round white gemstones or perhaps pearls (Paetz gen. Schieck 2010, 96, see also Parlasca & Seeman 1999, 194, cat. no. 97, 204, cat. no. 113, 238, cat. no. 145). Here, the brooches are executed with care, which is interpreted as a sign that they are indicators of (officer) rank.

A wall painting also commissioned by and depicting soldiers likewise shows them wearing brooches. It originally decorated the Temple of Bel in Dura Europos and dates to around AD 230 (James 2004, 39, fig. 18). It represents the soldiers of the *Cohors XX Palmyrenorum* and their tribune performing a sacrifice. The tribune Terentius, named in an inscription on the picture, wears a cloak fastened on the right shoulder with a disk brooch. His men wear their cloaks in a similar manner, but the painting is not preserved well enough to discern their brooches.

Most of the plate brooches are either depicted as flat disks or as a disk with an elevated middle. A few exceptions show a rosette type brooch with an outer ring resembling petals or an oval brooch with a round middle gemstone surrounded by smaller stones.

## *Imperial and private portraits*

Disk brooches also appear on 'military portraits' of emperors, mainly occurring in four media, namely sculpture, relief, cameos and coins. Here, the portrayed are shown wearing the traditional battle dress of military commanders consisting of a muscle cuirass with the *paludamentum*, often pinned by a disk brooch. During the Roman republic, the purple *paludamentum* (a large rectangular cloak), was put on by the Roman general when leaving Rome, indicating that he was now invested with the *imperium* (Smith *et al.* 1890, 'paludamentum'). This attire therefore signalled military prowess and success as a general. While the propaganda value of this apparel for a reigning Emperor – or a prince – is self-evident (Manders 2012, 71), it was also used for private portraits, but is less common (Borg in Borg *et al.* 2005, 91, n. 18). Rothe's statement made above, namely that the garments worn on 'portraits' are carefully chosen to make various social statements about the depicted person is even truer for imperial portraits, where the cloak is used to convey a clear propaganda message about the person (Rothe 2009, 24–27). The busts and statues will be cited here with the Ararchne number only, which can be used to find the relevant data and literature in the database. In the same manner, the list of coins in the appendix cites the numbers of the RIC and other large coin publication series.

The different media in which the type of 'emperor with *paludamentum* and brooch' was depicted each have their own drawbacks: Cameos and coins are so small that the representations of the brooches cannot be very detailed. Busts and statues bring a different set of problems: Bust portraits of emperors usually show the portrayed life-sized, while statues are commonly life-sized or larger. Accordingly, the brooches on these portraits are depicted large enough to be able to discern details, but unfortunately, brooches on statues and busts were easily damaged. Thus, many brooches on statues and busts are modern additions, meant to complement the portrait. Consequently, only those brooches that were clearly stated in the publication to have been untouched by later hands were included here.

Another problem is that quite often, old portraits were set into much younger statues or busts. This could happen in antiquity, but also often happened after the rediscovery of the heads during the Renaissance and later. As these statues and busts have so far mainly been researched by classical archaeologists interested in portrait art, the dates connected to them usually just relate to the head, making it impossible to accurately date the brooch on the statue or bust, if it was younger. These busts and statues have been disregarded here as well.

Many of the statues and busts of emperors and princes were copied and spread throughout the Roman world in antiquity, and usually, many coins of/for the same emperor/prince were struck with similar obverses. In order to avoid tedious repetitions of basically the same depictions, it seemed useful to limit the following to a number of examples that touch on as many emperors as possible and thus illustrate the general development.

The first example of the iconographic type of 'emperor with *paludamentum* and brooch' is an equestrian statue of Augustus, found in the Aegean Sea and today in the National Museum at Athens (Arachne 982). While it does belong to the type, the *princeps* does not wear the customary cuirass under the *paludamentum*, but a tunic. The cloak is fasted on the right shoulder by a disk brooch with a highly raised middle part resembling a gemstone surrounded by a narrow, flat edge.

The following four examples are depictions dated to the Augustan to Tiberian periods: A colossal seated statue of Tiberius in Madrid (Arachne 11789) shows a sketchily executed brooch that is nothing more than a slightly domed disk in the cloak's folds. The brooch pictured on the right shoulder of Tiberius on an onyx cameo (Arachne 615889) also is shown in a simplified form as a flat disk with a raised border. The brooch depictions are similarly abbreviated on two glass cameos of Tiberius (Arachne 615890 and Hertel 2013, 204, cat. no. 142, pl. 129).

The first coins to depict an emperor in *paludamentum* with a brooch on the obverse are *sestercii* of Nero (Woytek 2010, 73–74, pls iii–iv, bust variants f and h; Wolters &

Ziegert 2014, 59; Wolsfeld 2014, 196–197). They mostly show the brooch as a flat disk, sometimes with an accented edge. After the introduction of this iconographical type into the medium of coins, it is used occasionally by the emperors of the 1st and early 2nd centuries. However, most busts on coins still only show the bare neck, in concurrence with the bust portraits. In accordance with the development of the bust portraits (see below) showing more of the upper torso and thus also part of the dress of the emperor, the type 'Emperor with cuirass, *paludamentum* and disk brooch' becomes more common on coins in the Trajanic period and is regularly used for many of the coins minted by emperors from Marcus Aurelius onwards. From the early 3rd century, this manner of representing the emperor on coins becomes the standard on the obverse, only being displaced by the depiction in a cuirassed bust without a *paludamentum* (which demonstrates the emperor to be even more 'prepared for war') in the late 3rd century under the soldier emperors. As a list with all the coins depicting the emperor with a *paludamentum* and disk brooch would be very long indeed, the list given in the Appendix (Table 5.5) only includes examples of such coins from the emperors between Nero and Constantine. This seems enough to prove that this type was in use by most – perhaps even all – emperors after Nero.

From the Trajanic period onwards, bust portraits show larger amounts of pectoral muscles and shoulder, giving the sculptors the possibility to include characteristic parts of dress and other attributes, such as a *paludamentum* with a brooch. A number of cuirassed busts depict Hadrian with *paludamentum* and brooch, pinned either on the right or left shoulder. While some busts (Arachne 5940, 7077, 7822; Wegner 1956, 21–22, pl. 9b) show the brooch to be a flat disk, with a large domed centre leaving only a narrow edge, others show a disk inscribed with a rosette (Arachne 13571) or a mildly domed disk or rosette with a central bead on top (Arachne 19674, 28360).

The bust of a young man in a fringed *paludamentum* kept at Castle Howard is dated into the early Antonine period by B. Borg (Borg et al. 2005, 91–94, cat. no. 45, pl. 47; Arachne 3793). His brooch is pinned on the right shoulder (Figs 5.4 & 5.5). It has a raised edge enclosing a flower with four petals, each petal folded back on itself on its three sides, and a raised middle consisting of two disks, the smaller and higher of which has a hole. Another statue with a bearded man wearing a *paludamentum* dated by Goette to the mid-2nd century (Arachne 2250) also depicts the brooch in the form of a flower with a serrated edge and a central bead.

During the second part of the 2nd century AD, the bust with *paludamentum* and brooch becomes a very common type of depiction for emperors and princes. Often, the brooch is too worn to show much (Arachne 10520, 12568, 14920, 22794, 37932). The brooches that are better preserved seem to fall into three categories: (a) the brooch is simply domed, (b) it is domed and has an inscribed rosette or (c) it is domed

and topped by a bead, sometimes also depicting a rosette (Appendix, Table 5.6).

A group of statues of the same cuirass type but depicting different emperors and dating into the 2nd and 3rd centuries all carry the *paludamentum* loosely thrown over the left shoulder, with the brooch riding on top (Stemmer 1978, 66–68, cat. no. V19–V22, pls. 42–43). The brooches are all depicted as belonging to type (a). The brooch on a statue of an unknown emperor from the 3rd century from Alba Iulia (RO, Arachne 133) also shows a domed disk of type (a).

The representations of the emperors Gordian III, Philippus Arabs and Valerian on the famous triumphal reliefs of Shapur I at Bishapur and Nashq-e-Rustam are, of course, not imperial portraits in the Roman tradition; nevertheless they depict the dress and equipment of the emperors with a high degree of accuracy (Hoss 2015b). On both of the reliefs at Bishapur, the emperors are shown wearing a disk brooch on the right shoulder, while the kneeling emperor on the relief at Nashq-e-Rustam wears a brooch with a distinctive double edge that might indicate a gemstone in the centre (Fig. 5.6).

Of the two famous porphyry groups of the Tetrarchs now kept in Venice and the Vatican, the Vatican group are depicted with disk brooches slightly differing in form: While the two Augusti wear simple disks, the disk brooches of the Caesars are pictured with raised edges and a small raised middle part, representing a gemstone (Laubscher 1999, fig. 1, fig. 4). According to Laubscher (1999, 213), remains demonstrate that the brooches of the Venice group originally had been crossbow 'onion-headed' brooches (*Zwiebelknopffibel*). These had been chiselled off – perhaps under Theodosius II – and small stud holes added, in order to replace the brooches with real metal examples, probably made from gilded bronze and of the disk type with pendants favoured in the early 5th century AD (Laubscher 1999, 241–242, fig. 9).

Two possible types of brooches seem to be represented on the above depictions of princes and emperors: Some imperial portraits and the reliefs from Nashq-e-Rustam show a domed brooch with a flat edge, indicating a brooch with a central gemstone. Other portraits represent a rosette-type brooch, with the two portraits depicting very detailed flowers being the most obvious (Arachne 2250, 3793).

### Historical reliefs

Most Roman reliefs that fall into this category can be termed 'propaganda sculpture' (Bishop & Coulston 2006, 2). The term implies that they do not depict ancient reality, even though they pretend to do just that. The manner of depiction on these reliefs was quite formulaic and determined to a high degree by the artistic *koine* in which the sculptors worked (Coulston 1983, 24–25). Another drawback is that most figures are quite small and consequently the brooches are even smaller.

*Fig. 5.4: Bust of a young man with* paludamentum *(Castle Howard, GB), early Antonine period (Arachne 3793)*

*Fig. 5.5: Detail of Fig. 5.4*

*Fig. 5.6: Drawing of the rock relief at Nashq-e-Rustam: the Sassanidian ruler Sharpur with two Roman emperors, perhaps Valerian and Philippus Arabs (drawing R. Reijnen)*

On most of the historical reliefs dating to the 1st century AD, the actors are either dressed as civilians, who do not wear brooches (see introduction) or – if dressed as soldiers – are depicted either without a cloak or with a *paenula*. In the small number of reliefs, in which the depicted does wear a *sagum* or *paludamentum,* such as the Census-relief, also known as *ara Domitii Ahenobarbi,* now in the Louvre (Arachne 24409), the brooches are often unrecognizable in the folds of the cloak. An exception to this is one of the four reliefs from what traditionally is described as the base of a column in Mainz, dated to the Flavian period (Bishop & Coulston 2006, 4, fig. 5). The relief shows two legionaries on the march, with the one on the right carrying a *signum* and wearing a fringed *sagum,* closed at the throat with a round brooch with a V-shaped decoration.

From the turn of the 1st–2nd centuries onwards, brooches are increasingly depicted on historical reliefs. On the

*Fig. 5.7: Figure of Nero/Domitianus with paludamentum and disk brooch with head of Medusa, detail of the so-called 'Cancelleria'-Relief A (Rome, I), dating to AD 81–96 (Photo: Arachne 21573, negatives Research Archive for Ancient Plaster, University of Cologne)*

Cancelleria Relief A (Arachne 21573), commonly dated into the period of Domitian, the emperor (originally Domitian, re-worked into Nerva) wears a *paludamentum* pinned with a brooch which is shown to have a domed centre and a flat edge. The domed centre represents a cameo, as it is decorated with a Medusa's head (Fig. 5.7). One of the largest reliefs depicting brooches is the column of Trajan in Rome. In various scenes of the column, legionaries, auxiliaries, as well as Praetorians are pictured with a round brooch on the right shoulder, as are the Dacian enemies (scenes 16, 28, 52, 64, 83, 93, 104, 190, see Pogorzelski 2012, figs 30, 44, 78, 94, 120, 134, 149, 190). In some scenes, the emperor is wearing military attire, topped by a *paludamentum* pinned with a disk brooch (Gross 1940, pl. 37a–c, 38, c, 39, a, 40 a–d, 41b, 42c–d, f). The brooch is either shown as a flat disk or as a disk with a domed centre.

Some of the horsemen pictured on both the eastern and the western so-called *decursio* reliefs of the base of the column of Antoninus Pius (Arachne 2100275, see also pictures offered on the internet) wear cloaks billowing behind them as they ride, with round brooches at the right shoulder. This is also true of the soldier in muscle cuirass standing on the left of the group of Praetorians in the middle (Koeppel 1989, 63–70, figs 24–25).

In almost all of the scenes on the column of Marcus Aurelius in which the Emperor is pictured, he and his *lictors* and entourage wear cloaks pinned by a round brooch on the right shoulder. Soldiers, however, rarely are pictured wearing cloaks, but if they are, they wear a *sagum* pinned with a round disk brooch at the right shoulder. In all cases, the brooches appear undecorated (Burandt 2015, 199–207).

Eleven further reliefs with deeds of Marcus Aurelius were originally from a monument now unknown. Three are now at the Palazzo dei Conservatori in Rome and eight are integrated into the arch of Constantine. From the reliefs in the Palazzo dei Conservatori, one scene depicting the emperor on horseback with Barbarians begging for mercy shows him, an officer to the left of him and a horseman and two soldiers to the right wearing brooches on their right shoulders (Koeppel 1986, 47, fig. 27). The brooches of the officer, the emperor and the horseman are domed, the soldiers seem to wear simple disk brooches, but these are perhaps due to later supplements of lost parts. Four of the reliefs integrated into the arch of Constantine show brooches: The first depicts a *profectio* in which Marcus Aurelius is wearing a domed brooch on his right shoulder while a soldier with a *vexillum* wears a simple disk in the region of his sternum (Koeppel 1986, 56–58, fig. 31). The second shows prisoners being brought before the emperor on a rostrum; both Marcus Aurelius and the man behind him wear round brooches on the right shoulder (Koeppel 1986, 60–62, fig. 33). In a third scene picturing a *submissio,* the emperor is sitting on the rostrum and both he and the man behind him are wearing round brooches (Koeppel 1986,

63, fig. 34). The emperor also wears a brooch on his right shoulder in two other scenes (Koeppel 1986, 65–66, fig. 35, 70–72, fig. 38).

During the 3rd and 4th centuries, the number of historical reliefs is smaller, but they still show both emperors and soldiers wearing disk brooches. The triumphal scene on the arch of Septimius Severus at Leptis Magna (Arachne 1070178) shows several men in front of the *quadriga* of the emperor, wearing disk brooches on the right shoulder. The tetrarchs presented on the late 3rd century arch of Galerius in Thessaloniki (Arachne 1249663) also wear cloaks with a round brooch, but as the relief is severely abraded, any decoration of the brooches is lost. Of those reliefs on the arch of Constantine in Rome that date into the period of Constantine, the right corner relief of the *profectio* depicts a horseman with a disk brooch on the right shoulder (Koeppel 1990, 43, cat. no. 17, fig. 13)

We can conclude that while most historical reliefs seem to show only simple disk brooches, this is most likely connected to the fact that the depictions are too small to allow elaborate brooches. On those reliefs that depict the protagonists large enough, the brooches are shown as domed and the exceptionally well-executed brooch on the shoulder

of the emperor in the Cancelleria relief even depicts a cameo with a Medusa's head.

## Conclusions

While the representational evidence thus seems to point univocally towards (some) men using plate brooches to fasten their cloaks, the question remains whether this manner of depiction was chosen out of convenience for the sculptors, as a disk brooch could be more easily fashioned from stone than a bow brooch. The disk brooch would then be a substitute for the brooch worn in reality, which might have been a bow brooch.

That this is not the reason for choosing disk brooches is proven by the tombstones depicting bow brooches (Appendix, Table 5.1 & 5.2) and by the four tombstones depicting both a disk brooch and a bow brooch simultaneously: One tombstone found in Lauriacum (Enns, Austria, Lupa 497; Fig. 5.8) represents a family. The man on the left wears a (possibly domed?) disk brooch, while the man on the right wears a bow brooch. A similar depiction can be found on the tombstone of Aurelius Ianuarius, who died at age 10 (Lupa 4361). While the boy is wearing a bow brooch, his

*Fig. 5.8: Tombstone of a family depicting a woman and two men: detail with the two men (Enns-Lorch, AU, Lupa 497; drawing B. A. Burandt)*

father, a *tribunus legionis,* wears a disk brooch. The two other examples show couples, with the women wearing bow brooches, while the men wear disk brooches (Lupa 3827, 3985).

The latter examples underline the conclusion that the division into male (bow) brooches and female (plate) brooches is not borne out by the available evidence. It was already speculated for some time that if bow brooches were preferred for the closing of cloaks, women must also have used them for this purpose. As the representational evidence has just shown us, men also used plate brooches to fasten their cloaks, regardless of the small volume between the pin and the plate. The volume of folds a brooch can scrunch between pin and bow/plate thus seems to play no role in the use of brooches for cloaks.

As we have seen, the majority of the tombstones picturing men wearing brooches were erected for soldiers, while the *sarcophagoi* depicting men wearing cloaks with brooches were commissioned for high officers or generals. On the historical reliefs, most of the men wearing brooches are soldiers as well, and the wall painting of the *Cohors XX Palmyrenorum* in Dura Europos also undoubtedly depicts soldiers. While there are no inscriptions telling us whether the men represented on the mummy portraits were soldiers, the depictions of sword pommels are very good indicators that they indeed were. The depiction of late crossbow brooches ('onion-headed' brooches or *Zwiebelknopffibel*) on the Great Hunt mosaic of Piazza Armerina and the wall painting of the Silistra tomb confirms that the men pictured here were also soldiers. The emperors portrayed in busts,

coins, cameos, statues and reliefs are shown in their role as military commanders and as such either wear full military dress with a muscle cuirass and the *paludamentum* with a brooch or an abbreviation of it showing only the cloak and brooch. As the main difference between a soldier's *sagum* and a general's *paludamentum* was the larger size and purple colour of the *paludamentum*, the combination of a rectangular cloak and a brooch seems to have been the most enduring military outer garment in the Roman period. While the *paenula* was used from mid-1st to the early 3rd century AD, the *sagum* and *paludamentum* originate at an uncertain point in the Republican period and continue well into post-Roman times (Burandt 2015, 199–207).

Most of the men wearing a cloak and brooch can be identified as soldiers either by the inscription or additional visual proof (such as weapons) in the depiction. On the other hand, many representations of male civilians depict them wearing different outer garments, such as the Gallic and Treveran capes. While this may indicate that the combination of mantle and brooch was reserved to soldiers, and that civilian males had to wear different outer garb, it is no more than an indication at present. Testing this hypothesis would necessitate a complete examination of the large corpus of depictions being made available through various online and other publications, which would vastly exceed the confines of this article.

If we summarise the information gained on the form of the brooches from the different media, we can discern two general types: The first is a flat round or oval 'domed' brooch with a central gemstone or cameo/intaglio. The mummy

*Fig. 5.9: Brooch found in the Augustan proto-town of Waldgirmes (D; drawing B.A. Burandt)*

*Fig. 5.10: Adlocutio-brooch from Lackford (GB; drawing B.A. Burandt)*

portraits prove that the flat edge of these brooches could also be decorated with additional gemstones or pearls. The second type is a rosette brooch, represented in the better executed and preserved examples as either a full-blown flower or a domed fibula with an inscribed rosette, topped by a bead. The exceptionally well-preserved brooch with a Medusa's head hints at brooches with a central cameo.

The standard publications on brooches from the provinces along the Limes, which were populated by large numbers of soldiers, seem not to include many examples that resemble these depictions. In fact, there are only a small number of published brooches that do resemble them: The earliest example is a rosette brooch from the Augustan proto-town of Waldgirmes in Germany, which seems to have comparative parallels in Trier (Martin-Kilcher *et al.* 2008, fig. 3.38; Rasbach 2013, 119, fn 22, fig. 4; Fig. 5.9). The silver brooch is made from a round plate with a hinged pin on the underside, while the upper part forms a rosette (or a lotus flower) cut from silver sheet, partly gilded and decorated with glass stones riveted to the plate. A small group of brooches only found in Britain, dating to the mid–late 2nd century AD and picturing military subjects also has a disk-shaped form ('*Adlocutio*-brooches', see Hattat & Webster 1985; Mackreth 2011, 154–155, pl. 104, fig. 5.10). A later brooch from a hoard in southern Germany dated to the late 2nd/early 3rd century AD is made from silver, domed and decorated with finely granulated vines and grapes (Martin-Kilcher *et al.* 2008, fig. 3.29; Fig. 5.11). Even later is an oval brooch of 12 cm length, decorated with a central cameo and surrounded by small coloured gemstones, which was

discovered in Dura Europos and thus must have been lost before this city's abandonment in AD 257 (Martin-Kilcher *et al.* 2008, fig. 3.32; Fig. 5.12). A gold brooch with a sard intaglio from the Villa Borghese in Rome and now at the British Museum seems comparable to it; it is dated rather vaguely 1st–3rd century AD (Mackreth 2011, 161 BM 1772.0314.185).

A cheaper version of this type might be represented in the brooches of the type Riha 7.8, which are made up of three parts; a thin metal ground plate with a repoussé sheet metal decoration, in whose middle a round and domed glass "gem" sits, which is sometimes carved in the manner of a cameo (Riha 1979, 185; 1994, 157–158; Mackreth 2011, 178, type 23, pl. 121). In a similar manner the brooches Mackreth Type 3.b, which are oval and domed and often gilded may bee seen as cheaper variants (Mackreth 2011, 160–166, pls 106–109).

While these examples seem to agree fairly well with the representations, their number is not sufficient to account for the high number of these brooches that must have been worn by the soldiers during the Roman period. For this, several possible explanations can be offered. One possibility is that after the establishment of the iconographic type during the Julio-Claudian period, the depictions of the emperors and soldiers– at least in regard to *sagum/paludamentum* and

*Fig. 5.11: Brooch found in a hoard in Southern Germany dated to the late 2nd/early 3rd century AD (drawing B. A. Burandt)*

*Fig. 5.12: Brooch found at Dura Europos (SYR; drawing B.A. Burandt)*

brooch – became increasingly schematic. This is certainly true of the coins and cameos, but also noticeable in the reliefs and sculpture. This schematic manner of depiction may have meant that a certain type of brooch would continue to be represented on the depictions of soldiers and emperors, although it no longer was used or existed in reality. But the mummy portraits – which are generally held to have been fairly accurate in their depiction of accessories (Paetz gen. Schieck 2012, 95–96) – show that brooches with gemstones were still worn in 2nd century Egypt. That this is also true elsewhere is proven by the brooch finds dating to the 2nd and 3rd centuries.

Another possible explanation of the discrepancy between the small number of finds of brooches and the high number of depictions is that these brooches were too valuable to be thrown away or carelessly lost. Instead, their small numbers may be explained by their having been taken apart for their materials during antiquity. We could even speculate that the brooches decorated with real gemstones were the 'best' brooch a soldier had, used only for special occasions. The simple bow brooches named 'soldier's brooches' (for instance Drahtfibel Almgren type 15) found in masses in the forts and fortresses along the limes and in the neighbouring *vici* and *canabae* may then have been the cheaper 'everyday' version used to close the *sagum*. It is quite possible that this group of 'everyday' brooches also included a number of well-represented plate brooches, as there are some types among them that are conspicuous by their military subjects, such as military equipment or *beneficarii* insignia (see Hoss 2015a).

While the general form of the disk brooch is used too ubiquitously on the depictions (for instance on Trajan's column, see above) to have been a mark of rank, it is very likely that the quality of the metal and gemstone(s) of the brooches were indeed used as indicators of rank. This manner of expressing rank in Roman society is also known from other jewellery worn by men, for instance rings: an iron ring was the mark of the citizen and a gold ring denoted the higher equestrian and senatorial ranks (*ius annulorum*, see Schmitz 1875). As the reliefs and statues were painted, the brooches could have been coloured according to the metal and gemstones they represented. If this assumption is correct, it would fit with the statement by Rothe (2009, 24–27) mentioned above, that dress (and dress accessories) worn in 'portraits' are carefully chosen to make various social statements about the depicted person. It would also explain the depiction of the early and late crossbow brooches (*Armbrustfibel* and *Zwiebelknopffibel*) on some of the tombstones, as these types were used to denote rank (Paul 2011, 94–98).

We can thus conclude that far from being exclusively female dress accessories, disk brooches were not only worn by men, they were typical for military men: worn in combination, the rectangular cloak – be it the *sagum*

of the soldier or the larger purple *paludamentum* of the commander – and brooch seems to have signalled 'military man' in the Roman period. While the brooch used here could be – and indeed often was – a bow brooch, disk brooches (and probably also other plate brooches) were often worn as well.

The mistaken identification of disk and other plate brooches as characteristically female objects has shown that when speculating about the social usage of a class of objects in daily life, in addition to finds, it is important to use the depictions of objects wherever possible. Representations typically depict objects in a manner that is laden with meaning through their associations, illustrating the situation shown and/or commenting on the social station of the person(s) depicted (Rothe 2009, 24–27). This is especially true for items of dress, which – as mentioned in the beginning – were used to define and express those multi-layered clouds of social information about a person termed 'identities' by archaeologists. The evidence of the reliefs on the use of objects has not yet been fully made use of, but further work on them will surely more fully illustrate the many facets of Roman life.

## Databases

Arachne: Object database and cultural archives of the Archaeological Institute of the University of Cologne and the German Archaeological Institute at http://arachne.dainst.org/.

Ubi-erat-Lupa = F. and O. Harl, www.ubi-erat-lupa.org (Picture database of antique stone monuments)

## Bibliography

Allison, P. M. (2015) Characterizing Roman artifacts to investigate gendered practices in contexts without sexed bodies. *American Journal of Archaeology* 119(1), 103–123.

Andreae, B. (1980) *Die Sarkophage mit Darstellungen aus dem Menschenleben, Part II: Die römischen Jagdsarkophage (Die antiken Sarkophagreliefs Series)*. Berlin, Gebrüder Mann.

Balty, J. C. (1988) Apamea in Syria in the second and third century. *Journal of Roman Studies* 78, 91–104.

Beck, H., Steuer, H., Timpe, D. & Wenskus, H. (2000) *Fibel und Fibeltracht. Reallexikon der Germanischen Altertumskunde.* Berlin, De Gruyter.

Bergmann, M. & Lahusen, G. (1982) Die römischen Portraitbüsten der Saalburg. *Saalburg-Jahrbuch* 38, 12–25.

Bienkowski, P. von (1919) *Zur Tracht des römischen Heeres in der spätrömischen Kaiserzeit.* Beiblatt zu den Jahresheften des Österreichischen Archäologischen Instituts in Wien 19–20, 258–279.

Bishop, M. C. & Coulston, J. C. N. (2006) *Roman Military Equipment from the Punic Wars to the Fall of Rome.* Oxford, Oxbow Books.

Böhme-Schönberger, A. (1997) *Kleidung und Schmuck in Rom und den Provinzen.* Schriften des Limesmuseums Aalen 50. Stuttgart, Württembergisches Landesmuseum.

Böhme-Schönberger, A. (1998) Die proinzialrömischen Fibeln bei Almgren. In J. Kunow (ed.) *100 Jahre Fibelformen nach Oscar Almgren. Forschungen zur Archäologie im Land Brandenburg 5*, 351–366. Wünsdorf, Brandenburgisches Landesmuseum für Ur- und Frühgeschichte, 351–366..

Böhme-Schönberger, A. (2000) Römische Kaiserzeit im provinzialrömischen Gebiet und Beziehungen zur Germania Magna. In H. Beck, H. Steuer, D. Timpe & H. Wenskus (2000) *Fibel und Fibeltracht. Reallexikon der Germanischen Altertumskunde*, 101–113. Berlin, De Gruyter.

Boppert, W. (1992) *Militärische Grabdenkmäler aus Mainz und Umgebung*, CSIR Deutschland Bd II, 5, Bonn, R. Habelt.

Borg, B. (1996) *Mumienportraits: Chronologie und kultureller Kontext*. Mainz, Phillip von Zabern.

Borg, B., Hesberg, H. von & Linfert, A. (2005) *Die antiken Skulpturen in Castle Howard*. Monumenta Artis Romanae 31. Wiesbaden, Reichert.

Boschung, D. (1993) *Dir Bildnisse des Augustus*. Das römische Herrscherbild I. Berlin, Gebr. Mann.

Brüsing, H. (1911) *Antik Konst i Nationalmuseum*. Stockholm, Cederquist.

Bull, S. (2007) *Triumphant Rider. The Lancaster Roman Cavalry Tombstone*. Lancaster, Palatine.

Burandt, B. A. (2015) Die römische Armee und ihre Ausrüstung auf der Siegessäule des Marcus Aurelius in Rom. Unpublished PhD Thesis, University of Cologne.

Carandini, A., Ricci, A. & Vos, M. de (1982) *Filosofiana. The Villa of Piazza Armerina, the Image of a Roman Aristocrat at the Time of Constantine*. Palermo, Flaccovio.

Croom, A. (2010) *Roman Clothing and Fashion*. Stroud, Amberley.

Coulston, J. C. N. (1983) Arms and armour in sculpture. In M. C. Bishop (ed.), *Roman Military Equipment*, 24–26. Sheffield, University of Sheffield.

Coulston, J. C. (2007) Art, culture and service: the depiction of soldiers on furnerary monuments of the 3rd century AD. In L. De Blois & E. Lo Cascio (eds) *The Impact of the Roman Army (200 BC–AD 476). Economic, Social, Political, Religious and Cultural Aspects*, 529–561. Amsterdam, J. C. Gieben.

Eibl, K. (1994) Gibt es eine spezifische Ausrüstung der Beneficiarier? In Landesdenkmalamt Baden-Württemberg (ed.) *Der römische Weihebezirk von Osterburken Vol. II*, 273–299. Forschungen und Berichte zur Vor- und Frühgeschichte in Baden-Württemberg 49, Stuttgart: Konrad Theiss.

Faust, St. (2012) *Schlachtenbilder der römischen Kaiserzeit. Erzählerische Darstellungskonzepte in dder Reliefkunst von Traian bis Septimius Severus*. Tübinger Archäologische Forschungen 8. Rahden/Westfalen, Marie Leidorf.

Feugère, M. (1985) *Les fibules en Gaule méridionale de la conquête à la fin du 5. s. ap. J.-C.* Revue Archéologique de Narbonnaise Supplement 12. Paris, Éditions du Centre National de la Recherche Scientifique.

Franzoni, C. (1982) Il monumento funerario pataviano di un militare e un aspetto dei rapporti artistici tra zone provinciali. *Rivista Archaeologica* 6, 47–51.

Franzoni, C. (1987) *Habitvs atqve habitvdo militis. Monumenti funerari di militari nella Cisalpina Romana*. Studia archaeologica. Rome, L'Erma di Bretschneider

Grabherr, G., Kainrath, B. & Schierl, Th. (eds) (2013) *Relations Abroad - Brooches and Other Elements of Dress as Sources for Reconstructing Interregional Movement and Group Boundaries from the Punic Wars to the Decline of the Western Roman Empire*. IKARUS 8. Innsbruck, Innsbruck University Press

Greifenhagen, A. (1933) Antiken in Braunsberg. *Archäologischer Anzeiger* 48, 419–453.

Hattat, R. & Webster, G. (1985) New light on 'Adlocutio' repoussé disk brooches. *Antiquaries Journal* 61(2), 434–437.

Henig, M. (2004) *Roman Sculpture from the North West Midlands, Corpus Signorum Imperii Romani - Great Britain*; 1.9, Oxford, Oxford University Press.

Hertel, D. (2013) *Das römische Herrscherbild I: Die Bildnisse des Tiberius*. Wiesbaden, Reichert.

Hoss, S. (2015a) Zu einigen Dekorationsmotiven des 2. und 3. Jahrhunderts auf den Beschlägen von Soldatengürteln, Schultergurten und Fibeln. In P. Henrich, C. Miks, J. Obmann & M. Wieland (eds) *NON SOLUM...SED ETIAM. Festschrift für Thomas Fischer zum 65*, 199–206. Rahden/Westfalen, Marie Leidorf.

Hoss, S. (2015b) The origin of the ring buckle belt and the Persian wars of the 3rd century. In L. Vagalinski & N. Sharankov (eds) *Limes XXII. Proceedings of the 22nd International Congress of Roman Frontier Studies Ruse, Bulgaria, September 2012/* Bulletin of the National Archaeological Institute 42, 2015. Sofia, NIAM-BAS. 319–326.

Ivleva, T. A. (2012) Britons Abroad. The Mobility of Britons and the Circulation of British-made Objects in the Roman Empire. Unpublished Dissertation, University of Leiden.

James, S. (2004) *The Excavations at Dura-Europos conducted by Yale University and the French Academy of Inscriptions and Letters 1928 to 1937. Final report VII: The Arms and Amour and other Military Equipment*. London, British Museum Press.

Kähler, H. (1965) *Der Fries vom Reiterdenkmal des Aemilius Paullus in Delphi*. Berlin, Mann.

Kähler, H. (1966) *Seethiasos und Census. Die Reliefs aus dem Palazzo Santa Croce in Rom*. Berlin, Mann.

Koeppel, G. M. (1986) Die historischen Reliefs der römischen Kaiserzeit IV. Stadtrömische Denkmäler unbekannter Bauzugehörigkeit aus hadrianischer bis konstantinischer Zeit. *Bonner Jahrbücher* 186, 1–90.

Koeppel, G. M. (1989) Die historischen Relief der römischen Kaiserzeit IV. Reliefs von bekannten Bauten der augusteischen bis antoninischen Zeit. *Bonner Jahrbücher* 189, 17–72.

Koeppel, G. M. (1990) Die historischen Reliefs der römischen Kaiserzeit VII, Der Bogen des Septimius Severus, die Decennalienbasis und der Konstantinsbogen. *Bonner Jahrbücher* 190, 1–64.

Lagogianni-Georgkarakos, M. (1998) *Die Grabdenkmäler mit Portraits aus Makedonien. Corpus Signorum Imerii Romani, Griechenland*. Band III, Faszikel I. Athen, Athenian Academy.

Laubscher, H.-P. (1999) Beobachtungen zu tetrarchischen Kaiserbildnissen aus Porphyr. *Jahrbuch des Deutschen Archäologischen Instituts* 114, 207–252.

Mackreth, D. F. (2011) *Brooches in Late Iron Age and Roman Britain*. Oxford, Oxbow Books.

Manders, E (2012) *Coining Images of Power: Patterns in the Representation of Roman Emperors on Imperial Coinage, A.D. 193–284*. Impact of Empire 15. Leiden, Brill.

Martin-Kilcher, St., Amrein, H. & Hortisberger, B. (eds) (2008) *Der römische Goldschmuck aus Lunnern (ZH)*. Collectio archeologica 6, Zürich, Chronos.

Megow, W.-R. (1987) *Kameen von Augustus bis Alexander Severus*. Antike Münzen und geschnittene Steine 11. Berlin, Walter de Gruyter.

Mook, D. W. von (1998) *Die figürlichen Grabstelen Attikas in der Kaiserzeit*. Mainz, Philipp von Zabern.

Miks, Chr. (2007) *Studien zur römischen Schwertbewaffnung in der Kaiserzeit*. Kölner Studien zur Archäologie der römischen Provinzen 8. Rahden/Westfalen, Marie Leidorf.

Noelke, P. (1986) Ein neuer Soldatengrabstein aus Köln. In *Studien zu den Militärgrenzen Roms III(13)*, 213–226. Internationaler Limeskongress Aalen 1983, Forschungen und Berichte zur Vor- und Frühgeschichte in Baden-Württemberg 20. Stuttgart, Theiss.

Paetz gen. Schieck, A. (2012) A Late Roman Painting of an Egyptian Officer and the layers of its perception. On the relation between images and textile finds. In Nosch, M. L. (ed.) *Wearing the Cloak. Dressing the Soldier in Roman Times*, 85–108. Ancient Textiles Series 10. Oxford, Oxbow Books.

Panciera, S. (ed.) (1987) *La collezione epigrafica die Musei Capitoline*. Inediti – revisioni – contributi al riordino 6. Rome, Edizioni di storia e letteratura.

Parlasca, K. & Seemann, H. (eds) (1999) *Augenblicke – Mumienporträts und ägyptische Grabkunst aus römischer Zeit. Exhibition Schirn Kunsthalle Frankfurt*. München, Klinkhardt und Biermann.

Paul, M. (2011) *Fibeln und Gürtelzubehör der späten römischen Kaiserzeit aus Augusta Vindelicum / Augsburg*. Münchner Beiträge zur provinzialrömischen Archäologie 3. Wiesbaden, Reichert.

Pfug, H. (1989) *Römische Porträtstelen in Oberitalien. Untersuchungen zur Chronologie Tyopologie, und Ikonographie*. Mainz, Phillip von Zabern.

Pfuhl, E. & Möbius, H. (1978) *Die ostgriechischen Grabreliefs*. Mainz, Philipp von Zabern.

Phillips, E. J. (1977) *Corbridge, Hadrian's Wall East of the North Tyne*. Corpus Signorum Imperii Romani Great Britain Vol. I, Fasc. 1. Oxford, Oxford University Press.

Pogorzelski, R. (2012) *Die Traianssäule in Rom. Dokumentation eines Krieges in Farbe*. Mainz: Nünnerich-Asmus.

Rasbach, G. (2013) Zuhause in der Fremde – Die Fibelfunde aus der römischen Siedungsgründung in Waldgirmes an der Lahn. In G. Grabherr, B. Kainrath & Th. Schierl (eds) *Relations Abroad - Brooches and Other Elements of Dress as Sources for Reconstructing Interregional Movement and Group Boundaries from the Punic Wars to the Decline of the Western Roman Empire*, 109–126. IKARUS 8. Innsbruck, Innsbruck University Press.

Riha, E. (1979) *Die römischen Fibeln aus Augst und Kaiseraugst*. Forschungen in Augst 3. Augst, Römermuseum Augst.

Riha, E. (1994) *Die römischen Fibeln aus Augst und Kaiseraugst. Die Neufunde seit 1975*. Forschungen in Augst 18. Augst, Römermuseum Augst.

Rothe, U. (2013) Die norisch-pannonische Tracht – gab es sie wirklich? In G. Grabherr, B. Kainrath & Th. Schierl, Th. (eds) (2013) *Relations Abroad - Brooches and Other Elements of Dress as Sources for Reconstructing Interregional Movement and Group Boundaries from the Punic Wars to the Decline of the Western Roman Empire*, 33–49. IKARUS 8. Innsbruck, Innsbruck University Press.

Richthofen, J. von (2000) *Fibelgebrauch – gebrauchte Fibeln: Studien an Fibeln der älteren Römischen Kaiserzeit*. Bonn, Holos.

Schmitz, L. (1875) Annulus. In W. Smith (ed.) *A Dictionary of Greek and Roman Antiquities*, 95–97. London, John Murray.

Schmidt, S. (2003) *Grabreliefs im griechisch-römischen Museum von Alexandria*. Abhandlungen des Deutschen Archäologischen Instituts Kairo, Ägyptologische Reihe Band 17. Berlin, Achet.

Speidel, M. P. & Scardigli, B. (1992). Neckarschwaben (Suebi Nicrenses). In M. P. Speidel (ed.), *Roman Army Studies II*, 153–164. (MAVORS 2). Stuttgart, Steiner.

Speidel, M. A. (2011) Dressed for the occasion. Clothes and context in the Roman Army. In M.-L. Nosch (ed.), *Wearing the Cloak. Dressing the Soldier in Roman Times*, 1–12. Ancient Textiles Series 10, Oxford, Oxbow Books.

Susini, G. & Pincelli, R. (1960) *Il Lapidario: Museo Civico Bologna*. Bologna, Mareggiani.

Swift, E. (2011) Personal ornaments. In L. Allason-Jones (ed.) *Artefacts in Roman Britain*, 194–218. Cambridge, Cambridge University Press.

Touloupa, E (1988) Eine Bronze-Reiterstatue de Augustus. In K. Gschwandler & A. Bernhard-Walcher (eds) *Griechische und römische Statuetten und Grossbronzen. Akten der 9*. Vienna, Kunsthistorisches Museum.

Wegner, M. (1956) *Das römische Herrscherbild II,3: Hadrian, Plotina, Marciana, Matidia, Sabina*. Berlin, Mann.

Wolsfeld, A. (2014) Der Kaiser im Panzer. Die bildliche Darstellung Neros und Domitians im Vergleich. In S. Bönisch-Meyer, L. Cordes, V. Schulz, A. Wolsfeld & M. Ziegert (eds) *Nero und Domitian. Mediale Diskurse der Herrscherrepräsentation im Vergleich*, 181–216. Classica Monacensia. Tübingen, Narr.

Wolters, R. & Ziegert, M. (2014) Umbrüche – die Reichsprägung Neros und Domitians im Vergleich. In S. Bönisch-Meyer, L. Cordes, V. Schulz, A. Wolsfeld & M. Ziegert (eds) *Nero und Domitian. Mediale Diskurse der Herrscherrepräsentation im Vergleich*, 43–80. Classica Monacensia. Tübingen, Narr.

Woytek, B. (2010) *Die Reichsprägung des Kaisers Traianus (98–117)*. Moneta Imperii Romani 14, Denkschriften der phil.-hist. Klasse der Österreichischen Akademie der Wissenschaften 387, Veröffentlichungen der Numismatischen Kommission. Wien, Verlag der Österreichischen Akademie der Wissenschaften.

# Appendix

*Table 5.1: 3rd century AD tombstones depicting unidentifiable bow brooches*

| Soldiers (7): | |
| --- | --- |
| Lupa 78 | |
| Lupa 348 | |
| Lupa 579 | |
| Lupa 4361 | |
| Lupa 23384 | |
| Lupa 23771 | |
| Phillips 1977, No. 76, p. 30, pl. 22 | |

| No certain indicator of soldierly status (4): | |
| --- | --- |
| Lupa 497 | |
| Lupa 735 | |
| Lupa 1260 | |
| Lupa 2733 | |

*Table 5.2: 3rd & 4th century AD tombstones depicting late crossbow brooches (Zwiebelknopffibel), the ones with (G) are in graffito (all are soldiers)*

| 3rd century AD (4) | |
| --- | --- |
| Lupa | 643 |
| Lupa | 650 |
| Lupa | 9647 |
| Lupa | 9649 |
| **4th century AD (19)** | |
| Lupa | 2273 |
| Lupa | 3035 |
| Lupa | 3058 |
| Lupa | 3298 |
| Lupa | 3522 |
| Lupa | 3819 |
| Lupa | 4347 (G) |
| Lupa | 9647 |
| Lupa | 9649 |
| Lupa | 14846 |
| Lupa | 17126 (G) |
| Lupa | 20853 |
| Lupa | 23346 (G) |
| Lupa | 23373 (G) |
| Lupa | 23531 (G) |
| Lupa | 23540 (G) |
| Lupa | 23553 (G) |
| Lupa | 23601 (G) |
| Lupa | 23670 |

*Table 5.3: 3rd century AD tombstones depicting disk brooches*

| Soldiers (82) | |
| --- | --- |
| Lupa | 493 |
| Lupa | 495 |
| Lupa | 496 |
| Lupa | 575 |
| Lupa | 583 |
| Lupa | 642 |
| Lupa | 663 |
| Lupa | 685 |
| Lupa | 1414 |
| Lupa | 2846 |
| Lupa | 2896 |
| Lupa | 2910 |
| Lupa | 2937 |
| Lupa | 3110 |
| Lupa | 3243 |
| Lupa | 3418 |
| Lupa | 3421 |
| Lupa | 3534 |
| Lupa | 3549 |
| Lupa | 3590 |
| Lupa | 3594 |
| Lupa | 3596 |
| Lupa | 3602 |
| Lupa | 3632 |
| Lupa | 3801 |
| Lupa | 3840 |
| Lupa | 3878 |
| Lupa | 4141 |
| Lupa | 4565 |
| Lupa | 4361 |
| Lupa | 6049 |
| Lupa | 6261 |
| Lupa | 7573 |
| Lupa | 8035 |
| Lupa | 8510 |
| Lupa | 13281 |
| Lupa | 13284 |
| Lupa | 15318 |
| Lupa | 15334 |
| Lupa | 17644 |
| Lupa | 19305 |

*(Continued)*

*Table 5.3: 3rd century AD tombstones depicting disk brooches (Continued)*

*Table 5.3: 3rd century AD tombstones depicting disk brooches (Continued)*

| |
|---|
| Arachne Seriennummer 21906 |
| Arachne Seriennummer 80275 |
| Arachne Seriennummer 80373 |
| Arachne Seriennummer 80694 |
| Arachne Seriennummer 80284 |
| Arachne Seriennummer 80276 |
| Arachne Seriennummer 80278 |
| Arachne Seriennummer 80277 |
| Arachne Seriennummer 80279 |
| Arachne Seriennummer 80280 |
| Arachne Seriennummer 80281 |
| Arachne Seriennummer 80284 |
| Arachne Seriennummer 80374 |
| Katalog Augenblicke 1999, 254–255, cat. no. 259 |
| Balty 1988, pl. 14,1 |
| Bienkowski 1919, fig. 118 |
| Bienkowski 1919, 258–279, fig. 119 |
| Brüsing 1911, 81, 35 |
| Coulston 2007, fig. 1 |
| Coulston 2007, fig. 2. |
| Coulston 2007, fig. 5 |
| Coulston 2007, fig. 9. |
| Eibl 1994, 276f. fig. 5 |
| Franzoni 1987, no. 59, 86–87, xxviii, 3 & 4 |
| Greifenhagen 1933, 450–453, fig. 29 |
| Panciera 1987, 55, cat. no. 15 (fn 142), pl. xix, 1 |
| Panciera 1987, 55, cat. no. 15, pl. xix, 2. |
| Panciera 1987, 55, cat. no. 15, pl. xviii, 3 |
| Panciera 1987, 55, cat. no. 15 (fn 141), pl. xviii, 4. |
| Pfuhl & Möbius 1978, no. 307 |
| Pfuhl & Möbius 1978, no. 309 |
| Pfuhl & Möbius 1978, no. 315, 56 |
| Pfuhl & Möbius 1978, no. 316 |
| Pfuhl & Möbius 1978, no. 310 |
| Pfuhl & Möbius 1978, no. 303 |
| Pfuhl & Möbius 1978, no. 302 |
| Schmidt 2003, cat. no. 104, pl. 38 |
| Schmidt 2003, cat. no. 106, pl. 38 |
| Schmidt 2003, cat. no. 111, pl. 39 |
| Speidel & Scardigli 1992, 153–164 |
| Susini & Pincelli 1985, 151, 19. |

| *No positive indicator of soldierly status (25)* | |
|---|---|
| Lupa | 354 |
| Lupa | 450 |
| Lupa | 482 |
| Lupa | 492 |
| Lupa | 495 |
| Lupa | 497 |
| Lupa | 573 |
| Lupa | 644 |
| Lupa | 691 |
| Lupa | 694 |
| Lupa | 862 |
| Lupa | 980 |
| Lupa | 1267 |
| Lupa | 1403 |
| Lupa | 2633 |
| Lupa | 3139 |
| Lupa | 3636 |
| Lupa | 3995 |
| Lupa | 4050 |
| Lupa | 4064 |
| Lupa | 4219 |
| Lupa | 4255 |
| Lupa | 4825 |
| Lupa | 9200 |
| Lupa | 19185 |
| Arachne | 39329 |

*Table 5.4: Reliefs on* sarcophagi *depicting disk brooches.*

*Hunting sarcophagi*: Andreae 1980, 143–185, cat. no. 1, 8, 27, 32, 33–35, 41–42, 59, 65, 69, 71, 73–75, 77–78, 101, 122, 126, 128, 131, 149–150, 188, 190, 204, 206, 210, 213, 224, 235, 240–241; pls 3–4, 6–7, 10–11, 13, 19, 21–24, 27, 46–49, 53–55, 59–61, 64–65, 69–71, 74–75, 77, 79, 81–83, 90, 92, 97, 104, 106

*Battle sarcophagi*: Faust 2012, 197–212, pls 73, 77, 80–81 and Arachne 26590, 80541

*Table 5.5: Coins depicting the emperor (or prince) with paludamentum and disk brooch*

| Emperor | Publication |
|---|---|
| Nero | RIC 79 |
| Galba | RIC 271 |
| Vitellius | RIC 156 |
| Vespasianus | RIC 79 |
| Titus | RIC 371 |
| Domitian | RIC 512 |
| Traian | Traian 249 var. |
| Hadrian | RIC 63 |
| Antoninus Pius | RIC 147 |
| Marcus Aurelius | RIC 20 |
| Lucius Verus | RIC 535 |
| Commodus | RIC 128 |
| Pertinax | RIC 10 |
| Didius Julianus | RIC 3 |
| Septimius Severus | RIC 73 v |
| Pescennius Niger | Antioch Prieur 177var |
| Clodius Albinus | Prieur 177var |
| Caracalla | Caracalla 80 a |
| Geta | RIC 4 |
| Macrinus | RIC 26 |
| Elagabal | RIC 67 |
| Severus Alexander | RIC 43 |
| Maximinus Thrax | RIC 7a |
| Gordian I | Milne 33302 |
| Gordian II | RIC 1 |
| Balbinus | RIC 18 |
| Pupienus | RIC 2 |
| Gordian III | RIC 23 |
| Philippus Arabs | RIC 12 |
| Trajanus Decius | RIC 7a |
| Trebonianus Gallus | RIC 13 |
| Aemilianus | RIC 7 |
| Valerian | RIC 34 / 37 |
| Gallienus | RIC 102 |
| Postumus | RIC 50 |
| Marius | RIC 7 |
| Victorinus | RIC 71 |
| Tretricus | RIC 72 |
| Claudius Gothicus | RIC 32, 48 |
| Quintillius | RIC 9 a |
| Aurelian | RIC 16 |
| Tacitus | RIC 3 |

*Table 5.5: Coins depicting the emperor (or prince) with paludamentum and disk brooch (Continued)*

| Emperor | Publication |
|---|---|
| Florianus | RIC 40 |
| Probus | RIC 78 var 1 |
| Carus | RIC 3 var |
| Carinus | RIC 153 |
| Numerianus | RIC 353 |
| Diocletian | RIC V 38 |
| Maximinianus | V 492 |
| Carausius | RIC 69 (2) |
| Allectus | RIC 7 |
| Galerius | Cohen 137 |
| Severus II | RIC Trier 648 |
| Maxentius | RIC Rome 191 var |
| Constantinus I | Arles RIC VII 138 var |

*Table 5.6: Brooch types on imperial portraits after AD 150*

| Emperor | Arachne no. |
|---|---|
| *Type (a) domed brooch* | |
| Marcus Aurelius | 14923, 15854, 16056, 16057 |
| Lucius Verus | 8643, 10831, 14931, 14935, 14936, 16487, 19796, 24210, 80251 |
| Commodus | 14924 |
| Clodius Albinus | 18281 |
| Caracalla | 38242 |
| Macrinus | 80169 |
| Balbinus | 7429 |
| *Type (b) domed brooch with inscribed rosette* | |
| Antoninus Pius | 8631, 17128 |
| Lucius Verus | 38509, 50053 |
| Commodus | 7519, 17138 |
| Gordianus III | 19667 |
| *Type (c) domed brooch topped by a pearl, sometimes also depicting a rosette* | |
| Antoninus Pius | 12562, 13573, 33852 |
| Marcus Aurelius | 5372, 6914, 19792, 31242 |
| Commodus | 16054 |
| Didius Julianus | 19799 |
| Septimius Severus | 7516, 36117 |
| Caracalla | 2254, 16061, 17140, 17141, 22275, 38118, |
| Gallienus | 28748 |
| Claudius Gothicus | 8763 |

# Part 2

# Religion and ritual in the Roman north-west provinces

# 6

# Ordinary objects transformed: the compound natures of material culture

*Mara Vejby*

*Keywords*: Roman finds; votive deposits; utilitarian; megaliths; Neolithic; Brittany

*This chapter explores the phenomenon in which some materials possess a 'dual nature' and meaning. If found at a temple or shrine these deposits are interpreted as votive offerings. In another context, however, they would be considered utilitarian items. A few such materials within the Roman world include hobnails, tiles, bricks, pottery and coins. Some of these material types have been more extensively discussed than others within the context of votive or at least symbolic deposits, especially hobnails and coins, while others have been discussed to a lesser extent. This chapter aims to consider the different meanings, functions and values that these utilitarian items might possess in light of the alternative sacred contexts in which they are frequently found. The material deposits from a series of secular and sacred sites will be presented in order to compare the nature of the materials between these sites. It will then be seen how bringing the other half of their dual nature to bare in either context can affect the interpretation of the deposits and the site.*

## Introduction: bridging the sacred and the mundane

This chapter explores the grey area occupied by items that are used for utilitarian purposes, but which are frequently also found within 'ritual' or 'sacred' contexts. It argues that for such items the abstract meanings with which they are associated in ritual contexts are not necessarily absent when they are being used in a utilitarian manner. It also notes that, perhaps, the dual meanings or purposes of these items are frequently being overlooked and lost within archaeological interpretations, or that the items themselves are being overlooked due to their contexts. The exploration of this topic will focus on the geographic region of Brittany, during the Roman occupation of Gaul. It will consider the presence of Roman deposits at Neolithic sites, and the lack of attention paid to utilitarian materials from these contexts, in contrast to items without utilitarian functions. It will then explore a scenario in which the significance of subsequent deposits, materials placed at these tombs after their initial construction and use had ended, is interpreted based on the dual utilitarian and ritual meanings carried by some of these materials.

At the centre of the dichotomy between votive and utilitarian items is the context in which these materials are found. Whereas items that are primarily identified as 'votive materials' are most frequently found within 'ritual' contexts, utilitarian items are much more common and are found across a wider variety of site types. Examples of contexts that would typically be classified as 'ritual' include sanctuaries, temples, shrines and sometimes burials. Such sites are often associated with a specific deity (or deities) and/or the sites contain evidence of certain rituals or cult activities. Consequently, there are certain materials that tend to be repeatedly found within such contexts. Conversely, utilitarian sites cover a much broader spectrum of human activity. They include all other aspects of day-to-day living, incorporating evidence of material production, trade and economy, habitation, hunting/fishing, agriculture and the disposal of human material waste, among others.

When looking at the deposition of material culture in the past, there are certain 'object types' that are often considered to be ritual materials during the Roman occupation of Gaul, including 'cult accessories' such as small bells or metal amulets/votive offerings (Fauduet 1993a, 125; 1993b, 148–149). Other, more numerous 'object types' are frequently interpreted as utilitarian items. Some such materials, however, have also been found in ritual contexts, where they are interpreted as votive deposits, such as pottery and coins, both of which are typically produced and used within an economic, utilitarian, system. On a settlement site, such materials are interpreted as evidence of habitation, commerce and/or trade. However, at a Roman temple or sanctuary, these materials are seen as votive offerings. What is key for these objects is not just that the context in which they were ultimately deposited is used to define their significance, but that their significance can change rather drastically from site to site (Grahame 1998; Hamilakis 2010; Jones 2007). The objects themselves, however, whether ultimately found in a utilitarian or sacred context, often do not differ in production method, material, or, as far as has been determined, movement through trade. It is this indistinction leading up to their deposition that causes questions to be raised about using their final context as the main factor in their interpretation.

The presence of these object types at sanctuary sites may imply a more complex relationship to these items, and there are a few possible interpretations: 1) they are, in fact, strictly utilitarian items and we've been wrong in assigning a ritual function to them based on their context; 2) they gain a ritual significance based on their deposition at a ritual location; 3) these objects always possessed some kind of a dual ritual/utilitarian function within the past. In the case of the third interpretation, the presence of these objects in a settlement context does not negate their potential to be deposited at a ritual site. The underlying question becomes whether or not these forms of material culture carry their dual meanings with them over the course of their lives, from creation to deposition? Though it would be difficult to identify archaeological evidence that utilitarian items, in utilitarian contexts, were being treated in a manner implying the potential for ritual significance, it is at least possible to point to instances where apparent votive deposits have been overlooked partly because of the utilitarian nature of the materials.

Research completed in 2012 uncovered a number of these instances in the process of collecting evidence of Iron Age and Roman period activity at megalithic tombs across Atlantic Europe (Vejby 2012). The study created a catalogue of Neolithic megalithic tombs at which _any_ Roman material was found. Within Brittany alone subsequent deposits of Roman materials were identified at 65 different Neolithic tombs, and most of the materials were 'utilitarian' in nature. Because of the contexts of these deposits, and the lack of associated features, these subsequent materials had repeatedly been mitigated as 'lost items' in excavation reports and later discussions of these sites. The pattern of deposition that was uncovered as a result of this study,

however, indicates that these were probably not stray items that had been conveniently lost. Rather, it appears that these materials had been intentionally placed at Neolithic monuments significantly after the initial use of the tombs had ceased (Vejby 2012, 208).

Such a pattern of deposition, however, might never have been uncovered had these materials not been placed at megalithic tombs. If the deposits had instead been made without any association to megalithic structures or other features, then it is probable that they would have been identified as lost items, if indeed they were ever found. This scenario, and the natural conclusions to which it leads, are the basis for this discussion on the utilitarian materials deposited at the megalithic tombs in Brittany.

The following is an overview and brief analysis of some of the Roman materials deposited at the 65 megalithic tombs. 'Utilitarian' materials will be discussed first, along with the distribution of these deposits. The presence and distribution of materials that are more consistently interpreted as votive materials, such as Roman statuettes, will then be presented and discussed. It is important to keep in mind that these 65 tombs are a part of a much larger pattern of over 250 megalithic tombs across Atlantic Europe at which subsequent deposits from the Iron Age and Roman periods have been identified. They therefore represent a regional pattern of cultural activity that has contemporary parallels in other territories, as been discussed elsewhere (Vejby 2012).

## Subsequent deposits on the Breton peninsula

Of the 65 megalithic tombs in Brittany at which Roman materials were identified, the vast majority contained Roman pottery (Fig. 6.1). Roman tiles were found at roughly a third of these sites and in most cases the tiles appear to have been roofing tiles. Perhaps surprisingly, Roman coins were only recorded at 13 tombs. Though the nature of these materials is likely one of the reasons why Roman deposits at these sites have been historically disregarded, the large number of Neolithic sites in the Morbihan region of Brittany at which such materials were recorded indicates a clear concentration of deposits, which is worthy of further examination (Fig. 6.2).

Again, the term 'subsequent deposit' refers to the fact that these materials were placed at megalithic tombs once the tombs' initial construction and use had ended, and after a long period of disuse or abandonment. This disuse lasted for over five hundred to nearly a thousand years in some cases. Then, for reasons that are often not apparent, later cultures began to deposit materials at some of these sites. The term 'votive deposit' is used to refer to deposits accompanying a burial or sacrifice; ritual objects, such as miniatures or statuettes; or materials that are deposited at a sanctuary/shrine/temple. In other words, materials are

| | |
|---|---|
| Pottery (51) | 51 |
| Tiles (20) | 20 |
| Other Material | 17 |
| Bricks (17) | 17 |
| Coins (13) | 13 |
| Statuettes (10 | 10 |
| Hobnails (2) | 2 |

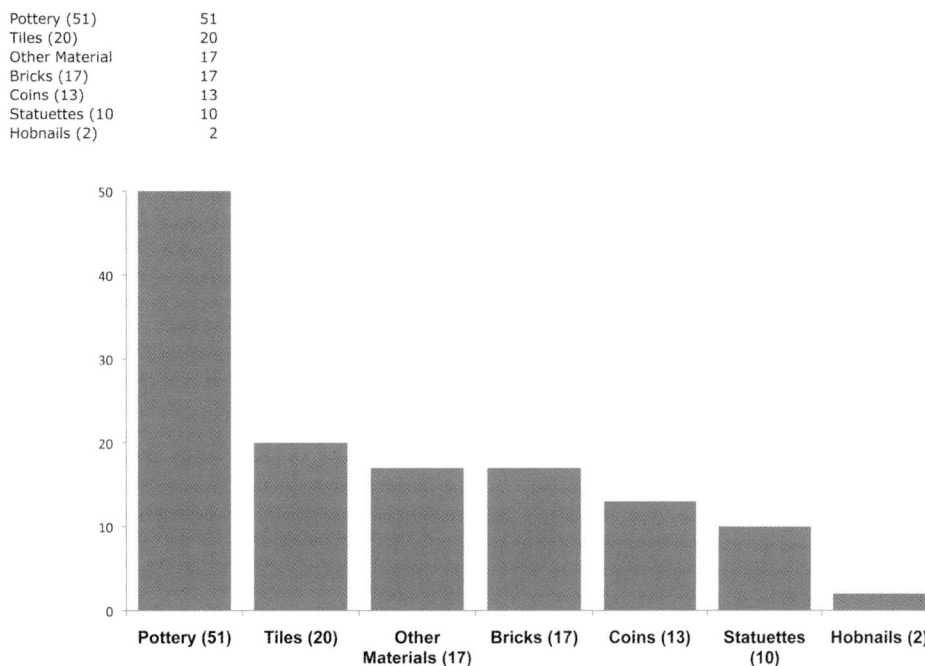

*Fig. 6.1: Graph of Roman materials found at megalithic tombs within Brittany (image: M. Vejby)*

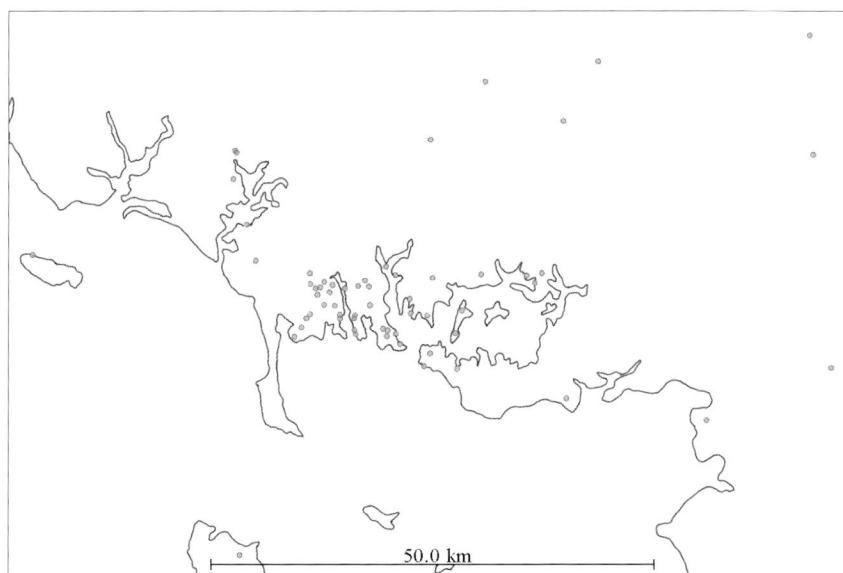

*Fig. 6.2: Distribution of megalithic tombs in Brittany at which Roman material has been found (image: M. Vejby)*

classified as votives based on their status as a ritual item and/or because of the ritual context in which they are uncovered. While it is tempting to use this term to refer to all the Roman materials placed at megalithic tombs in Brittany, the fact that these tombs are not Roman ritual sites means that the quality of the materials themselves is what is used to interpret their status upon being deposited. Thus,

deposits at these tombs which included only utilitarian Roman items, such as Roman pottery or roofing tiles, were dismissed entirely as rubbish or lost items, whereas a few of the Venus statuettes found at nearby tombs were referred to as 'votive items' and were comparatively more thoroughly discussed, though still only minimally compared to deposits at Roman ritual sites.

To be sure, megalithic tombs as a context are quite different from Roman temples/sanctuaries and shrines. Most megalithic tombs would have been over 2000 years old when these Roman materials were deposited. In addition, though their initial Neolithic use was connected to the internment of human remains, the Roman materials deposited at tombs in Brittany do not indicate a similar subsequent use, with the possible exception of two sites which will be more thoroughly discussed later: Tressé and Le Petit Mont. These interactions are therefore a part of these tombs being re-interpreted/re-purposed.

Sadly, the lack of significance generally attributed to these subsequent deposits has greatly affected the information that is available on this activity. An overly strong emphasis on the construction and initial use of Neolithic monuments has resulted in evidence of later interactions being either ignored, or only minimally recorded. Consequently, not only are we missing evidence that would more completely illuminate the extent to which Roman interactions with previous Neolithic monuments occurred, but the vast majority of records fail to provide details beyond the presence of these items, or speculations that these were 'lost materials.' Subsequent materials are not given added meaning or significance in these early excavation records, and only rarely are the conditions of these materials being recorded. It is therefore unknown whether materials were produced for deposit, or were deposited at the end of their use for another purpose. Given the limited deposits though the latter seems more likely. These challenges unfortunately put significant limitations on the analysis of these activities, as will be discussed in upcoming sections (Vejby 2012, 8). Votive deposits within the Roman period, however, are comparatively well documented in the contexts of Roman temples/sanctuaries and shrines (Bispham *et al.* 2000; Fauduet 1993a; Fauduet 1993b; Lecornec 2001).

While Roman material deposits at the sites in this region do not appear to be the result of utilitarian activities, most of the deposited materials themselves would be considered utilitarian items if they were uncovered in another context. Only two tombs, Crucuny and D'Er-Roc'h, are located within proximity of any Roman buildings, which could potentially explain the presents of building-related materials at the tombs. The rest, however, do not appear to be associated with any Roman construction. In the case of D'Er-Roc'h, Roman building foundations were found in the direct vicinity of the dolmen, and Roman pottery and brick were found inside the dolmen (André 1961, 250). Remains of buildings, presumed to be Roman, were found within the area of Crucuny and Roman tiles, along with sherds of Roman pottery, were found within the tomb (André 1961, 249).

Some of these material types are also frequently found at Roman temples, shrines and sanctuary sites in this region,

such as Roman coins, statuettes and pottery. However, they appear to be found in greater quantities at temples and sanctuaries than they are at megalithic tombs (Fauduet 1993a, 125–126; Lecornec 2001, 289). There are also shrine materials that have not been found at these tombs, including tablets with inscriptions and other 'cult accessories' such as small bells or metal amulets/votive offerings (Fauduet 1993a, 125; 1993b, 148–149). The one possible exception is the Roman altar and accompanying deposits found at Le Petit Mont. The evidence from this site will be discussed in the context of other ritual materials in the forthcoming section on Roman statuette deposits. Overall, however, though some of the materials deposited may be similar, there are distinctions in the material evidence found at megalithic tombs versus temple sites. Additionally, research done on the distribution of Roman shrines/temples in Brittany seems to negate the argument that the reuse of the tombs was an attempt to convert megalithic structures into Roman shrines/temples, as there are Roman sanctuaries found along the Gulf of Morbihan (Vejby 2012, 212). It is rather unlikely that the Roman materials deposited at megalithic tombs were the result of a high concentration of shrine use in the area, as much higher concentrations of these ritual sites are found to the northeast, near modern-day Rennes (Vejby 2012, 212).

## Roman utilitarian items

Pottery, tiles, bricks and hobnails are the most common types of utilitarian materials found deposited at megalithic tombs in Brittany. But, again, with the exception of two tombs, there are not any features or other evidence of nearby activities that might explain the presence of these materials. These item types have been found at 65 tombs, but at 43 of the tombs no other 'ritual' materials were present, only the utilitarian deposits.

### *Roman pottery*

Pottery was by far the most common subsequent material deposited at these tombs, and of the 51 tombs at which subsequent deposits of Roman pottery was found, 11 contained no other accompanying subsequent material. The majority of these tombs are centred along the north-western coast of Quiberon Bay (Fig. 6.3). Two additional sites, Kerjagu and Pray, are located north and north-east, respectively, of the bay. Though they may appear to be isolated from the other tombs at which only Roman pottery has been uncovered, they are in fact set among a collection of other tombs at which additional Roman materials accompanied the pottery. South of Pray is the tomb Carhon, which contained Venus Anadyomene and mother goddess statuettes of painted white clay, along with Roman pottery and coins (André 1961, 252). All of this material was found inside the tomb, which indicates both

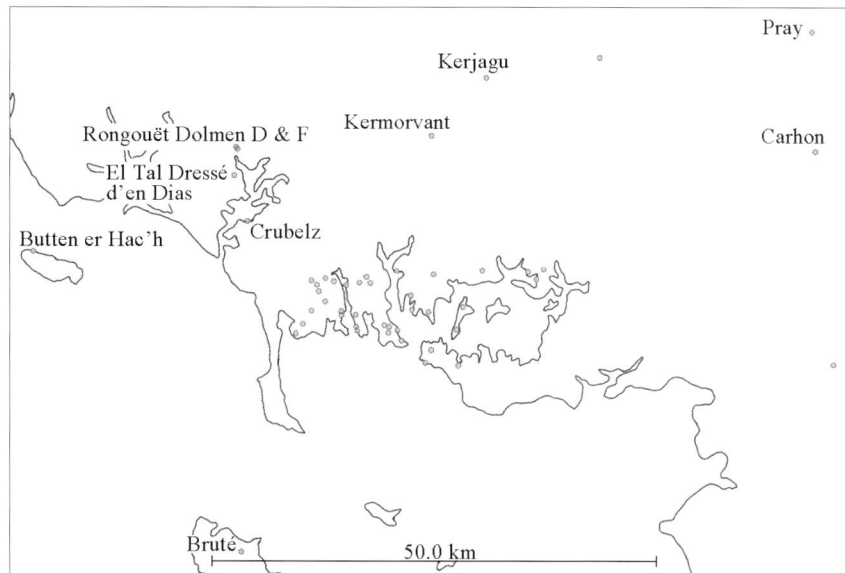

*Fig. 6.3: Distribution of megalithic tombs in Brittany at which Roman pottery has been found (image: M. Vejby)*

knowledge of the internal structure of the chamber, as well as a gained access to the interior after it was closed off at the end of its Neolithic use. Roman coins and pottery were similarly found in the dolmen of Kermorvant (André 1961, 250). Four additional tombs, Rongouët D and F, En Tal Dressé d'en Dias and Crubelz, contained Roman pottery and roofing tiles (*tegulae*) (André 1961, 252; 249; 52; De Closmadeuc 1864, 8–9).

With the exception of two dolmens, Tressé and Clos Pernel, megalithic tombs at which Roman materials have been uncovered are located within Morbihan, and are centred around the Gulf of Morbihan, Quiberon Bay and modern day Vannes. Clos Pernel is located along the southern coast of Finistere and contained Roman brick and pottery (André 1961, 250). Tressé, conversely, is a gallery grave located near the northern coast of Ille-et-Vilaine. There is far more information available on the subsequent activities at this site, where a single crouched inhumation was found during Collum's 1931 excavation, accompanied by Iron Age/Gallo-Roman pottery, a dagger and five steatite beads with some iron fragments (Bender & Caillaud 1986, 115; Collum 1935, 23–26; 49). The beads and iron fragments are thought to have originally been a beaded fibula, similar to the ones found at Etruria and the Gaulish cemetery at Tronoën, St Jean-Trolimon. A Domitian bronze was also uncovered in the allée couverte,[1] but it is not entirely clear whether the bronze was directly associated with the inhumation or not (Collum 1935, 49). Sherds of Gallo-Roman pottery and amphorae (some blackware, some reddish coarse ware and some buffed ware) were found in the covering mound of the tomb in addition to those found in association with the burial. Small breed of dog bones

and 'an ox bone' were also found at this site according to the excavator (Collum 1935, 33–39; 51). Charcoal samples were taken from all levels of the tomb (above the pavement from the bases of the collapsed uprights, the middle of the allée, and near the entrance, as well as beneath the pavement) indicating a fair amount of *in situ* burning within the monument (Collum 1935, 51–52). At the time, Collum was convinced that the structure had been built for the Iron Age/Gallo-Roman inhumation, but now it is clear that this activity took place significantly after the tomb's initial use (Bender & Caillaud 1986, 115). The subsequent inhumation found at this tomb makes it one of only two tombs where the later activity appears to be in-line with the initial use of the tomb.

There are an additional 40 megalithic tombs in the region at which other Roman period materials accompanied Roman pottery deposits, and they are also all located within the district of Morbihan. Most of these sites centre on the Bay of Morbihan, with eight additional tombs located further inland, at distances of 20–35 km from the bay. Butten er Hac'h, which is located on Île d'Groix to the north-west of the Bay of Morbihan, contained a bronze ring, iron dagger of undetermined age, Roman roofing tiles (*imbrices*), common pottery and *sigillata* pottery within the covering mound of the tomb (André 1961, 251). Two Roman pitchers and four Constantine II coins (AD 317–340) were found in the mound of Bruté on Belle-île en Mer, 30 km to the south-east of Île d'Groix (André 1961, 249; De Closmadeuc 1902, 308; Leins *et al.* 2003).

The megalithic tombs at which Roman pottery was recovered contain a range of accompanying materials, most commonly: tiles, coins, bricks and statuettes; however,

Other Materials (15)          15
Tiles (14)                    14
Coins (12)                    12
Bricks (10)                   10
Statuettes (9)                 9
Nails (2)                      2

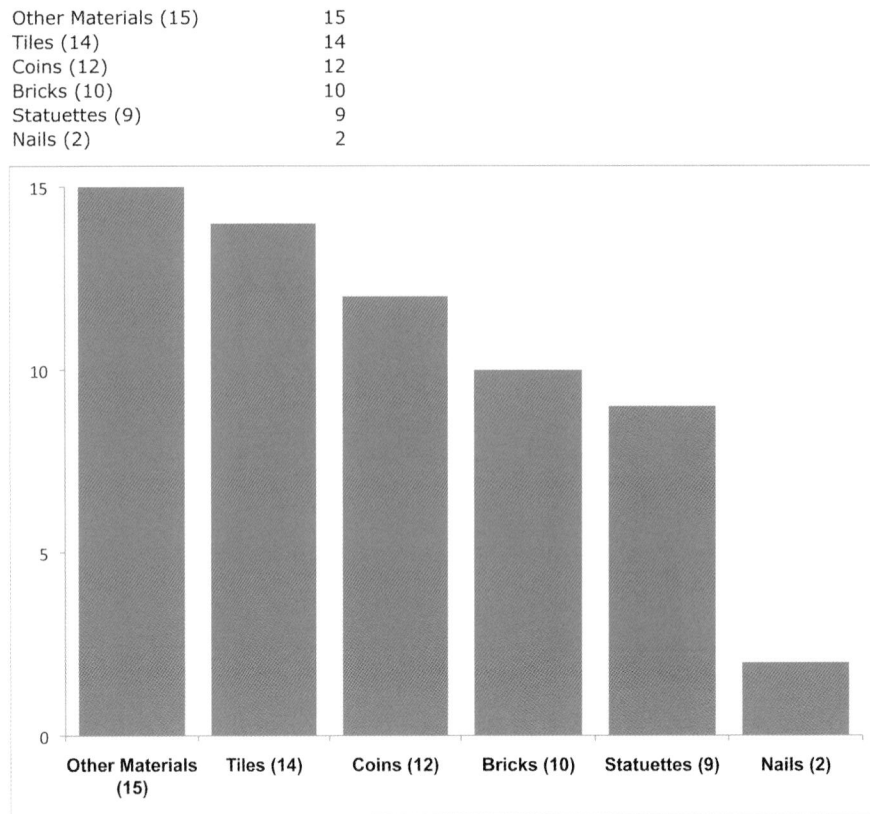

*Fig. 6.4: Graph of Roman materials found in association with Roman pottery at megalithic tombs in Brittany (image: M. Vejby)*

at 25% of these tombs an assortment of other materials were found in addition to Roman pottery (Fig. 6.4). These materials include: a bronze ring, iron dagger, an iron tool, small gold fragments, bracelets, beads, a Roman millstone, an inhumation, iron and bronze fragments, animal bones, charcoal, a bronze bell and glass (André 1961, 250–251; Bender & Caillaud 1986, 115; Collum 1935, 23–26, 33–39, 49–51; Z. Le Rouzic 1932, 24, 49; Lecornec 1994, 68–69). Some of these 'accompanying' materials may have been Iron Age deposits that were disturbed by later Roman period interactions, but it is also possible that during the Roman period these megalithic tombs appeared to be an appropriate place to deposit curated Iron Age materials. Unfortunately, there is insufficient information on the materials, or the stratigraphy of these sites to shed further light.

### Roman tiles

Though they have been found at fewer tombs than pottery, Roman tiles also appear to have been deliberately deposited at megalithic tombs within Brittany (Fig. 6.5). Sadly, an equally limited amount of information is available with respect to these deposits. Megalithic tombs with Roman tiles are also located primarily around Morbihan bay. Tile deposits have been identified at 20 megalithic tombs, and at four of these tombs, La Roche aux Fées, Mané Canaluye, Méarzein and Trenehue, these tiles are the only Roman materials recorded from these sites. The tomb at La Roche aux Fées is set furthest from the bay, and, according to Briard, it appears to have been emptied during the early Roman period. 'Border tiles' were found within the interior of the chamber (Briard 1991, 33). To the north of the bay a large amount of Roman tiles were found in the debris of Trenehue, which is now a destroyed cairn (André 1961, 252). Roman roofing tiles were found within the Mané Canaluye tomb, and in the upper layers of the mound at Méarzein (André 1961, 252, 53).

All of the Roman materials found at megalithic tombs discussed above were recorded in cursory detail, a problem that has already been discussed. In addition to being dismissed as 'lost materials' some materials were described as the leftover waste from picnickers, implying that they had a passing utilitarian purpose at most. Though such interpretations may be partially the result of finding small amounts of unanticipated Roman deposits at Neolithic sites, it is likely that they were also the result of the utilitarian nature of the materials (i.e. pottery, tiles and

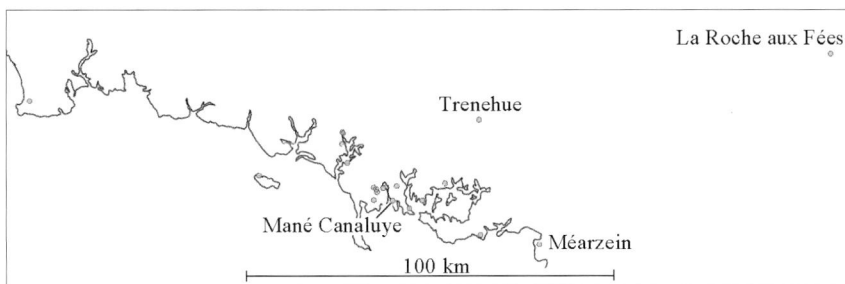

*Fig. 6.5: Distribution of megalithic tombs at which Roman tiles have been found (image: M. Vejby)*

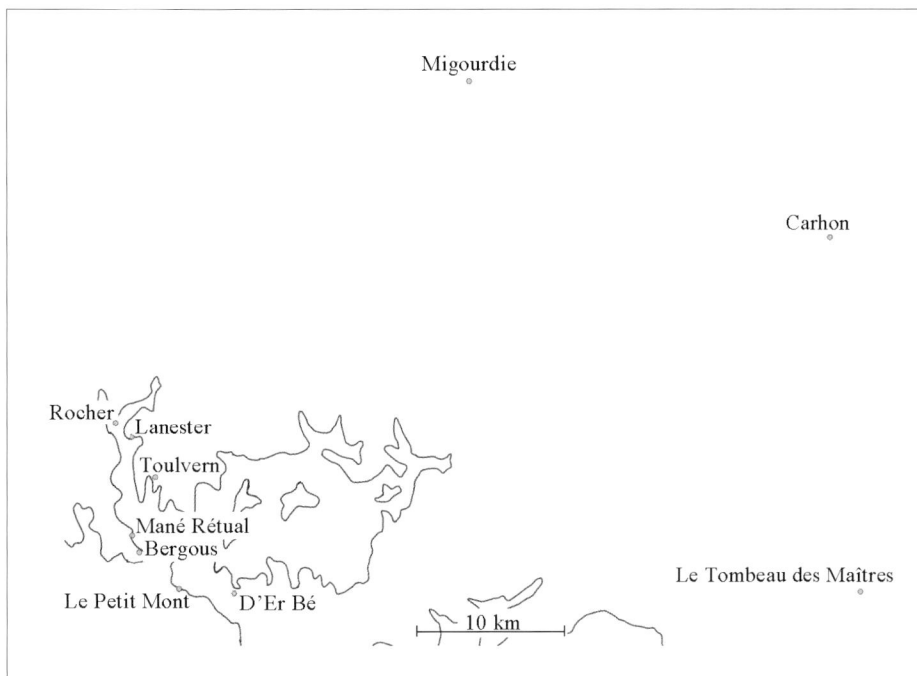

*Fig. 6.6: Distribution of megalithic tombs at which Roman clay statuettes have been found (image: M. Vejby)*

even coins). Such materials may have been more readily overlooked as compared to other more 'distinctive' votive deposits.

## Roman ritual items

Ritual or votive materials, on the other hand, have been given marginally more attention as subsequent deposits at megalithic tombs. Compared to materials at Roman temples and shrines though, they are still hugely overlooked. The most common materials deposited at megalithic tombs that could be classified as votive deposits are coins and statuettes. However, there is also limited evidence of inhumations with other accompanying ritual materials, including beads, a dagger, a bronze bell, animal bones and fragments of bronze and iron at two tombs.

## Roman statuettes

There are ten megalithic tombs in Brittany at which Roman period clay statuettes were uncovered, most of them figures of Venus Anadyomene ('Venus Rising From the Sea'), and they are all centred around the Gulf of Morbihan (Fig. 6.6) (Vejby 2015). At a few of these tombs the statuettes were either accompanied by more elaborate deposits, or were composed of a collection of different statuette types.

Le Tombeau des Maîtres is located near the La Vilaine River, close to the Pays de la Loire/Breton border, and contained fragments of Roman pottery and two white earthenware statuettes of Venus Anadyomene. Venus Anadyomene and mother goddess statuettes of painted white clay were also found in Carhon, less than 25 km to the north-north-east, accompanied by Roman pottery and coins (André 1961, 252). At the dolmen Migourdie Roman pottery and coins (Domitian and Germanicus) were found in association with statuettes of Venus Anadyomene and mother goddesses (André 1961, 252; Leins *et al.* 2003). Though these sites are slightly removed from the rest, they do not appear to distinguish themselves from the other seven sites in terms of the types of accompanying Roman materials.

The other seven megalithic tombs at which Venus statuettes were uncovered are located around the Gulf of Morbihan and Quiberon Bay. White clay Venus Anadyomene statuettes and vases (one with illegible initials) were found within the Lanester dolmen, which is now at the bottom of the bay of Kerdréan (André 1961, 249; Marsille 1919, 114). White earthenware statuettes, perhaps Venus statuettes, though details are not given, along with pottery with some glossy areas, and Constantine II coins (AD 317–340), were found in the dolmen Bergous on the northern shore of Quiberon Bay (André 1961, 251; Leins *et al.* 2003). 150 statuettes of Venus, Latona, mother of Apollo, and mother goddesses, along with common pottery, were found at a depth of 0.6 m in the sifted yellow earth of the D'Er Bé allée couverte (André 1961, 252). Toulvern contained statuettes of Venus Anadyomene and Minerva, along with Roman pottery and Domitian coins (AD 81–96) (André 1961, 249; M. Le Rouzic 1902, 298; Leins *et al.* 2003).

Back on the western peninsula north of Quiberon Bay, less than 5 km south-west of Toulvern and roughly 1 km north-west of Bergous, earthenware statuettes of Venus and mother goddesses were found in Mané Rétual accompanied by Roman roofing tiles, pottery vases, glass vases, marbles, spindle whorls and seven Trajan (AD 98–117) and Antoninus (AD 138–161) coins (André 1961,

251; Leins *et al.* 2003). The association of Roman roofing tiles with the Venus and mother goddess statuettes is unique, as are the vases, marbles and spindle whorls. For whatever reason, this particular site attracted deposits that extended beyond the more common 'pottery and coins,' which seem to be so closely associated with statuettes at all the other megalithic tombs with Roman materials in Brittany. There is only one tomb, Rocher, at which figurines appear to have been found without any other accompanying deposits. It is very likely, however, that there were other items that the 1872 excavation failed to identify or recover (André 1961, 249; Bain de la Coquerie 1872, 276). Probably the most compelling evidence for the ritual reuse of one of these megalithic tombs, however, is at Le Petit Mont. It contains the most extensive amount of Roman materials, including: Roman pottery, Gaulish and Roman coins, a blue bracelet from the 1st century BC, a 4th century BC blue La Tène bead and a small rectangular fragment of gold (Lecornec 1994, 66; 68–70). In addition, nearly 600 fragments of white earthenware Venus Anadyomene and Mother Goddess statuettes were found along the outside of the mound, within the passage and at the entrance to the chamber (Rouzic 1912, 118; Jousselandière & Marsille 1928, 21; Daniel 1960, 217; André 1961, 249; Briard 1991, 4; Lecornec 1994, 71; 2001). A Roman altar was also found at the entrance to the tomb with an inscription on its anterior face (Lecornec 1994, 75). The upper portion of this inscription has been significantly defaced, but the lower two lines read: QVINTVS SABINUS FILIVS VOTVM SOLVIT LIBENS MERITO ('the son of Quintus Sabinus has accomplished his vows freely and justly'). Lecornec believes that Quintus Sabinus may have

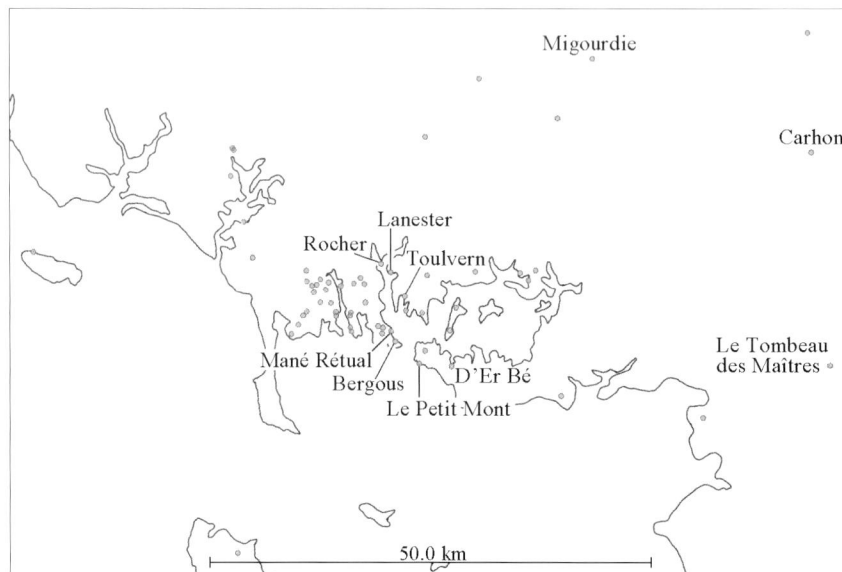

*Fig. 6.7: Distribution of megalithic tombs at which Roman clay statuettes were deposited, in the context of megalithic tombs at which other Roman materials have been uncovered (image: M. Vejby)*

been the General Quintus Sabinus who led the campaign against the Veneti (Lecornec 1994, 76; Vejby 2015, 175). This appears to be a compelling case in which a megalithic tomb is being reused in a ritual manner, in this case as a place of commemoration. No evidence of a subsequent inhumation was reported at this tomb, but the altar does make a personal connection clear, and then there are the hundreds of accompanying votive statuettes.

The distribution of megalithic tombs at which the Venus statuettes have been found is not wholly dissimilar from the distribution of tombs at which other Roman materials have been uncovered (Fig. 6.7). The vast majority of the tombs are situated around the Gulf of Morbihan, with a few additional sites slightly more removed. The statuettes at each of these tombs have been variously interpreted as indications that the sites were used as *fana*, *templa*, or *cella* at which ritual activities took place (Wellington 2002, 3). These terms, however, are heavily laden with modern connotations that these were cult/ritual sites, which may or may not reflect the nature of the interactions with these tombs. Such an interpretation would have to take into account the other materials found, the history of the region, and the known Roman temple sites in the area (Vejby 2015). Again, though some Roman materials associated with these statuettes are also found at sanctuary sites and temples, such as coins and pottery, they are found in lower quantities at megalithic tombs, and other materials typical of ritual sites, such as tablets and 'cult accessories', appear to be missing entirely from these Neolithic monuments (Fauduet 1993a, 125–126; 1993b, 148–149; Lecornec 2001, 289).

## Conclusion

These distinctions seem to imply Roman activities and interactions with megalithic tombs that are unique from those evidenced at Roman temples. It has been suggested that the concentration of reused tombs around the Gulf of Morbihan in Brittany may be linked to the Roman conquest over the Veneti and other allied tribes from Gaul and Brittany in 56 BC (for a complete discussion see Vejby 2015). The concentration of reused tombs along the gulf does not directly correspond to the distribution of megalithic tombs in Brittany, which seems to indicate that the location of these specific tombs may have had an affect on the Roman-period interactions. Though absolute dates for these subsequent activities are not available, analysis of the deposited Roman coins indicate activity some time after the 56 BC victory of the Roman fleet on the bay of Quiberon (Vejby 2015, 176). Though the distribution of mint dates can also be explained as the result of the Roman conquest, and the increase of Roman material in the area as a result of the Roman occupation, the concentration of the deposits around the bay implies that these activities were somehow linked to the location of the tombs, arguably connected to the historic

victory of the Roman fleet. This might further support the interpretation that these materials served as votive deposits. What is key with respect to the scope of this chapter is that the majority of the subsequent deposits at these tombs are traditionally classified as utilitarian items, and also differ from those found at Roman temples.

While there have been prolonged discussions within archaeology over the meaning of the term *ritual*, the dilemma is that there is ample cross-cultural evidence which demonstrates an 'inseparability and overlap of the sacred, and the mundane worlds' (Bell 2007; Kyriakidis 2007b; 2007b, 17; Renfrew 1994; Weekes 2002). Given these close links between the spheres of the mundane and the ritual, interpreting these items and giving them value based on their context alone is extremely difficult within archaeology (Kyriakidis 2007b, 18).

Regardless, however, there are some materials that are more archaeologically visible than others, and this in turn affects not only the value placed on these materials, but on the sites at which they are found. It is likely that one of the main reasons Roman materials were largely dismissed in the contexts of a Neolithic tomb site, in addition to being considered 'secondary' or 'intrusive,' is because the majority of these deposits consisted of what we might classify as utilitarian items, namely: pottery, bricks, tiles, nails and even coins. Lacking an explanation as to why utilitarian items would be found in a non-utilitarian context, they were therefore passed over as 'lost materials' perhaps on their way to being used elsewhere but not intentionally placed.

The patterns of deposition that were uncovered in Brittany, however, support the argument that these deposits were intentional. Many of these materials were placed within the internal structure of the tombs, rather than being 'dropped' near or on the mounds. Furthermore, the concentration of tombs at which subsequent deposits have been recorded is not simply analogous to the concentration of tombs. The distribution of megalithic tombs is far more widespread. The concentration of Roman materials at these sites is therefore a result of the activity itself, rather than being shaped by the availability of megalithic tombs at which to deposit these items. This pattern of Roman activity at megalithic tombs in Brittany is also only a part of the wider evidence for both Iron Age and Roman interactions with megalithic tombs across Atlantic Europe (Vejby 2012). Furthermore, ten of the sites at which Roman materials were uncovered contained clay statuettes whose deposition has been interpreted as votive in nature. It is, perhaps deceptively, easier to interpret the placement of a non-utilitarian item in a context such as this. A non-utilitarian item, frequently found as a votive deposit at sanctuary/ritual sites within the region, may reasonably be called a votive deposit when it is found in other ambiguous contexts nearby.

But what about utilitarian items? Particularly those that are also frequently found at the same sanctuary sites mentioned above? Is a utilitarian item that is frequently found in a ritual context ever really just a utilitarian item? And should this affect our interpretation of these items when they are found within a more utilitarian context? I would argue that not only is the categorisation of ritual versus utilitarian materials not absolute in the Roman period, but that there was a recognised overlap, wherein some materials always held the power/significance of a ritual item even as they were being produced, traded and consumed within secular contexts (such as pottery, hobnails and tiles, for example). Additionally there is the tradition in the Romano-Celtic world of votive miniatures to consider. These votive materials are diminutive reproductions of specific objects, such as: wheels, weapons (shields, swords, daggers, spearheads, axes), coins, ceramic vessels and jewellery (Kiernan 2009). That these utilitarian materials are being selectively reproduced in miniature to function specifically as votive offerings seems to imply that these materials held a more complex significance than the utilitarian functions they performed. With this in mind, it is probable that the archaeological record is missing a large collection of 'utilitarian items' that have been overlooked because of the context of their deposition.

The subsequent deposits discussed above have been largely dismissed and/or under-documented on an individual level. Past excavations, not limited to antiquarian investigations, often overlooked the importance of these items, limiting any mention of them to footnotes or appendices, and presenting them as intrusive to the Neolithic construction and material. Their importance was not analysed. Brought together though, these footnotes and 'supplementary materials' have created noteworthy regional patterns of Roman materials deposited at megalithic tombs across Atlantic Europe (Vejby 2012).

The presence of more traditional 'votive items' within some of the Roman period deposits in Brittany increased the visibility of other less 'ritually-charged' Roman materials at these tombs. Thus a greater spectrum of Roman deposits at megalithic tombs in Brittany, which includes 'utilitarian materials', became a part of a recognisable pattern of deposits. Whether or not the deposits are related to the Roman victory on Quiberon Bay, the concentration of subsequent deposits along the bay is noteworthy, and may have been overlooked without consideration of *both* the ritual and utilitarian materials in this context. This raises the question, how many utilitarian items have been overlooked, or misinterpreted, because of the lack of associated ritual features or materials?

## Note

1 In France passage graves are classified as dolmens à galerie or dolmens à couloir, and gallery graves are referred to as allées couvertes, although very occasionally this term is used to describe passage graves as well (Daniel 1960, 10).

## Bibliography

André, J. (1961) Les Dolmens Morbihannais Remployés à l'Époque Romaine. *OGAM: tradition celtique* 13(74–75), 248–254.

Bain de la Coquerie (1872) Liste des objets acquis, donnés, ou déposés au Musée Archéologique de Vannes pendant l'année 1872. *Bulletin de la Société Polymathique du Morbihan*, 273–276.

Bell, C. (2007) Response: defining the need for a definition. In E. Kyriakidis (ed.) *The Archaeology of Ritual*, 277–288. Los Angeles, University of California.

Bender, B. & Caillaud, R. (1986) *The Archaeology of Brittany, Normandy, and the Channel Islands*. London, Faber & Faber.

Bispham, E. & Smith, C. J. (2000) *Religion in Archaic and Republican Rome and Italy: Evidence and Experience*. Edinburgh, Edinburgh University Press.

Briard, J. (1991) *The Megaliths of Brittany*. Luçon, Éditions Jean-Paul Gisserot.

Collum, V. C. C. (1935) *The Tressé Iron Age Megalithic Monument: its Quadruple Sculptured Breasts and Their Relation to the Mother-Goddess Cosmic Cult.* London, Oxford University Press.

Daniel, G. (1960) *The Prehistoric Chamber Tombs of France: A Geographical, Morphological, and Chronological Survey*. London, Thames & Hudson.

De Closmadeuc, G. (1864) Fouille et découverte d'un dolmen tumulaire a Crubelz, Commune de Belz, Arrondissement de Lorient. *Bulletin de la Société Polymathique du Morbihan*, 6–13.

De Closmadeuc, G, (1902) Découverte de Cists Tumulaires a Belle-Ile, en 1896. *Bulletin de la Société Polymathique du Morbihan*, 305–309.

Fauduet, I. (1993a) *Atlas des Sanctuaires Romano-Celtiques de Gaule: les fanums*. Paris, Errance.

Fauduet, I. (1993b) *Les Temples de Tradition Celtique en Gaule Romaine*. Paris, Errance.

Grahame, M. (1998) Redefining Romanization: material culture and the question of social continuity in Roman Britain. *TRAC 1997: proceedings of the seventh annual theoretical Roman archaeology conference*, 1–10.

Hamilakis, Y. (2010) Re-collecting the Fragments: Archaeology as Mnemonic Practice. In K. Lillios & V. Tsamis (eds), *Material Mnemonics: Everyday Memory in Prehistoric Europe*, 188–199. Oxford, Oxbow Books.

Jousselandière, P. de La & Marsille, L. (1928) Les figurines en terre blanche de Pertu du Roffo, Commune de Nivillac (Morbihan). *Bulletin de la Société Polymathique du Morbihan*, 16–25.

Jones, A. (2007) *Memory and Material Culture*. Cambridge, Cambridge University Press.

Kiernan, P. (2009) *Miniature Votive Offerings in the Roman North-West*. Mainz, Franz Philipp Rutzen.

Kyriakidis, E. (2007b) Archaeologies of ritual. In E. Kyriakidis (ed.) *The Archaeology of Ritual*, 289–308. Los Angeles, University of California.

Kyriakidis, E. (2007b) Finding ritual: calibrating the evidence. In E. Kyriakidis (ed.) *The Archaeology of Ritual*, 9–22. Los Angeles, University of California.

Le Rouzic, Z. (1902) Fouilles faites dans la région: dolmen de Beg-Port-Blanc, Commune de Saint-Pierre-Quibéron. *Bulletin de la Société Polymathique du Morbihan*, 289–304.

Le Rouzic, M. (1912) Carnac. Restaurations faites dans la région. Dolmen à galerie de Petit Mont, Commune d'Arzon, Morbihan. *Bulletin de la Société Polymathique du Morbihan,* 118–123.

Le Rouzic, Z. (1932) *Tumulus du Mont St Michel, 1900–1906.* Vannes, Imprimerie Lafolye et J De Lamarzelle.

Lecornec, J. (1994) *Le Petit Mont, Arzon, Morbihan.* Rennes, Association pour la diffusion des recherches archéologiques dans l'Ouest de la France.

Lecornec, J. (2001) Réutilisation des Monuments Mégalithiques à l'Époque Gallo-Romaine. In C.-T. Le Roux (ed.), *Du Monde des Chasseurs a Celuides Métallurgistes. Hommage Scientifique à la Mémoire de Jean-L'Helgouac'h et Mélanges Offerts à Jacques Briard,* 289–294. Supplément 9: Revue Archéologique de l'Ouest

Leins, I. Moorhead, S. & Bauer, N. (2003) *The Portable Antiquities Scheme: Roman Coins.* <http://www.finds.org.uk/romancoins>.

Marsille, L. (1919) Séance Solennelle D'Inauguration de Chateau-Gaillard. *Bulletin de la Société Polymathique du Morbihan,* 103–123.

Renfrew, C. (1994) The archaeology of religion. In C. Renfrew & E. B. W. Zubrow (eds), *The Ancient Mind: Elements of Cognitive Archaeology,* 47–54. Cambridge, Cambridge University Press.

Vejby, M. (2012). Reinterpreting the Iron Age and Roman Reuse of Megalithic Tombs in Atlantic Europe. Unpublished PhD thesis, University of Reading.

Vejby, M. (2015) Enduring past: megalithic tombs of Brittany and the Roman occupation. In M. Díaz-Guardamino, L. García Sanjuán & D. Wheatley (ed.) *Outstanding Biographies: The Life of Prehistoric Monuments in Iron Age, Roman and Medieval Europe,* 163–182. Oxford, Oxford University Press.

Weekes, J. (2002) Acculturation and the temporal features of ritual action. *TRAC 2001: proceedings of the eleventh annual theoretical Roman archaeology conference,* 73–82.

Wellington, I. (2002) Considering continuity of deposition on votive sites in northeastern France from 200 BC to AD 100. *TRAC 2001: Proceedings of the Eleventh Annual Theoretical Roman Archaeology Conference,* 1–12.

# A Mars with breasts from Weißenburg in Bavaria

## *Nicole Birkle*

*Keywords*: Weißenburg; feathered plaques; votive offerings; Mars; Fortuna

*Roman votive plaques of silver, gold and bronze are well known, and have been recovered in metal or treasure hoards and temple remains. The group of the so-called feathered plaques was first studied by Ph. Buzon (1999) and then by the author in her PhD thesis in 2013. Among these finds, a group from Weißenburg in Bavaria comprising 11 high quality silver plaques shows amazing and exceptional features in the design of the figural reliefs. At first glance, the reliefs are not conspicuous. The gods depicted – Mars, Victoria, Fortuna, Apollo, Minerva, Mercury and Hercules, as well as a Genius – are all quite frequent on votive plaques and are represented here in very common types. But a closer inspection of them shows that at least some were made by using a variety of moulds consisting of single arms, legs, feet or a torso. The most distinctive representation is that of a Mars. The poor little warrior god shows a unique combination of the real head of Mars, a strangely twisted right arm leaning on a lance, the upper body of a woman with breasts wearing a dress, the lower body of an armoured Mars and, most unusual, backwards bare legs. It seems that in the absence of an appropriate mould, the manufacturers in Weißenburg improvised by using individual, mismatched moulds to create such a successful overall impression that no one studying the plaques before had noticed these discrepancies. This paper examines the group of the Weißenburg plaques by studying the special techniques that were applied in the production process. The use of individual moulds is well known in the production of clay or bronze statuettes and artistic metal work, but the unique Mars with breasts in Weißenburg merits a more detailed investigation.*

## A short introduction to Roman votive plaques

Votive plaques of silver, gold or bronze and bearing inscriptions and/or representations of the gods were well known and widespread in ancient times (Birkle 2013, 62–125). For centuries, they were used as valuable gifts to the gods. Often, the gift was preceded by a vow to offer the god a plaque if a certain wish was fulfilled as expressed by the Latin phrase *do ut des* ('give, so that you may be given'), as was also common with other larger dedications. Plaques made of precious metals can depict representations of deities with inscriptions, (healed) body parts (still common in the Catholic and Orthodox Christian Churches), or just a *tabula ansata* (Lat.: 'tablet with handles', a favourite form for votives) with the dedication inscriptions.

The feathered or rather pinnate plaques from the Roman Era (Fig. 7.1) are typical of the North-western Provinces. The main feature is a ribbed decoration covering at least part, but quite often the entire plaque. In their overall shape, many seem to imitate plants and consequently, scholars believed that a common model, most likely a palm branch, existed. In the first comprehensive study of the material, Buzon (1999) was so convinced that all the plaques imitate palms branches that he titled his study *Palmae argentae*. A different school of thought sees the plaques representing not just palms, but more generally different kinds of plants (Birkle 2013, 164–169).

The plaques' period of use can be bracketed by the oldest known example, found in Mainz (D) and dating to the

*Fig. 7.1: Silver votive plaques from Weißenburg in Bavaria (Archäologische Staatssammlung München, without a Film Neg. No. Photo: M. Eberlein)*

later 1st century AD and the Christian plaques from Water Newton (GB), which belong to the 4th century AD (Birkle 2013, 289, 373–378). Up to now, more than 500 plaques from at least 84 findspots are known, ranging from finds of individual plaques to treasure or scrap metal hoards. While the plaques had been studied before Buzon and the author, in most cases only a specific (new) group was published, and other examples were only added for comparison (Walters 1921, 55–64; Drexel 1924, 70 n. 40; Noll 1938; Toynbee 1978; Corrocher 1981, 251–257; Noll 1980; Bernhard *et al.* 1990; Piso 1993, 826–841; Kellner & Zahlhaas 1993, 67–78; Naumann-Steckner 167–191; Künzl, 1993, I 85–89; 1997).

Previous studies have shown that in many cases the plaques were probably stockpiled when half-finished and only completed with a personal inscription or a god's image when a worshipper bought them (Buzon 1999, 1, 29). For some sites, such as Barkway (GB), Hagenbach (D), Mauer an der Url (A), Stony Stratford (GB), Vichy (F), Water Newton (GB) and Weißenburg in Bavaria (D), it has been possible to prove that all the plaques came from one hand or at least one workshop (Birkle 2013, 34–42, with additional discussion and references). This can be proven best if the same moulds were used for different plaques, or when, as in Weißenburg (Fig. 7.2), the overall shape always follows the same pattern and decorative elements are used again and again. We can thus assume that generally, the plaques

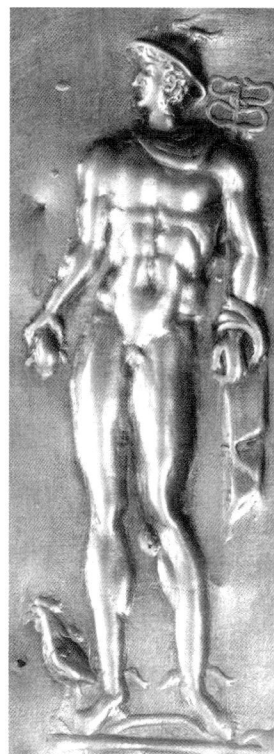

*Fig. 7.2: Mercury on W. 04 (Archäologische Staatssammlung München. without a Film Neg. No. Photo: M. Eberlein)*

*Nicole Birkle*

were made and sold in workshops directly connected to the sanctuaries where they were offered to the gods (Birkle 2013, 43). While studying these different workshops, some remarkable details were discovered, and the Weißenburg plaques present the most illustrative examples.

## The Weißenburg Group

Weißenburg in Bavaria, some 60 km south of Nuremberg, is the site of Roman Biriciana, one of the largest forts of the Roman Danube limes in Raetia. In 1979, a very important Roman hoard was discovered near the fort, which had most likely been buried in the first half of the 3rd century AD. Statuettes and vessels made of bronze were recovered, as well as iron equipment, decorative fittings and eleven votive plaques of a very high quality, evident in their overall shape, the configuration of their rib pattern parts and – at first glance – the gods' representations (Birkle 2013, 38–42, 378–387, pls 116–119).

On all of the plaques, the gods – whether represented individually or in groups – are framed in a small shrine (*aedicula*) partly designed free hand, partly stamped with a die. It is obvious that they were all made in one workshop, as they all are of the same type (Kellner & Zahlhaas 1983, 67). The workshop also used the same mould for other images,

for example, to create the images of Mercury on plaque numbers W.04 (Fig. 7.3) and W.05 (Fig. 7.4), although the heads may differ slightly from each other (Kellner & Zahlhaas 1983; Birkle 2013, 38).

Plaques W.06 (Fig. 7.5) and W.09 (Fig. 7.6) both depict Fortuna from the front, holding a *cornucopia*. Although the quality of the relief on W.09 is much better than on W.06, one can easily see the inorganic form of the right arm (Figs 7.7 & 7.8), which is too thin and too long in comparison with the other arm, has no real subdivision between the lower and the upper parts and meets with the shoulder in a strange way. But a much more amazing detail can be seen when looking at the feet of Fortuna on W.09 (Fig. 7.9). While the left foot is carried out only very roughly, the right foot emerges clearly under the dress. But what we see here is

*Fig. 7.3: Mercury on W. 05 (Archäologische Staatssammlung München, reproduction of a postcard bought in the museum. Photo: M. Eberlein)*

*Fig. 7.4: Fortuna on W. 06 (after Kellner & Zahlhaas 1993, pl. 64, Nr. 36. Photo M. Eberlain)*

the left foot of a figure seen from behind. The heel is lifted up, the toes are set aside.

Another mould was used for the Fortuna on W.07 (Fig. 7.10), but again, the image bears some distinctive elements. The goddess's hair looks more like a hat, similar to the *petasos* of Mercury (Fig. 7.11), and the masculine face does not really suit Fortuna. The upper part of the body is slightly shifted toward the *cornucopia* in her left arm and the breasts are really unequal in size (Fig. 7.12). It seems as if the right breast was enlarged to be able to connect the body to the

right arm, which again, as seen before, is much too long, too small and too weak to match the body. Some elements such as a part of the mantle, the wheel to her feet and the rudder seem to have been added in free hand. Overall, this Fortuna is a very inconsistent figure.

The most intriguing image among the Weißenburg plaques is without a doubt the presentation of Mars on W.11. (Fig. 7.13). Again, at first glance the image represents a common Mars type well known from all over the Roman Empire. But when analysing it section by section, it becomes obvious that the image is a pastiche. Where we would expect an ordinary Roman breastplate, we can recognize an upper female body, dressed in a garment fixed on the shoulders with a round brooch and showing tension wrinkles between the breasts (Fig. 7.14). This part is combined with the lower body of an armoured Mars and, in the most unusual feature, bare legs seen from behind (Fig. 7.15). In addition the right arm is strangely twisted to lean on the lance (Fig. 7.16). Both upper arms are much too thin for the body, while the lower right arm seems to be pretty muscular. The right hand grasps the upper part of the lance, which is bent almost in a right angle. This hand position would only have been possible with the left hand, which might be the reason why this right hand is connected to the right arm in an inorganic way. The position of the rounded shield in the left arm is too close to the body, and parts of the mantle, the shield, the lance and the plume are not made by using a mould but again added free-hand, with a *stilus* or something similar.

What we clearly can learn from this image is that the manufacturer of our plaque did not have high-quality moulds for each god or goddess to be portrayed on the plaques and therefore was forced to be innovative in creating a satisfying overall impression. The success of these improvisations can be seen in that nobody working on the Weißenburg

*Fig. 7.5: Fortuna on W. 09 (Archäologische Staatssammlung München, Detail from Neg. No. 23-83. Photo: M. Eberlein)*

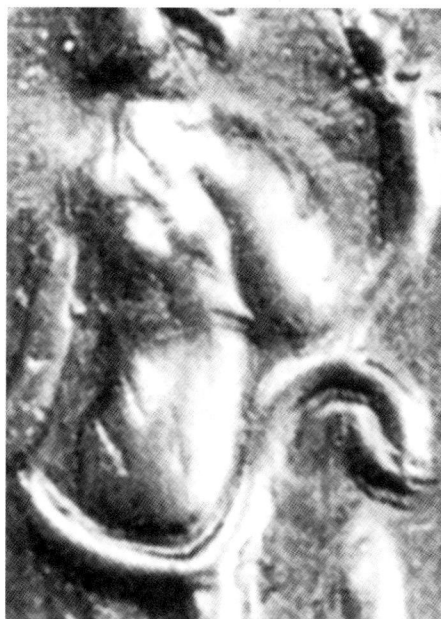

*Fig. 7.6: W. 06 (after Kellner & Zahlhaas 1993, pl. 64, Nr. 36. Photo: M. Eberlein)*

*Fig. 7.7: W. 09 (after Kellner & Zahlhaas 1993, pl. 64, Nr. 36. Photo: M. Eberlein)*

*Fig. 7.8: W. 09 (after Kellner & Zahlhaas 1993, pl. 64, Nr. 36. Photo: M. Eberlein)*

*Fig. 7.11: W. 07 (after Kellner & Zahlhaas 1993, pl. 63, Nr. 35. Photo: M. Eberlein)*

*Fig. 7.9: W. 07 (Archäologische Staatssammlung München, Details from Neg. No. 25–83. Photo: M. Eberlein)*

*Fig. 7.10: W. 07 (after Kellner & Zahlhaas 1993, pl. 63, Nr. 35. Photo: M. Eberlein)*

*Fig. 7.12: W. 11 (after Kellner & Zahlhaas 1993, pl. 67, Nr. 39. Photo M. Eberlein)*

plaques has ever mentioned these discrepancies in the representations of the gods; the author herself studied the plaques many times before recognising what had been done here.

We, of course, do not know why they used the pastiche technique for Fortuna and Mars, and perhaps Mercury, while the other gods, Victoria, Hercules, Genius and Apollo, do not reveal any 'abnormalities'. Maybe the reason was simply the absence of adequate moulds or dies, but perhaps it was already a very common technique to create such images in artistic metalwork and we just have not seen much of it until now. As E. Poulsen proved a long time ago, the use of partial moulds was very popular in the production of bronze statues (1977, 1–60). M. Y. Treister presents several moulds from the Hellenistic period found in Daors (Illyria), showing griffins lacking some parts of their bodies (2001, 436, fig. 79,1; 438, fig. 80, 1–2). These parts could be added separately using the special templates found on the same moulds. Another mould shows some female figures, who, by adding a pair of wings on the same mould, experienced a metamorphosis and became the goddess Nike (Gebhard 1991, 2–11).

So the technique of using partial moulds was not new when our manufacturer in Weißenburg was working, nevertheless, the way it was done here is unique, because our little warrior god in Weißenburg, as well as the images of Fortuna, are not a result of common techniques. Instead, their realisation seems to be improvised, perhaps because the worshippers wanted these gods and an adequate mould was not available. This creative way of working can also be seen in the representations of the framing architecture, which is sometimes just scratched in from the backside of the plaque, sometimes produced with single moulds or a combination of both techniques. None of the moulds appear to have included both the gods and the surrounding architecture.

We can only speculate today what the dedicants of the plaques may have thought about the unusual execution of their plaques. But perhaps how a god or goddess was depicted was of less importance than that he or she was recognizable and following a well known representational type, so even the non-Roman visitors of

Fig. 7.14: W. 11 (after Kellner & Zahlhaas 1993, pl. 67, Nr. 39. Photo: M. Eberlein)

Fig. 7.13: W. 11 (after Kellner & Zahlhaas 1993, pl. 67, Nr. 39. Photo: M. Eberlein)

Fig. 7.15. W. 11 (after Kellner & Zahlhaas 1993, pl. 67, Nr. 39. Photo: M. Eberlein)

the sanctuaries could register the relevant information instantly. And if there was no mould for Mars or Fortuna available – perhaps because these deities originally were not worshipped on this site – it was with no doubt appropriate to create one.

As a result of what we have learned from the Weißenburg plaques, it seems productive to take a new look at small-scale reliefs in metalwork to see if more examples of this technique exist, or if the Mars with breasts from Weißenburg is as unique and quaint as it seems to be.

## Bibliography

Bernhard, H., Engels, H.-J., Engels, R. & Petrovsky, R. (1990) *Der römische Schatzfund von Hagenbach.* Mainz, Verlag des Römisch-Germanischen Zentralmuseums.

Birkle, N. (2013) *Untersuchungen zur Form, Funktion und Bedeutung gefiederter römischer Votivbleche.* Bonn, Rudolf Habelt.

Buzon, P. (1999) Palmae argentae. Les feuilles votives dans l'Empire romain. I: Texte; II: Inventaire et documents. Unpublished PhD thesis, Toulouse.

Drexel, F. (1924), Römische Paraderüstungen. In M. Abramić & V. Hoffiller (eds), *Strena Buliciana* 55–72, Zagrebiae, Aspalathi.

Gebhard, R. (1991) Aus der Werkstatt eines antiken Feinschmiedes. Zum Depotfund von Ošanići bei Stolac in Jugoslawien. *Zeitschrift für schweizerische Archäologie und Kunstgeschichte* 48(1), 2–11.

Kellner, H. J. & Zahlhaas, G. (1993) *Der römische Tempelschatz von Weißenburgi. Bayern.* Mainz, Philipp von Zabern.

Künzl, E. (1993) *Die Alamannenbeute aus dem Rhein bei Neupotz: Plünderungsgut aus dem römischen Gallien.* Monographs

Römisch-Germanisches Zentralmuseum Mainz 34, Bonn, Habelt.

Künzl, E. (1997) Römische Tempelschätze und Sakralinventare. Votive, Horte, Beute. *Antiquité Tardive* 5, 57–81.

Naumann-Steckner, F. (1996) Privater Dank – Silbervotive aus Nordafrika. In E. N. Lane (ed.) *Cybele, Attis and Related Cults. Essays in Memory of M. J. Vermaseren*, 167–191. Leiden/New York, Brill.

Noll, R. (1938) *Führer durch die Sonderausstellung: "Der große Dolichenusfund von Mauer a. d. Url."* Wien, Kunsthistorisches Museum.

Noll, R. (1980) *Das Inventar des Dolichenusheiligtums von Mauer an der Url (Noricum)*, Römische Limes in Österreich 30. Wien, Österreichische Akademie der Wissenschaften.

Piso, I. (1993) La tablette de Baudecet (Gembloux, Belgique): Éléments d'étude comparative. *Latomus* 52, 826–841.

Poulsen, E. (1977) Probleme der Werkstattbestimmung gegossener römischer Figuralbronzen. *Acta archaeologica København* 48, 1–60.

Toynbee, J. M. C. (1963) *Art in Roman Britain.* London, Phaidon Press.

Toynbee, J. M. C. (1978) *A Londinium Votive Leaf or Feather and its Fellows.* In J. Bird, H. Chapman & J. Clark (eds) *Collectanea Londiniensia. Studies in London Archaeology and History Presented to Ralph Merrifield*, 128–147. London, London and Middlesex Archaeological Society.

Treister, M. (2001) *Hammering Techniques in Greek and Roman Jewellery and Toreutics*, Colloquia Pontica 8. Leiden/Boston/Köln, Brill.

Walters, H. B. (1921) *Catalogue of the Silver Plate, Greek, Etruscan and Roman in the British Museum.* London, British Museum.

# Metropolitan styling: metal figurines from London and Colchester

*Emma Durham*

*Keywords*: Bronze figurines; religion; eastern religions; votive deposits; London

*Bronze figurines are an important artefact category, providing insights into manufacture, art and religious beliefs. The figurines from London and Colchester make up some 14% of the figurines recorded in my recent PhD from all of Britain. As one might expect they range from high quality figurines, some imported from Italy, to stylised provincial examples, many of which may have been produced in Britain and possibly even London or Colchester. A wide variety of types is found within these two towns, but one factor that stands out is the concentration of Eastern deities, particularly those of the Cybele and Isis cults. This paper will review the collections from London and Colchester within the wider context of figurines from Britain as a whole and what they can tell us about the religious habits of their inhabitants.*

London and Colchester have produced the two largest collections of metal figurines from Roman Britain, including a number of types that are not found anywhere else in the province. As one might expect, these assemblages are varied in both composition and style, reflecting the religious and artistic life of Roman London and Colchester. There are particular differences in the proportions of certain deities such as Apollo and Harpocrates, and in the patterns of deposition within the two cities, which reflect differing populations and styles of worship. This paper will discuss the composition and distribution of the two assemblages, and then examine a particular group, those associated with the worship of deities of Eastern origin such as Isis and Harpocrates.

## The composition of the assemblages

The 87 metal figurines from Greater London form the largest group from any single site in Britain and represent 8.8% of the entire British assemblage (Durham 2012). An additional eight figurines that have been found in the Greater London area are also considered here (but not included in Table 8.1)

as they are all located on or near roads leading out from the city. The collection from Colchester is somewhat smaller, consisting of 50 figurines (5% of the whole assemblage) from the immediate area of the Roman town. A further ten come from locations outside the town, including three figurines from the Lexden tumulus, one from Gosbecks Farm and three from the temple at the Royal Grammar School.

The types represented in the groups from London and Colchester are listed in Table 8.1. There are multiple examples of some classical deities such as Hercules, Mars, Mercury and Minerva, but only single representatives of other less popular deities. The cosmopolitan nature of the London population is emphasised by the presence of imported 'genre' pieces such as gladiators. In addition there is a variety of birds and animals, many of which are associated with particular deities, such as the cockerel and goat with Mercury.

### Hercules

The two most common deities among the Roman figurines from London and Colchester are Hercules and Mercury, who

*Table 8.1: Figurines from London and Colchester. Other male deities: 1 Aesculapius, 1 Atlas, 2 Cautopates, 2 Genius cucullatus, 28 horse and rider, 2 Neptune, 13 Priapus, 1 River God, 1 Sucellus, 10 Vulcan. Other female deities: 1 Ceres, 1 Epona, 1 Flora, 11 Mother Goddess, 2 Vesta, 1 Muse. Other animals and birds: 2 Apis bull, 7 three-horned bull, 6 bull, 1 cat, 1 crocodile, 5 dolphin, 1 fish, 2 frog, 3 hare, 19 horse, 2 lizard, 6 mouse, 9 stag, 38 eagle, 1 ibis, 4 owl, 3 pigeon, 3 raven*

| | London | | | Colchester | | Total British assemblage | |
|---|---|---|---|---|---|---|---|
| Type | No | Uncertain | % | No | % | No | % |
| Apollo | 4 | 2 | 8 | 0 | 0 | 17 | 2.4 |
| Attis | 1 | | 1.3 | 0 | 0 | 7 | 1 |
| Bacchus and satyrs | 4 | | 5.3 | 1 | 2.9 | 24 | 3.4 |
| Cupid | 3 | | 4 | 2 | 5.9 | 32 | 4.6 |
| Dioscurus | 0 | | 0 | 1 | 2.9 | 3 | 0.4 |
| Genius paterfamilias | 1 | | 1.3 | 0 | 0 | 18 | 2.6 |
| Harpocrates | 4 | | 5.3 | 1 | 2.9 | 10 | 1.4 |
| Hercules | 11 | 2 | 17.3 | 5 | 14.7 | 59 | 8.4 |
| Jupiter | 2 | | 2.7 | 0 | 0 | 22 | 3.1 |
| Lar | 1 | | 1.3 | 1 | 2.9 | 18 | 2.6 |
| Mars | 3 | | 4 | 1 | 2.9 | 47 | 6.7 |
| Mercury | 8 | 1 | 12 | 8 | 23.5 | 116 | 16.6 |
| Other male deities | 0 | | 0 | 0 | 0 | 61 | 8.7 |
| Diana | 1 | | 1.3 | 0 | 0 | 9 | 1.3 |
| Fortuna | 0 | | 0 | 1 | 2.9 | 13 | 1.8 |
| Isis | 1 | | 1.3 | 0 | 0 | 5 | 0.7 |
| Juno | 1 | | 1.3 | 0 | 0 | 2 | 0.3 |
| Minerva | 4 | 1 | 6.7 | 2 | 5.9 | 33 | 4.7 |
| Venus | 2 | | 2.7 | 5 | 14.7 | 29 | 4.1 |
| Victory | 1 | 1 | 2.7 | 0 | 0 | 6 | 0.8 |
| Other female deities | 0 | | 0 | 0 | 0 | 17 | 2.4 |
| Human/uncertain i.d. | 7 | 1 | 10.7 | 4 | 11.8 | 93 | 13.3 |
| Fragments | 8 | | 10.7 | 2 | 5.9 | 58 | 8.3 |
| *Total* | 67 | 8 | | 34 | | 699 | |
| Boar | 0 | | 0 | 2 | 13.3 | 25 | 8.6 |
| Cow/boar | 1 | | 9.1 | 0 | 0 | 1 | 0.03 |
| Dog | 1 | | 9.1 | 1 | 6.7 | 30 | 10.3 |
| Goat | 2 | | 18.2 | 2 | 13.3 | 25 | 8.6 |
| Lion | 1 | | 9.1 | 1 | 6.7 | 6 | 2.1 |
| Panther | 1 | | 9.1 | 0 | 0 | 8 | 2.8 |
| Ram | 0 | | 0 | 1 | 6.7 | 11 | 3.8 |
| Snake | 1 | | 9.1 | 1 | 6.7 | 9 | 3.1 |
| Tortoise | 0 | | 0 | 1 | 6.7 | 2 | 0.7 |
| Other animals | 0 | | 0 | 0 | 0 | 64 | |
| Cockerel | 1 | | 9.1 | 3 | 20 | 44 | 15.2 |
| Duck | 0 | | 0 | 1 | 6.7 | 3 | 1 |

*(Continued)*

*Table 8.1: Figurines from London and Colchester. Other male deities: 1 Aesculapius, 1 Atlas, 2 Cautopates, 2 Genius cucullatus, 28 horse and rider, 2 Neptune, 13 Priapus, 1 River God, 1 Sucellus, 10 Vulcan. Other female deities: 1 Ceres, 1 Epona, 1 Flora, 11 Mother Goddess, 2 Vesta, 1 Muse. Other animals and birds: 2 Apis bull, 7 three-horned bull, 6 bull, 1 cat, 1 crocodile, 5 dolphin, 1 fish, 2 frog, 3 hare, 19 horse, 2 lizard, 6 mouse, 9 stag, 38 eagle, 1 ibis, 4 owl, 3 pigeon, 3 raven (Continued)*

| Type | London | | | Colchester | | Total British assemblage | |
|---|---|---|---|---|---|---|---|
| | No | Uncertain | % | No | % | No | % |
| Goose | 2 | | 18.2 | 0 | 0 | 3 | 1 |
| Peacock | 1 | | 9.1 | 0 | 0 | 2 | 0.7 |
| Other birds | 0 | | 0 | 0 | 0 | 49 | |
| Uncertain animals | 0 | | 0 | 2 | 13.3 | 4 | 1.4 |
| Sphinx | 1 | | | 1 | | 6 | |
| *Total* | *12* | *0* | | *16* | | *292* | |
| *Grand Total* | *79* | *8* | | *50* | | *991* | |

were also the most popular deities in the rest of Britain as well as Gaul (Boucher 1976). Hercules forms the largest single group among the male deities from London, while he is second to Mercury at Colchester. Two probably imported figures are an archer from Queen Street, Cheapside (Henig 1995a, 81; Durham 2012, no. 169; *CSIR* 1.10, no. 214) and, from a mid-1st century context at Swan Street, Southwark, a seated Hercules with a lion skin draped over his left arm and shoulder (Beasley 2006, 33, fig. 9.11; Durham 2012, no. 816; Wardle unpublished report).

One of the most common depictions of Hercules shows him with his left arm outstretched and draped in a lion skin while his right arm is raised and holds a club (Fig. 8.1). Six figurines from London and all five Hercules figurines from Colchester (Durham 2012, nos 84–88) show him in this stance.

There are three further examples of Hercules from London – two (nos 714 and 1045) depict him as a clean-shaven youth with his right hand resting on his hip and the left arm outstretched and draped with a lionskin (Fig. 8.2). One (no. 1064) depicts Hercules standing with his right foot resting against the left calf (Fig. 8.3). He wears a cap and holds a club in his left hand and a two-handled cup in the right. This is the only example of a Hercules in this style in Britain, but there is another standing Hercules holding a club and cup from Gaul (Rolland 1965, pl. 105).

## Mercury

Mercury is the second most common figurine type in London, but forms the largest group in Colchester. He is usually shown standing, wearing a *petasos* or with wings springing directly from his head, often with drapery over his left shoulder and arm and holding a purse in his right hand. Like Hercules, the style and quality of production varies from highly classical forms through

varying degrees of stylised examples (Durham 2012, nos 9 and 43).

There are also two examples of Mercury wearing a *petasos*, fully draped with a purse in his right hand and a *caduceus* in his left (Durham 2012, no. 36 from East India House, London; Crummy 2006, 60, 67, fig. 29 no. 4, pl. 6; Durham 2012, no. 1041 from St Mary's Hospital, Colchester).

The final form of Mercury depicts him reclining with a patera in his right hand and *caduceus* in his left (Durham 2012 no. 35). The figurine from London is the only example of this form in Britain. In addition to the figurines of Mercury, three *caducei* have been recovered from the temple at St Mary's Hospital in Colchester (Durham 2012, nos 1038, 1039 and 1040).

## Apollo

Figurines of Apollo are not found in any great number in Britain, but there are four definite and two possible examples from London. No figurines of Apollo have been found in Colchester. Identification of Apollo can be difficult as he often lacks obvious attributes, but he is generally depicted as a nude, youthful, standing male, such as two examples from the Thames (Durham 2012, nos 11 and 18). One of two figurines, which have been published as Mercury but could be Apollo is a fragmentary figure wearing only a baldric and holding an object against his left side (Green 1976, 224 no. 63; Pitts 1979, 54 no. 26; Durham 2012, no. 39 from the Royal Exchange).

## Mars

Mars is not common in either London or Colchester and is represented by only three figurines from London and one from Colchester. Two stylised pieces depict Mars in classical

*Fig. 8.1. Hercules figurine. Durham 2012, no. 86 from Colchester (with kind permission of Colchester and Ipswich Museum Service, accn no. COLEM 1936.900)*

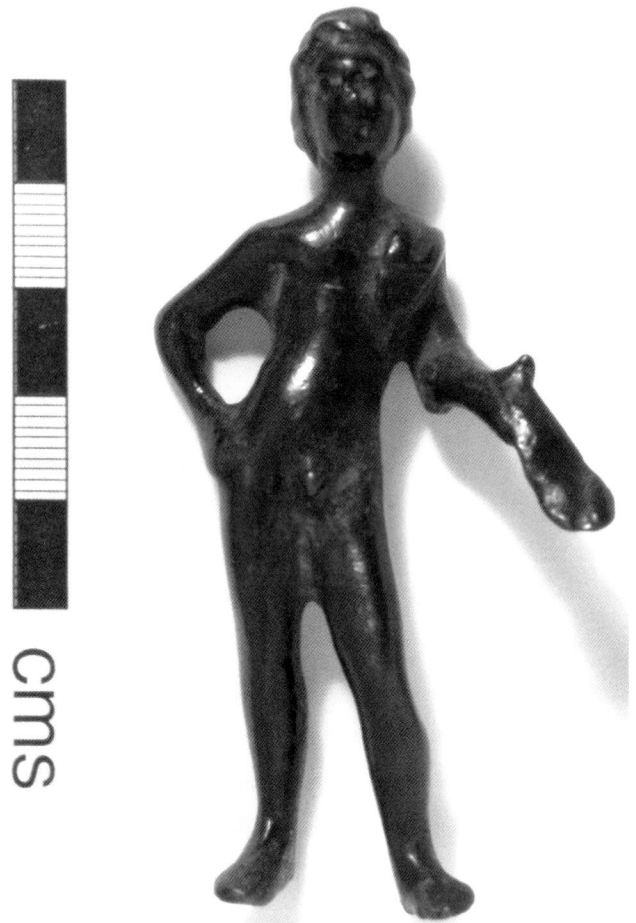

*Fig. 8.2. Hercules figurine. Durham 2012, no. 1045 (with kind permission of the Museum of London, accn no. 2076)*

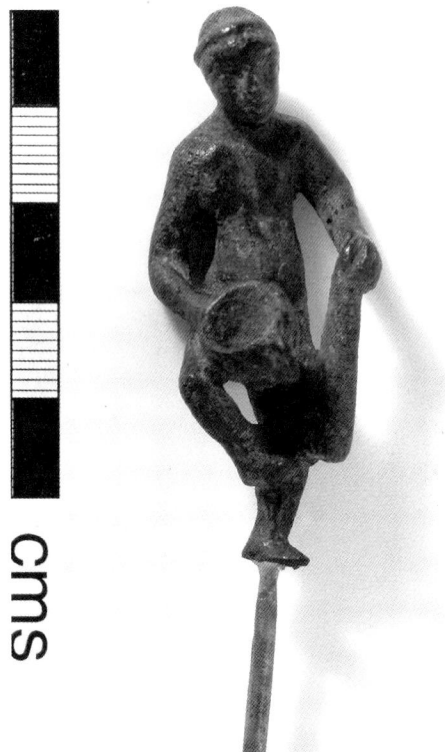

*Fig. 8.3. Hercules figurine. Durham 2012, no. 1064 (with kind permission of the Museum of London, accn no. 59.94/39).*

form with a helmet, short kilt, cuirass and greaves (Durham 2012, nos 23, 33). Of more interest is a figure which is similarly attired to the previous examples but depicted in a naïve style (Durham 2012, no. 24). It is the only example of a naïve figurine in London and is remarkably similar to an example from Tiel in the Netherlands (Jitta *et al.* 1969, 80 no. 33), which may suggest that the two come from the same workshop. The single Mars figurine from Colchester is a typically classical piece, but the execution is slightly stylised (Durham 2012, no. 26). It shows a nude Mars wearing a large crested helmet, with his right hand raised to hold a spear, and is the most common form of Mars in Britain.

## Other male deities

The final male deities are both of the type that one would expect to find displayed in a family *lararium*. One is a togate

*Genius paterfamilias* from London and the other two are Lares from Swan Lane, London and Colchester (Durham 2012, nos 113, 103 and 107). The Genius shows the fully draped male typical of these figurines. The Lares both depict a youth in a tunic with overfold and sash and are examples of the *Lar Compitalis*, a dancing figure associated with boundaries in Rome (Alcock 1986, 115). It is interesting that in such large groups there are only three examples of these family gods. As Alcock (1986, 129) points out, the use of these figures in Britain would be associated with Roman concepts, and one cannot know how widespread the idea of Genius was, even among the more Romanised sections of society.

## Minerva

In comparison with the 47 male deities from London and 20 from Colchester, only 12 figurines of female deities have been recovered from London and eight from Colchester, and among the female deities only Minerva and Venus are depicted in any number. London and Colchester are, in fact, the only sites in Britain from which more than one figurine of Minerva has been found. One example from Isleworth, Greater London is seated (Durham 2012, no. 119), while the five from within London itself and Colchester are standing and follow the conventions for the majority of Minerva figurines as they are dressed in long gowns, four have additional drapery and four also wear the aegis and

*Fig. 8.4. Minerva figurine. Durham 2012, no. 124 from Colchester (with kind permission of Colchester and Ipswich Museum Service, accn no. COLEM 1925.5062)*

*Fig. 8.5. Minerva figurine. Durham 2012, no. 120 (British Museum, accn no. 1853,0502.16)*

Corinthian helmet (Figs 8.4 & Fig. 8.5; Durham 2012, nos 120–124, 1117, 1150). All three of the London figurines, which still have arms have the right arm extended (two hold a patera, the hand of the third figure is missing) while the left arm is raised, but both Colchester examples have a raised right arm and lowered left.

## Venus

Only two Venus figurines have been found in London, but there are five examples from Colchester. One from Southwark is a Venus Pudica who stands with her left hand covering her groin (Durham 2012, no. 144). Three others (Durham 2012, no. 131 from London Bridge, 136 and 138 from Colchester) depict Venus Anadyomene as she rises from the sea and wrings the water from her hair. Examples of both of these types are found throughout Britain.

Two Venus figurines from Colchester are more unusual. One depicts a standing Venus (Durham 2012, no. 137). She holds her right hand out, palm up, while in her left hand she holds an apple. One other British Venus from St Albans (Durham 2012, no. 132) is depicted in a similar stance with an apple or pomegranate in her hand, but other examples of this form are

found on the Continent. Finally, one Venus is in poor condition and poorly executed, but is seated and holds what appears to be a mirror in her right hand (Durham 2012, no. 139).

## Human figurines

Apart from the deities and worshippers described above, a number of figurines depicting human characters have also been found. Of particular interest are the two gladiators, kneeling barbarian and rider from London (Durham 2012, nos 170–173). The heavily armed gladiators are of a type, which is found elsewhere in Europe but no others have been found in Britain. Similarly, the kneeling barbarian with his animal skin cap is unparalleled in Britain, but there are continental examples and this figurine was probably imported. Images of barbarians are common in the Roman world, especially on coins and military items, but less so in private art (Ferris 2000, 3). However, they are depicted in statuary and on friezes either dying or being killed in battle (e.g. Ferris 2000, figs 1, 10 & 40) or as captives (e.g. Ferris 2000, figs 11, 16 & 18).

Barbarians were also depicted in less trying circumstances, and a rider with a beard in thick locks, long moustache and corkscrew hair and holding a circular shield is another unusual and effective piece (Durham 2012, no. 172). He has been identified as an African or Indian elephant rider and is one of three known examples, which were probably produced in Italy in the mid-2nd to 3rd centuries (Eckardt 2014, 83–4).

Two interesting human figurines have also been found in Colchester. The first is a priapic comic actor from the Cups Hotel (Durham 2012, no. 177). The figure wears a mask, the top of his head is bald and his ears are large. His hooded tunic gives him a rather hunchbacked appearance, which is further emphasised by the loose folds of the tunic across his chest. He is shown lifting the hem of his skirt to reveal a large, erect phallus, and a pile of fruits is placed on top of the folds of the skirt. His feet are on a small, flat, rectangular base, and he does not stand upright but leans backwards slightly. Another similar Priapus holding the fruit in his hands rather than on his cloak was recently found at Thorrington, Essex (Worrell & Pearce 2011, 425 no. 20, fig. 21) and a number of figurines on the Continent show the same theme.

The second figurine was recovered during excavations at St Mary's Hospital and shows a draped priestess with her right arm raised to hold a missing object (Durham 2012, no. 1042) and in her left hand she holds a purse or pot. Crummy (2006, 61) believes the object is a purse, and thus favours an association of this figure with Rosmerta, the consort of Mercury. Meanwhile Black (2008, 10) believes that the object is a pot and accordingly suggests a link with Nantosuelta, consort of Sucellus. Whichever is correct, there seems little doubt that this figurine is meant to portray a priestess or deity associated with Romano-Celtic religious beliefs.

### *Birds and animals*

Finally there are the small groups of birds and animals (Table 8.1). Many birds and animals are associated with particular deities: cockerels, goats, rams and tortoises with Mercury, peacocks with Juno, panthers with Bacchus and snakes with Aesculapius. Dogs and snakes are associated with healing and snakes also with rebirth and the afterlife (Toynbee 1973, 123, 234). Some figurines, such as the cockerel from Hunt's House, Southwark (Taylor-Wilson 2002, 56, fig. 41.1, fig. 25) or tortoise from Balkerne Lane, Colchester (Crummy 1983, 143, fig. 173 no. 4273) could have been part of groups such as the Mercury from St Albans who is accompanied by a ram, cockerel and tortoise (Durham 2012, no. 55). It is also interesting to note that, given the number of eastern figurines in London, while the goose is perhaps more often associated with deities such as Venus or Juno, it is also associated with Isis and Osiris (Toynbee 1973, 263).

## Discussion of the figurine assemblages

In comparison with other large towns in Britain, London stands out not only because of the large number of figurines but also the variety of types represented and while Colchester has a slightly smaller collection of figurines it exhibits a similarly large range of forms. The proportions of the various male deities from London, Colchester and all of Britain are shown in Figure 8.6. Hercules and Mercury stand out as the largest groups in all three charts, but the number of Hercules figurines from London and Colchester is particularly high. The only other site from which more than two Hercules figurines have been recovered is St Albans, which indicates a certain popularity of Hercules among the urban population, many of whom may also have been immigrants.

Bird (2008) has recently discussed the evidence for the worship of Hercules in London, citing images in stone, on samian and wall plaster as well as the copper alloy figurines shown here. She points out that, apart from his presence on a monumental arch, fragments of which have been found reused in the Roman riverside wall, and a wall painting from Redcross Way, Southwark, all the finds are of a personal nature (Bird 2008, 139). While we know that three figures are from north of the river and two from Southwark, the lack of a good provenance for the majority does not allow the identification of any clusters that might indicate the presence of a temple.

The proportions of Mercury figurines from the two towns are quite different, and London has a relatively small number of this type. Mercury forms 40% of the Colchester assemblage of male deities, which is due in part to the large number of figurines associated with the temples at the Balkerne Gate (Crummy 2006). Meanwhile, the smaller proportion of Mercury figurines in London is offset by the relatively high numbers of Apollo and Harpocrates. While no figurines of Apollo have been found at Colchester, the six from London represent 35% of the assemblage of Apollo from Britain. Like London, Colchester has examples of some of the rarer Eastern figurines such as Harpocrates and the sphinx. There is, however, a concentration in London and the four Harpocrates represent 40% of the total number of Harpocrates from Britain. This concentration of Eastern figurines is in contrast to the lack of one of the better-known British types, the horse and rider, which is completely missing from both cities.

The female deities present a rather different picture (Fig. 8.7). It is immediately obvious that the groups from London and especially Colchester are rather less diverse. However, in spite of the small total number of female deities from these towns, they make up a slightly higher proportion of the figurine assemblages than that for Britain as a whole (London 14%, Colchester 16%, Britain 12%). Both towns contain concentrations of a particular female

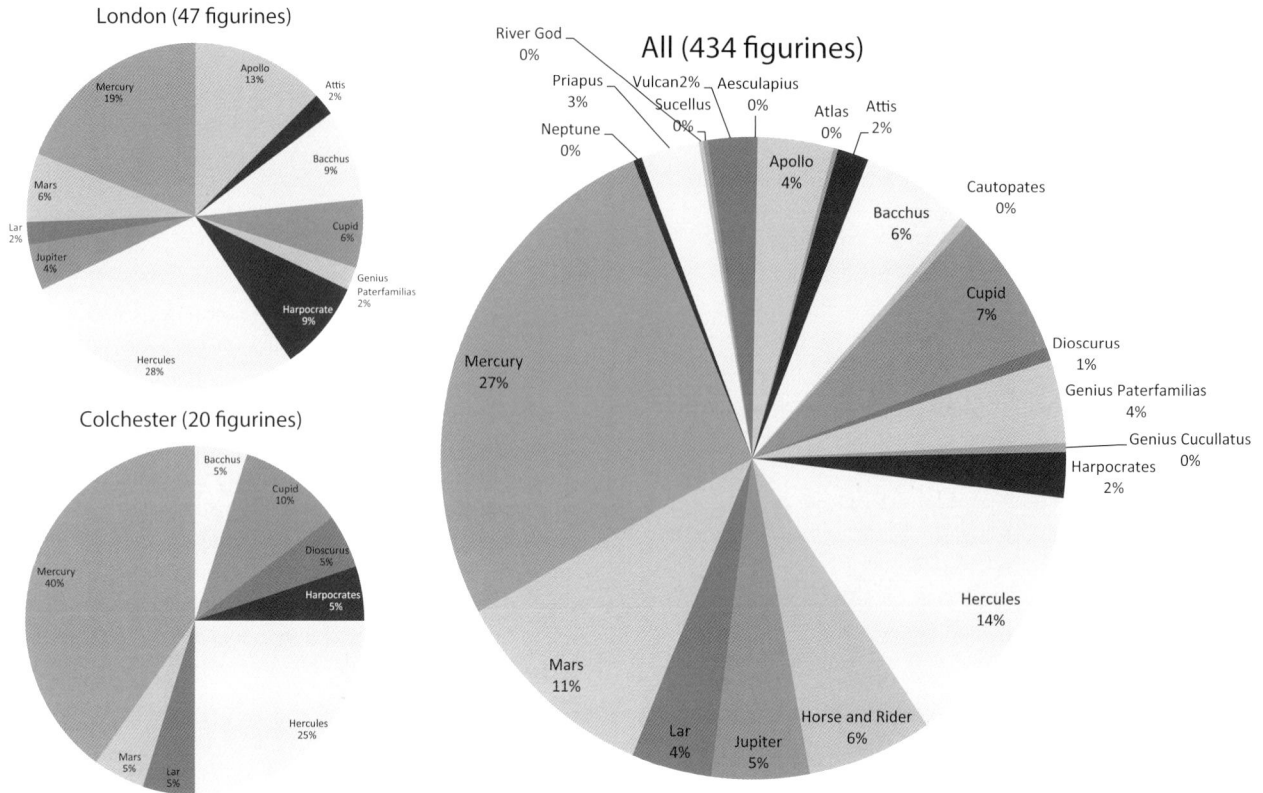

*Fig. 8.6. Proportions of male deities from London, Colchester and Britain*

deity. Minerva is by far the largest group in London (42% of female deities), and the five figurines comprise 15% of the total from Britain. Meanwhile, the largest group from Colchester is Venus (62% of female deities), representing 17% of the total number from Britain. However, Venus is rather under-represented in London, forming only 17% of the female assemblage there.

Finally the assemblages of birds and animals from these two sites are also rather different. Birds and animals represent 29.6% of the total figurine assemblage from Britain, but comprise only 13.8% of the assemblage from London, and thus are somewhat underrepresented. There are only single examples of all species except the goat and goose in London. Meanwhile birds and animals form 30% of the Colchester assemblage, which is almost exactly the same proportion as in the national assemblage. Given the high number of Mercury figurines from the town, it is not surprising that many are associated with this god, and include two goats, a ram, a tortoise and three cockerels. However, the second most common bird in Britain, the eagle, which typically is associated with Jupiter and the military, is not found at either London or Colchester.

The quality of the figurines from the two cities is also quite different. No examples of highly classical figurines have been recovered from within Colchester, but a total of 11 come from London. This represents 12.3% of the assemblage from London, while in Britain figurines in these two styles comprise only 5.1% of the total assemblage. In contrast, the number of stylised figurines in both London (11%) and Colchester (6%) is lower than that found in the total assemblage (14.1%). Thus the assemblage from Colchester is one dominated by moderately well executed and provincially produced pieces. This is also true in London, but to a lesser extent, due to the larger number of high quality imported pieces in the assemblage.

## Distribution

A major obstacle in determining the distribution of figurines in Britain is the lack of a good provenance for many of the pieces. A small number of the figurines from London have been recovered from modern excavations, but often even these are from residual contexts. The majority were found in the 19th century. Some do come with minor details of their discovery, but many more have no specific details of

London (12 figurines)

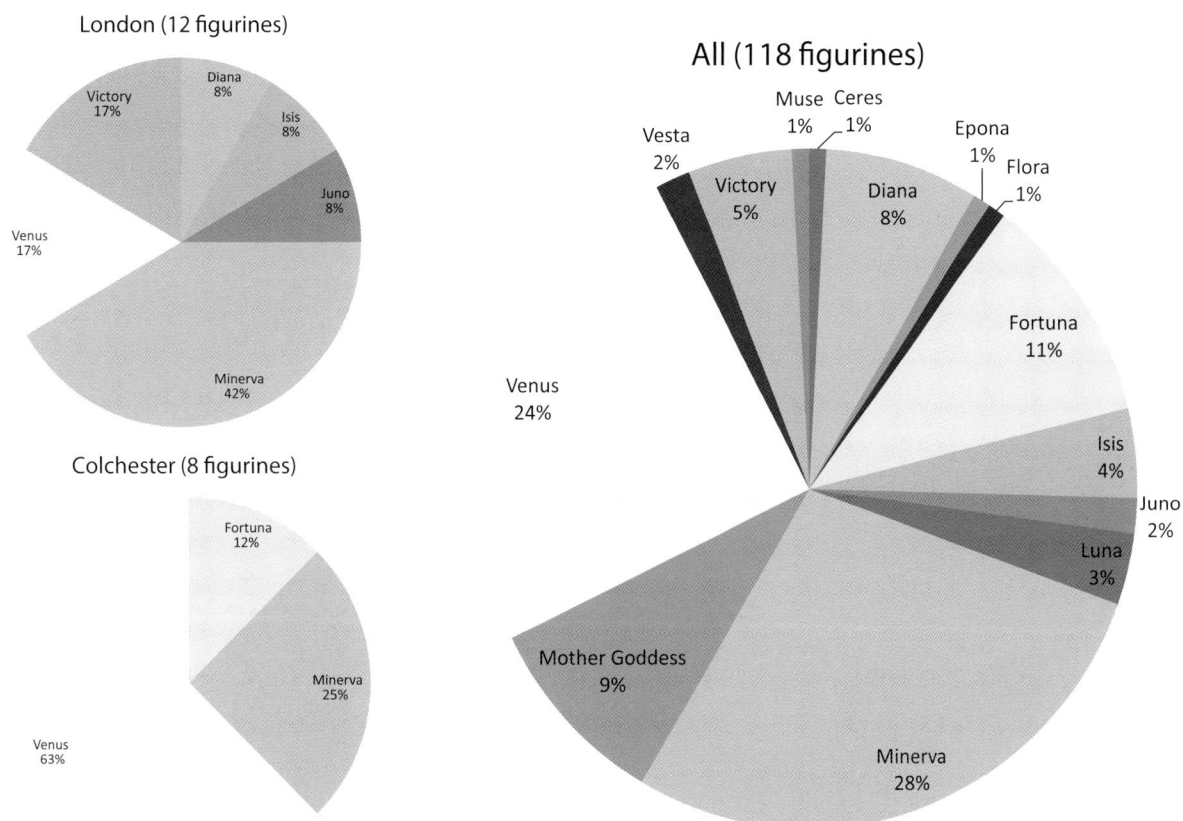

Colchester (8 figurines)

All (118 figurines)

*Fig. 8.7. Proportions of female deities from London, Colchester and Britain*

either when or where they were found, and it is possible that some may not be from London at all.

Thus many of the figurines discussed above are known only to have come from somewhere in London while others have a general area location such as Southwark (8 figures), Lambeth (1), Isleworth (1) and Lewisham (1). This means that only 44 of the 87 figurines could be plotted on a map (Fig. 8.8). As might be expected the majority fall within the line of the Roman wall around Londinium north of the Thames, while five are from south of the river in Southwark. Three figurines were found in the vicinity of London Wall and a Mercury was found just outside the wall to the north. Other outlying pieces tend to occur on the roads leading out of London such as the Bacchus from Enfield and dog from Brockley Hill (Durham 2010, fig. 116; 2012, nos 830 and 815).

Within the Roman city wall there does appear to be a slight concentration along the lines of the two major east–west roads through the city and from the forum south to the Thames. A small cluster of four figurines also occurs along the roads just inside Aldgate, while two figurines have been found in the cemetery just outside the gate (Hall 1996, 74).

There has been much discussion about the deposition of finds in the Walbrook valley (e.g. Maloney & de Moulins 1990; Merrifield 1995), but, while several figurines do appear to come from this area, there is no real concentration. Merrifield and Hall (2008, 126) note that many of the finds from the Middle Walbrook are of copper alloy or iron and are predominantly dress or personal ornaments. However, while few figurines have come from the Walbrook, 16 figurines have been recovered from the River Thames in London. Five of these were found at the same time (Athlete, Mercury, Jupiter, Apollo and Attis) at old London Bridge, and it is possible that they were deposited together. Other figurines that have been found near London Bridge are a Venus, Harpocrates and rider while figurines from unspecified locations in the Thames include two Apollos, Isis, a Satyr, goat and goose. In addition two figurine fragments in Winchester City Museum are listed as having been found in the River Thames: a club from London Bridge and a lower right leg from an unspecified location. Prestige finds such as swords and shields, as well as human skulls, were being deposited in the Thames for many years before the arrival of the Romans (Wait & Cotton 2000, 108; Schulting

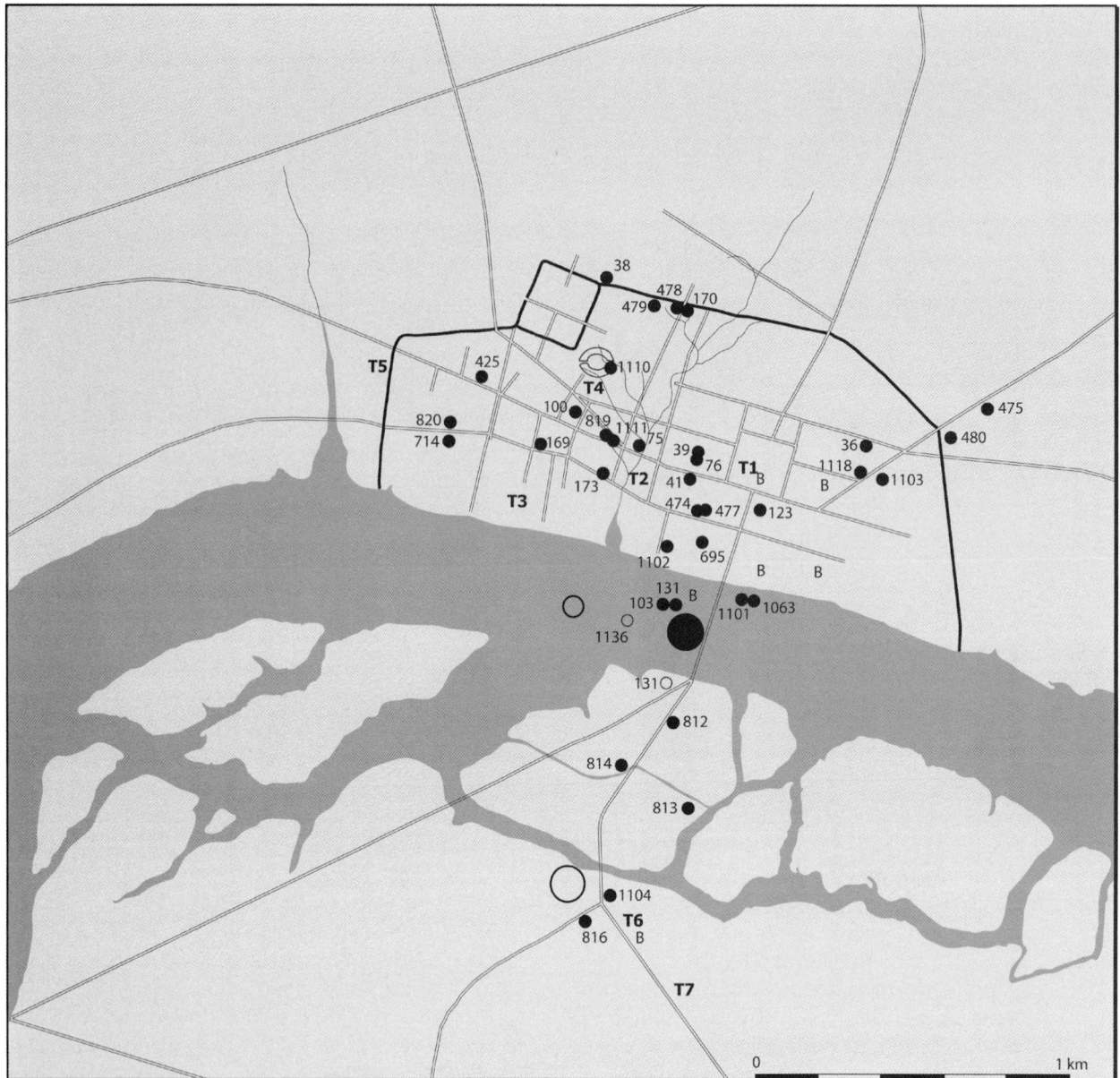

Fig. 8.8. The distribution of figurines in London. The map does not represent the city at any one point in time but includes the major constructions of the first to third centuries including the city wall, fort, amphitheatre and road system. Also indicated on the map are the locations of life size or larger bronze statue fragments. T1 – classical temple built adjacent to the forum in the first century AD (Marsden 1987); T2 – mithraeum built in the mid-third century on the eastern bank of the Walbrook (Shepherd 1998); T3 – temple complex in the south-west of the city near St Peter's Hill (Hill et al. 1980); T4 – a small shrine and possible temple at Gresham Street (Bateman et al. 2008, 118); T5 – possible octagonal temple just outside the western wall at Old Bailey (Schofield and Maloney 1998, 277); T6 – two temples and associated structures, including a ritual shaft containing an inscription to Mars Camulus, were built at Tabard Square in the second century (Durrani 2004); T7 – possible temple of second to third century date associated with a cemetery at Great Dover Street (Mackinder 2000, 9–10)

& Bradley 2013), and it is interesting to note that not only did the practice continue into the Roman period, but that the quality of the figurines thus deposited is high. Another high quality object from the Thames at London Bridge is the head from a statue of Hadrian (British Museum Accn No. 1848,1103.1). A number of arms and hands from life-size, or larger, statues have also been found in the city (Durham 2012, nos 465, 466, 467, 468 and a hand from Gresham Street), most of which are in an uncorroded condition which suggests their deposition in waterlogged deposits (Bayley *et al.* 2009; Hall & Shepherd 2008, 40). All of this indicates a long-lived tradition of making votive offerings in the Thames. The Thames is not the only body of water from which offerings have been recovered; in particular there is a large group of material from the river at Piercebridge, County Durham. The finds date from the 1st to 4th centuries AD and include figurines (Durham 2012, nos 697, 920) as well as coins, brooches, rings and pins. Figurines, as well as being personal objects, might help the supplicant target specific deities or attributes.

Apart from votive deposits in the Thames, some figures from London have been found in other ritual contexts. A Hercules was recovered from a 1st century AD ditch in Southwark on a site where offerings in wells or ritual shafts were found (Beasley 2006), while a goat and club were recovered from the cemetery just outside Aldgate (Hall 1996, 74). Finally a stamped lead figure possibly representing Juno was buried in the arena floor at the eastern entrance to the amphitheatre, and a small unidentified fragment from a copper alloy figurine was also found at the amphitheatre (Wardle 2008, 194, 199; Durham 2012, no. 1110).

A location in the city where one might expect to find figurines is at temples. Recent excavations both north and south of the river have uncovered several temples, but the evidence for religious sites in London is still limited. The sites that we do know of are all marked on Figure 8.8. Slightly further afield, there is a probable temple on the line of Watling Street in Greenwich Park from which several inscriptions and a fragment of a stone statue of Diana have been recovered (Wallower 2002a, 52; 2002b, 80).

While a variety of votive objects, altars and inscriptions have been found, no metal figurines have been recovered from any of these sites, although there is a life-size bronze foot from the temple at Tabard Square (Hall and Shepherd 2008, 30). This is in contrast to Colchester where a number of the figurines are associated with specific temple sites. However, the large number of Apollo figurines from London might be related to the octagonal temple at Old Bailey (T5). Merrifield (1996) has made a case for stone statues from Southwark Cathedral, Goldsmith's Hall and Bevis Marks to represent a Celtic hunter-god who was popular in south-west Britain. The statues depict a youthful figure wearing a cap, with a bow and arrow and quiver. Merrifield goes on to associate this god with Apollo Cunomaglos, to whom an octagonal temple at Nettleton, Wiltshire was dedicated, and suggests that the temple at Old Bailey could also be associated with this god (Merrifield 1996, 110; CSIR 1.10,

43). Although the metal figurines are all classical in style, the presence of a cult to a Celticised version of Apollo in London could account for the number of figures found in the town.

Since figurines were not being deposited at temples in the city, perhaps many were personal objects, either carried with the owner or placed in a domestic *lararium*. Excavated figurines often come from domestic sites, such as the Victory from a rubbish deposit associated with a 1st century building at St Martin Orgar Churchyard (Schofield & Maloney 1998, 233), sphinx from a 3rd/4th century rubbish deposit on Fenchurch Street (Bluer & Brigham 2006), cow/boar from a post-Roman layer at the possible *mansio* site on Southwark Street (Cowan 1992) and cockerel from a late Roman rubbish deposit at Guy's Hospital, Southwark (Taylor-Wilson 2002).

Although Colchester, like London, has a large number of figurines with no contextual details some 23 have been recovered from excavations carried out at various sites both within the town wall and on the outskirts of the city, and it was possible to plot 29 out of the 50 figurines from Colchester (Fig. 8.9). The distribution is somewhat biased towards areas where excavations have taken place (Durham 2012, nos 1032 and 1033 from Lion Walk, 1000–1002 from Culver Street, 1034–1037 Balkerne Lane), but others have been found by chance (nos 26, 51, 150, 177 and 1030) which suggests that the slight concentration towards the western side of Colchester is real.

The primary difference between London and Colchester is the number of figurines that have been found in association with temples. The Mercury, goat, cockerel and tortoise found just outside the Balkerne Gate to the west of Colchester and associated pieces such as three *caducei* and two cockerel fittings can be related to the temples on Balkerne Hill near the Balkerne Gate (Crummy 2006). Slightly further west, along the road to London, a stag was found in a pit associated with the temple to Silvanus at the Royal Grammar School (Hull 1958, 238–239; Durham 2012, no. 414). Two other figurines have also been found at the site (Durham 2012, Duck 1148 and Mars 1149), although not from excavated contexts. However, further association with Mercury also appears in the form of two figurines of the god from the area of the western cemetery between Colchester and the Royal Grammar School site (Durham 2012, nos 45 and 50). Crummy (2006, 58) suggests that these figurines could have come either from graves or a shrine to Mercury within the cemetery area.

A final association with Mercury can be seen in the high quality figurine from the temple at Gosbecks Farm, a long-lived site with Iron Age occupation, Roman fort, theatre and Romano-Celtic temple which is located some 4 km to the south-west of Colchester (Hawkes & Crummy 1995, 7, 97–103; Durham 2012, no. 43).

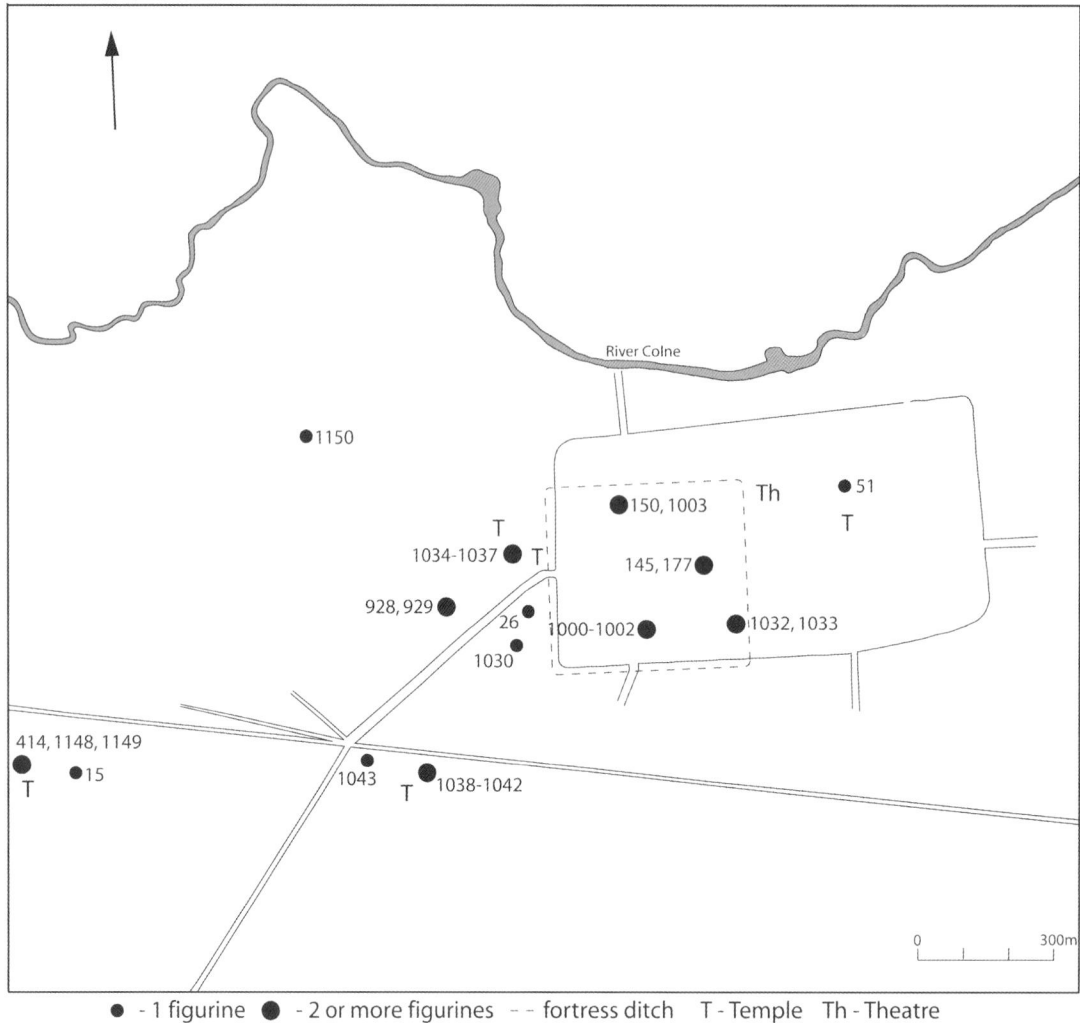

Fig. 8.9. The distribution of figurines in Colchester

*Fig. 8.10. Isis from London. Durham 2012, no. 127 (with kind permission of the Museum of London, accn no. A25383).*

## Eastern religions

Moving on from the assemblages as a whole, I will briefly look more closely at figurines associated with eastern religions, in particular those of Cybele and Isis. The fertility goddess Cybele, or *Magna Mater*, and her consort Attis originated in Asia Minor (Henig 1995b, 110). Evidence for the worship of the cult of Cybele is limited in Britain but does include bronze figurines of Attis from London and Retford, Nottinghamshire (Durham 2012, nos 12 and 1156). There are also heads from Mildenhall, Suffolk and Lincoln and an arm holding a pine branch from Hockwold-cum-Wilton, Norfolk may have belonged to an Attis figurine (Green 1976, 212; Durham 2012, nos 441, 499 and 630).

One of the main attributes used to identify Attis is the Phrygian cap, as seen on the head from Mildenhall. The figurine from London also wears this cap, as well as a tunic and trousers which are open at the front from the waist to the knee, thus exposing the genitalia. The figurine from Retford is quite different and depicts a pensive, seated figure with rather feminine breasts whose head rests on his right hand, the elbow of which is on his right knee (Henig, pers. comm.).

Other evidence for the worship of Cybele and Attis in London includes an altar (Tillyard 1917), three steelyard weight busts of Cybele (Green 1976, 222 no. 15), a terracotta figurine from Paul Street (Vermaseren 1986, 168 no. 490, pl. clxv) and a castration clamp from the Thames, decorated with busts of Cybele and Attis, which may have been used to castrate the priests of Cybele (Henig 1995b, 110–111). Finds associated with these gods from other British sites are limited but include altars from Gloucester (Green 1976, 171; Vermaseren 1986, 169–170 no. 496) and Corbridge (Vermaseren 1986, 170 no. 497; *RIB* 1135), a jet plaque of Attis from Whitton, Suffolk (Green 1976, 218; Toynbee 1962, 184 no. 136), a pipeclay Cybele from Corbridge (Green 1978, 57), and a steelyard weight bust of Cybele from Cirencester (Green 1978, 173). Thus the evidence for this cult is geographically widespread but sparse.

Somewhat more common is worship of the fertility goddess Isis, along with her consort Osiris, or Serapis as he was known in the Roman world, and son Harpocrates. The murdered Serapis was brought back to life by Isis and as such is a god of the Underworld (Alvar 2008, 44–47). Metal figurines of Isis include examples from London; Dorchester, Dorset and Thornborough, Buckinghamshire (Durham 2012, nos 127, 594 and 734). There are no figurines of Serapis in Britain, but Harpocrates is more common than Isis, and there is a silver figurine from the Thames in London and bronze examples from London, Colchester, Chester and St Albans (Durham 2012, nos 147, 148, 1101, 1102, 1043, 210 and 726).

The figurine of Isis from London shows her seated with her head resting against her right hand, while in her left she holds ears of corn or the base of a cornucopia (Fig. 8.10). She wears a tunic and mantle and a coronet on her head. The presence of the corn or cornucopia led to her initial identification as Ceres (e.g. Toynbee 1964, 85; Wheeler 1930, 46), but there is little doubt that she is in fact Isis. Not only is she wearing a mantle tied at the front with an Isis knot, which replicates the ankh, the hieroglyphic symbol for life (Turcan 1996, 80), but she is seated in a pose that is seen in a number of other figures of Isis which are discussed by Bricault (1992) who suggests a date in the 1st or 2nd century AD for the London piece. The figurine from the Thames, however, is the only example of this form in copper alloy.

Another goddess with whom Isis was frequently associated in the Roman world was Fortuna. A figurine from Crewelthorpe, Yorkshire has also been published as Ceres (Green 1978, 58), but this time the figure is actually Isis-Fortuna (Durham 2012, no. 227). The goddess is standing clothed in a long gown and wears a *modius* and diadem on her head. The *modius* was used as a corn measure in Egypt but was also worn as a cylindrical head-dress by the deities Harpocrates, Serapis and, less commonly, Isis (Clerc 1998, 82). The Crewelthorpe piece is missing both arms, but may have held a rudder and a cornucopia.

Depictions of Harpocrates are slightly more common than those of Isis. A Harpocrates from the River Thames at London Bridge is a high quality piece in silver with a gold body chain and was probably imported while a second figurine wears a *modius* (Durham 2012, nos 147 and 148). Two other London examples from Lower Thames Street and Martin Lane are fairly crude depictions in the same stance in which the right hand is held to the mouth and the left hand is behind the body resting on the buttocks (Durham 2012, nos 1101 and 1102). Both pieces are small and are in the same stance as a Harpocrates amulet with a suspension loop on the back which was also recovered from the Thames in London (British Museum Accn No. 1891, 0418.15). One final Harpocrates from Great Winchester Street, London is in terracotta (Green 1976, 222 no. 12; Harris and Harris 1965, 81). Apart from the figurines from Chester, St Albans and Colchester, there are also amulets from Colchester and possibly Woodeaton, Oxfordshire (Bagnall Smith 1995, 182; Durham 2012, nos 210, 726, 1043, 1152, 536). Finally, an example from Worcester was identified as Angerona (Haverfield 1901, 206, fig. 2; Durham 2012, no. 865), but the stance is the same as many of these Harpocrates figurines with one hand to the lips and the other behind the back.

Gods of the Isis cult are also depicted in other media. Isis is seen on several bone hairpins from London (Hall & Wardle 2005, 174; Johns 1996), bronze steelyard weights from London (Toynbee 1964, 95, pl. xxiia) and Cirencester (Green 1976, 173), a lead bust from Groundwell Ridge, Wiltshire (Schuster 2011), an intaglio of Isis-Fortuna from London Wall (Henig 2008, 229 no. 30), a cameo of Isis or a Ptolemaic queen from Friday Street, London (Henig 2008, 232 no. 82), an intaglio from Wroxeter (Henig 2008, 119) and a bust from York (Green 1978, 75). There are three stone heads of Serapis – one in marble from the Walbrook mithraeum in London (Toynbee 1986, 13 no. 3, pls 8, 9 and III), one in porphyry from Highworth, Wiltshire (*CSIR* 1.2, 31 no. 113; Passmore 1944, 99–100), and one in oolitic limestone from Silchester, Hampshire (Boon 1973; Toynbee 1964, 94–95) – as well as intaglios from London (Henig 2008, 232 no. 72); Beckford, Gloucestershire; Wroxeter and Stanwix, Cumbria (Henig 1978, 93 nos 357, 356 and 354), and a lamp depicting Jupiter Serapis and Cerberus from Great Winchester Street, London (Harris & Harris 1965, 79). There are also three lamps depicting Anubis, an Egyptian god of the afterlife who was assimilated with Osiris (Wilkinson 2003, 187), from a burial on the site of a temple on Great Dover Street, London (Mackinder 2000, 12) and one from Caerleon (Bricault 2001, 110).

One animal associated with the Isis cult is the Apis bull from Memphis who is depicted with a sun disc between his horns (Wilkinson 2003, 171). Two examples of Apis bulls have been found in Britain at York and St Just, Cornwall, although the find from St Just may be a modern import (Durham 2012, nos 310 and 752).

Other figurines with Egyptian associations are the Sphinx, ibis and crocodile. Copper alloy examples of the Sphinx have been found in London; Colchester; Watchet, Somerset; Caerwent, Monmouthshire and Epperstone, Nottinghamshire (Durham 2012, nos 1103, 412, 443, 554 and 779) and there is a stone sphinx on a tombstone from Colchester (*RIB* 211). The sphinx from Fenchurch Street, London was excavated from a 3rd- or 4th-century rubbish layer and was found with a copper alloy link chain around its left leg (Kiely 2006, 155). Although the figure is in poor condition, the fine detail depicting the feathers on the wings indicates that this was a good quality, provincial, piece and is of a much higher quality than the simple depictions from Colchester and Watchet.

The ibis, which represented the deity Thoth (a moon god who became associated with writing and knowledge), protected Osiris and is most commonly depicted as an ibis-headed man (Wilkinson 2003, 215–216), has been found on three sites: a possible figurine from Chiddingfold, Surrey and attachments from Caerwent and Rochester, Kent (Durham 2012 nos 582, 545 and 666). Of interest is the figurine of a crocodile from the villa at Fullerton, Hampshire (Durham 2012, no. 319). This well-modelled piece shows the animal with its head raised and tail curling upwards. The jaws are open to reveal teeth, three ridges along the back are created by cross-hatched grooves and the sides of the body are decorated with circular stamps. The crocodile appears in Egyptian art, both as an animal and as the god Sobek (a fertility deity and god of water), who often appears as either a crocodile or a crocodile-headed man (Wilkinson 2003, 218–220). The crocodile and Sobek are also associated with the Isis cult. Although no parallels for this figurine have been found, there is a mount from Saxton, North Yorkshire in the shape of a crocodile (PAS SWYOR−76B161).

Unlike the cults of Jupiter Dolichenus and Cybele, there is believed to be a temple to Isis in London, although the location is as yet unknown (Henig 1995b, 113), and a serapeum outside the fortress at York (Harris & Harris 1965, 75). A foundation inscription found at the serapeum indicates that it was built by the Legate Claudius Hieronymianus of the Sixth Legion in the second half of the 2nd century (*RIB* 658). The legate's second name suggests he was of Egyptian

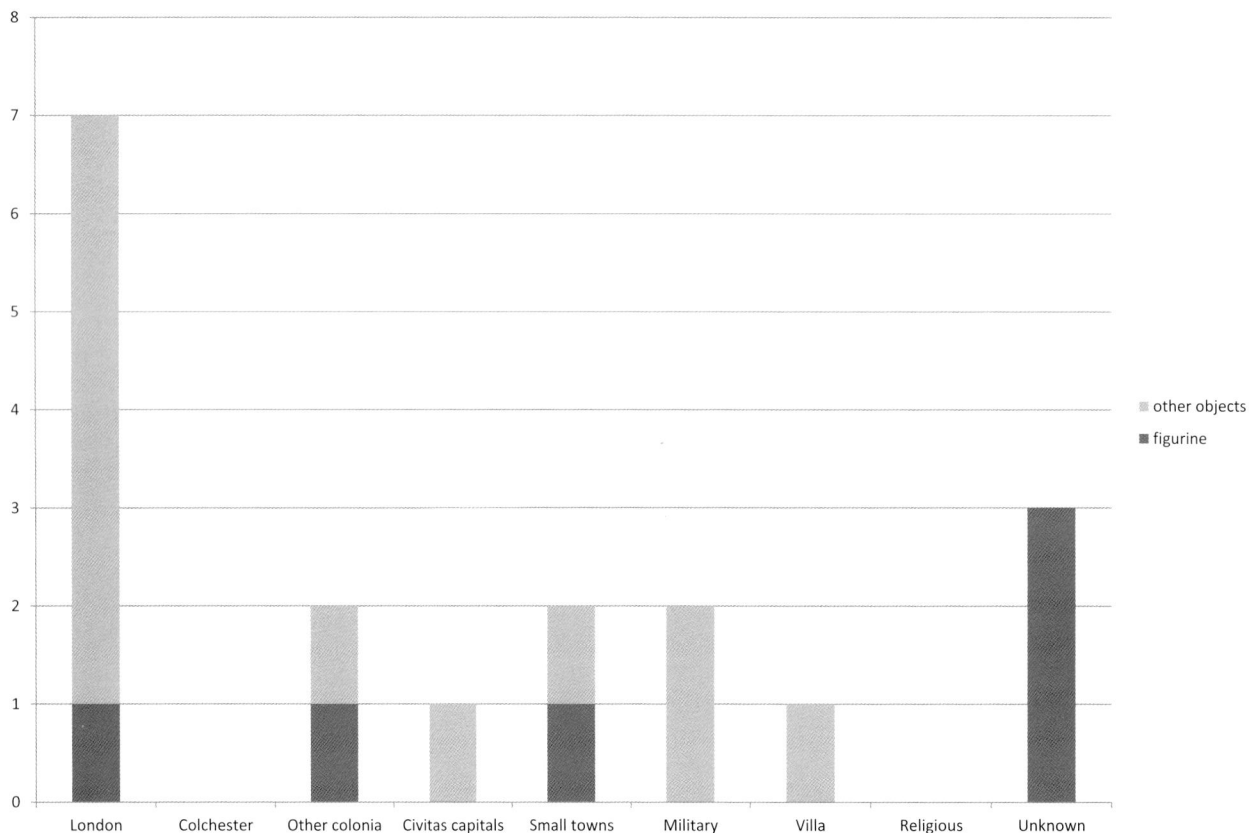

*Fig. 8.11. The distribution of all objects associated with Cybele and Attis (17 pieces)*

origin (Ottaway 2004, 114). Finds providing evidence for a temple in the city of London include a late 1st century jug from Tooley Street, Southwark which is inscribed with the grafitto *Londini ad Fanum Isidis* or 'At the temple of Isis, London (*RIB* II 2503.127). An inscription dedicating the restoration of a temple to Isis was also found during excavations at Baynard's Castle on Upper Thames Street where a collapsed section of riverside wall contained a number of re-used blocks from an arch and a screen of gods as well as a relief of four Mother Goddesses and two altars (Hill *et al.* 1980, 2). One of the altars, while broken, is largely complete and contains the inscription: 'In honour of the divine (i.e. imperial) house, Marcus Martiannius Pulcher, deputy (?) imperial propraetorian legate of two emperors ordered the temple of Isis ... which had fallen down through old age, to be restored' (Hassall 1980, 196–197; *RIB* III

3001). Dendrochronology dates from various sites along the wall suggest a construction date in the late third century (Brigham 1990, 101, 124). Hassall (1980, 198) believes that the location of the altar north of the river and the grafitto in Southwark could point to the presence of two temples to Isis in London, one on each side of the river.

### Distribution of eastern deities

Thus the evidence for Eastern religions in Britain is somewhat sparse, but fairly widespread and varied, especially if one considers the figural evidence in conjunction with other objects such as altars, statues and personal objects. The total number of objects associated with the cult of Cybele and Attis, and the types of sites from which they were recovered, is listed in Figure 8.11. From

*Fig. 8.12. The distribution of figurines associated with Eastern religions*

this one can see that the number of figurines is very small (all five depict Attis), and that the other objects associated with the cult greatly add to the evidence for its worship in Britain. The figurines are all found towards the eastern side of the country (Fig. 8.12), but this could just be a result of the small number of figurines since other objects associated with the cult have been found on Hadrian's Wall and further west in Gloucester and Cirencester. However, the distribution does highlight the concentration of material in London and sites associated with the military.

Figure 8.11 also shows that London dominates the assemblage of Cybele and Attis depictions, but that overall the majority of finds come from major urban centres, with a small number from military sites and their associated settlements. Interestingly, there are no pieces from Colchester or religious sites, but the distribution does suggest that the majority of adherents to this cult were urban and immigrant. Jones and Mattingly (2002, 272, Map 8:8) cite the concentration of dedications along Hadrian's Wall as evidence for the association of this cult with the military, but, as is the case for other deities such as Mars, this largely reflects the military use of dedications, and the scattering of other finds around the country are primarily found south of the Wall.

Britain has a similar figural assemblage to other Continental provinces such as Gallia and Germania, although Attis is more often represented in those provinces. Several figurines of Attis with open fronted trousers like the Attis from London have also been found (Menzel 1966, 28 no. 58a from the Moselle at Trier; Vermaseren 1986, 109–10 no. 318 possibly from Marseille; 158 no. 466 from Seine-Maritime and 160 no. 476 from Tournai). Stone altars and statuary are, however, much more common in Gaul (see Vermaseren 1986, 84–94 nos 222–243, 99–101 nos 268–274). Britain is generally considered to have little in the way of stone sculpture compared to other provinces in the Empire (Stewart 2008, 157) so this is not unexpected.

As London does so dominate the assemblage from Britain (while Colchester conspicuously has no objects associated with Cybele and Attis) it is of interest to see how it compares to other major urban centres in north-west Europe. The four cities of Cologne, Mainz, Bordeaux and Trier were chosen as suitable comparative urban sites with well-published assemblages. All four are also situated on rivers and major road routes (Woolf 1998, 87), and so, as London and Colchester, they are suitable sites for the trade and redistribution of objects. Like London, Cologne was a provincial capital (of Germania Inferior) with no evidence

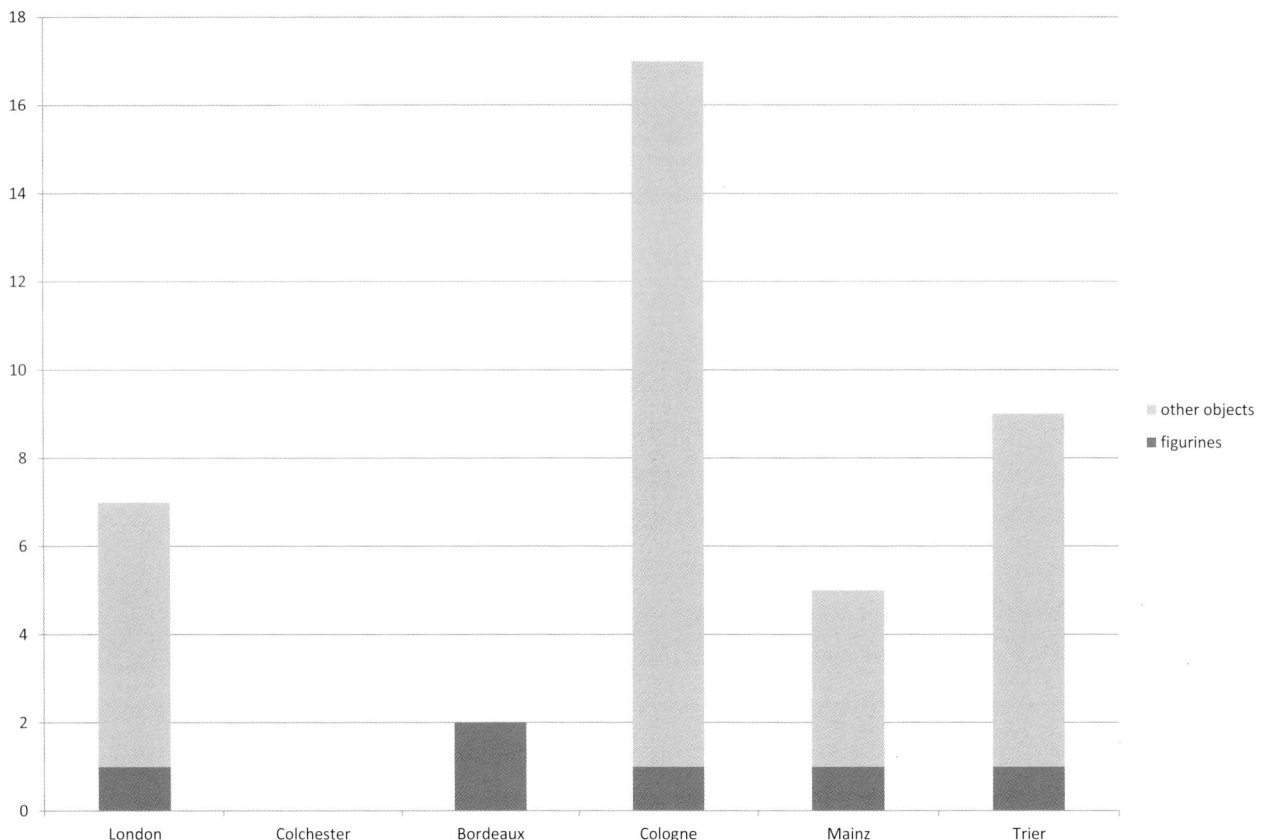

*Fig. 8.13. The objects associated with Cybele and Attis from selected cities (40 pieces)*

for pre-Roman settlement and Mainz the provincial capital of Germania Superior (Carroll 2001, 41–42). Bordeaux was particularly well-situated for Atlantic trade and was probably the home of a provincial governor for a time (Woolf 1998, 134), while Trier was a *civitas* capital which became a *colonia* under Claudius (Carroll 2001, 42–43). The objects associated with this cult from Bordeaux, Cologne, Mainz and Trier, which have been published by Vermaseren (1977; 1986; 1989), are listed in Figure 8.13. Here it can be seen that London has an assemblage which in size is second only to Cologne, and that only Colchester shows no trace of the cult. The single figurines from London, Cologne, Mainz and Trier are all of Attis. The bulk of the other objects from the continental cities are stone altars or reliefs, but there are also terracotta figurines of Cybele from Mainz (one example), Trier (four examples) and Cologne (eight examples). Figurines of this type are rare in Britain, although there are single examples from London (Vermaseren 1986, 168 no. 490) and Corbridge (Green 1978, 173).

The Egyptian deities are the most commonly represented of the Eastern religions in Britain, especially those associated with Isis. Figure 8.14 illustrates the various deities and creatures represented, and as with Cybele and Attis the figural assemblage is small in comparison to the other objects. Isis, Serapis and Harpocrates are the largest groups, while Anubis is less popular, and figurines of these deities are found in similar proportions on the Continent (Leclant 2004, 95).

Urban sites which were important ports or on trade routes became centres for the cults of Isis and Serapis in Italy, which then spread further west across the Mediterranean into Spain, France and beyond (Heyob 1975, 14; Turcan 1996, 97–103). In comparison to other parts of the Roman Empire, Isis was more popular in Britain than Germany or Spain, but less so than in Gaul (Leclant 2004, 95). Isis-Fortuna was the patron of traders and sailors, thus the cult was spread around the empire by merchants and officials rather than soldiers and was more prevalent where temples were built (Heyob 1975, 23; Turcan 1996, 104). The serapeum at York could, perhaps, be accounted for by the fact that Serapis was more popular than Isis with the military (Perrissin-Fabert 2004, 450–452). No temples to Isis or Serapis have been found in Gaul, but inscriptions at Arles, Nimes, Grenoble and Lyon indicate that they did exist (Leclant 2004, 97–98). A review of the figurines published in Continental catalogues shows that there are more figurines of Isis in Gaul than Britain, although more often of the Isis-Fortuna type (Bricault & Podvin 2008, 7), and there are similar numbers of Isis in Britain and Germany. It is also

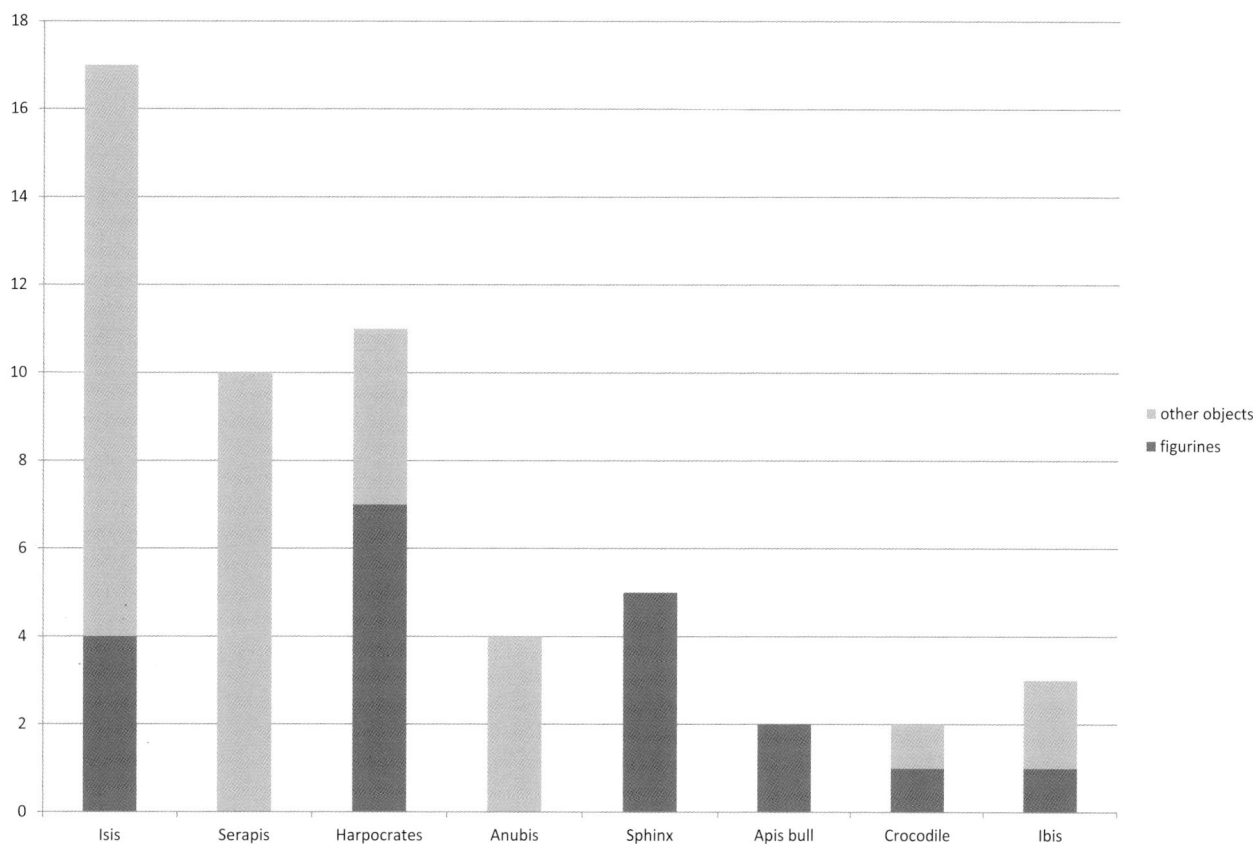

*Fig. 8.14. Objects associated with Egyptian deities (54 pieces)*

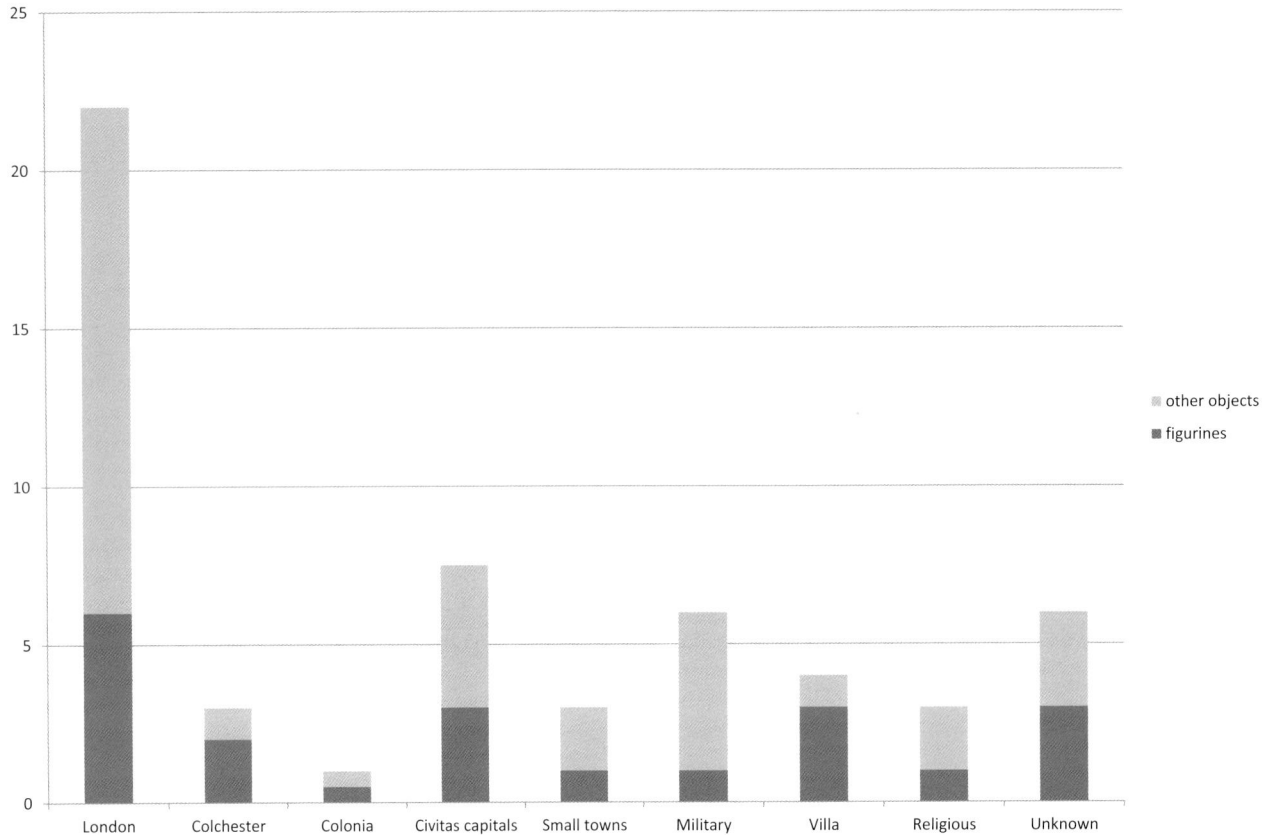

*Fig. 8.15. Distribution of objects associated with Egyptian deities (54 pieces)*

of note that figurines of Isis, Osiris and Harpocrates from Gaul and Britain are more often depicted in a Roman provincial style than those from areas such as Austria (Fleischer 1967, Tafn 74 & 75 nos 137–140 & 142) or Switzerland (Kaufmann-Heinimann 1977, Taf. 44 no. 44, Taf. 86 no. 79) which closely follow the Egyptian style and were probably imported. This indicates that the more widespread worship of these deities in Britain and Gaul encouraged the production of appropriate figurines for the local market.

Figure 8.12 shows that Egyptian figurines are scattered throughout Britain, while the distribution of figurines and other objects among various site types is illustrated in Figure 8.15. The most obvious difference between this and the distribution of Cybele and Attis is that figurines are found at all site types, although often in very small numbers, and again the majority of finds come from major urban centres which usually have a military presence, such as London, Exeter, Gloucester, Cirencester, Silchester, Wroxeter, York and Corbridge. However, there are also examples from villas at Fullerton, Chiddingfold and Whitton and religious sites at the temples at Thornborough and Woodeaton.

As London dominates the British assemblage of objects associated with the Isis cult, in Figure 8.16 this group

is again compared with those from selected continental cities, as published by Bricault (2001). Once again London is second only to Cologne in the size of its assemblage. However, unlike the assemblage of objects associated with the cult of Cybele and Attis, which on the Continent is dominated by stone inscriptions or altars, the assemblages from both Britain and the Continent are largely comprised of figurines, statues or other small objects such as busts, lamps and sistra (ibid. 98, 100, 114, 116). Perhaps this reflects the type of worshippers associated with the Isis cult which was popular with traders as well as women, both groups which might be less inclined to set up the stone dedications which were obviously popular with the worshippers of *Magna Mater*, who were more likely to have military connections.

In Britain, London would have represented the perfect milieu for the development of the Isis cult, as is indicated by the presence of one, possibly two, temples in the city. Finds associated with the Egyptian religions are found scattered throughout the city (Fig. 8.17) and so do not help to indicate where these temples might have been situated, except for the fact that the majority come from within the city walls or the river itself. The map shows that a high proportion of finds associated with Eastern religions, in

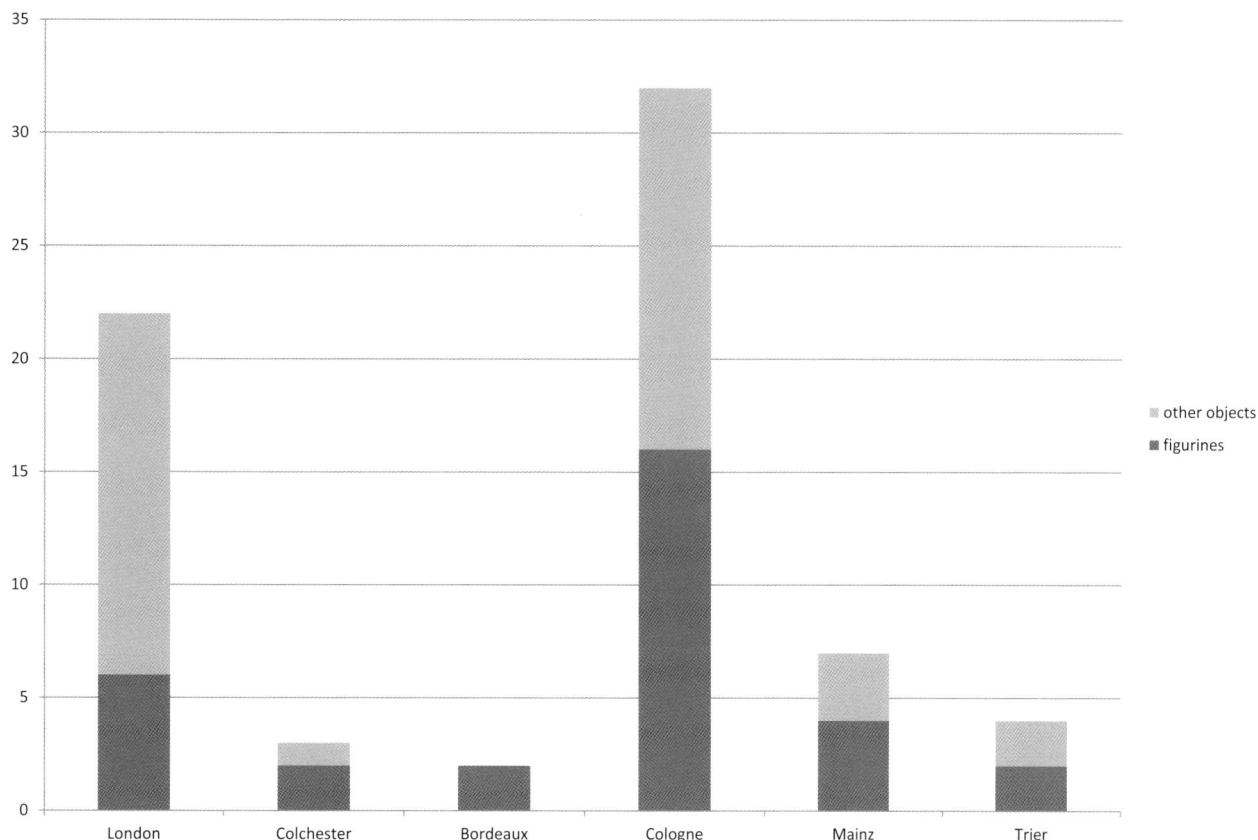

*Fig. 8.16. Objects associated with Egyptian deities from selected cities (70 pieces)*

particular the bronze figurines and castration clamp, have come from the river. Twelve other figurines of classical deities have also been recovered from the river, and it has been suggested that this could indicate the continued deposition of high class material in water. Certainly, given the association of the Isis cult with water, this practice would accord well with the deposition of the figurines of Isis and Harpocrates.

**Conclusion**

It is difficult to assess how the use of figurines from London and Colchester may have changed over time since the lack of provenance from well-dated, non-residual contexts means that dates often can only be assigned on stylistic grounds. This is not easy to do, and is further complicated by the fact that these objects may have been in use for some time before deposition. In only a very few cases, such as a Hercules from a ditch at Swan Street, Southwark or *caduceus* from a pit at St Mary's Hospital, Colchester, an early date can be assigned due to the context from which they were recovered. The higher quality figurines, which were probably imported, tend to be assigned dates

in the first or second century. Many provincial figures are undated, but dates in the 2nd and 3rd centuries are often suggested.

The important role that London played in the administration of the province meant that it would have attracted people from all over the Roman Empire to live and work. Figurines are small, portable objects and no doubt some were brought as part of people's own religious practices; others were probably imported for sale. As well as deities such as Mercury, Minerva or Isis supporting the health and wealth of their supplicants, figurines might also serve to maintain links with families and homelands. The personal nature of figurines meant that they may have been carried with their owners for years, and some do show wear from repeated handling.

These practices could account not only for the presence of interesting genre pieces such as the gladiators from London, but also for the high quality imported pieces of 1st and 2nd century date, when the city was thriving. The concentration of items associated with Eastern religions in London was no doubt due to the popularity of the Isis cult with merchants and officials (Heyob 1975, 23; Turcan 1996, 104).

Altar - A; B - bust; C - clamp; F - terracotta figurine; I - inscription; L - lamp; P - hairpin; R - finger ring; S - stone statue; T - temple
● - 1 figurine;  ○- 1 figurine, uncertain location;  ● - 2-5 figurines, uncertain location

*Fig. 8.17. The distribution of objects associated with Eastern religions in London*

Figurines have been recovered from a variety of context types at London and Colchester. Where found at public sites such as the forum or amphitheatre, they have clearly been deposited as votive offerings. Those from domestic contexts are usually found in residual rubbish layers and so would appear to be casual losses rather than deliberate deposits, and this is common among the figurines from other urban sites in Britain, as is the general absence of figurines in burials (Durham 2012, 4.3). The primary

difference between London and Colchester is the lack of figurines at temple sites in London, which may reflect a difference in the people living in the two towns. Stone inscriptions were predominantly dedicated by military men in both towns, but there are also a number set up by foreign officials in London. Inscriptions were far more popular among these groups than civilians in Britain as the distribution of certain figurine types shows (Durham 2012, 4.4.1). This is not to say that soldiers did not carry figurines themselves; a figurine base was recovered from a first-century destruction layer in barracks at Colchester (Crummy 1992, 193, fig. 5.61 no. 1704) and figurines have been found at many military sites. Figurines would make a more personal offering and their presence at the temples in Colchester, reflects this. Indeed Colchester better represents the people of Roman Britain who regularly deposited figurines at temples, and in particular figurines associated with Mercury, as seen at temple sites such as Uley, Lydney and Brigstock.

The possible figurine of Rosmerta from Colchester also illustrates the use of Roman practices in Romano-Celtic religion. There is evidence for the development of figurine types representing non-Roman deities, such as the horse and rider in eastern/central Britain or the hoard group from Southbroom, Wiltshire (Durham 2014) and the lack of these types from London in particular is striking. However, the use of Roman images to depict local deities, such as the Minerva plaques used in the worship of Senuna is also known (Jackson & Burleigh 2007) and it is perhaps this that accounts for the large number of Apollo figurines in London which were actually representing a Romano-British hunter god, Apollo Cunomaglos.

The figurines from London and Colchester form impressive and interesting collections. They are dominated by classical types and although they contain none of the British types such as the horse and rider figurines, there is evidence that Classical deities may have been used to represent Romano-Celtic deities. The range of types and the different deposition patterns in the two towns illustrate the variety of practices in Roman Britain where both Roman and regional deities were represented by metal figurines and used and deposited in a range of ways.

## Bibliography

*CSIR* 1.2 Cunliffe, B. & Fulford, M. G. (1982) *Corpus Signorum Imperii Romani. Great Britain Vol. 1. Fasc. 2 Bath and the Rest of Wessex.* Oxford, Oxford University Press.

*CSIR* 1.10 Coombe, P., Grew, F., Hayward, K. & Henig, M. (2015) *Corpus Signorum Imperii Romani. Great Britain Vol. 1. Fasc. 10 Roman Sculpture from London and the South-East.* Oxford, Oxford University Press.

PAS Portable Antiquities Scheme. https://finds.org.uk/database.

*RIB* Collingwood, R. G. & Wright, R. P. (1965) *Roman Inscriptions of Britain I. Inscriptions on Stone.* Oxford, Clarendon Press.

*RIB* II Frere, S. S. & Tomlin, R. S. O. (1995) *The Roman Inscriptions of Britain Vol. II, Fasc. 8.* Stroud, Alan Sutton.

*RIB* III Tomlin, R. S. O., Wright, R. P. & Hassall, M. (2009) *The Roman Inscriptions of Britain III. Inscriptions on stone found or notified between 1 January 1955 and 31 December 2006.* Oxford, Oxbow Books.

Alcock, J. P. (1986) The concept of Genius in Roman Britain. In M. Henig & A. King (eds) *Pagan Gods and Shrines of the Roman Empire,* 113–133. Oxford, Oxford University Committee for Archaeology Monograph 8.

Alvar, J. (2008) *Romanising Oriental Gods. Myth, salvation and ethics in the cults of Cybele, Isis and Mithras.* Leiden, E. J. Brill.

Bagnall Smith, J. (1995) Interim report on the votive material from Romano-Celtic temple sites in Oxfordshire. *Oxoniensia* 60, 177–203.

Bateman, N., Cowan, C. & Wroe-Brown, R. (2008) *London's Roman Amphitheatre: Guildhall Yard, City of London.* London, Museum of London Archaeological Service Monograph 35.

Bayley, J., Croxford, B., Henig, M. & Watson, B. (2009) A gilt-bronze arm from London. *Britannia* 40, 151–162.

Beasley, M. (2006) Roman boundaries, roads and ritual: excavations at the Old Sorting Office, Swan Street, Southwark. *Transactions of the London and Middlesex Archaeological Society* 57, 23–68.

Bird, J. (2008) A samian bowl by Crucuro and the cult of Hercules in London. In J. Clark J. Cotton, J. Hall, R. Sherris & H. Swain (eds) *Londinium and Beyond. Essays on Roman London and its Hinterland for Harvey Sheldon,* 134–141. York, Council for British Archaeology Research Report 156.

Black, E. (2008) Pagan religion in rural south-east Britain: Contexts, deities and belief. In D. Rudling (ed.), *Ritual Landscapes of Roman South-East Britain,* 1–25. Oxford, Heritage Marketing/Oxbow Books.

Bluer, R. & Brigham, T. (2006) *Roman and Later Development East of the Forum and Cornhill: Excavations at Lloyds Register, 71 Fenchurch Street, City of London.* London, Museum of London Archaeology Service.

Boon, G. C. (1973) Sarapis and Tutela: a Silchester coincidence. *Britannia* 4, 107–114.

Boucher, S. (1976) *Recherches sur les bronzes figurés de Gaule pré-romaine et romaine.* Rome, Ecole Française de Rome.

Bricault, L. (1992) Isis dolente. *Bulletin de l'Institut Français d'archéologie Orientale* 92, 37–49.

Bricault, L. (2001) *Atlas de la diffusion des cultes Isiaques (IVe s. av. J.-C. - IVe s. apr. J.-C.).* Paris, Diffusion de Boccard.

Bricault, L. & Podvin, J.-L. (2008) Statuettes d'Isis en argent et en bronze. *Biblioteca Isiaca* I, 7–21.

Brigham, T. (1990) The late Roman waterfront in London. *Britannia* 21, 99–183.

Carroll, M. (2001) *Romans, Celts and Germans. The German provinces of Rome.* Stroud, Tempus.

Clerc, G. (1998) Une Isis-Fortuna en Alsace. In W. Clarysse, A. Schoors & H. Willems (eds) *Egyptian Religion. The Last Thousand Years. Studies Dedicated to the Memory of Jan Quaegebeur,* 81–90. Leuven, Uitgeverij Peeters.

Cowan, C. (1992) A possible mansio in Roman Southwark: Excavations at 15–23 Southwark Street, 1980–86. *Transactions London and Middlesex Archaeological Society* 43, 3–191.

Crummy, N. (1983) *The Roman Small Finds from Excavations in Colchester 1971–9.* Colchester, Colchester Archaeological Report 2.

Crummy, N. (1992) The Roman small finds from the Culver Street site. In P. Crummy (ed.) *Excavations at Culver Street, the Gilberd School, and Other Sites in Colchester 1971–85,* 140–205. Colchester, Colchester Archaeological Report 6.

Crummy, N. (2006) Worshipping Mercury on Balkerne Hill, Colchester. In P. Ottaway (ed.) *A Victory Celebration. Papers on the archaeology of Colchester and Late Iron Age-Roman Britain presented to Philip Crummy,* 55–68. Colchester, Friends of Colchester Archaeological Trust.

Durrani, N. (2004) Tabard Square. *Current Archaeology* 192, 540–547.

Durham, E. (2010) Metal Figurines in Roman Britain. Unpublished PhD thesis, University of Reading.

Durham, E. (2012) Depicting the gods: metal figurines in Roman Britain. *Internet Archaeology* 31, http://intarch.ac.uk/journal/issue31/durham_index.html.

Durham, E. (2014) Style and substance: some metal figurines from South-West Britain. *Britannia* 45, 195–221.

Eckardt, H. (2014) *Objects and Identities. Roman Britain and the North-Western Provinces*. Oxford, Oxford University Press.

Ferris, I. (2000) *Enemies of Rome. Barbarians through Roman eyes*. Stroud, Sutton.

Fleischer, R. (1967) *Die römischen Bronzen aus Österreich*. Mainz, P. von Zabern.

Green, M. J. (1976) *A Corpus of Religious Material from the Civilian Areas of Roman Britain*. Oxford, British Archaeological Report 24.

Green, M. J. (1978) *A Corpus of Small Cult Objects from the Military Areas of Roman Britain*. Oxford, British Archaeological Report 52.

Hall, J. (1996) The cemeteries of Roman London: A review. In J. Bird, M. Hassall & H. Sheldon (eds) *Interpreting Roman London. Papers in Memory of Hugh Chapman*, 57–84. Oxford, Oxbow Monograph 58.

Hall, J. & Shepherd, J. (2008) Places of worship in Roman London and beyond. In D. Rudling (ed.) *Ritual Landscapes of Roman South-East Britain*, 27–43. Oxford, Heritage Marketing and Publications/Oxbow Books.

Hall, J. & Wardle, A. (2005) Dedicated followers of fashion? Decorative bone hairpins from Roman London. In N. Crummy (ed.) *Image, Craft and the Classical World. Essays in Honour of Donald Bailey and Catherine Johns*, 173–179. Montagnac, Editions Monique Mergoil/Monographies *instrumentum* 29.

Harris, E. & Harris, J. (1965) *The Oriental Cults in Roman Britain*. Leiden, E. J. Brill.

Hassall, M. (1980) The inscribed altars. In C. Hill, M. Millett & T. F. C. Blagg (eds), *The Roman Riverside Wall and Monumental Arch in London*, 195–198. London, London and Middlesex Archaeological Society Special Paper 3.

Haverfield, F. (1901) Romano-British remains. *Victoria County History of Worcestershire* Vol. I, 199–221.

Hawkes, C. F. C. and Crummy, P. (1995) *Camulodunum 2*. Colchester, Colchester Archaeological Report 11.

Henig, M. (1978) *A Corpus of Roman Engraved Gemstones from British Sites*. Oxford, British Archaeological Report 8 (2nd edn).

Henig, M. (1995a) *The Art of Roman Britain*. London, B. T. Batsford.

Henig, M. (1995b) *Religion in Roman Britain*. London, B. T. Batsford.

Henig, M. (2008) Intaglios from Roman London. In J. Clark, J. Cotton, J. Hall, R. Sherris & H. Swain (eds) *Londinium and Beyond. Essays on Roman London and its Hinterland for Harvey Sheldon*, 226–238. York, Council for British Archaeology Research Report 156.

Heyob, S. K. (1975) *The Cult of Isis Among Women in the Graeco-Roman World*. Leiden, E. J. Brill.

Hill, C., Millett, M. & Blagg, T. F. C. (1980) *The Roman Riverside Wall and Monumental Arch in London*. London, London and Middlesex Archaeological Society Special Paper 3.

Hull, M. R. (1958) *Roman Colchester*. Oxford, Report of the Research Committee of the Society of Antiquaries of London 20.

Jackson, R. & Burleigh, G. (2007) The Senuna treasure and shrine at Ashwell (Herts.). In R. Haeussler & A. C. King (eds) *Continuity and Innovation in Religion in the Roman West* Vol. 1, 37–54. Portsmouth, RI, Journal of Roman Archaeology Supplementary Series 67.

Jitta, A. N. Z.-J., Peters, W. J. T. & van Es, W. A. (1969) *Roman Bronze Statuettes from the Netherlands. Vol. 2. Statuettes from South of the limes*. Groningen, J. B. Wolters.

Johns, C. (1996) Isis, not Cybele: A bone hairpin from London. In J. Bird, M. Hassall & H. Sheldon (eds) *Interpreting Roman London. Papers in Memory of Hugh Chapman*, 115–118. Oxford, Oxbow Monograph 58.

Jones, B. & Mattingly, D. (2002) *An Atlas of Roman Britain*. Oxford, Oxbow Books.

Kaufmann-Heinimann, A. (1977) *Die Römischen Bronzen der Schweiz. I Augst und das Gebiet der Colonia Augusta Raurica*. Mainz, Zabern.

Kiely, J. (2006) The accessioned finds. In R. Bluer & T. Brigham (eds) *Roman and Later Development East of the Forum and Cornhill: Excavations at Lloyds Register, 71 Fenchurch Street, City of London*, 142–59. London, Museum of London Archaeology Service.

Leclant, J. (2004) La diffusion des cultes isiaques en Gaule. In L. Bricault (ed.) *Isis en Occident*, 95–105. Leiden. E. J. Brill.

Mackinder, A. (2000) *A Romano-British Cemetery on Watling Street. Excavations at 165 Great Dover Street, Southwark, London* London, Museum of London Archaeology Service Archaeology Studies Series 4.

Maloney, C. & de Moulins, D. (1990) *The Upper Walbrook Valley in the Roman Period*. London, Council for British Archaeology Research Report 69.

Marsden, P. (1987) *The Roman Forum Site in London. Discoveries before 1985*. London, HMSO.

Menzel, H. (1964) *Römische Bronzen*. Hannover, Bildkataloge des Kestner-Museums Hannover 6.

Menzel, H. (1966) *Die Römischen Bronzen aus Deutschland. II Trier*. Mainz, Zabern.

Merrifield, R. (1995) Roman metalwork from the Walbrook – rubbish, ritual or redundancy? *Transactions London and Middlesex Archaeological Society* 46, 27–44.

Merrifield, R. (1996) The London hunter-god and his significance in the history of Londinium. In J. Bird, M. Hassall & H. Sheldon (eds), *Interpreting Roman London. Papers in Memory of Hugh Chapman*, 105–113. Oxford, Oxbow Monograph 58.

Merrifield, R. & Hall, J. (2008) In the depths, what treasures – the nature of the Walbrook stream valley and the Roman metalwork found therein. In J. Clark J. Cotton, J. Hall, R. Sherris & H. Swain (eds), *Londinium and Beyond. Essays on Roman London and its Hinterland for Harvey Sheldon*, 121–127. York, Council for British Archaeology Research Report 156.

Ottaway, P. (2004) *Roman York*. Stroud, Tempus.

Passmore, A. D. (1944) Roman burial at Highworth. *Wiltshire Archaeological Magazine* 50, 99–100.

Perring, D. (1991) *Roman London*. London, Seaby.

Perrissin-Fabert, A. (2004) Isis et les dieux orientaux dans l'armée Romaine. In L. Bricault (ed.), *Isis en Occident*, 449–478. Leiden, Brill.

Pitts, L. F. (1979) *Roman Bronze Figurines from the Civitates of the Catuvellauni and Trinovantes*. Oxford, British Archaeological Report 60.

Rayner, L., Wardle, A. & Seeley, F. (2011) Ritual and religion. In J. Hill & P. Rowsome, *Roman London and the Walbrook stream crossing. Excavations at 1 Poultry and vicinity, City of London. Part II*, 404–408. London, Museum of London Archaeology Monograph 37.

Rolland, H. (1965) *Bronzes Antiques de Haute Provence (Basses-Alpes, Vaucluse*. Paris, Gallia Supplément 18.

Schofield, J. & Maloney, C. (1998) *Archaeology in the City of London 1907–91: A Guide to Records of Excavations by the Museum of London and its Predecessors*. London, Museum of London.

Schulting, R. J. & Bradley, R. (2013) 'Of human remains and weapons in the neighbourhood of London': New AMS $^{14}$C dates on Thames 'river skulls' and their European context. *Archaeological Journal* 170, 30–77.

Schuster, J. (2011) A lead bust of the goddess Isis from Groundwell Ridge, Swindon, Wiltshire. *Britannia* 42, 309–313.

Shepherd, J. (1998) *The Temple of Mithras, London. Excavations by W. F. Grimes and A. Williams at the Walbrook*. London, English Heritage Archaeological Report 12.

Stewart, P. (2008) *The Social History of Roman Art*. Cambridge, Cambridge University Press.

Taylor-Wilson, R. (2002) *Excavations at Hunt's House, Guy's Hospital, London Borough of Southwark*. London, Pre-Construct Archaeology Monograph 1

Tillyard, E. M. W. (1917) A Cybele altar in London. *Journal of Roman Studies* 7, 284–288.

Toynbee, J. M. C. (1962) *Art in Roman Britain*. London, Society for the Promotion of Roman Studies.

Toynbee, J. M. C. (1964) *Art in Britain Under the Romans*. Oxford, Clarendon Press.

Toynbee, J. M. C. (1973) *Animals in Roman Life and Art*. London, Thames & Hudson.

Toynbee, J. M. C. (1986) *The Roman Art Treasures from the Temple of Mithras*. London, London and Middlesex Archaeological Society Special Paper 7.

Turcan, R. (1996) *The Cults of the Roman Empire*. Oxford, Blackwell.

Vermaseren, M. J. (1977) *Corpus Cultus Cybele Attidisque (CCCA) Vol. VII Musea et Collections Privatae*. Leiden, E. J. Brill.

Vermaseren, M. J. (1986) *Corpus Cultus Cybele Attidisque (CCCA) Vol. V Aegyptus, Africa, Hispania, Gallia et Britannis*. Leiden, E. J. Brill.

Vermaseren, M. J. (1989) *Corpus Cultus Cybele Attidisque (CCCA) Vol. VI Germania, Raetia, Noricum, Pannonia, Dalmatia, Macedonia, Thracia, Moesia, Dacia, Regnum Bospori, Colchis, Scythia et Sarmatia*. Leiden, E. J. Brill.

Wait, G. A. & Cotton, J. (2000) The Iron Age. In T. Brigham (ed.) *The Archaeology of Greater London. An assessment of archaeological evidence for human presence in the area now covered by Greater London*, 102–17. London, Museum of London Archaeology Service.

Wallower, B. (2002a) Roman temple complex in Greenwich Park? Part 1. *London Archaeologist* 10(2), 46–54.

Wallower, B. (2002b) Roman temple complex in Greenwich Park? Part 2. *London Archaelogist* 10(3), 76–82.

Wardle, A. (2008) The accessioned finds. In N. Bateman, C. Cowan & R. Wroe-Brown (eds) *London's Roman Amphitheatre, Guildhall Yard, City of London*, 191–202. London, Museum of London Archaeology Service Monograph 35.

Wheeler, R. E. M. (1930) *London in Roman Times*. London, London Museum Catalogues 3.

Wilkinson, R. H. (2003) *The Complete Gods and Goddesses of Ancient Egypt*. London, Thames & Hudson.

Woolf, G. (1998) *Becoming Roman. The Origins of Provincial Civilization in Gaul*. Cambridge, Cambridge University Press.

Worrell, S. & Pearce, J. (2011) Finds reported under the Portable Antiquities Scheme. *Britannia* 42, 399–437.

# Staring at death: the jet *gorgoneia* of Roman Britain

## *Adam Parker*

*Keywords:* Pendant; inhumation; jet; Medusa; Roman Britain; grave goods; jewellery

*Pendants made of jet are rare in Roman Britain, despite the prominence and availability of the material. The jet pendant subclass depicting an image of the Medusa is even smaller, numbering only ten from this province. These pendants are assessed in terms of their stylistic similarities and, where possible, depositional conditions. Although the sample is small, it is concluded that the jet gorgoneia of Roman Britain represent a dispersed group of stylistically and contextually similar grave goods associated with adult female inhumations in the later Roman period. A further discussion attempts to assess these objects within an applied framework of magical theory.*

## Introduction

Objects of jet from the Roman world are some of the most enigmatic to survive to the current day. As a material it is important in the study of archaeology in the north-western Roman provinces, especially that of Britain. *Eboracum* (York) and *Arbeia* (South Shields) are the major workshops for this material in Roman Britain (Allason-Jones 1989, 128), the popularity of the industry reaching its height in the 3rd to mid-4th centuries AD. Jet itself (in Latin: *gagates)* is well attested as a material in the archaeological record of Britain and elsewhere.

The jewellery industry within Britain incorporates other shiny, black geological specimens (the 'jet-like' materials) and includes shale, kimmeridge coal, durain, lignite and cannel coal (Allason-Jones and Jones 2001, 234–237). Jet itself is a material restricted to the North and East Yorkshire coastline in Britain, although this type of Toarcian (lower Jurassic) jet does outcrop in Germany and Kimmeridgian jets can be found in Portugal and Spain (Allason-Jones & Jones 2001, 237). The level of distinction made between jet and jet-like materials within contemporary Roman society is unclear; cautious use of the terms is advised by Allason-Jones' (2001) spectroscopy study. That being said, I use the term 'jet' in the following article as a catch-all, unless otherwise

clearly disproven, because petrological analysis of jet has a limited application at this time.

Jet-like materials are most frequently employed to produce a quite finite variety of object types, namely hairpins (and several other objects seen in the creation of hairstyles), beads, bracelets, rings, bangles, furniture fittings and pendants. Jet is usually used for whole, individual objects and is rarely used in conjunction with other materials, but bone hair pins with jet finials have been found at York and South-Shields (Allason-Jones 1996, 44–45, nos 275–280; Allason-Jones & Miket 1984, nos 2.443–6).

Jet pendants can take the form of animal figurines (bears – Crummy 2010, 38, foxes – Allason-Jones & Miket 1984, and eagles – Guinio 2010, 198) or the more commonly seen flat-backed ovular discs incised with low relief decoration on the obverse. The decoration is variable but frequently includes portrait busts, family groups and betrothal scenes in Britain (Allason-Jones 1989, 128). This paper is focused on the pendant sub-class depicting Medusa, the so-called *gorgoneia*. There are, currently, no cohesive reports looking solely at these objects as a group. This article brings together the few examples from Roman Britain, identifies their features and discusses their context when available. The magical functions traditionally attributed to jet are discussed in a following section, in conjunction with depositional contexts and iconographical details.

## Roman jet

Jet as a grave good in funerary contexts is particularly important in the latter two centuries of Roman Britain especially in the north of England. The author Pliny famously notes that:

> The kindling of jet drives off snakes and relieves suffocation of the uterus. Its fumes detect attempts to stimulate a disabling illness or a state of virginity. Moreover, when thoroughly boiled with wine it cures toothache, and if combined with wax, scrofulous tumours. The Magi are said to make use of it in what they call 'divination by axes', and they assert it will not burn away completely if a wish is destined to come true. (Pliny, Natural History 36. 142)

Solinus notes its aesthetic use as jewellery (*Coll. Mem.* 22.11) and the Greek Physician Galen advocates its use in the treatment of bleeding and, in particular, as a female medication (*De. Simp. Med. Facul.* 9.203). These ancient sources, in discussing jet and jet-like materials, do not mention objects but raw materials (Eckardt 2014, 112).

The actual procurement of jet is, presumably, based on a beach-combing industry due to the existence of jet on the north-east Yorkshire coast. Beach-combing would be entirely dependent on the chance discovery of such material on the shoreline – influenced by submarine, meteorological and environmental conditions. A small-scale cottage industry may even have developed to extract jet from the coastal rock face (Allason-Jones and Jones 2001, 242). The use of shale and other materials show that the 'jet' industry involves more than just jet proper; examples of pendants in shale from London (Barber *et al.* 1990, 10) and cannal coal from York (Allason-Jones & Jones 2001, 247; Allason-Jones 1996, 24–25, no. 4; Pendant in the Yorkshire Museum YORYM : H1028) provide evidence that in some cases the exact material is either unimportant or the petrological differences are largely unknown.

## Form and iconography

### *The ten Romano-British gorgoneia*

A total of ten jet *gorgoneia* are currently known from Roman Britain (Appendix: Table 9.1): one from a cemetery at Chelmsford (No. 1; Fig. 9.1), one from an inhumation grave at Colchester (No. 2; Fig. 9.2), two from inhumation graves at London (Nos 3–4, Figs 9.3 & 9.4) and one from Rochester (No. 5; Fig. 9.5). The assemblage of jet artefacts at York contains an unusually high number

*Fig. 9.1: Chelmsford* gorgoneion *(no.1), photographed before conservation (© Chelmsford Museum)*

*Fig. 9.2: Colchester* gorgoneion *(no. 2) (© Colchester Archaeological Trust/Colchester Museum)*

of pendants (seven), of which three can be labelled *gorgoneia* (Nos 6–8; Figs 9.6–9.8). A fourth example, of which we have no recorded image or contextual details, was lost before 1962 (No. 9). The final *gorgoneion* is tentatively given a London provenance, but this is not secure (No. 10).

*Gorgoneia* are a visually striking form of pendant – all are ovular, flat-backed and include a transverse perforation on the uppermost side. The engraved decoration, from which their name derives, depicts a hand-carved relief of a Medusa or Gorgon visage facing forwards and incised with a classically proportioned face in some detail. As well as hair, the Gorgon image has snakes growing from her head, as she is usually represented in antiquity. Grouped in mirrored,

*Fig. 9.3: Hooper Street, London* gorgoneion *(no. 3) (© Museum of London)*

*Fig. 9.4: Hayden Street, London* gorgoneion *(no. 4) (© Museum of London)*

S-shaped pairs, the snakes number either four or six. Nos 6–7 and 10 have a squat pair below the chin and one pair rising from behind the jaw line diagonally upwards to the edge of the frame. No. 3 is represented with four snakes in the manner of the above, with the added detail of cross-hatched scales on the snake bodies. A similar arrangement is evident from Colchester (No. 2) and Rochester (No. 5). The third York example (No. 8), in addition to the above, has a third pair of snakes rising from behind eye-level to the hair line, bringing her total to six. No. 3, from London, has six snakes, but whereas the additional third pair rise from above the eye-line on no. 8, the third pair extend from beneath the chin in a U- rather than S-shape. This third pair also appears to have detailed scales. It is unclear whether the degraded example from Chelmsford (No. 1) has four or six pairs.

In all cases the gorgon has a cropped or bunched hairstyle (better preservation from the amulets at Colchester and London show the hair in some detail) atop which she wears a winged helm. The wings are each represented through roughly incised groups of cross-hatched parallel lines in irregularly spaced groups of twos or threes. Her face shape is subject to some minor variation with examples of both an elongated ovular shape (Nos 3 & 7) or a rounded circular face (Nos 1, 2, 4, 5, 6, 8 and 10); a factor which may be dependent on the overall shape of the amulet as a frame into which the image is carved, whereby an ovular frame lends itself to an ovular face within it. Some limits will be applied by the availability of suitably large jet

pebbles coming ashore which can be worked, although an exceptionally large roughout plank from York demonstrates that large roughouts were certainly available on occasion; a large roughout plank (raw jet cut in advance of further working) measured 90 mm length and is now in the Yorkshire Museum (YORYM : 1995.197). Attempts at symmetry of decoration are visible through the position of snakes and the cross-hatched incisions of the winged helmet. In all cases but one, the Medusa remains expressionless, staring forward.

The single exception to this formulaic depiction of Medusa on a jet pendant is the first such example found in Britain, from 1838 at Rochester. Whilst she displays a winged helmet and four snakes (two from beneath the chin and two from behind the jaw line; in keeping with the other examples with four snakes), this amulet is noticeably different in terms of her orientation – the head is physically turned to the right (her left). A single, large eye is depicted slightly out of proportion to her nose and mouth. Her hair is styled into four parts pulled back from a large fringe, but does not stretch below the neckline. The helm and snake figures are incised in the same orientations as the forward-facing examples, making the image seem somewhat abstract.

The bunched and parted hairstyle from Rochester (No. 5) may also be visible on Colchester (no. 2); three globular pellets can be seen on each side of the cheeks, lightly incised in linear lines in the same manner as the fringe. The fringe of No. 4 also parallels this design, and it is certainly suggested by a similar fringe outline from York (No. 7).

*Fig. 9.5: Rochester* gorgoneion *(no. 5) (© Ashmolean Museum)*

*Fig. 9.6: Railway Station, York* gorgoneion *(no. 6). (© York Museums Trust, Yorkshire Museum)*

*Fig. 9.7: York* gorgoneion *(no. 7) (© York Museums Trust, Yorkshire Museum)*

*Fig. 9.8: Walmgate, York* gorgoneion *(no. 8) (© York Museums Trust, Yorkshire Museum)*

The preservation of the latter prevents any conclusion on the matter.

### The Medusa image

The structural similarities between the *gorgoneia* represented lend themselves more to an accepted tradition of Gorgon representation within the province than the finer points of a local production centre. Martin Henig notes six individual onyx cameos which conform to a similar formulaic depiction of the Medusa head (Henig 1974, nos 725–731), and a gold ring with a cameo inset from early 3rd century *Vindolanda* (Birley & Green 2006, 123) is certainly similar in this depiction, even if the inclusion of snake-imagery can be disputed. The number of intaglios depicting such an image in Britain is, perhaps surprisingly, quite small and appears as a secondary feature within the iconography: an intaglio from Winteringham (PAS: NLM-382206) depicts Perseus holding the severed head of the Medusa and four intaglios depicting a bust of Medusa show the snake imagery on her cuirass (St Margaret's Street Baths, Canterbury; St Albans; 24–30 Tanner Row, York; Charterhouse on Mendip. I thank Ian Marshman for this information.). On the intaglios from York and St. Albans, the snakes appear to be leaping outwards from the cuirass and have a very real physical presence in the image. The Gorgon also appears as the decorative

focus of metal furniture fittings (PAS: NMS-650F10, Fig. 9.9; PAS: LVPL-1DEDD5). The Medusa image was widely circulated on coinage, but the Republican issues (PAS: SF-773CB3, Fig. 9.10; PAS: CAM-DE4215) do not correlate with the major chronological rise of the jet working industry in Britain and it is only a minor feature on a small number of late 2nd century issues (PAS: SF-C64838; PAS: WMID-34E581). Within York, other Medusa images are known including architectural *antefixae* (*RCHME.* 1962, 114) and mosaics (YMH 1881, 28). An additional Medusa mosaic in Yorkshire is also known from Dalton Parlours Villa (YMH 1881, 82)). A Lydion brick from London (MOL12819) is certainly comparable with the *antefixae,* with a stylised female face and fly-away, snake-like incised lines radiating from her head. The stylistic execution prevents a clear-cut identification as either hair or snakes, though the small quantity might suggest the latter.

The point is that the Medusa image is, of course, attributable to a wider range of objects in Roman Britain, but that the form which this takes has a level of uniformity associated with it. It is clear from the few available examples of *gorgoneion* pendants that there is a group of features acceptable for inclusion on such an amulet. Largely these will have been informed by the dispersal of the well-established use of Medusa's image in the Classical world as a religious, mythological, artistic or apotropaic icon via

*Fig. 9.9: A copper-alloy roundel depicting a winged Gorgon visage facing forwards from Norfolk (PAS: NMS-650F10; © Portable Antiquities Scheme)*

*Fig. 9.10: A republican denarius of 47 BC from Suffolk (PAS: SF-773CB3; © Portable Antiquities Scheme)*

media such as those listed above. It is interesting to note the structural similarities within this group as a result of this process: the majority are forward-facing and include a winged helm, 4-6 snakes at similar positions, a blank expression, an oval or sub-ovular frame and a transverse perforation for suspension. Whereas variation between other pendant classes (the betrothal charm and family group) is justified by the variability in the human form and the social requirements of the images contained within them, a degree of aesthetic uniformity can be seen within the *gorgoneia* sub-class. It would be crass to suggest that these objects are mass-produced on any scale. They are certainly each produced by craftsmen with the knowledge of the Medusa image generally. Given the similarity of features in the jet *gorgoneia* group and the small number known to archaeology, it is tempting to suggest a single production site (an argument made by Allason-Jones (1996, 24)), which remains a distinct possibility. However, it is important to point out that the variability in execution of this image is ultimately indicative of the individuality of the production process. The jet *gorgoneia* could represent a series of bespoke commissions, homemade projects or exquisitely expensive and hard to come by products. Equally they could be underrepresented in the archaeological record because of a whole range of excavation biases, predominant use in cremation (jet burns very well), or because they represent a particularly short-lived inhumation rite. All sides of this argument remain inconclusive.

Analyses undertaken as part of the collation and cataloguing by Lindsay Allason-Jones in 1995 of jet material in the collections of the Yorkshire Museum have definitively identified the three examples of *gorgoneia* at York to have been sourced from Whitby jet (Allason-Jones 1996, 24–25). These are the only examples that have been objectively analysed using modern scientific investigation for which we can attribute a Yorkshire genesis for the material. The depositional locations of these pendants within York certainly suggest that they have been manufactured locally. Further investigation is required to establish the source and exact nature of the fabric of the other *gorgoneia*.

Henig notes the export of Whitby jet towards the Rhineland (Henig 1995, 134), likely in both raw and carved forms (Todd 1992, 246), so it is unsurprising that the small number of *Gorgoneion* pendants from elsewhere in Europe have similar features to those in Britain. The potential production of comparable forms of jet pendants in provinces outside of Britain adds an additional dimension to the discussion of jet working, pendant manufacture and the *gorgoneia* development – one that is dependent upon the better understanding of jet exportation. Jet is apparent in Northern Gaul, particularly following the Rivers Seine and Marne and a single composite pendant is recorded from Tournai (Todd 1992, 247–248), depicting the Gorgon on one face and a full-face portrait of a young man on the other; there is currently no recorded parallel for another dual-sided Medusa pendant. After Britain's total of nine, the second largest distribution of *gorgoneia* within a single province comes from *Germania,* which can claim a total of eight.

Taking Cologne as a case study, the three (of four) illustrated Medusa pendants from this single site feature the major anatomical features as the British examples: the first (E11) is depicted in an ovular frame, wider than it is tall (Hagen 1937, Cologne examples; E11 (Accn No. 5167), E17 (Accn No. 5166), E18. A fourth example, E16 is not illustrated, but is from Cologne and published in the Bonner Jahrbücher 1849, 47, Taf. V.4 (Allason-Jones 2014, pers. comm.)). The Medusa is expressionless with a narrow face, slightly off centre in the frame. She has wavy hair flying away from her hair and six snakes visible within these. She wears a wide winged helm. The second Cologne pendant (E17) is circular. The Medusa has a rounded face (an expected feature given the frame type), bunched hairstyle,

pursed lips and is shown with four large snakes. A final illustrated Cologne example (E18) is also circular and simply incised with a rounded face and pursed lips. A further four European jet *gorgoneia* are recorded by Hagen in 1937 as coming from Bonn (now in the Ashmolean Museum, AM 1927.560), Trier, Krefeld-Gellep and Neuss (Hagen 1937: E18, Bonn; E12, Trier; E13, Krefeld-Gellep (Accn No. 05.2946); E13a, Neuss; E14, Bonn (Accn No. 12055)). Of these, the Bonn example is notable as the only such jet *gorgoneion* to be depicted in a teardrop-shaped frame. Two additional European examples are recorded from the Evans collections in the Ashmolean Museum: a circular-framed example from Amiens, which includes a gold suspension loop in situ, and a fragmentary example from Rheims (AM 1927.560, 1927.562).

## The context of death

### York

The four jet g*orgoneia* from York (Nos 6–9) are all known to modern archaeology from antiquarian excavations in the modern city; the exact contextual information is thus less complete than examples discovered using modern excavation techniques (RCHME 1962, 142). Unhelpfully all details and a secure contextual location for one of these (No. 9) has now been lost, but its attribution to the site of York is almost certainly assured. A secure context from York is given to the example (No. 6) from a grave group in the Railway Station excavations of 1890, immediately west of the colonia. A female skeleton was found with three cylindrical beads 'at the neck' along with the gorgon amulet proper (RCHME 1962, 142). Copper-alloy armlets and a glass vessel are also associated. The earliest of York's *gorgoneia* (No. 7), regarded in the RCHME volume as 'the first, found in 1841 … also the best' (RCHME 1962, 141–142; YMH 1881, 109, j, iii) is certainly well preserved. Unfortunately, much of the contextual information for this amulet is missing; the Yorkshire Museum handbook from 1881 identifies it as being from York but otherwise unprovenanced (YMH 1881, 125). The final surviving jet *gorgoneion* in York (No. 8) was unearthed in 1892 by a road running south-east from the site. It represents one significant part of the grave assemblage of a female inhumation burial within a lead coffin containing gypsum. Other finds include two necklaces (one consisting of 297 beads and the other of 93), an armlet of glass and pearl beads, sixteen jet hairpins (four of which survive) and two glass bottles. The glass can be tentatively dated to the 4th century. Other funerary remains are certainly known from the area (Evans 2005, 7).

### Colchester

An inhumation burial at Colchester contained the *gorgoneion* (No. 2) most recently discovered, but

## London

No. 3, from London, was originally attributed to a male inhumation grave, rich in burial goods: a pewter bowl, two ceramic vessels, a copper alloy bracelet and a huge glass and jet necklace accompanied this person to the afterlife, interred within a wooden coffin. The original 2000 publication of this 1988 excavation by Barber and Bowsher noted the sex of the human remains as male, aged 19–25. Although the skeletal remains are in a poor state of preservation, recent osteological analysis by the Museum of London has reidentified these human remains as those of a female, 25–35 years old (WORD 2014; Rebecca Redfearn, pers. comm.). Jet artefacts are noted from a small number of male inhumation graves in London (Barber & Bowsher 2000, burials 197, 673, & 577). In the discussion of the potential *Gallus* priest at Catterick, Hilary Cool makes note of the rarity of jet necklaces in male graves (Cool 2002), originally noting only four others in addition to the Catterick example. There are now only three.

A second pendant from London (No. 4) was recorded above the grave of a 19–25 year old female inhumation burial. Contextual details could not define whether this was deliberately deposited above or is a chance loss in the final funerary rites of the young woman (Barber & Bowsher 2000, 146). If the 'chance loss' scenario can be given credence, it opens a new contextual window on the use of these amulets – the use of the Medusa amulet as an appropriate form of funerary dress for those attending the funeral as well as those being interred. Given that in other examples of inhumations with jet *gorgoneia* there is a consistency of funerary rites encountered (inhumation graves, usually within a coffin, of an adult female accompanied by many grave goods including jet), this is much more likely to be an example of a deliberate deposition later in the funerary ceremony.

A third pendant, now in the Ashmolean Museum, is circumstantially associated with a London provenance (No. 10). No secure provenance or contextual information has survived with this pendant.

## Chelmsford

Chelmsford's jet Medusa (No. 1) is associated with an inhumation cemetery and was traditionally seen as part of a hitherto unparalleled context in a votive hoard of jet (PastScape monument no. 879342). Crummy, however, argues convincingly that the find location and soil conditions are indicative of a inhumation in which no skeletal remains have survived and that this was thus not

a votive deposit, but a (now degraded) inhumation burial (Crummy 2010, 81–82).

## Rochester

The find spot for the Rochester amulet is unstratified on the banks of the River Medway, near Strood. This can be associated with the nearby Church Field cemetery site, in use from the second to fourth centuries, with numismatic evidence terminating with coins of Gratian (AD 375–383) (PastScape monument no. 416145). As a single find, there is no explicit relationship between this *gorgoneion* and any skeletal remains.

## Discussion

Of the surviving sample from Roman Britain, five come from stratified inhumation burials (Nos 2, 3, 4, 6, 8), one is from a cemetery context and likely originally accompanied human remains (No. 1) and four have no contextual information associated (Nos 5, 7, 9, 10). Given the close similarity between the inhumation graves of the former group, it is a reasonable assumption to expect the unstratified examples to have originally been deposited within inhumation graves.

Following the reidentification of No. 3, the entire currently available sample of skeletal remains surviving from inhumations with a *gorgoneion* are adult females. Although this only represents four individual inhumations, for which sweeping conclusions are impossible, this is an important and salient observation for the future study of this material. The association between jet and later Roman female inhumation rites is strong, and one that can be further developed through the reidentification of the male skeleton at London as female.

The surviving evidence from Britain does not include the suspension loops, straps or threads originally associated with these amulets. Locality on the chest of inhumed individuals on Nos 3 and 8 (RCHME 1962, 79, 114, 142) and the association with beads for strung necklaces on Nos 6, 7 and 3 provides a small amount of evidence that these pendants were worn around the neck, perhaps on a beaded necklace (Barber & Bowsher 2000, 146). Whilst the Rochester amulet was originally dated to the later Iron Age by Sir Arthur Evans, in 1915 he does note, that 'it was suspended to a ring of bronze wire, and had been probably worn round the neck' (Evans 1915, 572). A bronze wire, described as a 'torc', is mentioned as still being in situ through the amulet's suspension loop in the accession register of the Ashmolean Museum when the collection was donated in the 19th century, but the 'torc' is now missing (Susan Walker, pers. comm.) A label in the Museum from 1927 identifies the wire as being part of the Humphrey Wickham Collection in 1894, although its current location is unknown; there is no record of its accession to the Ashmolean with the amulet. Fortunately, a single example of a *gorgoneion*, also from the Evans collections in the Ashmolean (AM 1927. 560), does have a single gold loop retained in situ through the suspension block. The amulet, from Amiens 1872, has a rounded frame with a circular visage, prominent winged helm, four snakes in the positions noted above, and a wide suspension block at the top. Through the block is threaded a single-piece gold wire, bent into an overlapping, annular fixing. Both terminals are wrapped onto themselves. The suspension loop is not cut laterally through the block, but at a distinct curve, allowing simple attachment to the ring. One result of attachment to a small ring such as this has been additional wear to the sides of the perforation on the suspension block, widening the opening and creating a visibly worn 'teardrop' shape at the edges. Similar steep-angled use-wear visible on the upper part of the exit holes on the suspension block on pendant Nos 3, 4, 5 and 8 suggests that these too were attached to a metal ring, which is then strung onto a larger strap or necklace and facilitating it hanging at the chest. A strung *gorgoneion* would hang flat against the chest at the lowest point of any necklace arrangement and be conspicuously facing outwards.

A rare example of a classical statue depicting Minerva adorned with the slain Medusa visage on her chest, in a manner wholly comparable with the use of these amulets, is recorded from an antiquarian drawing of a figure discovered at Sibson, Huntingdonshire in the 19th century (Henig 1995, 88). The depiction of Minerva with a medusa emblazoned upon her cuirass is a traditional classical image, and one replicated into the Roman World – the mosaic of Alexander at the battle of Tarsus from Pompeii includes a Medusa visage embossed into his chest armour. In these cases, there is a very poignant physical aspect to the locality of this image as an object of protection – the Medusa is associated with the chest as a literal form of protection, comparable with the intended use of the jet *gorgoneia* as necklaces. It is safe to say that the significance of *gorgoneia* in such contexts has not been fully explored in the literature.

The colour of jet may have had a particular efficacy in the funerary contexts in which these amulets are found. As a glossy black material it *may* have been comparable with the dark-coloured cloth of the *toga pulla,* a type of clothing used in mourning. We should be wary of considering use of the *toga pulla* in the third and fourth centuries in Britain, but as a comparable feature it is worthy of notice (see Kaster 2006, 111 for a commentary on Cicero's description of the usage of the *toga pulla*.)

If the darkness itself is taken as a chthonic or psychopompic symbol then the jet *gorgoneia* may be appropriate for both the deceased (as the individual travelling to the underworld) and the funeral guests (in their capacity as deliverers of the dead to a final resting place). The case of the London amulet (no. 4) and the potential loss during the backfilling of the grave is a tantalising insight into this practice, but the evidence here remains circumstantial at best.

We might also consider the use of these amulets in a crematorial context. As a form of coal, jet burns very well and any chemical trace left would be minimal to modern analytical techniques. It is certainly placed within some cremation deposits, alongside the ashes, as a post-crematory grave good as shown by 14 elliptical beads from a third century cremation at Brougham (Cool 2004). Pliny twice mentions the interaction between jet and fire to unlock its medicinal and magical properties (*'kindling of jet'* and *'its fumes'*), with its supernatural efficacy, at some level, dependent upon it burning. Although this evidence is circumstantial, we must consider the possibility that a substantial quantity of worked jet objects have been lost to modern archaeological consideration because of their use on funeral pyres.

## Apotropaism

Certainly the electrostatic properties of jet undoubtedly fascinated contemporary Roman society, leading to the apotropaic and positive healing functions attributed to it by Pliny, Galen and Solinus. A combination of its supposed magical properties and aesthetic beauty made it particularly appropriate in funerary contexts.

The heavy use-wear on the face of Nos 6, 8 and 10 is most likely as a result of its physical manipulation in the hands of its owner, such as the face being rubbed by hand and interacted with. Is this direct evidence of a casual apotropaic ritual? The wear associated with these pendants is the product of a significant period of time spent interacting with the object; a suggestion that the amulet was used over a long period (certainly one individual's lifetime, and, potentially, more than one). It would be dangerous to suggest this is a universal practice associated with the jet *gorgoneia*. At the very least it can be stated that non-*gorgoneia* jet pendants do not bear the obvious marks of such a practice, although the jet lion figurine associated with the Medusa amulet from Chelmsford has received similar treatment. Unfortunately, minimal evidence prevents a unified discussion of use-wear on these amulets. That being said, a question can be asked: what if apotropaic qualities of all jet amulets are activated through their physical manipulation in the hands? Jet is electrostatic, so there could be a very physical reaction to its manipulation (such as the static attraction of human hair to the amulet) as an indication of the reality of its supernatural properties.

If this were true, what could be learned? Firstly, evidence for both the supernatural efficacy and agency of *gorgoneia* survives in the archaeological record. Secondly, any magical power or qualities associated with the amulets were activated through their physical manipulation and there were, consequently, appropriate times when such power can (or needs to) be used. Thirdly, the high quality preservation of the other jet *gorgoneia* would suggest either that they were interacted with less intensively or in a physically different way (manipulating the edges of the frame, for example, would not damage the visage). Fourthly, the use of such amulets as grave goods is particularly noteworthy because there would be an incontrovertibly direct association with apotropaic use of these gorgon images in life as well as death.

There are further ideas of apotropaism that, in this author's opinion, have not yet been fully explored in relation to the image represented on the Gorgon amulets. Snake or 'anguimorphic' iconography becomes more prevalent in the archaeological record in Britain at the same time as the rise of jet in the 3rd and 4th centuries AD. Snakes are a readily recognisable icon, simple to represent artistically and steeped in well known religious, magical and mythological lore. The connection with snakes as symbols both of healing and continuity through associations with deities such as Asclepius (a cult of Asclepius is well attested in the north of Roman Britain, with six altars known: Maryport, *RIB*: 808; Binchester, *RIB*: 1028; South Shields, *RIB*: 1052; Lanchester, *RIB*: 1072; Chester (with *Fortuna Reduci*), *RIB*: 445; Overborough (with *Hygaeia*), *RIB*: 609) and Ouroboros is significant in this context. The connection of this image to Abrasax, the cockerel-headed, snake-legged warrior related to ideas of eternity (Henig 1983, 31. cf. *RIB*: 2423.15 and 2423.16) and Chnoubis the lion-headed serpent, associated with the healing of stomach ailments (RCHME 1962, 'inscribed object' no. 139) is also worthy of consideration. These four deities are all attested in the region, and Chnoubis specifically at York: both a gold *lamella* or charm to Chnoubis from the Railway Station Excavations (YORYM : H20) and an incomplete copper-alloy ovular ring bezel incised with a lion-headed serpent (YORYM : 2012.378, cf. *RIB*: 2423.33) are in the collections of the Yorkshire Museum. *Lamellae* may have been inserted into amulet cases, like the example from York (see Henig 1984, 187). It is not a coincidence that such snake imagery is incorporated into these amulets. The Medusa image is an additional form of the snake-icon and has an intrinsic relationship with ideas of death and continuity. An argument can be made that the snake imagery is the absolute defining icon on the *gorgoneia* amulets without which the faces represented would simply be solemn female portraits, thus the importance of the snake imagery should not be underestimated when applied to these objects.

Although the number of *gorgoneia* in Britain is not extensive, those with contextual information all come from inhumation burials. This does suggest that they are being deliberately chosen as a suitable form of imagery to accompany an individual into the afterlife. One of the suggestions of Pliny, that the fumes can *detect attempts to stimulate disabling illness*, could be revealing of an additional use of jet. The well-documented and wide ranging cursing tradition (via *defixiones*) in Britain has been well explored in the past and is not something that shall be repeated here (see Tomlin 1988). A connection between the functions of curse-tablets (that they intend to deliberately and significantly damage the personal, social, economic or spiritual well being of an individual) and such assertions of Pliny are obvious. The relationship to the underworld of chthonic powers in the delivery of curses and within the magical formulae represented in the *Papyri Graecae Magicae* is also particularly present (Betz 1996, PGM IV, 296–466). In these curses and spells, the deceased often act as messengers or vessels to facilitate the demands of the writer.

If we can be so bold to accept an extrapolation of a collection of Graeco-Roman spells from the 2nd century BC to the 5th century AD into the latter half of Roman period in the north-western provinces, the role of jet as an apotropaic material might here be continuing a literal form of protection against physical and supernatural malignant influences interfering with the deceased. Representation of the Medusa in this capacity could also be considered as an addition to the chthonic potency – the image of the head divorced from the remainder of the body, courtesy of Perseus in the Classical myth, was perhaps more familiar to the majority of contemporary viewers than the more archaic image of the Medusa in her complete, living body. The gorgon head is an active symbol, as the Gorgon is slain and the trophy of her head takes on a protective capacity on the shield or cuirass of Athena/Minerva. She has an intrinsic relationship with ideas of both death and continuation which cannot be underestimated.

The Rochester amulet is unique, amongst the known examples, in facing to the right of the frame. When worn as a strung amulet the head would then be facing towards the left side of the body. A complex linguistic association with the left-side and 'evil' or 'bad luck' is difficult to apply to a physical amulet, but what is known is the dual-meaning of the Latin word *sinister* as both 'left' and 'unlucky' or, perhaps more accurately, 'inauspicious' due its association with the *auspicia* (*Nec coelum servare licet: tonat augure surdo, Et laetae iurantur aves, bubone sinistro* 'It is not permitted to watch the sky: it thunders, but the augur is deaf and they swear the omens are favourable, although an owl flies to the left' (Lucan. *Pharsalia* V, 395)). Given the forward-facing gaze of the Medusa on the remaining amulets and the innate importance of her stare in the myth, the deliberate unorthodox positioning of this single example may owe as much to an application of superstitious knowledge as it does to a craftsman's interpretation of a known image.

## Jet *gorgoneia* and *magical* theory

The supernatural properties ascribed to jet are interesting; they allow us to see jet as apotropaic or medicinal – both features that can come under the larger umbrella of 'Magic'. Magic is particularly complex because of its close association with religion. The fundamental and utilitarian differences between magic and religion, in terms of the ancient world at least, have been suggested by Versnel, who claims there are several areas in which we can seek to define objects as magical (Versnel 1991, 178). The first is 'intention'. Magic is employed to achieve clear and immediate goals for an individual whereas religion is less purpose motivated and has its sights set on longer term goals. The second is 'attitude' – magic is manipulative as the process is entirely in the hands of the user (a sentiment paralleled by Luck 2000, 204). Versnel describes this more clearly as 'instrumental, coercive manipulation' opposed to the religious attitude of 'personal and supplicative negotiation.' Versnel's third area of difference is 'action.' Magic is a technical exercise that often requires professional skill (such as the making of curse-tablets or carving of amulets) whereas religion is not dependant on these factors but the favour of the Gods. The final area that Versnel uses to define the difference between magic and religion is the 'social' aspect. Magical goals run counter to the interests of society (i.e. if an individual stands to gain any benefit, this would give him an advantage over his peers and therefore stands against the interests of society as a whole) whereas religion has more positive social functions.

Given the lack of a formalised approach for the application of magical theory to empirical archaeology, these four areas highlighting difference should not be used as concrete definitions but as guides in attempting to define how (or *if*) the label of religion or magic can be applied to an object. 'Magic' can be defined as the:

> 'actions, beliefs and institutions predicated upon the assumptions of the existence of either supernatural entities with powers of agency, or impersonal powers or processes possessed with moral purpose who may be explicitly employed to achieve specific, personal goals through their technical and deliberate manipulation by an individual.' (Parker 2010)

A definition like this is useful, but the inherent complications in approaching magic will need to be addressed in future work.

As a case study, the jet *gorgoneia* offer an excellent opportunity to discuss Versnel's position on magic in applied terms. The 'intention' of the *Gorgoneia* in a mixture of burial and unstratified contexts is difficult to consider. In terms of achieving a deliberate goal an entirely circumstantial argument could be made that the amulet intends to offer supernatural protection beyond death and into the afterlife. Conversely any protection offered might only last until the inhumation ceremony is complete. Perhaps the protection offered is as much to protect the funeral party from chthonic or malignant influences as it is for the deceased? Versnel's ideas of intention largely only apply to *living* magical users, such as the writers and dedicators of the *defixiones* across the Empire.

To move to the second area of interest, the attitude of 'instrumental, coercive manipulation' does indeed seem relevant to this type of artefact as the 'magical' properties being garnered by use of these amulets are constructed through the application of appropriate imagery (the Medusa visage) to a specific material (in this case, jet). They are deliberately constructed to serve an explicit function and are not related to any formalised form of religious supplication that can be deduced from the surviving evidence.

Within its action, the amulets require technical expertise to construct, but only as far as skill with a sculptor's or jeweller's toolbox is concerned. As far as can be identified, there is no suggestion that the explicit skills of a *magos* (magician) need to be employed – certainly not in the ways suggested for the mass-production and sale of *defixiones* within the Empire (Ogden 1999, 55). In this sense the ability both to create and utilise such an object is theoretically open to everyone. Versnel argues that magical goals run counter to general interests of society (in that personal advantage is not beneficial for a society), but any supernatural benefits provided by these amulets in life (as the use wear on many do show a functional lifespan) end somewhat permanently once they are inhumed. That they may then take on an alternative supernatural function after this point is entirely up for debate.

The point of this discussion is to raise a warning in relation to the uncritical attribution of magical properties to a group of objects. Pliny provides some tantalising magical functions, but is the use of all jet objects magical by extension? Unless there is significant contextual information to suggest as much, we should be particularly careful with such labelling. Jet objects may have all been used solely for their protective properties, but we can't prove this without both an understanding of magic and superstition in the Roman world and the close contextual observation of the surviving artefact. These two criteria would prevent the vast majority of jet objects as being labelled as magical. In the case of the Medusa image on jet artefacts, I would argue that the combination of evidence from literature, context and an application of Versnel's theory would suggest that Medusa amulets are magical, based on our current understanding and nomenclature, but that this will be forever open to reinterpretation and debate.

## Conclusions: staring at death

The jet *gorgoneia* take the form of pendants with a Medusa image depicted within a circular or ovular frame. She faces forwards, wears a winged helmet and is depicted with a total of four or six snakes, in mirrored pairs, rising around her face. Of the ten known from Romano-British contexts, five are from inhumation burials (Nos 2, 3, 4, 6, 8) and an additional two (Nos 1, 5) are closely associated with inhumation practices. Although skeletal remains have only survived from four of the inhumations, all of these are now known to be adult females.

There is some evidence to suggest the extensive use of such amulets in life as an interactive amulet intended to be worn around the neck, but we should perhaps see their primary efficacy within a funerary context – indeed this is what the evidence in Britain points to. The dispersed collection of the *gorgoneia* is difficult to collate, but a tentative total of 21 from north-west Europe is now established. *Britannia* has ten (four at York, three from London and one each from Colchester, Chelmsford and Rochester,), *Gaul* has three (Tournai, Rheims, Amiens), *Germania* has eight (four at Cologne and one each from Bonn, Trier, Neuss and Krefeld-Gellep) (Eckardt 2014, fig. 4.10 for a distribution map).

No confined date range can feasibly be suggested for the production and use of *gorgoneia* due to difficulties encountered with depositional conditions. We are currently prevented from attributing a finer date-range to the objects beyond safely asserting their use in the 3rd and 4th centuries AD. If the development of this pendant type could ever be associated with a particular phase of the development of jet within the material culture of Britain, the evidence for this currently remains elusive. This shortcoming is somewhat facilitated by the extensive number of question marks that still stand over the collection, distribution and manufacture of jet within the region. It is a somewhat invisible industry and, as with all such things, the level of resulting detail is tempered.

Whilst the distribution of the jet *gorgoneia* in Britain is slight (Fig. 9.11), there is a significant bias towards the east side of the island. With the existence of comparable examples on the continent factored into the equation, it is clear that there is a very small, cross-provincial industry relating to these objects. The group of five in the south-east of Britain are all located at sites with immediate access to major rivers with close access to the North Sea and the continent. Any suggestion of transport and trade is unfortunately, at this time, only circumstantial.

Henig remarked that 'living creatures are used in art to express two, frequently contradictory ideas; burgeoning

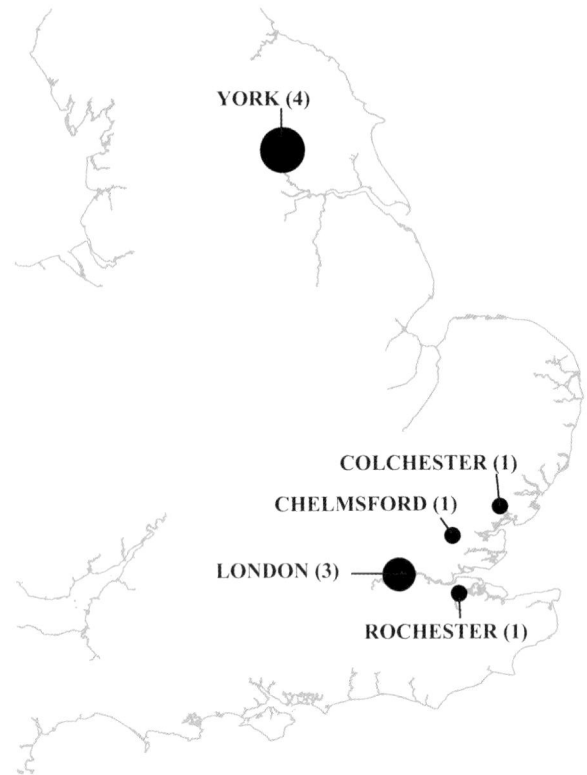

*Fig. 9.11: Spatial distribution map of* gorgoneia *in Britain. Total numbers from each site shown in brackets.*

life and violent death' (Henig 1977, 356) – an idea that is expressed immaculately through the jet *gorgoneia*. The supernatural properties of the jet material are used in combination with appropriately apotropaic symbolism on an object both depicting and designed for use in death.

*Acknowledgements*

I am grateful to the past work of Lindsay Allason-Jones on the subject of Jet and its uses and her encouragement of this interest. Many thanks for access to and information on material from the Ashmolean Museum, Chelmsford Museum, Colchester Museum, the Yorkshire Museum and the Museum of London. Thanks also to Birgitta Hoffman, Ian Marshman, Andrew Featherstone, Emma Holloway and Glynn Davis for their correspondence, advice and information on this subject and, of course, Stefanie Hoss and Alissa Whitmore for organising the TRAC session and commenting on several versions of this paper.

## Abbreviations

PAS: Portable Antiquities Scheme
PGM: *Papyri Graecae Magicae*
RCHME: Royal Commission on Historic Monuments England

*RIB*: Roman Inscriptions of Britain
YMH: Yorkshire Museum Handbook (see Wellbeloved 1881)

## Ancient Sources

Pliny, *Natural History*
Solinus, *Collecteanea rerum Memorabilium*
Galen, *De simplicium medicamentorum temperamentis et facultatibus*
Lucan, *Pharsalia*

## Bibliography

Allason-Jones, L. (1989) *Women in Roman Britain.* London, British Museum.

Allason-Jones, L. (1996) *Roman Jet in the Yorkshire Museum.* York, Yorkshire Museum.

Allason-Jones, L. & Jones, J. M. (2001) Identification of 'jet' artefacts by reflected light microscopy. *European Journal of Archaeology* 4, 233–251.

Allason-Jones, L. & Miket, R. (1984) *The Catalogue of Small finds from the South-Shields Roman Fort.* Society of Antiquaries of Newcastle-upon-Tyne Monograph Series 2. Gloucester, Alan Sutton.

Barber, B., Bowsher, D. & Whittaker., K. (1990) Recent excavations of a cemetery of Londinium. *Britannia* 21, 1–12.

Barber, B. & Bowsher, D. (2000) *The Eastern Cemetery of Roman London:Excavations 1983–1990* London, Museum of London Archaeological Service Monograph 4.

Betz. H. D. (ed.) (1996) *The Greek Magical Papyri in Translation (including the Demotic Spells) Volume 1: Texts* (2nd edition). Chicago & London, University of Chicago Press.

Birley, B. & Green, E. (2006) *The Roman Jewellery from Vindolanda.* Research Reports, New Series, Volume IV. Fascicule V: Beads, Intaglios, Finger Rings, Bracelets and Ear-Rings. Greenhead, Vindolanda Trust

Colchester Archaeology Trust (forthcoming) *Archaeological Evaluation and Excavation at Colchester Garrison Area H (former Butt Road Car Park) Butt Road, Colchester Essex.* Colchester, Colchester Archaeology Trust.

Collingwood, R. G. & Wright, R. P. (1991) *Roman Inscriptions of Britain: Volume II, Fascicule III.* Stroud, Alan Sutton.

Cool, H. E. M. (2002) An overview of the small finds from Catterick. In P. Wilson (ed.) *Cataractonium: Roman Catterick and its Hinterland. Excavations and Research 1958–1997. Part II.* York, Council for British Archaeology Research Report 129.

Cool, H. E. M. (2004) *The Roman Cemetery at Brougham, Cumbria: Excavations 1966-67.* Britannia Monograph 21. London, Society for the Promotion of Roman Studies.

Crummy, N. (2010) Bears and coins: the iconography of protection in late Roman infant burials. *Britannia* 41, 37–93.

Eckardt, E. (2014) *Objects and Identities: Roman Britain and the North-Western Provinces.* Oxford, Oxford University Press.

Evans, A. (1915) Late-Celtic dagger, fibula, and jet cameo. *Archaeologia* 66, 570–573.

Evans, D. (2005) *Report on an Archaeological Watching Brief: 60 Lawrence Street, York.* York, York Archaeologist Trust. Report available via Archaeological Data Service, accessed 02/07/2013.

Giunio, K. A. (2010) Nakit od gagataiz fundusa Arhaeoloŝkog Muzeja Zadar. *Histria Antiqua* 19/2010.

Hagen, W. (1937) Kaiserzeitliche Gagatarbeiten aus dem rheinischen Germanien. *Bonner Jahrbucher* 142, 77–144.

Henig, M. (1974) *A Corpus of Roman Engraved Gemstones from British Sites.* Oxford, British Archaeological Report 8.

Henig, M. (1977). Death and the maiden: funerary symbolism in daily life. In J. Munby & M. Henig (eds) *Roman Life and Art in Britain*, 347–366. Oxford, British Archaeological Report 41.

Henig, M. (1983) The gemstones. In C. Johns & T. Potter (ed.) *The Thetford Treasure: Roman Jewellery and Silver*, 30–32. London, British Museum.

Henig, M. (1984) *Religion in Roman Britain.* London, B. T. Batsford.

Henig, M. (1995) *The Art of Roman Britain.* London, B. T. Batsford.

Kaster, R. A. (2006) *Cicero: Speech on Behalf of Publius Sestius.* Oxford, Oxford University Press.

Luck, G. (2000) *Ancient Pathways and Hidden Pursuits: Religion, Morals and Magic in the Ancient World.* Ann Arbor, University of Michigan Press.

Ogden, D. (1999) Binding spells: curse tablets and voodoo dolls in the Greek and Roman World. In V. Flint, R. Gordon, G. Luck & D. Ogden (eds) *The Athelone History of Witchcraft and Magic in Europe, Vol 2: Ancient Greece and Rome*, 1–90. London, Athlone Press.

Parker, A. (2010) Supernatural: Magic and Identity in Roman Britain. Unpublished MA Rome and Its Neighbours Thesis, University of Leicester.

Royal Commission on Historic Monuments England (RCHME) (1962) *Eburacum, Roman York.* London, Royal Commission on Historic Monuments England.

Todd. M. (1992) Jet in Northern Gaul. *Britannia* 23, 246–248.

Tomlin, R. S. O. (1988) The curse tablets. In B. Cunliffe (ed.). *The Temple of Sulis Minerva at Bath: Volume 2 The Finds from the Sacred Spring.* Oxford, Oxford University Committee for Archaeology

Versnel, H. S. (1991) Some reflections on the relationship magic-religion. *Numen* 38(2), 177–195.

Wellbeloved, C. (1881) *Handbook to the Antiquities in the Grounds and Museum of the Yorkshire Philosophical Society.* York, YPS.

WORD Database, Museum of London. Accessed by R. Redfearn on 12/11/2014.

## *Websites*

www.pastscape.org.uk (English Heritage), accessed 16/11/2014

**Appendix**

Table 9.1: Catalogue of jet gorgoneia in Roman Britain

| Cat. | Provenance | Date | Human remians? | Associated objects | Dims | notes | Location details | References |
|---|---|---|---|---|---|---|---|---|
| 1 | Hall Street, Chelmsford | 1972 | Although originally rejected, recent scholars have argued strongly in favour of remains associated. | Deposit including bangles, pins & a lion of jet. | — | Damaged during conservation | Chelmsford Museum | Crummy 2010, 81-2 |
| 2 | GAL: Garrison Alienated Land, Colchester | 2012 | Presumed but destroyed by soil conditions | n/a | — | GAL Area H (former Butt Road Car Park) Colchester Museum site code 2012.50. Finds number (793) feature HF468 (grave), Small Find no. 108 | Colchester Archaeology Trust/Colchester Museums Trust | Colchester Archaeological Trust forthcoming |
| 3 | Hooper Street, London. | 1988 | Female inhumation in wooden coffin, aged 25–35 | Associated with glass & jet necklace of 260 beads, colour-coated flagon, jar, copper-alloy bracelet, jet shell-shaped pendant, tin-alloy bowl. | L: 39 mm W: 43.5 mm Th: 15 mm | — | Museum of London HOO88<754> | Barber & Bowsher 2000, 226-7, no. B709 |
| 4 | Hayden Street, London | 1986 | Female? inhumation in wooden coffin. Aged 26–45. | In grave backfill; deliberate deposition assumed but not confirmed | L: 35 mm W: 28 mm Th: 12 mm | — | Museum of London HAY86<39> | Barber and Bowsher 2000, 146, no. B164 |
| 5 | Church Field, Strood, Rochester | 1838 | n/a | Copper-alloy necklace | L: 51 mm W: 45 mm Th: 9 mm | Associated copper-alloy necklace was accessioned to the Ashmolean; a label from 1927 identifies is as part of the 'Humphrey Wickham Collections' from 1894. The necklace remains unlocated. | Ashmolean Museum, AN1927.563 | Evans 1915, 572, Henig 1974, no. 755 |
| 6 | Railway Station (N. Side, York | 1890 | Female inhumation | 4 copper-alloy bracelets & 3 jet beads. | L: 33.4 mm, W: 26.1 mm Th: 8.6mm | Significant wear on obverse. | York Museums Trust (Yorkshire Museum). YORYM : H320.1 | RCHME 1962, 142; Allason-Jones 1996; Henig 1974 (cat. ref: 751), Allason-Jones & Jones 2001, 249 |

*(Continued)*

*Table 9.1: Catalogue of jet* gorgoneia *in Roman Britain (Continued)*

| Cat. | Provenance | Date | Human remians? | Associated objects | Dims | notes | Location details | References |
|---|---|---|---|---|---|---|---|---|
| 7 | York | 1841 | | | L: 39.3 mm W: 30.9 mm Th: 15.7 mm | Provenance lost. | York Museums Trust (Yorkshire Museum). YORYM : H2443 | RCHME 1962:142, Allason-Jones 1996, Henig 1974 (catalogue ref: 752), Allason-Jones and Jones 2001, 249 |
| 8 | Walmgate, York | 1892 | Female inhumation in lead coffin | 7 necklaces, 16 pins, 3 glass bottles and 2 coins. | L: 42.6 mm W: 34.4 mm Th: 9.5 mm | Lead coffin accessioned to YMT as YORYM : 2010.1227.1 | York Museums Trust (Yorkshire Museum). YORYM : H321.14.1 | RCHME 1962:142, Allason-Jones 1996; Henig 1974 (cat. ref: 750), Allason-Jones & Jones 2001, 249 |
| 9 | York | ? | ? | ? | ? | All information lost prior to 1962 | – | YMH 1881 |
| 10 | London? | – | – | – | – | Auction | Ashmolean Museum AN1948.72 | Eckardt 2014, Appendix 6 |

# Part 3

# Artefacts, behaviours and spaces

# 10

# Dining with Mithras – functional aspects of pottery ensembles from Roman *Mithraea*

## Ines Klenner*

*Keywords*: Mithras; pottery; Roman religion; mystery cults; Mithraeum; Güglingen

*Early Christian authors tell us of a cult meal which took place in the Temples of Mithras, and seemed to be similar to the last supper. We also know this feast from reliefs depicting scenes, where Mithras is eating together with Sol. Other objects show the followers gathering for a meal in the temple. But because Mithraism was a secretive religion, we have only sparse information about the cult meals in* Mithraea.*

*This paper attempts to gain more information on the cult meals in* Mithraea *by studying the pottery found inside two* Mithraea *in Güglingen (G), which were exceptionally well preserved. The ensembles found are analysed in their composition and compared to pottery from common settlement waste found in two small towns nearby in order to ascertain whether the food was prepared in the temple building or whether it was delivered from elsewhere. The ensembles are also compared to pottery ensembles from other* Mithraea *in order to see if the Güglingen* Mithraea *are typical in their pottery ensembles and the conclusions from this case study can be seen as representative for cult meals in* Mithraea.*

## Introduction and research questions

The mystery cult of Mithras was popular from the end of the 1st century until the end of the 4th century AD throughout the Roman Empire. The cult spread predominantly along the frontiers in the North-western provinces as well as the Danube region. Its huge popularity is reflected by the large amount of archaeological evidence that has come down on us, mainly sculptures, inscriptions and *Mithraea*, the cult's worship buildings.

Unfortunately, our knowledge about the cult's theology and liturgy is very limited. Most studies on Mithraism were mainly based on the interpretation of the iconography in addition to the small amount of written sources extant, which mostly reflect the view of early Christian authors. As a result, the studies are highly hypothetical in regard to the ritual practice of the cult, especially on the so called 'cult meal'. In contrast to this, the structured analysis of *Mithraea*

excavated to a modern standard is very promising, especially in regard to the small finds.

Some reliefs depict a scene in which Mithras and Sol are having a meal together (Heddernheim, Ladenburg, Fig. 10.1). The early Christian authors Tertullian and Justin claim that there are similarities between the Christian Eucharist and the activities taking place in the *Mithraea*. According to them, the followers of Mithras are obviously simulating this divine meal inside their sanctuaries, even using the same liturgy and the same words as in the divine service (Justinian, *Apologie* 1, 66; Tertullian, *De praescriptionem haereticorum* 40, 3–4).

There are only a few iconographic representations of the cult meal, such as the reliefs from the Konijc and Stockstadt *Mithraea* (Fig. 10.2). In contrast to this, the architecture reflects the enormous importance of the cult meal for the community, as the cult rooms were designed with two large

*Translated by Stefanie Hoss.

*Fig. 10.1: Relief from Ladenburg (D)*

side benches as banquet rooms. The large amounts of pottery and animal bones found inside the temples further support the idea of cult meals. Some *Mithraea* even had small hearths, which raises the question of meal preparation and cooking inside the temple building.

But what happened at a cult meal? Did the participants just eat or drink and where was the food been prepared? Is the high ritual status of this activity reflected in elaborate pottery or can any difference in the functional composition be detected that is characteristic for the use in the temples? In order to make it possible to answer these questions, it is necessary to have both well-preserved *Mithraea* and modern excavations.

Even if small finds were not at all the focus of the early excavators in the 19th century, most of them noted numerous beakers inside the *Mithraea*. Furthermore, there were several *Mithraea* with an unusual high number of mortars compared to settlement contexts. The distinctive Mithraic pottery was not systematically analysed up to now because of two main difficulties: First, the uneven state of publication; with only very few publications detailed enough for such an analysis, a wider comparison of *Mithraea* is still impossible. In addition, some of the modern excavations in the last decades are still unpublished. The second problem is that up to now there were no *Mithraea* with complete interiors surviving. In several cases, the occupation layers were mixed up with

*Fig. 10.2: Relief from Konjic (BIH)*

finds that were simply waste, thrown into the big pit of the destructed *Mithraeum*.

## The Güglingen *Mithraea*

One of the few detailed modern excavations of a very well preserved temple has been found in a small town in south-western Germany. In 1999 and 2003 two *Mithraea* were excavated in the periphery of a small *vicus* at the modern town of Güglingen am Neckar, district of Heilbronn, about 45 km north-west of Stuttgart (Fig. 10.3). Both temples fell victim to a fire. Due to its rapidly decaying wooden walls, the *Mithraeum* II 'disappeared' rather quickly and thus dedications, relief and sculpture escaped medieval stone robbers. As a result, the ruin was preserved to an as yet unrivalled degree of completeness. Beneath the roof tiles, the podia and altar zone with three dedicatory inscriptions as well as the altar itself still were intact. Several offerings and liturgical objects were found in situ, including oil lamps, the ceremonial crown, a votive sword, parts of a bow, a torch and others. In addition to that, the excavators found a huge amount of pottery and animal bones in the *cella* (not uncommon in well-preserved *Mithraea*). Many sherds and bones were found in several depositions and a large amount coming from the backfilling of the *podia*, which consists of rubbish from an earlier phase of the *Mithraeum*. Others were lying on the floor in the *nave* at the moment of excavation. Because of its excellent state of preservation, the Güglingen *Mithraeum* II gives us the unique opportunity to analyse the composition of the pottery forming part of the interior of a *Mithraeum* – and thus to reconstruct the ritual praxis in this *Mithreaum*.

## *Dating and phasing*

*Mithraeum* II was built under the reign of Hadrian and therefore is the oldest *Mithraeum* with a known architectural structure. It had been renovated two times before it was intentionally burnt down around AD 230/40, as evidenced by the presence of four so-called 'primary hotspots' in the corners of the cult room, places where a fire started and burned the hottest, indicative of deliberate burning. The stratigraphy clearly shows a succession of three different cult rooms, two of them built on the ruins of their predecessor. Most of the pottery can be connected to one of the three phases of the temple.

The larger *Mithraeum* I was built some years after the *Mithreaum* II in the mid-2nd century AD and boasted a stone basement. The interior structure shows at least one renovation of the floor, the altar zone and a drainage system inside the cult room. As the walls probably were still standing when the modern town of Güglingen nearby emerged, it was robbed of all its stones, sculptures and dedications. The podia and the nave were still intact, but due to the poor conditions at the rescue excavation, there is not much documentation left.

## *Methodology and problems*

The pottery analysis of *Mithraeum* II will be done summarily, mainly reviewing the types found and the amounts in which they were found. To get an idea whether and to what extent Mithraic pottery differs from common settlement pottery ensembles, the results will be then compared with cellar fillings from a *vicus* and a *villa rustica* nearby. Finally, the

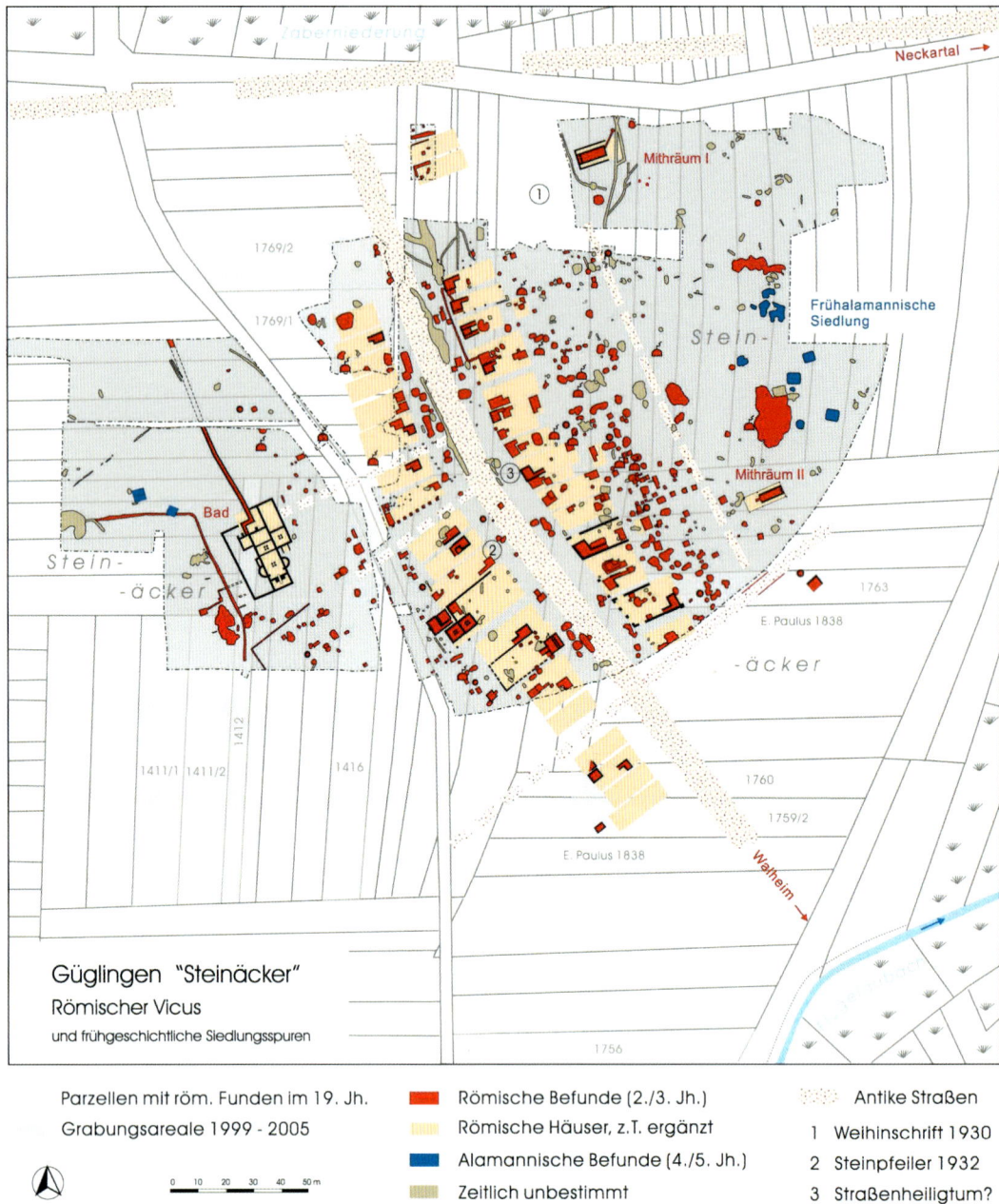

*Fig. 10.3: Plan of Güglingen vicus*

results will be looked at in comparison to other pottery studies from *Mithraea* excavated in a modern manner.

Let me start with some remarks on the methodological and statistical background: the entire pottery assemblage of both temples consists of almost 6000 sherds. Sixty per cent of them were found related to *Mithraeum* II. The other 2000 fragments belong to *Mithraeum* I and two pits next to it. One of these pits was filled with rubbish from both *Mithraea*, as is proven by shards, which join to others found in both *Mithreaum* I and II. The other structure contained a snake appliqué, a typical Mithraic icon that

can be connected to *Mithraeum* I. As far as possible, each fragment was related to a ware and a vessel type. On the basis of significant fragments (rims, handles, base sherds, etc.), the minimum number of individuals (MNI) was ascertained for each of the two *Mithraea* structures. If there were more insignificant (body sherds) than significant fragments in a structure, the MNI was counted on their basis.

High and closed forms like jugs are probably underrepresented when treated with this method, because of their fragile bodies and few significant fragments like base

## Mithraeum I - vessel types

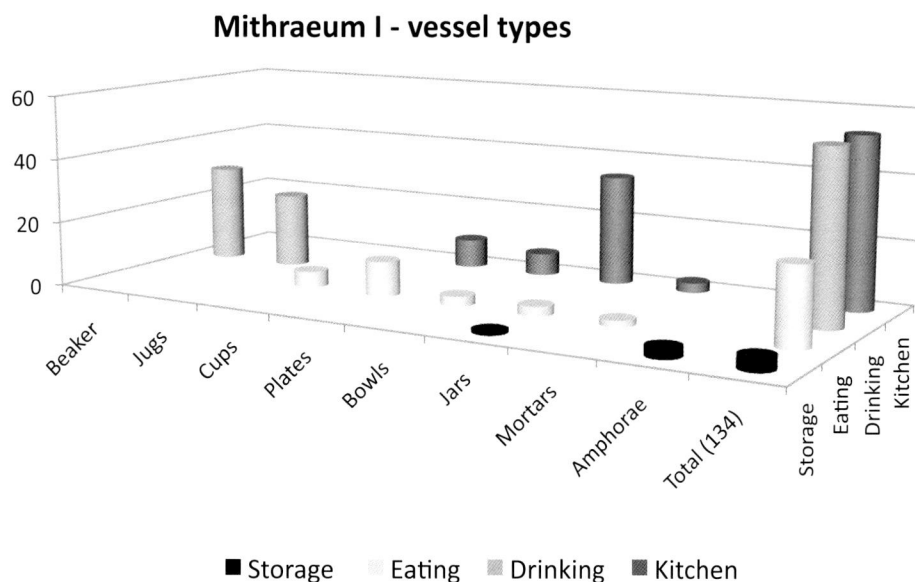

**Storage** ■    **Eating**    **Drinking** ■    **Kitchen** ■

## Mithraeum I - functional groups

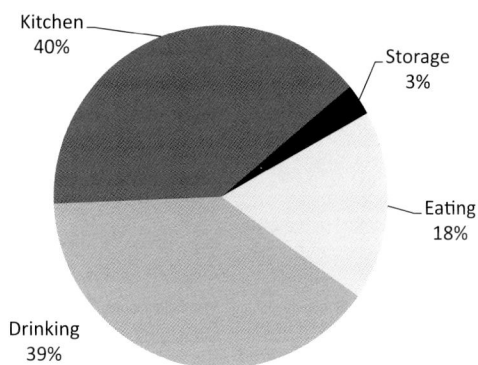

*Fig. 10.4: Complete ceramic assemblage of Mithraeum I*

sherds, rims and handles when compared to open vessels like bowls and dishes.

The opposite may often be the problem in the analysis of decorated Samian Ware. Very often, just one decorated wall sherd is enough to identify the vessel form and thus count as one vessel. As the decorated sherds outnumber the base sherds, rims and handles, this leads to a higher number of Samian ware than may have been originally present. This methodological problem is apparent in all the pottery reports of the region. We may thus assume that when comparing the pottery from different buildings the error ratio will be constant. Because of the different state of documentation of the Güglingen temples, this method of determining the MNI seemed to be the most useful manner to sort the pottery according to function.

An exact correlation between the small finds and the stratigraphy was not possible for all small finds. In order to prevent errors in the dating of features, objects with an insecure origin were put one layer upwards. Accordingly, some objects may have ended up in a layer younger than the one they originated from. This will not be a problem for our study of the pottery assemblage here, as we will be looking at the pottery of each *Mithreaum* collectively.

### Functional groups of pottery

For a utilisation study of the pottery with regard to the ritual practice in *Mithraea*, we have to sort all vessels by their function and assign them to functional groups. Some objects such as fragments of incense burners, a

## Mithraeum II - vessel types

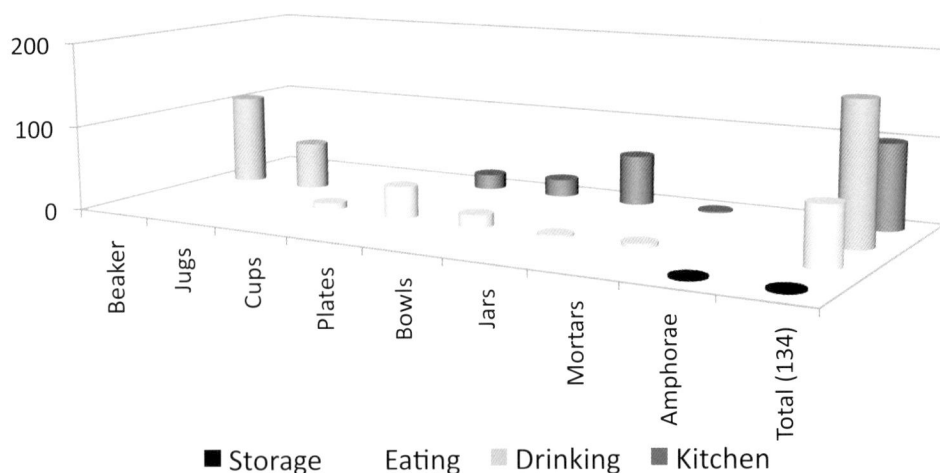

## Mithraeum II - functional groups

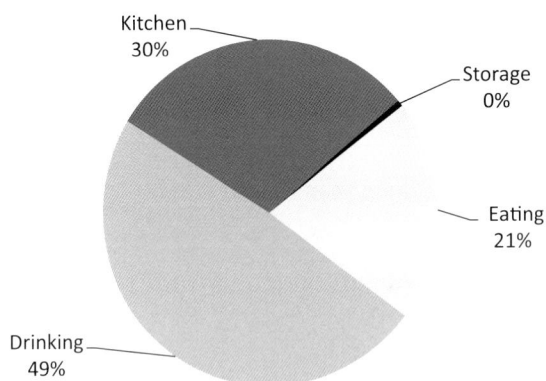

*Fig. 10.5: Complete ceramic assemblage of Mithraeum II*

handful of glass objects as well as the fragments of bronze strainers were not included in the analysis. Unfortunately, the only part of a Mithraic cult vessel recovered is an applique, which doesn't tell us the vessel form that it was originally applied to and as such cannot be factored into our analysis.

All lids were basically counted as individuals, but as they are not independent vessels, they were not included in the analysis of the functional groups. This is also the case with individual vessels that could not be assigned to a specific type. The results are displayed in bivariate charts, where the number of vessels per type and the dispersion within the functional groups are visible.

Tableware and drinking ware are all vessels used directly during the meal. Beakers and jugs with one handle are

defined as drinking ware, while the tableware consists of dishes, bowls and pots in fine wares like Samian (Terra Sigillata) or *Terra Nigra*, as well as plates with or without a slip. It is generally impossible to tell whether a plate was used to prepare food in the kitchen or for serving the meal – or both. Plates unsuited to the high temperatures of the open fire due to their particular internal composition (consisting of a significantly finer temper) were counted to the group used during the meal. Only Samian mortars are counted as tableware, even though it is possible that the red slipped Raetian versions were also used at table.

Coarse ware pots and bowls as well as non-Samian mortars are counted as kitchenware. As the coarse ware plates were probably used as baking plates they are also counted among the kitchenware, as well as storage vessels of all types too large to be used at the table. This includes all amphorae, big jars with two handles and a kind of smaller storage jar known as *Honigtopf* (honey pot), although the latter did not play a major role in the pottery ensemble of Güglingen.

### Mithraeum I

*Mithraeum* I has a MNI of 135 vessels, with the vessels used during dining representing the largest portion at 57% (Fig. 10.4). Split up into eating and drinking, the tableware makes up just 18%, while the drinking equipment makes up nearly 40%. The kitchenware is also 40%, more than half of which were pots (64%). There was only one fragment of a *Honigtopf*, which was possibly used as a storage vessel. Even if we consider that the preservation conditions for storage vessels in side rooms were not very good, we can state that there was no storage of food or wine and water inside the cult rooms. Only 3% of the vessels were for storage: one pot and three amphorae. One of the latter belongs to a very popular type used to store wine and beer (type Nb. 74). The second (Dressel 20) usually contained oil, probably for the lamps lighting the ceremonies.

### Mithraeum II

Due to the remarkably good preservation of the wooden cult room, we have a much more complete ensemble of the interior of the second temple from Güglingen. There was a minimum total of 375 individual vessels from all features of the building, including occupation layers, levelling layers filled with building debris, backfillings, depositions and pits near the temple. This is about three times the amount that was found in *Mithraeum* I. If we take into account the possible loss of an uncertain amount of vessels, this seems to be a large number for a small building like this, which could only hold 12–20 persons for a cult meal. However, these fragments come from different layers of all three of the phases, which stretch over about 100 years. As we cannot include lids and uncertain vessels into the functional analysis, only 334 vessels remain.

The result of the pottery analysis in *Mithraeum* II is much clearer (Fig. 10.5): the table and drinking wares play a major role (70%). With 49%, the percentage of the drinking vessels is higher than in *Mithraeum* I, and most of them are beakers. Only a fifth of all vessels belong to the tableware (21%), most of them being plates. Compared to *Mithraeum* I, we have less kitchenware (30%), but again, pots are the biggest group in this category, followed by bowls and plates for baking food. Only two fragments were assigned to storage vessels, so this group did not play a big role in *Mithraeum* II.

## Comparison to settlement pottery from the Neckar-region

After sorting the pottery finds from the two *Mithraea* into functional groups, the question arises if it is possible to reconstruct the cultic activities in the sanctuaries from them. Working with the premise that differences in drinking or eating and in the preparation and storing of food and drink would appear in a comparison between the functional pottery groups of the sanctuaries and those of ordinary households, the Güglingen pottery will be compared with settlement pottery, taking finds from the same region and period in order to ensure comparability. Like Güglingen, the two settlements of Walheim am Neckar and Lauffen am Neckar lie in the Heilbronn district, both at a distance of about 12 km from Güglingen. They can be assumed to have similar supply lines and food traditions as those in Güglingen.

Household pottery sets from settlement contexts are probably best represented in the ceramic assemblages found in cellar fillings. Even if the proportion of storage vessels that might have been in the cellar is unknown, it seems quite safe to assume that pottery sets originally stored and used in the rooms above the cellar have been preserved in its filling after the abandonment of the household. But cellar fillings present their own problems: When a house destroyed, its cellar was often used as a rubbish pit and filled with pottery from elsewhere. Some cellar contexts contain the debris collected during the clearing of the ruins of the house, with rubble from the house construction mixed into the collection of objects used inside the house. Such contexts were disregarded for this comparison. The cellars chosen also show no signs of modifications, repairs or other indicators of secondary use. While the find ensembles used for the comparison bear all the marks of having fallen from the ground floor or upper floors into the cellar during the destruction of the house, we cannot of course prove this with absolute certainty.

### Walheim am Neckar

In the northern *vicus* of Walheim, several cellars in total were documented, dating to the latest phase of the settlement (Kortüm & Lauber 2004, 201, tab. 5). In order to examine the functional pottery groups, a cellar with a very large pottery ensemble was selected. According to my studies of the other cellar fillings (cellar 1686; Kortüm & Lauber 2004), this cellar reflects the distribution of pottery recovered from the other cellars in Walheim a.N. and is not the depot of a pottery merchant or exceptional in any other way. From the non-Samian wares, only the rim fragments were counted during the ceramic inventory of the Walheim *vicus*. Therefore, the MNI of a pottery ensemble may be slightly lower, but this is insignificant in the face of the large amount of vessels and our research question.

The selected cellar (number 1686) contained an extensive pottery ensemble of at least 309 vessels (Fig. 10.6). The kitchenware makes up about two-thirds of the vessels, while the serving wares for eating and drinking are just under a third of the total number of vessels. Again, the amount of pitchers is double the amount of cups. In this cellar filling, at least seven amphorae were found, but because of the large number of vessels, they make up only 3% of the total.

### Lauffen am Neckar (find complex 26)

The ceramic assemblage from the find complex 26 in a side room of the *villa rustica* of Lauffen exhibits a very similar distribution pattern: The kitchenware amounts to 57% of all the individual vessels and is mostly composed of pots and bowls. The drinking equipment constitutes 15% of the total and the tableware is only slightly more at about 20%. The only storage pottery is made up of large jugs with two handles and is just 6% of the total (Fig. 10.7).

### Results

The results of the pottery analysis of the Güglingen *Mithraea* demonstrates among other things that the pottery from the temples came from the same producers as that used in the households in the surrounding *vici*. The proportion of high-quality imported pottery such as Samian ware is almost as high in the temples as in the nearby *vicus* of Walheim. I. Huld-Zetsche has expressed the view that *Mithraea* were equipped with pottery of a significantly higher quality (Zetsche 2008, 69). Apart from a few exceptions such as Samian mortars and beakers, the high quality pottery seems to be limited to the cult vessels specifically produced for the *Mithraea*, although even those were barely detectable in Güglingen. The pottery inventories of some temples in the Limes area, like *Mithraeum* III of Heddernheim (Huld-Zetsche 1986, 32–38), *Mithraeum* II of Stockstadt (Stade 1933, 38–44) and the Dieburg *Mithraeum* (Behn 1928, 39–42) show similar ratios of distribution within the pottery ensembles. They all have only a small number of expensive metal or glass vessels and exhibit a proportion of Samian ware that is similar to the finds from household in settlements around the *Mithraea*. The distribution of the different wares among the pottery from a *Mithraeum* was ultimately derived from the regional supply, i.e. from what was available at the time of acquisition. It consequently differs from temple to temple.

What ultimately sets the pottery ensembles from the *Mithraea* apart from the household ensembles of the surrounding settlements is their functional composition. This is clearly demonstrated by the Güglingen examples, where the high proportion of drinking vessels is immediately

apparent. A particular feature of the pottery ensemble in the Güglingen *Mithreaum* II is a set of at least 18 similar Samian cups in the nave, which seem to have been lying on the altar and fell onto the floor during the destruction. This seems to imply that at that time, the *Mithraeum* congregation had at least 18 members. The comparison of the Güglingen *Mithraea* pottery ensembles with those from households in the Walheim *vicus* shows that the proportion of cups and jugs in the latter is much less, only about 10–15%. In addition, the temple ensembles from Güglingen are characterized by the fact that hardly any storage pottery was found. This is to be expected considering the confined spaces of the rather small vestibules. The few fragments of *amphorae* found here could have served for the storage of oil for lighting in general and lighting the cult room in particular. Another 30% of the pottery from the two Güglingen temples was made up of locally produced kitchenware. It is no surprise that the proportion of this functional group is usually twice as high in household ensembles from settlements. However, this raises the question whether the food was cooked in the temples themselves or brought in ready to eat. The detailed documentation in *Mithraeum* II allows a differentiated analysis of vessel shapes in terms of function and find position. It is striking that among the masses of kitchenware, the so-called baking plates (plate forms with a coarse temper) are underrepresented compared to settlement ensembles. Bread and other baked goods apparently were brought into the temple as finished goods. Contrary to common opinion, I think that the comparatively large amount of pots found on the last floor of the centre aisle of *Mithraeum* II can be interpreted as an indicator of their use in transporting and / or serving the food they contained during the meal, i.e. that all the food consumed in the temple was brought in cooked and at best re-heated there.

### Comparison of the Güglingen pottery ensembles with other *Mithraea* pottery ensembles

The pottery from the cult pits of the Tienen *Mithraeum* in Belgium have a similar distribution of functional groups to those from the Güglingen *Mithraea*, with cups and jugs again taking up a surprisingly large proportion. As expected, almost no storage containers were found. Residue analysis of the pitchers was able to prove that they must have been used repeatedly to heat liquids containing lime on the fire (Martens & de Boe 2004, 32).

Although the finds of the temple of Pfaffenhofen (*Ad Enum*, D) were obviously mixed with settlement finds, the ensemble still exhibits a high proportion of cups in Samian ware, colour-coated ware and even glass (Garbsch 1985, esp. figs 17 & 27).

A comparison with other pottery ensembles from *Mithraea* like the one from Strasbourg-Königshofen (F, see Forrer 1915, esp. figs 35–38) or Riegel (Meyer-Reppert

## Walheim Filling Cellar 1686 - vessel types

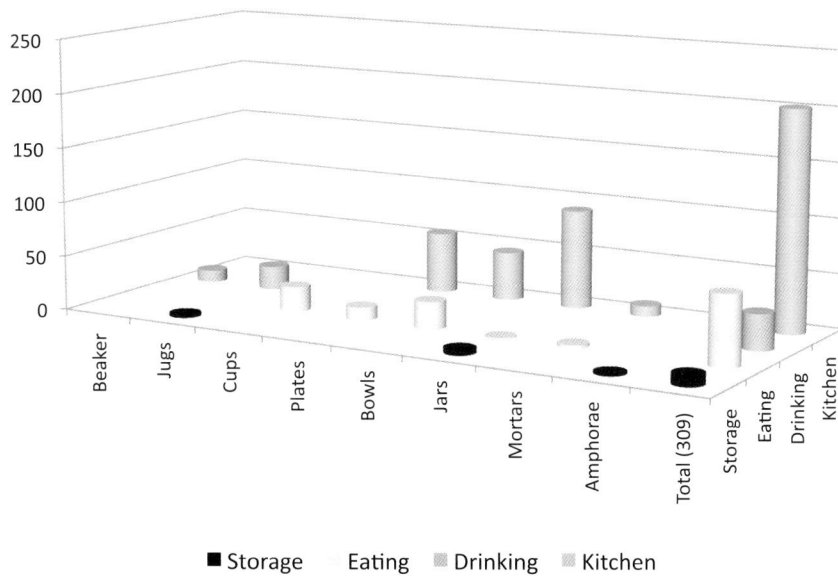

■ Storage   Eating   ▨ Drinking   ▨ Kitchen

## Walheim Filling Cellar 1686 - functional groups

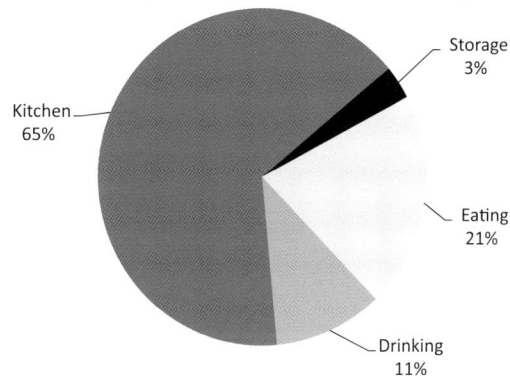

Fig. 10.6: Ceramic assemblage of cellar 1686, Walheim a.N.

2007, esp. tab. 19) with the settlement material from Walheim shows that a high proportion of cups and jugs seems to be a characteristic of all *Mithraea*. P. Meyer-Reppert (2007, 373–375 esp. tab. 19) established for the pottery of the *Mithreaum* in Riegel that beakers and jugs make up c. 44 % of the pottery. She did not include cooking pots into this statistic.

Some of these cups have a conspicuous design or bear inscriptions, emphasizing the importance of drinking in the Mithraic cult. Particularly prominent is a mug from the *Mithraeum* found in Ad Enum / Pfaffenhofen on which the complex Mithraic bull-killing scene has been applied in Barbotine technique (Garbsch 1985, 400–401, fig. 8.9).

In the Bliesheim *Mithraeum* in France, several very elaborately decorated beakers were found, which also bear inscriptions indicating that they are dedications to Mithras (Fortuné 2011, 243–244, fig. 13.8 no. 5).

Some Samian ware shapes such as the bulbous cup Drag. 52–54 and the *kantharoi* Nb. 26 have been frequently found in *Mithraea* (for instance in the Heddernheim *Mithraeum* III: Huld-Zetsche 1985, 36 fig. 18), but are rare in settlement contexts. Because of their significant association with *Mithraea*, these forms were long suspected to be almost an indicator of the cult of Mithras. Recent discoveries have revised this picture; while this beaker type seems to be an indicator of sacred contexts, it does not always have to be a *Mithraeum* (see Scholz 2008, 267).

## Lauffen, Building IV, Find Complex 26  - vessel types

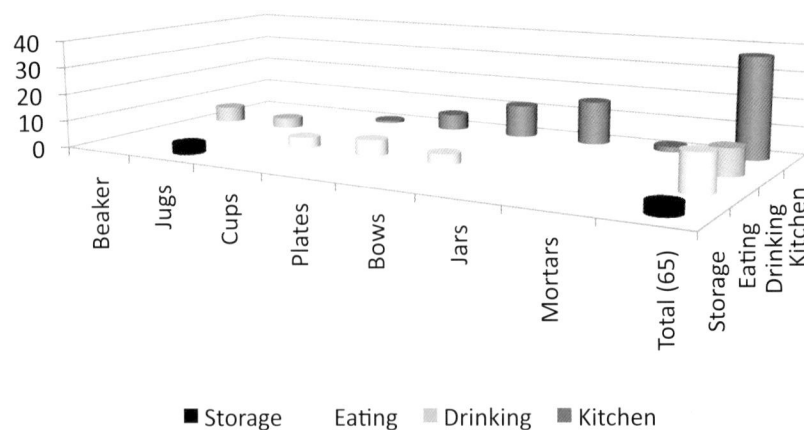

## Lauffen, Building IV, Find Complex 26, functional groups

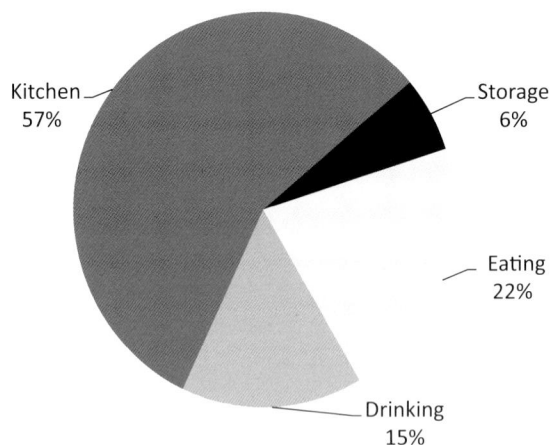

*Fig. 10.7: Ceramic assemblage of find complex 26, Lauffen a.N.*

The functional composition of the pottery indicates that communal drinking more than sharing a meal was of considerable cultic (and certainly also social) relevance in the Mithraic cult. Storage jars are generally known from *Mithraea* in only small amounts. By contrast, it seems that food was of more importance elsewhere than in Güglingen. The foods consumed were often prepared with the help of *mortaria*, as suggested by strikingly large quantities of *mortaria* fragments found in the temples of Mundelsheim (D, J. Hohendorf pers. comm.), Pfaffenhofen (D, Garbsch 1985, fig. 19), Carrawburgh (GB, Richmond & Gillam 1951, fig. 12) and Septeuil (F, Gaidon-Bunuel *et al.* 2006, 139, fig. 6).

Compared to other *Mithraeum* ensembles, the one from Güglingen *Mithraeum* II is notable for the sheer mass of stratified pottery and the completeness of the ensemble. Despite this relative completeness of the pottery ensemble (especially of the last phase), it is striking that indicators for specially designed vessels, for instance mixing vessels or other forms are completely absent. It seems that the preparation of food in mortars in Güglingen was also either organised differently or played a less important role than indicated elsewhere through the mass occurrence of *mortaria* in other *Mithraea*. Apart from these two aspects the functional composition of the pottery from the Güglingen *Mithraea* does not differ from that of other *Mithraea*.

The analysis of the Güglingen pottery could thus confirm a theory based on tableware ensembles in other *Mithraea*: communal drinking was of particular importance to the cult and was probably enjoyed with a communal meal. Storage of food in the *Mithraeum* was unimportant, because whereas the cult meals were held at the temple, the food consumed in them was brought in ready made and only kept warm or re-heated on the premises.

## Bibliography

Behn, F. (1928) *Das Mithrasheiligtum zu Dieburg*. Römisch-Germanische Forschungen 1. Berlin, Leipzig.

Forrer, R. (1915) *Das Mithras-Heiligtum von Königshofen bei Strassburg*. Stuttgart, Kohlhammer.

Fortuné, C. (2011) Le mithraeum, une fouille ancienne revisitée. In M. Reddé (ed.) *Oedenburg 2. L'Agglomération civile et les Sanctuaires 2. Matérial et études*, 227–256. Mainz, Römisch-Germanisches Zentralmuseum Monographien.

Gaidon-Bunuel, M.-A., Barat, Y. & van Ossel, P. (2006), Les céramiques du mithraeum de Septeuil (Yvelines): un ensemble du troisième quart du IVe siècle de notre ère dans la région parisienne. In P. van Ossel (ed.) *Les céramiques de l'Antiquité tardives en Île-de-France et dans le Bassin parisien 1. Ensembles régionaux. Dioecesis Galliarum*, 137–160. Document de travail 7. Nanterre, Action collective de recherche Organisation et occupation du territoire dans le nord de la Gaule lyonnaise.

Garbsch, J. (1985) Das Mithräum von Pons Aeni. *Bayerische Vorgeschichtsblaetter* 50, 355–462.

Gillam, J. P. & Richmond, I. A. (1951) The Temple of Mithras at Carrawburgh. *Archaeologia Aeliana* 4th ser. 29, 1–92.

Huld-Zetsche, I. (1986) *Mithras in Nida-Heddernheim*. Frankfurt, Archaeologische Reihe Museum Vor- und Frühgeschichte Frankfurt a. Main 6.

Huld-Zetsche, I. (2008) *Der Mithraskult und das Mithräum am Ballplatz*. Mainz, Mainzer Archaeologische Schriften 7.

Kortüm, K. & Lauber, J. (2004) *Walheim. 1. Das Kastell II und die nachfolgende Besiedlung*. Esslingen, Forschungen und Berichte zur Vor- und Frühgeschichte Baden-Württemberg 95.

Martens, M. (2004) The Mithraeum in Tienen (Belgium): small finds and what they can tell us. In M. Martens & G. de Boe, *Roman Mithraism: the Evidence of the Small Finds*. Archeologie in Vlaanderen 4, 25–48. Tienen, Vlaams Instituut Voor Het Onroerend Erfgoed Vioe.

Mayer-Reppert, P. (2006) Das römische Mithräum von Riegel am Kaiserstuhl im Spiegel des Fundmaterials. *Fundberichte Baden-Württemberg* 29, 327–532.

Scholz, M. (2008) Auswertung. In W. Czysz and A. Faber, Die *villa rustica* am Kühstallweiher in Marktoberdorf-Kohlhunden. *Berichte Bayerische Bodendenkmalpflege* 49, 247–267.

Spitzing, T. (1988) *Die römische Villa von Lauffen a.N. (Kr. Heilbronn)*. Stuttgart, Materialhefte Vor- und Frühgeschichte Baden-Württemberg 12.

Stade, K. (1933) Der Obergermanische-Raetische Limes des Römerreiches A3 Strecke 6 Supplement to Section B Nr. 33 Kastell Stockstadt, 29–70. Heidelberg/Berlin/Leizig, Otto Petters.

# Cloth working in the baths? Site formation processes, needles and spindle whorls in Roman bathhouse contexts

*Alissa M. Whitmore*

*Keywords*: Site formation; deposition; bathhouse; cloth working; military; gender; class

*The recovery of needles, spindle whorls, loom weights and other cloth working instruments from Roman public and military bathhouses raises the question of whether sewing, spinning and weaving – activities otherwise unattested in the baths – took place in these spaces. This paper evaluates the possibility of cloth working in Roman bathhouses by examining site formation processes, focusing on drains as the most probable context for artefacts related to the normal use of the baths. A review of the alternative functions and possible owners of textile implements discovered in bathhouse drains suggests that while these activities were uncommon, sewing and spinning occurred in a few baths and these needles, spindle whorls and related objects likely offer physical evidence for the activities of lower class bathers and bathhouse attendants.*

## Introduction

The last three decades have witnessed an increase in artefact studies in a wide range of ancient spaces. This research has greatly enriched our understanding of how people actually used built space, particularly when comparing artefacts to information provided in ancient texts. Lisa Nevett's study (1999) of small finds in ancient Greek houses indicates that there was little gender segregation in the use or storage of men's and women's objects, overturning decades of scholarship which tried to locate women's quarters in ancient Greek houses. Penelope Allison's research (2004) on artefacts and furniture in Roman houses illustrates the multifunctional use of many spaces and the dangers of depending upon ancient texts alone. Studies of small finds have also suggested the presence of women and children in Roman forts and barracks (van Driel Murray 1994; Allason-Jones 1999; Allison 2006). Caution is necessary, however, when interpreting artefacts for the presence and activities of ancient peoples, since object findspots do not always indicate places of use. Significant questions, for example, have been raised about the contexts of women's and children's

items in barracks, since relatively few were recovered in clear stratigraphic levels linked to the occupation of barrack buildings, rather than construction deposits or later dumps (Hodgson 2014; Becker 2006). Careful attention to deposition practices is crucial when evaluating small finds and offers the potential for a better understanding of ancient spaces and behaviour. This is especially the case when evaluating unique finds in settings without previous studies of small finds assemblages, such as cloth working items in Roman bathhouses.

With this in mind, I seek to critically interpret the discovery of needles, spindle whorls, weaving tablets and loom weights found in Roman public and military bathhouses. While cloth working artefacts make up a very small percentage of bathhouse finds assemblages (typically less than 3%, see Whitmore 2013), and they are absent entirely from many sites, these objects have been found in a number of baths and provide potential evidence for an activity that is otherwise unattested in these spaces. To evaluate whether these needles, spindle whorls and weaving tools provide evidence for a new activity in

Roman bathhouses, or if the objects are simply intrusive, this paper focuses upon the Roman construction, demolition and deposition practices and archaeological site formation processes behind the stratigraphic contexts in which these objects were found. First, however, an introduction to Roman bathing is useful.

### A brief overview of Roman bathing

Only the wealthiest individuals could afford spaces in their homes that were dedicated to bathing, which for the Romans entailed more than simply cleaning the body. Instead, the vast majority of the population bathed at the public baths: large, multi-room structures which offered a variety of bathing options, including hot and cold pools, dry and wet sweat rooms and rooms devoted to massaging, cleaning and grooming the body. Ancient texts suggest that the majority of bathhouses were visited by people of all genders, ages and classes, and the presence of bathhouses in ancient literature, inscriptions and the archaeological record attests to their popularity in large and small towns and military communities throughout the Roman Empire (Fagan 1999; Yegül 2010). In the Northwest provinces, public baths were associated with military forts and large urban centres and are often viewed as spaces involved in the creation and maintenance of Roman identity (Nielsen 1993, 73–84; Revell 2009, 172–179).

Written sources also attest to the important function of Roman baths as social centres. It was here that the Romans met with friends and lovers, caught up on the latest news and occasionally struck business deals and forged political alliances (Ovid, *Ars amatoria* 3.639–640; CIL IV.10677; Martial 3.36; Digest 50.1.27.1). Passages from Seneca (*Epistles* 56), Martial (11.82) and Juvenal (*Saturae* 6.419–425) mention a number of activities which occurred in these lively spaces, including eating and drinking, exercise, massage, depilation and sex. Many rooms in public and military bathhouses lack pools or other obvious architectural markers of hygienic activities, which may underline the importance of the socialization, and spaces for it, in the baths (DeLaine 1992; Revell 2007). Artefacts recovered from bathhouse contexts (Whitmore 2013; forthcoming) provide material evidence for many of these social activities, especially grooming, eating, drinking and status displays, and also indicate others, such as gaming, medical procedures and, perhaps, cloth working.

### Artefact deposition and site formation processes in Roman baths

Before turning to the cloth working artefacts, it is first necessary to consider how the architecture of Roman baths, ancient behaviour and site formation processes, affected the

ways in which objects became part of the archaeological record. Like any other site, the artefact assemblages recovered in baths provide only a partial picture of what once occurred in these spaces, and several factors assuredly limited or prevented many objects from becoming interred. The majority of bathhouse floors are flagstone or mosaic, and these solid surfaces would have made it easy for bathers to retrieve lost possessions and for attendants to clean the floors, an activity which ancient sources and modern scholars suggest occurred with some frequency (Seneca, *Epistulae* 86.10; Pliny, *Epistulae* 10.32.2; *CIL* II.5181; Zienkiewicz 1986a, 243). Thus, lost items and debris would not accumulate or be trod into floors and many objects used in the baths will never be recovered in these spaces.

Furthermore, not all objects recovered at bathhouse sites reflect the activities of ancient bathers. The most common findspots for bathhouse artefacts are discussed below, many of which do not diverge strongly from contexts at other Roman period sites. While each bath must be evaluated individually, I offer general guidelines for interpreting these types of contexts, drawing upon scholarship on Roman construction and demolition practices, rubbish disposal and archaeological site formation processes.

### Topsoil, post-abandonment and demolition accumulations: the afterlife of baths

Roman period artefacts are often recovered in the upper, poorly stratified layers of excavations, as at the Ribchester military baths (UK), where ancient and medieval robbing, antiquarian excavations and backfill trenches have resulted in mixed deposits (Godwin n.d.).

At some sites, there is clear evidence of artefacts being introduced into abandoned baths via natural processes, as at Mirobriga (near Santiago do Cacém, P), where soil, bone, Roman ceramics and a glass bracelet have washed into the courtyard and service yard of the West Baths from a nearby hill (Biers & Biers 1988a, 73; 1988b, 172, 175; cf. Schiffer 1985, 30). While these poorly stratified finds offer a general picture of life in the neighbourhood of the baths, they cannot be used to populate the baths with activities and people, even if the debris includes bathing instruments.

While the floors of buildings are often considered occupation contexts (e.g. Gardner 2007, 70), it seems unlikely that we can interpret assemblages in the majority of bathhouses in this way. If left standing, abandoned baths were often reused by squatters or became industrial workshops during Roman and later periods (e.g. Ellis 2000, 75–78; Gregory 2010, 15), and some bathhouse features and accumulations can be tied to these activities. A large quantity of rubbish, mostly cooking pots, pottery and animal bones dating to the 4th century, was found in the Vindolanda 3rd century baths (UK), and are believed to have been dumped there by squatters or stone robbers after the baths were abandoned (Birley 2001, 6–7). While these contexts and finds provide fascinating insight into the afterlife of bath buildings and the individuals living and working in these repurposed spaces, they do not provide any evidence relevant to the bath's period of use. Aside from sites with rapid abandonment and interment, it is unlikely that objects used in the baths would have remained in these spaces, since salvagers or squatters presumably would have collected any valuable, functional or recyclable materials (cf. Schiffer 1985, 26–28; Zienkiewicz 1986a, 42–45; Philp 2012, 75–84; Keller 2005; Peña 2007, 250–271).

Many bathhouses were demolished during the Roman period for their architectural materials or land, and these activities can clearly affect our interpretations of these spaces. Workshops were sometimes set up within buildings to recycle construction materials (cf. Munro 2010), which occurred in a late 3rd century abandonment phase at the Caerleon legionary baths (UK), when a metalworking furnace was built over the *frigidarium* floor drain, introducing slag and architectural materials into the drainage system (Zienkiewicz 1986a, 253–254). Robber trenches, both ancient and modern, often cut through numerous bathhouse features and layers to access stone foundations and drains, mixing different strata and artefacts (e.g. Gillam *et al.* 1993, 1; Barker *et al.* 1997, 6; Philp 2012, 75–76; Proctor 2012, 68–69). Before, during and after demolition, abandoned baths could also become local dumps (cf. Schiffer 1985, 29). The abandoned Baths of the Swimmers in Ostia (IT) were infilled with ceramics and small finds which are interpreted as neighbourhood rubbish (Carandini *et al.* 1968, 8), and this may also explain the medical instruments found below a layer of destruction rubble in a room off the *palaestra* of the Xanten baths (DE, Hoss forthcoming). During demolition, bathhouse spaces, especially hypocausts, were often filled with building rubble (e.g. Daniels 1959, 92–93; Perkins 2004, 42–43; Philp 2012, 62, 67).

Interpreting these infills is particularly challenging, as they may represent rubbish generated in the baths, waste produced by construction or demolition crews, or materials which were imported from outside areas as fill. While some finds might relate to activities in the baths, they are not from primary occupation layers and could easily originate from elsewhere. This is also true of objects recovered from the spoil heaps of earlier excavations.

### Occupation floors in rapidly abandoned baths: the baths of Pompeii and Herculaneum

While most artefacts recovered directly on bathhouse floors are more likely related to post-abandonment activities, a possible counter-example are baths which were

rapidly abandoned and buried, since these sites may have preserved occupation floors and avoided the squatting or demolition activities which introduce outside artefacts. The best known rapidly abandoned baths are in Pompeii and Herculaneum (IT), but as scholars of Campanian finds assemblages have warned (Allison 1992; Wallace-Hadrill 2011, 272–280), the notion of *in situ* artefacts at these sites can be misleading.

The baths at Pompeii and Herculaneum are greatly affected by their early excavation dates. Data on excavated artefacts must be recovered from early published sources (e.g. Fiorelli 1862) and unpublished inventories (*Libretti d'Inventario*) and excavation books (*Giornali degli Scavi*), and oftentimes, information in these sources leaves much to be desired. Descriptions of artefact contexts are woefully uneven, with findspots ranging from very general ('the baths') to more specific ('between the columns on the north side of the *peristyle*'). Rarely is the vertical position of artefacts from Pompeian bathhouses described, but on occasion, finds were noted as recovered from a meter or more above the pavement, presumably in ash and rubble layers. Whether these objects fell from shelves or terraces when roofs collapsed, or were swept into rooms from elsewhere on ash, pumice or lava flows, is unknown, but this does call into question where precisely many of these objects originated (cf. Allison 1992, 50).

A particularly significant point when interpreting artefact assemblages in Pompeii's baths, however, is that few of these buildings were open at the time of the eruption. Possible interruptions to the water supply and evidence for incomplete repairs following the earthquake of AD 62 suggest that part of Pompeii's Forum Baths (Eschebach 1982, 319; Koloski-Ostrow 2008, 231) and potentially all of the Stabian Baths (Maiuri 1931, 574; Eschebach 1979, 70) were closed. The Sarno Baths (Koloski-Ostrow 2008, 240) and Baths of Julia Felix (Parslow 2000) may also have been under renovation, the Central Baths were not yet open (Koloski-Ostrow 2008, 224) and the Republican Baths had been demolished decades prior to the eruption (Maiuri 1950, 113–116).

Recovering a true occupation floor that relates to the use of Roman bathhouses is thus difficult, if not impossible. While the Stabian Baths have a particularly rich artefact assemblage, the fact that these baths were closed and still under reconstruction at the time of the eruption means that these objects might have arrived into these spaces through any number of ways. The artefacts might relate to the normal use of the baths, and were stored here awaiting their reopening, but they could easily be associated with squatters, an altered use of the structure, or construction fill or workers. At Pompeii and Herculaneum, we must be more, rather than less, observant of context and potential disruptions to the day-to-day functioning of these spaces.

## Construction deposits: levelling layers and foundation trenches

Many bathhouses were in use for several centuries, and the long lives of these buildings resulted in numerous construction phases and deposits (Zienkiewicz 1986a, 46–50; Nielsen 1993, 82; Rook 1992, 6; Fagan 1999, 180). In the later centuries of the High Empire, pools in the North-west Provinces were regularly closed and infilled with rubbish while the rest of the baths remained in use (e.g. Zienkiewicz 1986a, 253–255; Ellis 2000, 68). Waste was also used to fill up no longer used hypocausts while the rest of the bath was still in use.

Many of these deposits include artefacts. Ceramic sherds and broken tile are common ingredients in Roman levelling layers and floor make-up (Peña 2007, 250; Vitruvius, *De Architectura* 7.1.1–5), and construction fills from the Baths of Caracalla (IT) contained numerous ceramic fragments, including amphorae, *terra sigillata* and coarse wares, mixed with *pozzolana*, clay, mortar and fragments of brick and marble (DeLaine 1997, 138). Glass sherds, coins and small finds are also occasionally recovered in these fill layers. Beads, fibulae, pins and toilet instruments were recovered in and around the foundation trenches of the Caerleon Castle baths (Lee 1850, 17) and intaglios, beads, gaming counters and a finger ring have been recovered from various make-up layers at the Caerleon Legionary baths (Zienkiewicz 1986b, 133, 142, 149, 156). Objects recovered from these layers often provide a date for the construction or renovation of baths, but since many bathhouses have multiple construction phases, it is tempting to interpret finds in these contexts as potentially providing hints about life during the earlier periods of the baths. We must, however, be cautious when interpreting the assemblages from such contexts.

Kevin Dicus has presented a compelling argument for the potential origins of artefacts found in Pompeian construction trenches and layers. Large-scale construction projects, such as the creation of levelling layers or infilling pools, would have required large quantities of sediments and materials, likely originating from outside the construction area. At Pompeii, the probable source for such fill appears to be rubbish dumps outside town walls, which included construction and demolition materials and refuse originating from numerous sources dating to various occupation periods. As a result, artefacts found in levelling layers or infilled features likely came from the community's garbage dumps, rather than within the construction area itself (Dicus 2014, 70–76; cf. Liebeschuetz 2000, 51–54). Undoubtedly, similar construction practices occurred outside of Pompeii as well, and this suggests that finds from the vast majority of bathhouse construction layers cannot provide evidence for activities taking place during the normal use of these spaces, even if these objects fit our conception of bathhouse material culture. Since strigils and bath flasks, the quintessential

bathing artefacts, are frequently recovered in settings other than baths (Wardle 2008, 207–211; Whitmore forthcoming), presumably because people carried them to the baths from home (Shelton 1981, 26–28; Carandini *et al.* 1982, 334; Dickey 2012, 121–125, 201; Juvenal, *Saturae* 6.419–420), any notion of 'exclusive' bathhouse material culture seems overly simplistic.

There are some scenarios, however, which might allow for materials from inside or around the baths to be interred in construction layers during small-scale projects. The Romans may have set aside soil removed when digging foundation or water pipe trenches for later backfilling. Any finds in such soil, however, are still unlikely to have originated from occupation layers, and subsequently would be mixed with objects from other strata (Dicus 2014, 72–76). Two levelling layers and a foundation trench at the Caerleon Legionary Baths might provide a possible exception (Zienkiewicz 1986a, 244–249). In this case, similarities in sediment colour and consistency, as well as finds assemblages, suggest that the materials in these construction deposits originated from a cleaning of the drainage system, a context which Zienkiewicz interprets as related to the daily operation of the baths.

## Floor and pool drains: traps for accidental losses and small rubbish disposal

Although not every bathhouse drain contains an artefact assemblage, material culture, occasionally in very large quantities, has been recovered in the sediments of some bathhouse drains. Objects could enter drainage systems through bathhouse pools or floor drains, the latter of which were often covered with slotted stone grates to allow water (and small objects) to enter (cf. Zienkiewicz 1986a, 35–36, 196–199). At least some of these drain artefacts likely represent items lost by bathers or small rubbish swept toward floor drains by bath attendants, thus this context may represent the closest thing to an occupation or primary rubbish layer in the baths (cf. Schiffer 1985, 24–25).

When interpreting drainage contexts, it is critical to isolate the strata and objects that represent the normal functioning of the baths. Material culture related to construction and post-abandonment activities can enter drainage systems, and a mass of lead, iron nails, glass and coins attributed to renovation activities was found under the Phase IV *frigidarium* floor drain in the Silchester Public Baths (UK; Hope & Fox 1905, 351–352). The infilling of pools surely could have introduced some material culture into adjacent drain segments, and rubbish and debris were dumped into sections of the Caerleon drain on at least two occasions after the closure of the baths (Zienkiewicz 1986a, 249, 253–255). The robbing of drains can also result in the removal of sediments and the introduction of artefacts, which occurred in the Dover Shore Fort Baths (UK), where 4th century coins are believed to have entered sediments when the drains were robbed in antiquity (Philp 2012, 76). At sites where detailed stratigraphic excavation of drain sediments occurred, as at Caerleon, it is possible to isolate drain strata associated with construction, dumping and robbing, and eliminate objects that are likely unrelated to bathers.

Using the Caerleon drain stratigraphy as a model, the sediments and materials most likely associated with the normal use of the baths are the horizontal layers found throughout the length of the drain, often consisting of fine, silty sand that was presumably gradually laid down while the baths were in operation (Zienkiewicz 1986b, 13). Since waterborne materials could also flow through the drain after the closure of the baths, objects found in lower drain strata are more likely tied to the use of the structure, though distinctions between drain layers cannot always be made, and it is always possible that heavier items could sink through the fine, viscous drain sediments (Zienkiewicz 1986a, 244–249). Detailed stratigraphic drain excavation and documentation, however, is absent from many sites, and it is often possible to only associate artefacts with specific segments of the drain, or merely with the drain itself. In such cases, especially when there is evidence that demolition or salvage work may have affected sediments, drain assemblages can only be viewed as possible evidence for bathhouse activities.

### Latrines, pits and furnaces: bathhouse rubbish deposits?

No ancient texts reveal what happened to the broken ceramics, bath flasks, toilet instruments and animal bones that were inevitably produced during a typical day in the baths. Ancient sources and scholarship on Greco-Roman rubbish practices, however, can provide some suggestions. Salvagers collected and purchased recyclable broken metals, glass and ceramics (Keller 2005; Peña 2007, 253; Martial 1.41, 10.3; Statius, *Silvae* 1.6.73–74; Juvenal, *Saturae* 5.48), and surely these individuals would have regularly stopped at the baths. Other sources indicate that carts may have removed various types of rubbish from town (Thüry 2001, 7–8; Tactius *Annales* 11.32; Cicero *De Divinatione* 1.57; CIL I² 593). Studies of artefact assemblages and refuse disposal at South Shields and York, in contrast, suggest that there may have been relatively little movement of objects from their original places of use, perhaps indicating that materials from ditches and dumps may illustrate activities occurring in spaces nearby (Gardner 2007, 85–87).

Contexts in or around bathhouses may have functioned as disposal sites for garbage produced in the baths. Artefacts are often recovered in bathhouse latrines, which were frequently located at the end of a bath's drainage system. These objects may have entered the latrine from bathing spaces further upstream in the drainage system or were lost or thrown in

as rubbish via the seat openings (Van Vaerenbergh 2011a). While serving as a rubbish dump wasn't the primary function of latrines, excavations of Campanian latrines and sewers have illustrated that the Romans threw kitchen waste and broken items into latrines and presumably lost intact objects down household and commercial toilets (Jansen 2000, 38; Wallace-Hadrill 2011, 282–285; Camardo 2011). Public latrines could not have been permanent or official garbage dumps, however, as large objects would remain and eventually compromise the latrine's functionality, requiring that it be cleaned out with greater regularity. Instead, it is more probable that the majority of rubbish was inserted into latrines after they fell out of use, and only the lowest latrine layers might contain objects that entered through bathhouse drains or were lost down a still functioning toilet (Daniels 1959, 145–157).

In addition, bathers were not the only individuals using bathhouse latrines. Many were located near entrances or courtyard areas, somewhat separate from the main bathing block, suggesting that latrines could be accessed without entering bathing spaces that required an entrance fee (Van Vaerenbergh 2011b; Koloski-Ostrow 2015, 11, 21). Since anyone potentially had access to these public bathhouse latrines, material culture from this context might better exemplify items that the Romans lost or threw down the toilet, rather than activities taking place in baths.

Coins, ceramics and occasionally small finds have been recovered in furnaces and hypocausts, begging the question of whether bathhouse rubbish was thrown into furnaces. Since hypocausts were often infilled with rubbish during demolition or renovations, and sometimes flooding introduced sediments and materials into hypocaust systems (Philp 2012, 67), careful attention must be paid to stratigraphy in hypocaust layers. Ceramics and coins have been recovered in ash layers thought to reflect the use periods of hypocausts and stokeholes at the Bewcastle (UK) and Dover Shore Fort baths (Gillam *et al.* 1993, 41; Philp 2012, 59). In the Late Roman baths at Corinth (GR), fragments of glass cups, a broken bronze finger ring, a marble mortarium, ceramics and a coin were recovered in ash attributed to the use of the *tepidarium*'s hypocaust, though these layers also contained building materials (Sanders 1999, 460–461), suggesting perhaps that there is some contamination from the demolition layer above.

While the vast majority of hypocaust and stokehole finds can likely be attributed to infill or destruction layers, it remains to be explained how objects might enter a stokehole or hypocaust and become part of an ash layer during normal use. Broken ceramics and other finds certainly wouldn't be suitable as fuel, but perhaps they entered stokeholes with the wood, chaff and/or charcoal that was used to heat hypocausts (Nielsen 1993, 19–20; McParland *et al.* 2009). The long term disposal of solid debris, such as ceramic sherds or building materials, in hypocausts would not be practical, since they would simply accumulate, requiring that the hypocaust be swept out more often and the rubbish disposed of elsewhere. The majority of ash layers, in fact, contain little material culture, suggesting that hypocausts were not regularly used for the burning or disposal of rubbish. It is possible that hypocausts simply may have served as a convenient garbage for bath attendants on occasion, though it seems unlikely that these objects necessarily represent the possessions or on site eating and drinking activities of these attendants, as the heat of the hypocaust furnace would not encourage workers to linger unnecessarily.

Rubbish produced in the baths may also have been disposed of in pits nearby. At Wroxeter (UK), excavations in the portico, courtyard and precinct near the baths recovered several pits containing jewellery, bath flasks, broken glass and ceramics and other small finds which may represent garbage from the baths. It is equally plausible, however, that these pits contain rubbish from the nearby market, houses or other buildings (Cool 2000, 162, 185; Mould 2000, 138), and it is impossible to discern to which structures this garbage belongs. While pits may have provided a means for bathhouse rubbish disposal, the urban setting of most baths makes it difficult to associate pits and rubbish exclusively with bathhouses.

## Cloth working items in Roman baths

The artefact data in this paper come from a larger study of published and unpublished small finds assemblages from Roman public and military bathhouses, the aim of which is to reconstruct social life in the baths using these objects (Whitmore 2013; forthcoming). As discussed above, drains seem to be the least problematic context for objects which were actually used by bathers, since the artefacts found in drain layers definitely entered from within the baths, likely during the normal functioning of the building, and this context is less affected by construction or demolition activities than any other bathhouse space. Thus, I have concentrated much of my research on sites with excavated drainage systems. This method of site selection assuredly has some bias since only a small fraction of bathhouses have excavated drains with finds assemblages. Large imperial *thermae*, for instance, are entirely absent from this study, since few have excavated drains and most are published without finds catalogues (cf. Hoss forthcoming). As a result, the artefacts in my study are best suited to illustrate social life in specific bathhouses, regions and time periods, and only tentatively can these data be extrapolated elsewhere.

The majority of cloth working tools in Roman baths were recovered from drains, destruction or demolition layers and unstratified or unspecified contexts (Table 11.1). Needles are by far the most commonly recovered cloth working artefact, followed by loom weights and spindle whorls. The majority of the objects from demolition contexts were

recovered from generalized destruction layers or infilled rooms and pools. Most of the unstratified or unspecified finds can only be traced to certain rooms or spaces. In Pompeii's Stabian Baths, for instance, spindle whorls, awls and a sacking needle were found in the *palaestra* and nearby rooms, likely those containing hip baths (Fiorelli 1862, 638, 646–647, 650; *Libretti d'Inventario*). These finds, however, lack a vertical context and the stratigraphic details necessary to discern how they might have entered the archaeological record.

The vast majority of needles, spindle whorls and loom weights in Table 11.1 are not from contexts that can be interpreted as bathhouse occupation layers. A few needles and a loom weight were recovered in the Mirobriga and Vindolanda bathhouse latrines, but it is impossible to determine whether these items were used and lost in the baths. While the description of the silty fill in Mirobriga's latrine seems comparable to other bathhouse drain sediments which reflect normal use, the latrine fill was not excavated stratigraphically (Biers and Biers 1988b, 179–180), making it difficult to distinguish which materials may be from the more promising lower layers. Details on the Vindolanda latrine drain's stratigraphy have not yet been published. Both of these bathhouse latrines, like many others, are also located at the end of their respective drainage systems (Figs. 11.1 & 11.2). One of the main entrances to the Mirobriga East Baths is located quite close to the latrine, and the latrine was entered through the courtyard, rather than directly from a bathing room. The Vindolanda latrine is detached from the main bathing block and robbing has obscured the location of its entrance. While it is probable that this latrine could have been entered from within the changing room of the baths (Birley 2001, 7), it is also likely that it could have been entered from the street. As a result, the objects recovered in these latrines could have plausibly been introduced by passersby rather than bathers, and with the currently available data, it is impossible to determine which latrine finds, if any, may have originated from the baths.

The only probable bathhouse occupation context that produced cloth working tools is the drains. In looking closer at these drainage contexts, however, some finds cannot be definitively tied to the use of baths. The Cataractonium (Catterick, UK) needle was found in the rubble fill of a drain dating to the last period of the baths (Wilson 2002, pt 1, 68; pt 2, 182), making it a likely demolition context, and four of the bone needles from Caerleon were recovered directly under or near the open *frigidarium* floor drain, a section which also may have been impacted by demolition activities (Zienkiewicz 1986b, 173, 201). While the York Sewer finds (UK) are commonly identified as a bath assemblage (MacGregor 1976; Cool 2006, 207–210), no sewer segments have been directly connected with bathhouse spaces. Furthermore, while the sewer may have drained a bath, it likely also served other nearby buildings (Whitwell 1976,

*Table 11.1: Cloth working artefacts in Roman bathhouses, by context.*

| Site | Finds | Unstratified / Uncertain | Contexts Near Baths | Topsoil / Post-Baths | Destruction / Demolition | Construction | Pits in Courtyards | Latrine | Drains | Total |
|---|---|---|---|---|---|---|---|---|---|---|
| Caerleon Legionary 1st – 3rd c AD Caerleon, UK | Needles | | | | 2 | | | | 13 | 18 |
| | Weaving Tablet | | | | | | | | 2 | |
| | Spindle Whorl | | | | | | | | 1 | |
| Stabian Baths 2nd c BC – 1st c AD Pompei, Italy | Needle | 1 | | | | | | | | 17+ |
| | Spindle Whorls | 4 | | | | | | | | |
| | Loom Weights | | | | 4 | 'many' | | | | |
| | Awls | | | | 4 | | | | | |
| | 'Women's Tool' | 3 | | | | | | | | |
| Frauenthermen 1st – 4th c AD Augst, Switzerland | Needles | 5 | 1 | | 3 | 6 | 1 | | | 16 |
| York Church Street 2nd – 4th c AD York, UK | Needles | | | | | | | | 12 | 12 |
| Baths of the Swimmers 1st – 3rd c AD Ostia, Italy | Needles | 3 | | 1 | 2 | 2 | | | | 10 |
| | Weaving Tablet | | | | | 1 | | | | |
| | Shuttle | | | | | 1 | | | | |
| Cataractonium Baths Late 1st – 4th c AD Catterick, UK | Needles | | | 1 | | 1 | | | 1 | 10 |
| | Spindle Whorls | | | 5 | | | | | | |
| | Awls | | | 2 | | | | | | |
| Republican Baths 2nd – 1st c BC Pompei, Italy | Loom Weights | | | | 7 | | | | | 7 |
| Vindolanda 3rd – 4th c AD Bardon Mill, UK | Needles | 1 | | | | | | 1 | | 5 |
| | Spindle Whorls | | 2 | | 1 | | | | | |
| Wroxeter 1st – 4th c AD Shrewsbury, UK | Needles | | 2 | | | | 1 | | | 5 |
| | Weaving Tablet | | 1 | | | | | | | |
| | Spindle Whorl | | 1 | | | | | | | |
| Mirobriga East 2nd – 3rd c AD Santiago do Cacém, Portugal | Needles | | | | | | | 2 | | 4 |
| | Loom Weights | | | | | 1 | | 1 | | |

*(Continued)*

*Table 11.1: Cloth working artefacts in Roman bathhouses, by context. (Continued)*

| Site | Finds | Unstratified / Uncertain | Contexts Near Baths | Topsoil / Post-Baths | Destruction / Demolition | Construction | Pits in Courtyards | Latrine | Drains | Total |
|---|---|---|---|---|---|---|---|---|---|---|
| Mirobriga West 2nd – 3rd ? c AD Santiago do Cacém, Portugal | Needle | | | 1 | | | | | | 1 |
| Caerleon Castle ? Caerleon, UK | Needles | | | | | 2 | | | | 2 |
| Ribchester 2nd – 3rd c AD Ribchester, UK | Needles | | | 1 | | | | | 1 | 2 |
| Dover Shore Fort 2nd – 4th c AD Dover, UK | Spindle Whorls | 1 | | | 1 | | | | | 2 |
| Herculaneum Forum 1st c BC – 1st c AD Ercolano, Italy | Loom Weight | | | | | | | | 1 | 1 |
| Carsulae Baths 3rd c BC – 4th c AD San Gemini, Italy | Needle | | 1 | | | | | | | 1 |
| Abbey Villa Baths 1st – 3rd c AD Minster-in-Thanet, UK | Needle | | | | | | | | 1 | 1 |
| Cramond Baths 2nd – 3rd c AD Cramond, UK | Needle | | | 1 | | | | | | 1 |
| Bewcastle Baths 2nd – 4th c AD Bewcastle, UK | Needle | 1 | | | | | | | | 1 |
| **Subtotal** | Needles | 11 | 4 | 5 | 7 | 11 | 2 | 3 | 28 | 71 |
| | Weaving Tablets | | 1 | | | 1 | | | 2 | 4 |
| | Spindle Whorls | 5 | 3 | 5 | 2 | | | | 1 | 16 |
| | Loom Weights | | | | 11 | 2+ | | 1 | 1 | 15+ |
| | Shuttle | | | | | 1 | | | | 1 |
| | Other | 3 | | 2 | 4 | | | | | 9 |
| **Total** | | 19 | 8 | 12 | 24 | 15+ | 2 | 4 | 32 | 116 |

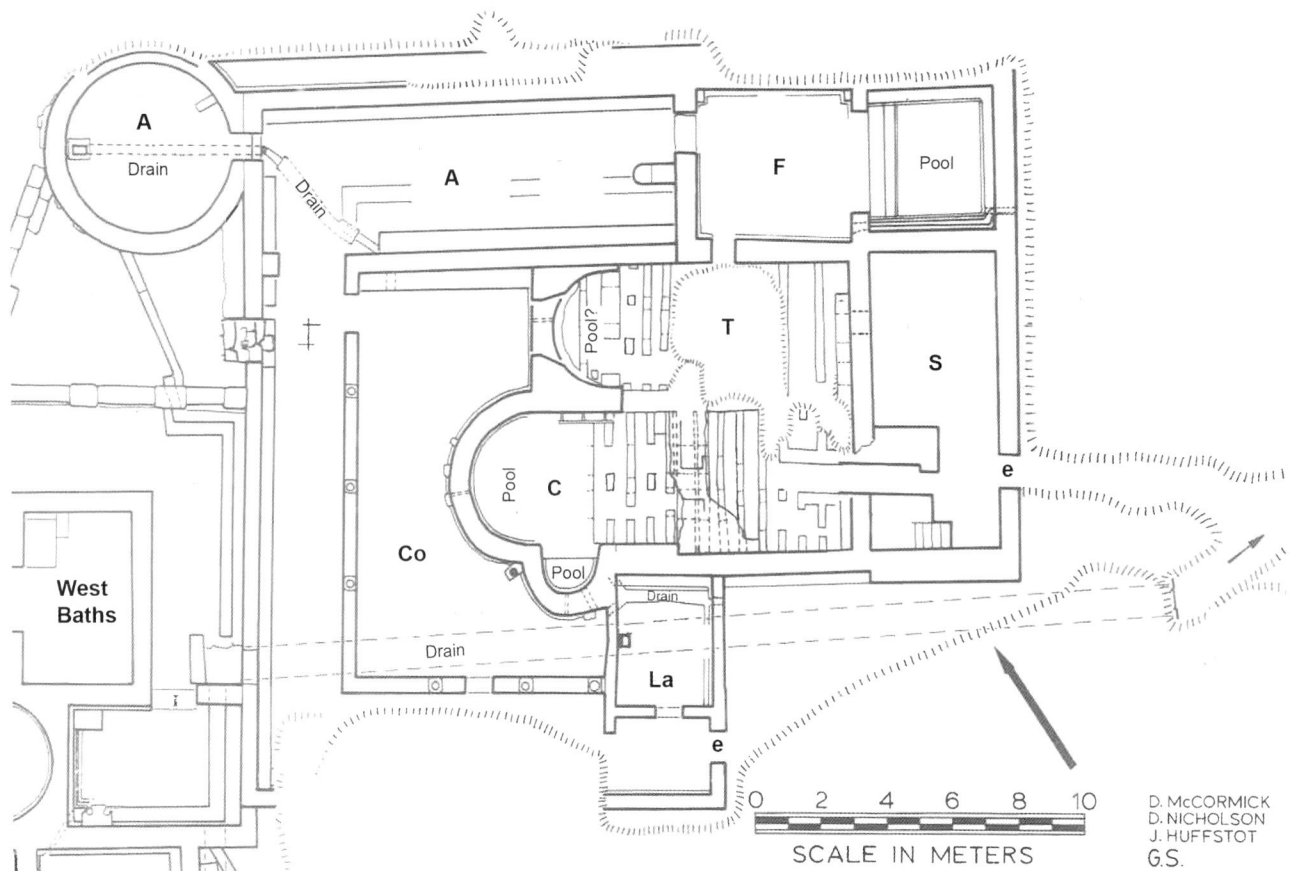

*Fig. 11.1: Mirobriga east baths. Note location of latrine (La) at bottom center. A:* apodyterium, *F:* frigidarium, *C:* caldarium, *T:* tepidarium, *S: service area/*praefurnium, *Co: courtyard, e: entrance (after Biers 1988, fig. 75. image: William R. Biers and Jane C. Biers)*

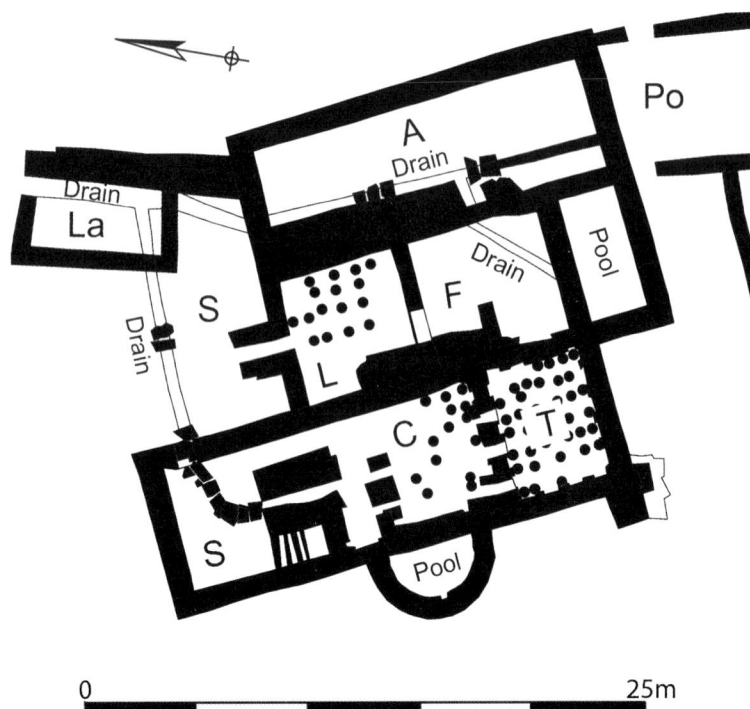

*Fig. 11.2: Vindolanda 3rd–4th century baths. Note location of latrine (La) at top left. A:* apodyterium, *F:* frigidarium, *C:* caldarium, *T:* tepidarium; *S: service area/*praefurnium, *L:* laconicum *(sweat room), Po: porch (image: Andrew Birley)*

24, 32). As a result, we cannot be certain that these finds only represent activities in the baths. Although the York sewer artefacts resemble expected finds from bathhouse drains (MacGregor 1976, 18; Cool and Baxter 2002), it is possible – given the rarity of well published Roman sewer assemblages – that Roman drains, whether connected with baths or not, simply have similar types of material culture.

After eliminating the problematic drain artefacts, ten needles, two weaving tablets, one spindle whorl and one loom weight remain from drainage contexts in three baths, with the vast majority stemming from the Caerleon legionary bathhouse (Table 11.2 and Figs 11.3–11.5). The majority of these finds and contexts are strongly associated with the normal functioning of the baths. Cloth working artefacts were spread throughout an 18-metre stretch of Caerleon's main drain (from contexts N-1 to 4), with an additional weaving tablet from Inlet 3, a separate but adjacent section of the drainage system (Figs 11.6 & 11.7) and several objects (Caerleon Needles #13 & 36, Spindle Whorl #40 and possibly Ribchester Needle #445) were recovered from the lower layers of their respective drains.

While these 14 artefacts represent the best evidence for cloth working in Roman public baths, this is only a small fraction – 12% – of the 116 bathhouse cloth working finds from Table 1. The vast majority of needles, spindle whorls and loom weights come from strata that cannot be strongly related to activities taking place in a functioning bathhouse. Furthermore, only 3 of the 19 baths in this sample have cloth working artefacts from use contexts and they typically make up a very minor percentage – 1–2% – of the total small finds drain assemblage (Whitmore 2013). The relatively low occurrence of these artefacts suggests that cloth working activities in bathhouse spaces were even less common than first appeared.

## Interpreting cloth working tools from bathhouse drains

Since artefact evidence for cloth working is so rare in the baths, and this activity is otherwise unattested in bathing spaces, it is worth considering whether these objects were actually used for sewing, spinning and weaving. The most problematic cloth working object found in a bathhouse drain is the very fragmentary loom weight recovered from the Herculaneum Forum Baths. While needles and spindle whorls are tools for small scale, portable cloth working activities, loom weights require a large, stationary loom. While it is hard to imagine this activity in the baths, loom weaving is more efficient in humid environments (Kemp & Vogelsang-Eastwood 2001, 327). It is possible that the moist, warm bathhouse air may have facilitated this activity, which could have been performed by bath attendants in side rooms or after hours. The context of the Herculaneum loom weight sheds little light on its use, as

it was uncovered not during a stratigraphic excavation, but a cleaning of the drain, whose entry points are uncertain but likely include the *palaestra*, men's *apodyterium* and the latrine (Pagano 1999, 181).

More problematic than its context, however, is that only one loom weight was found. The Roman warp-weighted loom most likely had two separate rows of loom weights, with a number of threads tied to each weight (Wild 1973, 62–64). The total number of weights used on a loom at a given time would depend upon the diameter of the yarn, the weight and thickness of the loom weights, and width and desired thread count of the fabric being woven (Mårtensson *et al.* 2009). Archaeological finds of loom weights in rows, as well as hoards of weights presumably in storage, suggest that all but the narrowest fabrics would require anywhere from 30 to 70 weights (Hoffmann 1964, 311–315; Wallace-Hadrill 1996, 112; Allison 1999, 70). In an experiment using loom weights based upon Bronze Age examples, one weaver used as many as 100 light, narrow loom weights (each weighing 177 g and 2 cm thick) to successfully produce a 1 sq. m fabric (Mårtensson *et al.* 2009, 394–396).

It seems probable that isolated finds of loom weights, such as this one from the Herculaneum Forum Baths, might reflect chance loss or use as simple weights, rather than on-site weaving (Wild 1970, 63 n.1). Weights may have been used in the sale of foods, drinks and perfumes in the baths, though admittedly selling these products in containers would be easier. Heavier loom weights may have been used to automatically close bathhouse doors, a practice known from the more recent 19th century (T. Fischer 2015, pers. comm.). While loom weights could have been used for other functions at any time, the fact that warp-weighted looms were beginning to wane in popularity when all these baths were in operation (Seneca, *Epistulae* 90.20; Wild 1970, 67), might make it even more probable that loom weights had additional functions.

The weaving tablets are also challenging to interpret. Only two broken weaving tablets were recovered at Caerleon, and while this small number is characteristic for the recovery of these objects at other types of sites, additional tablets, perhaps as many as 16–150 more, would have been required to weave a border (Wild 1970, 73; Knudsen 2010, 153–156). While tablet weaving can be more mobile than loom weaving, it still requires a fixed warp of some kind to stabilize the threads, and smaller tablets, such as those from Caerleon, may have been used with a warp-weighted loom, rather than individually (Knudsen 2010, 153). Regardless, while in use, the tablets would have been attached to threads, likely making them more difficult to lose. The fact that the broken Caerleon tablets were found in a drainage section that only received materials from pool and floor drains may suggest that these objects were damaged in the baths, perhaps while someone was weaving a band or border. It is equally plausible,

*Table 11.2: Cloth working artefacts from probable use contexts in Roman bathhouses.*

| Description | Context | Date | Source |
|---|---|---|---|
| **Caerleon Legionary Baths** | | | |
| *Needles* | | | |
| Broken bronze needle<br>L 62 mm; T 1–1.5 mm<br>Bronze Obj. #13 | Lowest layer of early drain silts between bath building and drain curve (1302:C) | AD 75–90 | Zienkiewicz 1986b, 173 |
| Bronze shaft of possible sacking needle<br>L 94 mm; T 0.5–2 mm<br>Bronze Obj. #116 | Upper drain silts between bath building and drain curve (DG 4 [-5]) | AD 160–230 | Zienkiewicz 1986b, 181 |
| Complete bone needle, rectangular eye<br>L 112 mm; T 1–4.5 mm<br>Bone Needle #32 | Upper drain silts under frigidarium floor between inlets from the north central pool and the NW pool (DG 4 [4]) | AD 160–230 | Zienkiewicz 1986b, 201 |
| Head of bone needle, rectangular eye<br>L 22 mm; T 4 mm<br>Bone Needle #35 | Upper drain silts between bath building and drain curve (DG 4 [-4]) | AD 160–230 | Zienkiewicz 1986b, 201 |
| Head of bone needle, rectangular eye<br>L 17 mm; T 4 mm<br>Bone Needle #36 | Middle layer of upper drain silts, just outside bath building (DG 4 [1] / 936:1) | AD 160–230 | Zienkiewicz 1986b, 201 |
| Complete bone needle with figure 8 eye<br>L 68 mm; T 1–4 mm<br>Bone Needle #39 | Upper drain silts between bath building and drain curve (DG 4 [-4]) | AD 160–230 | Zienkiewicz 1986b, 201 |
| Complete bone needle with figure 8 eye<br>L 69 mm; T 0.5–4 mm<br>Bone Needle #40 | Upper drain silts between bath building and drain curve (DG 4 [N-1]) | AD 160–230 | Zienkiewicz 1986b, 201 |
| Broken bone needle with figure 8 eye<br>L 59 mm; T 4.5–5 mm<br>Bone Needle #41 | Upper drain silts between bath building and drain curve (DG 4 [N-8]) | AD 160–230 | Zienkiewicz 1986b, 201 |
| Head of needle with prob. figure 8 eye<br>L 19 mm; T 4.5 – 5 mm<br>Bone Needle #42 | Upper drain silts, near drain curve (DG 4 [N-5]) | AD 160–230 | Zienkiewicz 1986b, 201 |
| *Weaving plates* | | | |
| Broken triangular bone weaving plate<br>T 1 mm<br>Bone Obj. #12 | Fill of Drain Inlet 3 from NE Apodyterium or Basilica (1182) | AD 160–230 | Zienkiewicz 1986b, 207 |
| Near complete triangular bone weaving plate.<br>L 39 mm; T 1.5 mm<br>Bone Obj. #13 | Upper drain silts between bath building and drain curve (DG 4 [N-7]) | AD 160–230 | Zienkiewicz 1986b, 207 |
| *Spindle whorl* | | | |
| Stone spindle whorl<br>D 34 mm; T 5 mm; Perf. D 6.8 mm<br>Stone Obj. #40 | Lower layer of upper drain silts, near drain's exit from bath building (DG 4 [2] / 939:2) | AD 160–230 | Zienkiewicz 1986b, 214–215 |
| **Ribchester Military Baths** | | | |
| *Needle* | | | |
| Broken bone needle<br>Inv. #445 | Clay in unrobbed portion of Drain 157 (687) | 2nd–3rd century AD | Ribchester Inventory |
| **Herculaneum Forum Baths** | | | |
| *Loom Weight* | | | |
| Broken loom weight with suspension hole<br>L 40 mm; W 25 mm; T 20 mm; Hole D 5 mm | Drain fill near entrance to Men's Baths | 1st century BC–1st century AD | Herculaneum Depot |

n.b. For the Caerleon finds, the bracketed number indicates which main drain segment the object was found in (see Fig. 11.7)

*Fig. 11.3: Bone needles from Caerleon* frigidarium *drain (© National Museum of Wales. Photo: A. Whitmore)*

*Fig. 11.4: Bone weaving tablets from Caerleon drains (© National Museum of Wales. Photo: A. Whitmore)*

*Fig. 11.5: Stone spindle whorl from Caerleon* frigidarium *drain (© National Museum of Wales. Photo: A. Whitmore)*

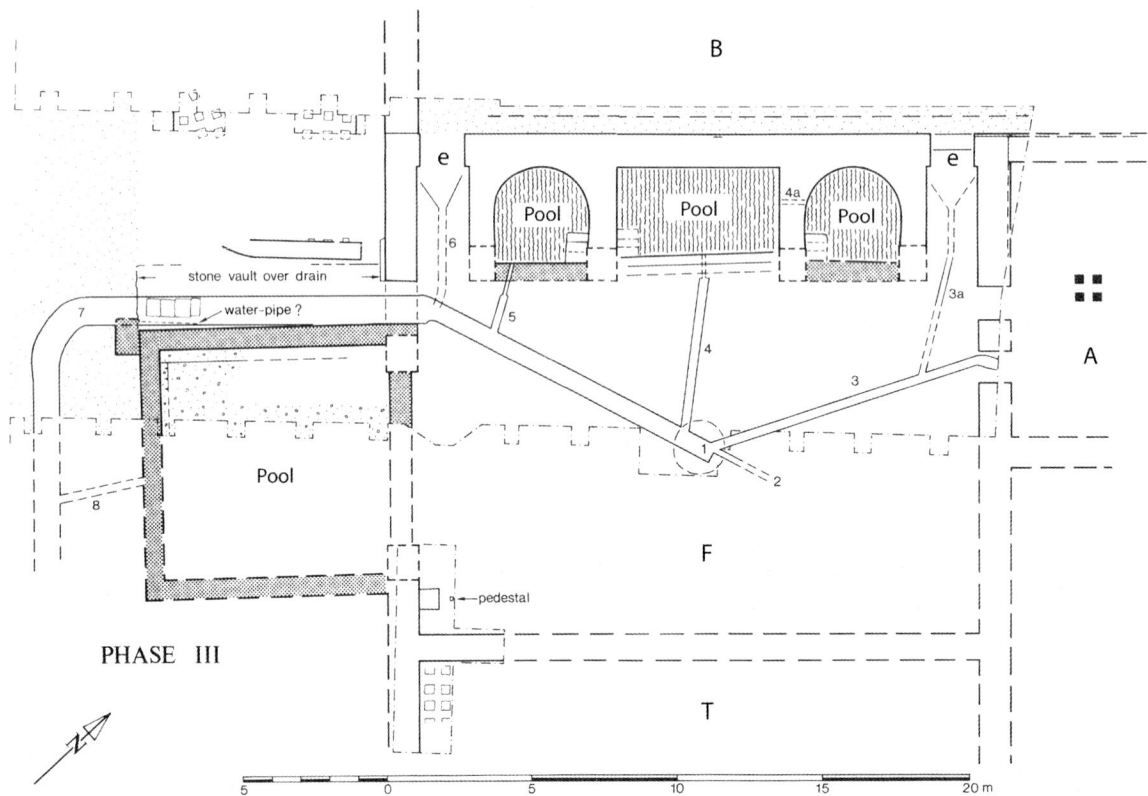

*Fig. 11.6: Location of Caerleon* frigidarium *drain. Smaller drain segments and inlets are numbered, with1 representing the position of the floor drain. 7 indicates the position of a a small inlet or manhole of uncertain purpose in the drain roof, which has been obscured by robbing. A:* apodyterium, *F: frigidarium, T: tepidarium, B: basilica, e: entrance (after Zienkiewicz 1986a, fig. 70, 196–199. © National Museum of Wales)*

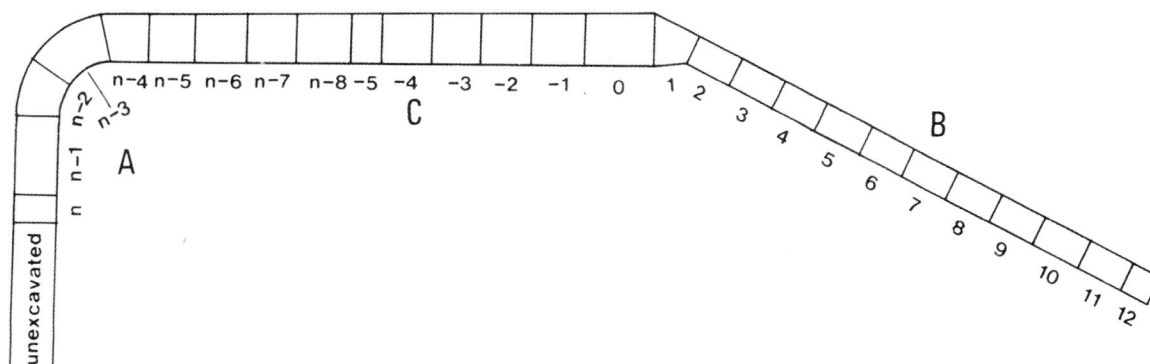

*Fig. 11.7: Segments of Caerleon* frigidarium *main drain . The drain segments are divided in two ways. The labels A–C divide the early drain sediments into three large, differently oriented segments. The later drain sediments (Drain Group 4 or DG 4) were excavated in 27 smaller, roughly metre-long segments, labeled n–12. (Zienkiewicz 1986b, fig. 1, 15. © National Museum of Wales)*

however, that these tablets could have been broken while stored in the *apodyterium* with their owner's clothing, and subsequently thrown away or abandoned in the baths. The limited evidence for this activity makes tablet weaving in the baths only a possibility.

Needles and spindle whorls may also have had alternative functions. Needles were used in toilet and medical activities (Juvenal, *Saturae* 2.93⁻9, Celsus, *De Medicina* 7.7.4, 8), though it is more probable that metal, especially iron, needles longer than 150 mm were preferred for suturing or medical activities (Jackson 1994; 2011, 250). Since the majority of needles from bathhouse drains are bone, with the exception of two broken bronze needles from Caerleon (Table 11.2), it seems improbable that most were used for medical activities. Janet Stephens has suggested that some bone needles, especially those longer than 90 mm, may have been used to create women's hairstyles (Stephens 2008). While one needle from Caerleon fits this criterion, and could potentially have been used in hair styling (#32, 112 mm), other complete examples fall short of the required length (Caerleon #39, 68 mm; #40, 69 mm). Spindle whorls may also have functioned as items of adornment. In the Romano-British cemetery at Poundbury, shale spindle whorls were recovered near and under the heads of three female skeletons, which may suggest that they were used as hair ornaments (Farwell & Molleson 1993, 85–86, 100). However, since needles and spindle whorls would be interpreted as evidence of cloth working if found in any other context (cf. Crummy 1983, 65; Manning 2011, 85–86), seeking alternative, non-cloth working explanations for these objects may be overly conservative. These artefacts can be reasonably interpreted as evidence for sewing, spinning and perhaps tablet weaving in the Caerleon, and possibly Ribchester, military baths (Zienkiewicz 1986b, 20; Allason-Jones 2011, 240).

## Sewing, spinning and weaving in Roman military baths

If we conclude that sewing and spinning occasionally took place in a few Roman military bathhouses, what additional information does this provide on life in the baths? One of the challenges with interpreting drain assemblages as occupation 'floors' is that the majority of drain contexts cannot be associated with specific bathhouse rooms, thus drain artefacts reflect only activities occurring somewhere in the baths. Robbing and modern disturbances have eliminated direct connections between drains and bathing spaces at Ribchester, so we can only speculate where materials may have entered. The Caerleon baths and drainage system, however, is better preserved. The majority of the cloth working finds – all of the needles, the spindle whorl and one of the weaving tablets – were recovered in the main *frigidarium* drain (Fig. 11.6). Inlets to this drain include a floor drain in the *frigidarium*, the cold plunges in the *frigidarium* and presumed floor drains in the north-east *apodyterium* and the basilica. A more specific point of origin can be given to a broken weaving tablet (Caerleon #12), which was found in a drain segment (Inlet 3) coming from the north-east *apodyterium* or basilica. While only part of the Caerleon baths have been excavated, leaving us without comparable data from heated rooms, these drain entry points permit the location of sewing, spinning and perhaps tablet weaving at Caerleon in unheated bathing spaces, some of which included pools (the *frigidarium*) and some without (the *apodyterium* and basilica). Notably, Caerleon's basilica and *frigidarium* are both very large rooms, and the pools take up only a fraction of the total available space in the *frigidarium*, suggesting that these spaces would be well suited, and perhaps designed, to accommodate socialization and other activities, as well as bathing (DeLaine 1997; Revell 2007).

Who would have been sewing, spinning or tablet weaving in the Caerleon and Ribchester military baths? Roman men and women were involved in sewing and weaving (Moeller 1969; Allason-Jones 1999), but spinning was more strongly associated with women alone (Allison *et al.* 2005). While both sites have military associations – the Caerleon legionary bathhouse was located within the walls of the fort, while the extramural Ribchester baths were situated in the surrounding settlement – the presence of women in military spaces is not unexpected (van Driel Murray 1997; Allason-Jones 1999; Allison 2013), and material culture associated with Roman women, such as beads, hairpins and bracelets, have been recovered in the drains of several military bathhouses (Whitmore forthcoming). While the gender of the individuals sewing and weaving in the baths cannot be plausibly surmised, the spindle whorl from Caerleon suggests that at least one woman brought a spindle whorl into, and perhaps spun in, the baths (Allason-Jones 1989, 179). Beyond gender, however, who were these individuals?

At Caerleon, where the largest and most diverse assemblage of cloth working artefacts was found, it is suggested that bathers (Allason-Jones 2011, 240), soldiers or craftspeople might have been involved with cloth working activities (Zienkiewicz 1986b, 20). Since needles were regularly part of a soldier's equipment (van Driel-Murray 1994, 357; Allason-Jones 1999, 1), it is possible that soldiers were sewing in military baths. But would bathers – soldiers or otherwise – have brought their chores into the baths, a space predominantly associated with leisure? Lower class bathers – a designation which may fit many soldiers – might multi-task by mending in the more enjoyable atmosphere of the baths, but it seems improbable that upper class individuals were engaged in cloth working activities.

It is possible that these needles, weaving tablets and spindle whorl provide evidence for the activities of slaves. In addition to slaves that were owned by the baths, domestic slaves came as bathers and attendants (Fagan 1999, 199–206). While some slaves actively assisted their owners with bathing (Martial 7.35, 11.75; Ammianus Marcellinus 28.4.6–9), others may have been left guarding their clothes elsewhere in the baths (Fagan 1999, 200; Lucian *Hippias* 5), and these individuals may have been expected to complete various tasks, such as spinning wool or mending the household's clothing.

While ancient texts focus on the experiences that were offered to bathers, it is important to recall that there were labourers, slaves and free, who provided these services. In addition to those who kept the baths in operation (Nielsen 1993, 125–130), sausage makers, confectioners and other peddlers advertised food, hair pluckers removed unwanted body hair, and masseurs offered massages (Seneca, *Epistulae* 56.1–2). Other commercial services may also have been offered in the baths, and a darning amenity might have been especially well suited for this space, since bathers would not need their clothing during their stay. While Roman soldiers were entirely capable of mending their own clothes, some likely had the resources to take advantage of such a service.

## Conclusions

It often takes an unusual find in an unexpected place for scholars to critically evaluate the impact of deposition practices and site formation on archaeological contexts, processes that affect every site regardless of how typical and mundane the assemblages appear. The necessity of critically appraising the impact of these forces is evidenced here: very few cloth working tools in Roman baths likely represent activities that actually occurred in these spaces. Caerleon, with its ten needles, two weaving tablets and a spindle whorl from the drain, provides the strongest case for this practice. The virtual absence of cloth working artefacts from other bathhouse drain assemblages is interesting, but difficult to interpret. The Caerleon legionary bathhouse is one of the largest baths in this sample, and has – by far – the most plentiful and diverse small finds assemblage recovered in any bath. This makes comparisons with other assemblages, especially those from smaller baths, problematic, as it is difficult to judge the significance of the absence of artefacts from an already small assemblage. Given the current evidence, we can only speculate whether cloth working was a unique occurrence only at Caerleon and Ribchester, or a more common, but invisible, activity within other bathhouses and bathing spaces.

Cloth working is absent from ancient texts and artistic depictions of life in the baths. When comparing these sources with artefact assemblages, significant areas of overlap exist, particularly the presence of jewellery, status displays and eating and drinking. Other activities that are never mentioned in ancient texts appear either regularly (gaming) and occasionally (medicine) in the archaeological record of baths. Conversely, the quintessential Roman bathing instrument, the strigil, is absent from the vast majority of bathhouse artefact assemblages, most likely due to a combination of ancient behaviours and taphonomic processes (Whitmore forthcoming). If sewing and spinning did occur in some baths, and was performed by slaves, the lower classes and women, its absence from ancient texts wouldn't be surprising, given the relatively few sources that offer detailed information on daily life in the baths (Fagan 1999, 7–8). Furthermore, the probable low status of those sewing and spinning, and the fact that these individuals – especially women – were engaged in socially acceptable pursuits, would make these individuals and activities unlikely to attract the attention of male authors. Though cloth working doesn't neatly fit with our conception of the Roman baths as a leisure space, these sewers, spinners and tablet weavers may have been craftsmen, servants or slaves, rather than paying customers, and these finds may provide material evidence of the countless, largely invisible, individuals for whom the baths were a place of work.

*Acknowledgements*

I could not have completed this research without the access granted to unpublished reports and finds at several of these sites, and I am especially grateful for the assistance of Stephen Bull (Lancashire County Museum Service), Andrew Birley and Barbara Birley (Vindolanda Trust), Tamara Tännler (Augusta Raurica Research Archives), the Soprintendenza Speciale per i Beni Archeologici di Napoli e Pompei, Jane Whitehead (Valdosta University) and Mark Lewis (National Roman Legion Museum). This research was funded in part through the Hugh Last and Donald Atkinson funds, the assistance of which I greatly appreciate, and I would also like the thank the staff at the Des Moines Area Community College and Perry Public libraries. My thoughts on bathhouse contexts have benefited greatly from discussions with the participants of the Thermae in Context Congress (Luxembourg 2013), and the current paper is much improved by comments from Stefanie Hoss, Barbara Köstner, and Molly Swetnam-Burland. All errors remain mine alone.

## Ancient sources

Ammianus Marcellinus, *History*, vol. 3. Trans. J. C. Rolfe (1939). Loeb Classical Library 331. Cambridge MA, Harvard University Press.

Celsus, *De Medicina* (On Medicine), vol. 3. Trans. W. G. Spencer (1938). Loeb Classical Library 336. Cambridge MA, Harvard University Press.

Cicero, *De Divinatione*. In *On Old Age. On Friendship. On Divination*. Trans. W. A. Falconer (1923). Loeb Classical Library 154. Cambridge MA, Harvard University Press.

*Corpus Inscriptionum Latinarum*, vol. 1², pars II, fasc. 1: *Inscriptiones Latinae antiquissimae*. Ed. A. T. Mommsen & E. Lommatzsch (1918). Berolini apud G. Reimerum.

*Corpus Inscriptionum Latinarum*, vol. 2: *Inscriptiones Hispaniae Latinae*. Ed. E. W. E. Hübner (1869). Berolini apud Georgium Reimerum.

*Corpus Inscriptionum Latinarum*, vol. 4: *Inscriptiones parietariae Pompeianae Herculanenses Stabianae*. Ed. C. Zangemeister and R. Schoene (1871). Berolini apud Georgium Reimerum.

*The Digest of Justinian*, vol. 4. Trans. A. Watson (1985). Philadelphia, University of Pennsylvania Press.

Juvenal, *Saturae*. In *Juvenal and Persius*. Ed. and Trans. S. M. Braund (2004). Loeb Classical Library 91. Cambridge MA, Harvard University Press.

Lucan, *Hippias*. Trans. A. M. Harmon (1913). Loeb Classical Library 14. Cambridge MA, Harvard University Press.

Martial, *Epigrams*, vol. 1 and 2. Ed. & Trans. D. R. Shackleton Bailey (1993). Loeb Classical Library 94 & 95. Cambridge MA, Harvard University Press.

Ovid, *Ars amatoria (The Art of Love)*. Trans. James Michie (2002). New York, Penguin Random House.

Pliny, *Epistulae (Letters)*, vol. 2. Trans. Betty Radice (1969). Loeb Classical Library 59. Cambridge MA, Harvard University Press.

Seneca, *Epistulae (Epistles)*, vols 1–2. Trans. R. M. Gummere (1919/1920). Loeb Classical Library 75 & 76. Cambridge MA, Harvard University Press.

Statius, *Silvae*. Ed. & Trans. D. R. Shackleton Bailey (2015). Loeb Classical Library 206. Cambridge MA, Harvard University Press.

Tacitus, *Annals*, vol. 4. Trans. J. E. Jackson (1937). Loeb Classical Library 312. Cambridge MA, Harvard University Press.

Vitruvius, *De Architectura (Ten Books on Architecture)*. Trans. I. D. Rowland (1999). Cambridge MA, Cambridge University Press.

## Bibliography

Allason-Jones, L. (1989) *Women in Roman Britain*. London, British Museum.

Allason-Jones, L. (1999) Women and the Roman army in Britain. In A. Goldsworthy & I. Haynes (eds) *The Roman Army as a Community*, 41–51. Journal of Roman Archaeology Supplementary Series 34. Portsmouth RI, Journal of Roman Archaeology.

Allason-Jones, L. (2011) Recreation. In L. Allason-Jones (ed.) *Artefacts in Roman Britain: their Purpose and Use*, 219–242. Cambridge, Cambridge University Press.

Allison, P. M. (1992) Artefact assemblages: not the 'Pompeii Premise.' In E. Herring, R. Whitehouse & J. Wilkins (eds) *Papers of the Fourth Conference of Italian Archaeology 3: New Developments in Italian Archaeology*, 49–56. London, Accordia Research Centre.

Allison, P. M. (1999) Labels for ladles: interpreting the material culture of Roman households. In P. M. Allison (ed.) *The Archaeology of Household Activities*, 57–77. New York, Routledge.

Allison, P. M. (2004) *Pompeian Households: an Analysis of the Material Culture*. Cotsen Institute of Archaeology Monograph 42. Los Angeles, University of California.

Allison, P. M. (2006) Mapping for gender: interpreting artefact distribution inside 1st and 2nd century AD forts in Roman Germany. *Archaeological Dialogues* 13(1), 1–20.

Allison, P. M. (2013) *People and Spaces in Roman Military Bases*. Cambridge, Cambridge University Press.

Allison, P. M., Fairbairn, A. S., Ellis, S. J. R. & Blackall, C. W. (2005). Extracting the social relevance of artefact distribution in Roman military forts. *Internet Archaeology* 17. http://dx.doi.org/10.11141/ia.17.4.

Barker, P., White, R., Pretty, K., Bird, H. & Corbishley, M. (1997) *The Baths Basilica Wroxeter*. London, English Heritage.

Becker, T. (2006) Women in Roman forts – lack of knowledge or a social claim? *Archaeological Dialogues* 13(1), 36–38.

Biers, W. R. (1988) *Mirobriga*. British Archaeological Report S451. Oxford, British Archaeological Reports.

Biers, W. R. & Biers, J. C. (1988a) The baths. In W. R. Biers (ed.) *Mirobriga*, 48–117. British Archaeological Report S451. Oxford, British Archaeological Reports.

Biers, W. R. & Biers, J. C. (1988b) The baths, locus summaries and catalogue of finds, catalogue of architectural blocks. In W. R.

Biers (ed.) *Mirobriga*, 164–205. British Archaeological Report S451. Oxford, British Archaeological Reports.

Birley, A. (2001) *Vindolanda's Military Bath Houses*. Northumberland, Vindolanda Trust and Roman Army Museum.

Camardo, D. (2011) Case study: Ercolano: la ricostruzione dei sistemi fognari. In G. C. M. Jansen, A. O. Koloski-Ostrow & E. M. Moormann (eds) *Roman Toilets: their Archaeology and Cultural History*, 90–91. Leuven, Peeters.

Carandini, A., Fabbricotti, E., Gasparri, C., Gasparri Tatti, M., Giannelli, M., Moriconi, M., Palma, B., Panella, C., Polia, M. & Ricci, A. (1968) *Le terme del nuotatore: scavo dell'ambiente IV*. Rome, De Luca Editore.

Carandini, A., Ricci, A., De Vos, M. & Medri, M. (1982) *Filosofiana: The Villa of Piazza Armerina. The Image of a Roman Aristocrat at the Time of Constantine*. Palermo, Flaccovio.

Cool, H. E. M. (2000) The Roman vessel glass. In P. Ellis (ed.) *The Roman Baths and Macellum at Wroxeter*, 162–185. London: English Heritage.

Cool, H. E. M. (2006) *Eating and Drinking in Roman Britain*. Cambridge, Cambridge University Press.

Cool, H. E. M. & Baxter, M. J. (2002) Exploring Romano-British finds assemblages. *Oxford Journal of Archaeology* 21(4), 365–380.

Crummy, N. (1983) *The Roman Small Finds from Excavations in Colchester 1971–9*. Colchester, Colchester Archaeological Trust.

Daniels, C. M. (1959) The Roman bath house at Red House, Beaufront, near Corbridge. *Archaeologia Aeliana* 37, 85–176.

DeLaine, J. (1992) New models, old modes: continuity and change in the design of public baths. In H. J. Schalles & P. Zanker (eds) *Die römische stadt im 2. Jahrhundert n. chr.: der funktionswandel des öffentlichen raumes*, 257–275. Bonn, Rheinland-Verlag.

DeLaine, J. (1997) *The Baths of Caracalla: a Study in the Design, Construction, and Economics of Large-scale Building Projects in Imperial Rome*. Journal of Roman Archaeology Supplementary Series 25. Portsmouth RI, Journal of Roman Archaeology.

Dickey, E. (2012) *The Colloquia of the Hermeneumata Pseudodositheana, vol. 1. Colloquia Monacensia-Einsidlensia, Leidense-Stephani, and Stephani*. Cambridge, Cambridge University Press.

Dicus, K. (2014) Resurrecting refuse at Pompeii: the use-value of urban refuse and its implications for interpreting archaeological assemblages. In H. Platts, J. Pearce, C. Barron, J. Lundock & J. Yoo (eds) *TRAC 2013: Proceedings of the 23rd Theoretical Roman Archaeology Conference*, 65–78. Oxford, Oxbow Books.

Ellis, P. (2000) *The Roman Baths and Macellum at Wroxeter*. London, English Heritage.

Eschebach, H. (1979) *Die Stabianer Thermen in Pompeji*. Berlin, Walter DeGruyter.

Eschebach, H. (1982) La documentazione delle terme del foro a Pompei. In *La Regione sotterrata dal Vesuvio: studi e prospettive*, 313–328. Naples, Università degli Studi di Napoli.

Fagan, G. (1999) *Bathing in Public in the Roman World*. Ann Arbor, University of Michigan Press.

Farwell, D. E. & Molleson, T. I. (1993) *Excavations at Poundbury, 1966–80, vol. 2: the cemeteries*. Dorchester, Dorset Natural History and Archaeological Society.

Fiorelli, I. (1862) *Pompeianarum antiquitatum historia*. Naples.

Gardner, A. (2007) *An Archaeology of Identity: Soldiers and Society in Late Roman Britain*. Walnut Creek, Left Coast Press.

Gillam, J. P., Jobey, I. M. & Welsby, D. A. (1993) *The Roman Bath-house at Bewcastle, Cumbria*. Kendal, Cumberland and Westmorland Archaeological and Antiquarian Society.

Godwin, E. G. (n.d.) Unpublished preliminary report following 1979 excavation of Ribchester baths. Preston, Lancashire Museum Service.

Gregory, R. (2010) Ribchester Roman Bathhouse: Desk-based research and archive assessment. Unpublished Site Assessment. Oxford Archaeology North and Lancashire Museums.

Hodgson, N. (2014) The accommodation of soldiers' wives in Roman fort barracks – on Hadrian's Wall and beyond. In R. Collins & F. McIntosh (eds) *Life in the Limes: Studies of the People and Objects of the Roman Frontiers*, 18–28. Oxford, Oxbow Books.

Hoffmann, M. (1964) *The Warp-Weighted Loom*. Norway, Universitetsforlaget.

Holmes, N. (2003) *Excavation of Roman Sites at Cramond, Edinburgh*. Edinburgh, Society of Antiquaries of Scotland.

Hope, W. H. S. J. & Fox, G. E. (1905) Excavations on the site of the Roman city at Silchester, Hants, in 1903 and 1904. *Archaeologia* 59, 333–370.

Hoss, S. (forthcoming) Small finds in Roman thermae: an introduction. In A. Binsfeld, S. Hoss, & H. Pösche (eds) *Thermae in context: Roman bathhouses in the town and in daily life*. Archaeologia Mosellana 10. Luxembourg, Musée national d'histoire et d'art.

Jackson, R. (1994) Medical instruments in the 'Antiquarium' at Pompeii. In L. J. Bliquez, *Roman Surgical Instruments and Other Minor Objects in the National Archaeological Museum of Naples*, 189–207. Mainz, Philipp von Zabern.

Jackson, R. (2011) Medicine and hygiene. In L. Allason-Jones (ed.) *Artefacts in Roman Britain: Their Purpose and Use*, 243–268. Cambridge, Cambridge University Press.

Jansen, G. C. M. (2000) Systems for the Disposal of Waste and Excreta in Roman Cities. The Situation in Pompeii, Herculaneum, and Ostia. In X. D. Raventós & J. A. Remolà (eds) *Sordes urbis: la eliminación de residuos en la ciudad Romana*, 37–49. Rome, L'Erma di Bretschneider.

Keller, D. (2005) Social and economic aspects of glass recycling. In J. Bruhn, B. Croxford, & D. Grigoropoulos (eds) *TRAC 2004: Proceedings of the 14th Theoretical Roman Archaeology Conference*, 65–78. Oxford, Oxbow Books.

Kemp, B. J. and Vogelsang-Eastwood, G. (2001) *The Ancient Textile Industry at Amarna*. London, Egypt Exploration Society.

Koloski-Ostrow, A. O. (2008) The city baths of Pompeii and Herculaneum. In J. J. Dobbins & P. W. Foss (eds) *World of Pompeii*, 224–256. New York, Routledge.

Koloski-Ostrow, A. O. (2015) *The Archaeology of Sanitation in Roman Italy: Toilets, Sewers, and Water Systems*. Chapel Hill, University of North Carolina Press.

Knudsen, L. R. (2010) Tiny weaving tablets, rectangular weaving tablets. In E. B. A. Strand, M. Gleba, U. Mannering, C. Munkholt, & M. Ringgard (eds) *NESAT X: The North European Symposium for Archaeological Textiles*, 150–156. Oxford, Oxbow Books.

Lee, J. E. (1850) *Description of a Roman Building and Other Remains Lately Discovered at Caerleon*. London, J. R. Smith.

Liebeschuetz, W. (2000) Rubbish disposal in Greek and Roman cities. In X. D. Raventós & J. A. Remolà (eds) *Sordes urbis: la eliminación de residuos en la ciudad Romana*, 51–61. Rome, L'Erma di Bretschneider.

MacGregor, A. (1976) *Finds from a Roman Sewer System and an Adjacent Building in Church Street*. Archaeology of York 17/1. York, Council for British Archaeology.

McParland, L. C., Hazell, Z., Campbell, G., Collinson, M. E. & Scott, A. C. (2009) How the Romans got themselves into hot water: temperatures and fuel types used in firing a hypocaust. *Environmental Archaeology* 14(2), 176–183.

Maiuri, A. (1931) Pompei: pozzi e condotture d'acqua nell'antica città. Scoperta di un antico pozzo presso "Porta Vesuvio." *Notizie degli Scavi di Antichità* Ser. 6, Vol. 7, 546–576.

Maiuri, A. (1950) Scoperta di un edificio termale nella Regio VIII, Insula 5, nr. 36. *Notizie degli Scavi di Antichità*, Ser. 8, Vol. 4, 116–136.

Manning, W. H. (2011) Industry. In L. Allason-Jones (ed.) *Artefacts in Roman Britain: Their Purpose and Use*, 68–89. Cambridge, Cambridge University Press.

Mårtensson, L., Nosch, M.-L. and Andersson Strand, E. (2009) Shape of things: understanding a loom weight. *Oxford Journal of Archaeology* 28(4), 373–398.

Moeller, W. O. (1969) The male weavers at Pompeii. *Technology and Culture* 10(4), 561–566.

Mould, Q. (2000) Small finds from the portico pits. In P. Ellis (ed.) *The Roman Baths and Macellum at Wroxeter*, 137–141. London, English Heritage.

Munro, B. (2010) Recycling in late Roman villas in southern Italy: reappraising hearths and kilns in final occupation phases. *Mouseion* Ser. 3, 10(2), 217–242.

Nevett, L. (1999) *House and Society in the Ancient Greek world*. Cambridge, Cambridge University Press.

Nielsen, I. (1993) *Thermae et balnea: the Architecture and Cultural History of Roman Public Baths*. Aarhus, Aarhus University Press.

Pagano, M. (1999) Ufficio Scavi di Ercolano. *Rivista di Studi Pompeiani 8 – 1997*, 180–183.

Parslow, C. (2000). The hydraulic system in the *balneum venerium et nongentum* of the Praedia Iuliae Felicis in Pompeii. In G. C. M. Jansen (ed.) *Cura Aquarum in Sicilia*, 201–214. Leiden, Stichting BABESCH.

Peña, J. T. (2007) *Roman Pottery in the Archaeological Record*. New York, Cambridge University Press.

Perkins, D. R. J. (2004) The Roman villa at Minster-in-Thanet. Part 1: introduction and report on the bath-house. *Archaeologia Cantiana* 124, 25–49.

Philp, B. (2012) *Discovery and Excavation of the Roman Shore-fort at Dover, Kent*. Dover, Kent Archaeological Rescue Unit.

Proctor, J. (2012) *Faverdale, Darlington: Excavations at a Major Settlement in the Northern Frontier Zone of Roman Britain*. London, Pre-Construct Archaeology Monograph 15.

Revell, L. (2007) Military bath-houses in Britain: a comment. *Britannia* 38, 230–237.

Revell, L. (2009) *Roman Imperialism and Local Identities*. Cambridge, Cambridge University Press.

Rook, T. (1992) *Roman Baths in Britain*. Princes Risboro, Shire.

Sanders, G. D. R. (1999) A Late Roman bath at Corinth: excavations in the Panayia Field, 1995–1996. *Hesperia* 68(4), 441–480.

Schiffer, M. (1985) Is there a "Pompeii Premise" in archaeology? *Journal of Anthropological Research* 41(1), 18–41.

Shelton, K. J. (1981) *The Esquiline Treasure*. London, British Museum.

Stephens, J. (2008) Ancient Roman hairdressing: on (hair)pins and needles. *Journal of Roman Archaeology* 21, 111–132.

Thüry, G. E. (2001) *Müll und marmorsäulen: siedlungshygiene in der Römischen antike*. Mainz am Rhein, Philipp von Zabern.

van Driel Murray, C. (1994) A question of gender in a military context. *Helinium* 34(2), 342–362.

Van Vaerenbergh, J. (2011a). Flush water for toilets in and near the baths. In G. C. M. Jansen, A. O. Koloski-Ostrow & E. M. Moormann (eds) *Roman Toilets: their Archaeology and Cultural History*, 78–86. Leuven, Peeters.

Van Vaerenbergh, J. (2011b). Location of toilets within baths. In G. C. M. Jansen, A. O. Koloski-Ostrow & E. M. Moormann (eds) *Roman Toilets: their Archaeology and Cultural History*, 115–119. Leuven, Peeters.

Wallace-Hadrill, A. (1996) Engendering the Roman house. In D. E. E. Kleiner & S. B. Matheson (eds) *I Claudia: Women in Ancient Rome*, 104–115. Austin, University of Texas Press.

Wallace-Hadrill, A. (2011) *Herculaneum: Past and Future*. London, Frances Lincoln.

Wardle, A. (2008) Bene lava: bathing in Roman London. In J. Clark, J. Cotton, J. Hall, R. Sherris & H. Swain (eds) *Londinium and Beyond*, 201–211. York, Council for British Archaeology.

Whitehead, J. K. (2006) Excavation of the baths at Carsulae 2006. *Etruscan News* 7, 9–10.

Whitmore, A. (2013) Small Finds and the Social Environment of Roman Public Baths. Unpublished doctoral thesis, University of Iowa.

Whitmore, A. (forthcoming) Artefact assemblages from Roman baths: expected, typical and rare finds. In A. Binsfeld, S. Hoss, & H. Pösche (eds) *Thermae in context: Roman bathhouses in the town and in daily life*. Archaeologia Mosellana 10. Luxembourg, Musée national d'histoire et d'art.

Whitwell, J. B. (1976) *The Church Street Sewer and an Adjacent Building*. Archaeology of York 3/1. York, Council for British Archaeology.

Wild, J. P. (1970) *Textile Manufacture in the Northern Roman Provinces*. Cambridge, Cambridge University Press.

Wilson, P. R. (2002) *Cataractonium: Roman Catterick and its Hinterland*. York, Council for British Archaeology.

Yegül, F. (2010) *Bathing in the Roman World*. New York, Cambridge University Press.

Zienkiewicz, J. D. (1986a) *The Legionary Fortress Baths at Caerleon: the Buildings*. Cardiff, National Museum of Wales and Welsh Historic Monuments.

Zienkiewicz, J. D. (1986b) *The Legionary Fortress Baths at Caerleon: the Finds*. Cardiff, National Museum of Wales and Welsh Historic Monuments.

# The complexity of intramural and extramural relationships on the northern frontier of Roman Britain – a Vindolanda case study

*Andrew R. Birley*

*keywords:* Roman Frontier; Artefacts; combatants; non-combatants; spatial deposition; extramural settlements

*In 2008 the Vindolanda Trust embarked upon an ambitious 5 year research project. It was aimed at exploring whether or not modern definitions of fort and vicus, which have so often been regarded as being binary, with soldiers portrayed as being mainly inside their forts and civilians confined to the adjacent 'vicus,' hindered rather than clarified the interpretation of military settlements and their communities. The site of Vindolanda has one of the largest datasets of material culture from Roman Britain, taken from both intramural and extramural contexts under modern archaeological conditions, which is robust enough to attempt to answer such a question. The spatial deposition of three domains of material culture were examined in this project to indicate the presence, location and activities of soldiers (combatants), non-combatants as exemplified by adult women, and shared activities that may have been common bonds across the whole community. A series of new excavations was started in 2008 which explored large sections of the 3rd century fort and vicus simultaneously, providing a thorough contextual perspective to historical datasets from the site and further broadening the material available for this study. The results of the project have provided new and often surprising perspectives into life at Vindolanda, questioning some of the current perceptions of military life and suggesting that there were more complex inter-relationships between the inhabitants of the fort and vicus than a simplistic or binary explanation of the two can easily provide.*

## Introduction

From the end of the 1st century AD to the beginning of the 5th century, the northern frontier of Roman Britain was a place of constant change and transition. The complex and often impressive archaeological monuments, as exemplified by Hadrian's Wall, with its linear barrier from the Solway Firth to the River Tyne estuary – curtain walls, milecastles, turrets, signal stations, forts, towns, roads and infrastructure are vivid reminders of the presence of a series of interconnected communities who would have used these facilities (Breeze 2013, 7). For such communities and groups to function well they undoubtedly needed a series of networks and inter-relationships, reflecting a complex society made up of many thousands of individuals. The daily lives of these people of the frontier would have been influenced by often

conflicting or competing elements including; rank and status (both social and economic), legal status (such as citizenship or slavery), physical geography (where an individual or group physically resided within the wide area covered by the frontier), age, gender, cultural background, family and friendship groups, political affiliations and the directives of the state, ethnicity, education, profession/professions, social mobility, religious affiliations, preferred leisure activities and social groupings to name but a few.

The challenge for scholars has been to study the body of evidence in both a nuanced and digestible way. Past research has been hampered by simple barriers, such as the clear historical bias in the quantity and quality of archaeological data gathered from frontier settlements. This is an area where an intramural military perspective has until relatively recently dominated research on the northern frontier of Roman Britain, with excavations and research concentrating on the areas within the walls of Roman forts (Birley A. R. 2013a, 85).

One area of frontier archaeology that has been poorly represented are extramural settlements, often termed as *vici* and normally situated adjacent to forts. These have largely been left unexplored, their occupants often labelled simply as 'civilians' (Birley A. R. 2013a, 85). This has led to a wider perception that the *vicani* were second class settlers on the Roman frontier, peripheral rather than integral. This classification is a largely accepted consequence of the historical archaeological bias towards intramural spaces and an over reliance on historical and epigraphic sources to fill in the gaps. While some scholars, such as Eric Birley (1935), Salway (1965), Robin Birley (1976) and Sommer (1984; 1988; 2006) promoted interest in the study of *vici*, it is only relatively recently that we have come to appreciate that in many cases the largest component parts of a military sites on the northern frontier of Roman Britain were the extramural settlements (Sommer 2006, 95–145, Biggins & Taylor 2007, 15–30, Birley A. R. 2013a, 85).

However, despite a growing appreciation of the potential size of extramural settlements, there remains little consensus or a better understanding on how their inhabitants actually used those spaces. It is here that there is perhaps the greatest potential for artefact studies to offer new perspectives. The study and analysis of the distribution and deposition of a range of artefacts from both inside and outside the walls of Roman forts can be considered by adapting and building upon the principles of the methodologies applied to intramural sites in Germany by scholars such as Allison (2006, 2013). However, to do this type of analysis the foundations for the work have to be sound, and therefore the artefacts discussed in this paper are only those that were solidly recovered from known structural and contextual spaces.

By using information gathered from tightly contextualised data, we can examine intramural and extramural spaces side-by-side. This will allow for a wider appreciation of how these contexts may have related to one another. We can also explore Vindolanda in the 4th century, in a period after the extramural settlement had been abandoned and the fort heavily modified, to see what happened next. Did all the *vicani* disappear with the extramural settlement? Did they move inside the fort? Or was there always a greater and more complex set of relationships at frontier settlements like Vindolanda than has been previously understood or recognised? This paper does not promise all of the answers to the above, but what it does offer is a way in which we can start to question the perceived wisdoms through the analysis of available archaeological dataset of material culture. For this purpose we shall consider how an

examination of the spatial deposition of three domains of material culture may differ from the current narrative. Those domains can be associated with the location and activities of soldiers (combatants), non-combatants as exemplified by adult women, and shared activities from case study site of Vindolanda may offer a pathway beyond the difficulties associated with such terminology. Through the spatial deposition of these artefact categories we may begin to see some of the complexities in the relationships across a single site as a whole, and without prejudice.

Before we can look at the material culture from Vindolanda we must first properly consider what is currently understood about how the people of the frontier might have used the term *vicus*, from a literary and epigraphic perspective, and whether or not modern conceptual interpretations of the term may have clouded our perception of the potential complexity of intramural and extramural relationships. This provides a broader contextual framework to what will follow with the discussions on the spatial patterning of material culture from the site.

## *Vicus* and the use of the term – ancient authors

Many of our modern conceptions of extramural settlements, their roles and functions, have been based upon the discussion of literacy and epigraphy mentioning the term *vicus* perhaps as much as any interpretation of the archaeology of those sites (Birley & Keeney 1935; Salway 1965; Sommer 1984; 1988; 2006). It is therefore important to consider how the term has come to be used to label or define extramural settlements in military contexts. The majority of literary and epigraphic evidence for the use of the term *vicus* has come from purely civil contexts, and it could be that civil associations may be misleading when trying to understand the complexities of intramural and extramural relationships.

Ancient literary and epigraphic evidence for the meaning and use of the term *vicus* have now been comprehensively collected and discussed by Tarpin in his monograph on *vici* and *pagi* in the Roman west (Tarpin 2002). He notes that the supposed derivative of the word *vicus*, from *via*, 'road' (Varro, *De lingua Latina* 5.145) is fictional. *Vicus* is related to the Greek οικος, meaning 'house' or 'household', and words derived from it refer to settlements.

The standard ancient authors generally quoted on the meaning of *vicus* are Festus and Isidore of Seville. Sextus Pompeius Festus, a grammarian of the late 2nd century AD, wrote a lexicon of Latin, which was an abbreviated version of a work by the earlier grammarian, Marcus Verrius Flaccus (*c.* 55 BC? –*c.* AD 20?), *De verborum significatione* (see OCD[3] 1589). Festus' passage on *vicus* (Lindsay 1930, 460–461) is incomplete, textually corrupt and not particularly helpful for understanding the role and function of this settlement type in a military context (Birley A. R. 2010, 12).

The 7th century AD bishop of Seville, Isidore (Isidorus), *Etymologiae* (ed. Lindsay 1911), in his book 15, *De aedificiis et agris*, 'On buildings and the countryside [fields]' also mentions the term *vicus*. This late source should be treated with caution, as the meaning of the term *vicus* may have changed from 2nd–4th century contexts (where it is most often applied to extramural settlements by archaeologists). Disappointingly, neither of these authors refers to the use of the term *vicus* for settlements outside military bases.

The *Digest* of Justinian also makes several brief references to the status of a *vicus*. At 50.1.30, Ulpian states that 'whoever is born in a village (*vicus*) is regarded as a member of the *patria* to which the village in question belongs'. A *vicus* then answered to an immediate higher authority; presumably a rural *vicus* would answer to the nearest larger town to which it was 'attributed'. It would be strange to suggest that a military *vicus* would not answer to the nearest immediate 'higher' authority, i.e. the Roman army itself, the local commanding officer or perhaps a regional centurion.

The *Digest* 30.1.73 also cites Gaius on the Praetor's Edict, Legacies book 3. 1: '*Vici* may receive legacies as may *civitates*, according to a rescript of our emperor.' So that as a collective, a *vicus* may be bequeathed inheritances of land or resources, underlining the legal importance of *vicus* status. Clearly then, having a recognised status as a *vicus* or as a *pagus* had its benefits, but also a responsibility to look after the highways and byways that passed through its territories. The legal writers clearly refer to civilian *vici*, villages or (mainly) smaller rural settlements, not to those that existed outside military bases.

The legal responsibility for maintaining the roads running through a settlement regarded as having *vicus* status seems fairly clear-cut (not least in *Digest* 30.1.73). Local councils in Britain are still responsible for the upkeep of all minor roads and the state, the Department of Transport, is responsible for all major highways. However, in the context of extramural settlements, the responsibility for roads may have not been in the hands of the local people or minor officials, as the roads invariably ran to or from fort gateways, and their upkeep may have been a matter for the garrisons. The legal status of a military community could have been significantly different from that of a similar size community with no military aspect.

Festus's statement that the 'rural settlements' that he calls *vici* had limited self-government is confirmed by the numerous inscriptions listed by Tarpin. Likewise, Pliny, *Naturalis Historia* 3.65–67, refers to the 265 *vici*, or 'wards' of Rome, pointing out that all of them had *magistri* who were responsible for aspects of their administration. It can be speculated that in the early stages on the foundation of extramural settlement next to a fort, the higher authority (*magister*) could have been a military official. It may be that such a task could have been entrusted to a centurion, or even an *optio*. A military official could well have regarded such duties in an extramural area as an important addition to his military rank, and possibly financially remunerative. In the 3rd century some kind of self-government seems to have been in place, to judge from inscriptions from continental extramural settlements, but the limited British inscriptions from military contexts are far less explicit.

Ancient authors' observations about the term *vicus* therefore need to be seen for what they are, a generality at best, referring to a house, a street, a village, a place. They do not refer to military contexts, make no statements about the nature and significance of extramural settlements at such sites or allude to how relationships may have worked either within extramural areas or between them and their adjacent intramural spaces.

We cannot divine significant answers about the complexity of intramural and extramural relationships from such simple binary comprehensions of the terms 'vicus' or 'fort' without understanding the contexts in which they were applied by those who dwelt within them. We must consider what light a study of artefacts might shed upon this matter, starting with inscriptions that mention the term *vicus*.

## Epigraphic sources for *vici* – a brief review

Like the ancient literary sources, epigraphic evidence for extramural settlement mainly comes in the form of inscriptions that mention the word *vici* or *vicus*. In Britain, as on the continent, these consist of just a handful of undisputed texts that have been recovered from outside the walls of military bases and a few examples from former military establishments which could have been regarded as having a mainly 'civilian population' by the time the inscriptions were carved. The dates of the inscriptions vary, but generally cover a period from the mid-2nd century to the end of the 3rd century. The 1st and 4th centuries have yet to provide direct epigraphic evidence of the presence of *vici*. Extramural settlements certainly existed during these times, as shown by the recently excavated early 2nd century extramural settlement at Vindolanda (Blake J. 2014) and the continuation of extramural settlements at military sites such as Binchester and Catterick into the 4th century (Wilson 2002). There is also a strong case to be made for the continuation of extramural activities within the walls of frontier forts in the 4th century (Birley A. R. 2013a, 36–46, Brickstock 2013, 121–126).

The earliest inscription is from the eastern end of the Antonine Wall, and is unlikely to be later than *c.* AD 160

(RIB III 3503). Others inscriptions, mainly thought to be 3rd century in date, include: *RIB* 1700 which records an altar set up by the *vicani Vindolandensses*; *RIB* 1616 a gift from the *vicani* at Housesteads; *RIB* 899 from Old Carlisle and *RIB* 1749, a fragmentary tombstone from the fort of Great Chesters.

Inscriptions from the two German provinces are conveniently listed by Tarpin (Tarpin 2002, 369–379). But they mostly come either from sites where there were no longer forts or are too fragmentary to provide clear evidence on the administration. Therefore the present body of evidence from the German provinces is no stronger than that from Roman Britain.

It is perhaps worth mentioning that most of the references to *vicani* in the form of altars or inscriptions have connections to particular deities: *RIB* 1700 from Vindolanda, the '*vicani Vindolandesses*' altar refers to the god Vulcan, the god of metalworking, while *RIB* 270 from Lincoln '*vic[us] hrapo Mercuresium*' refers to 'the … ward of the guild of Mercury' (although as already discussed this could be a misreading of a now lost stone); the inscription on lead from London refers to the '*vicus* of Jupiter' (Collingwood & Wright 1991, 92). The altar from Carriden in Scotland was set up by 'The *vicus* dwellers at the fort of Velunias' as '*vikani con[sis]tentes castel[lo] Veluniate*' to '*Jupiter Optimus Maximus*' (RIB III 3503).

If all of the inscriptions mentioning the *vicani* from extramural settlement in Roman Britain are religious dedications this may suggest that if there was a corporate identity or collective responsibility attached to the use of the term, one that may have been in some way separate from that of the army, it may have been through religious expression, rather than self-government or self-determination. In any case, the use of the term *vicus* does little to shed light upon the potential complexities of such settlements, nor their relationships with adjacent forts.

*Fig. 12.1: The site of Vindolanda in 2014, as seen from the south-west of the extramural settlement*

## The case study site – Vindolanda

Vindolanda lies in south-west Northumberland, in the district of Tynedale (Fig. 12.1), almost halfway between the North Sea east of Newcastle and the Irish Sea to the west of Carlisle, situated not directly on Hadrian's Wall (a frontier which it later becomes a part of), but on the road south of it known by its medieval name, the Stanegate. Material culture datasets from the site, collected during 44 years of research and excavation, can be used to gain a more detailed appreciation of some of the complex interwoven relationships that were present at the site in the 3rd and 4th centuries (Birley A. R. 2013a, 85–104).

This paper significantly builds upon previous research (Birley, A. R. 2013a, 85–104) by incorporating new datasets of material culture from the 2009–2011 excavations, including a series of three barracks, ramparts, roads, a temple and granaries located in the north-western quadrant. I also add a new category of artefacts not included in the previous study: finds associated with shared activities and skills such as literacy (stylus pens), industry (crucibles) and gaming (gaming counters).

## The archaeological context of Vindolanda and its site formation processes

It is now believed that there were nine successive Roman forts/settlements constructed at Vindolanda (Birley & Blake 2007, 3–4, Birley R. E. 2009). Few of the forts and associated settlements were the same size or shape; some parts of the site were covered by all nine periods of construction, while others were only intermittently part of intramural/extramural areas of the site. New levels of construction were regularly superimposed over the demolished remains of earlier settlements. Before construction took place the earlier buildings were demolished and the ground levels sealed with layers of turf and clay, sometimes to a depth of half a metre and often covering the entire site including former roadways and fort defences (Birley R. E. 1977, 103). In most cases this style of site preparation made the post-depositional movement of artefacts, by human or animal intervention, from one layer to another, less probable. When such movement did occur, as when deep foundation trenches or ditches were dug, earlier occupation material could be re-deposited.

By the end of the 4th century, parts of the site had risen above the pre-Roman landscape by more than 6m, creating either anaerobic or waterlogged conditions, in which almost all organic/inorganic objects could survive (Birley R. E. 2009, 51). The fort and associated extramural settlement of the third and fourth centuries, which are of particular relevance to this study, represented the last major construction project on the site and they were not completely sealed by new layers of construction. Here, the patterns of deposition are more open to different processes, including disturbance by stone robbers involved in quarrying activities and by later agricultural practices. This created a layer of unstratified material across the site, covering the last remains of occupation, to varying depths in different areas. Over the remains of the 3rd century extramural settlement, some 20–30cm of soil represented the plough zone, and all of the artefacts that were recovered in this zone have been omitted from this analysis. Inside the fort, which continued in occupation beyond the end of Roman Britain, a similar layer of de-contextualised soil and associated artefacts has been excavated and datasets from these levels have been discounted from this analysis.

It is possible that some of the material in extramural contexts was deposited by intramural inhabitants of 4th century or later date, while stone robbing for their own buildings. The paucity of 4th century pottery and coinage, even in the plough zone above the ruined remains of the 3rd century extramural settlement suggests that the 4th century inhabitants did not venture far beyond the walls of the fort, or into the fort ditches (which may have already been silted up) to deposit their waste.

The evidence for the abandonment of the 3rd century extramural settlement comes from a significant drop in the quantity of coinage, post-*c.* AD 280. This is supported by an almost complete absence of 4th century pottery from this part of the site. The use of coins and pottery continue within the walls of the adjacent fort into the 4th century although there is a possibility that the entire site was briefly abandoned in the latter part of the 3rd century with re-occupation from the early 4th century onwards limited to areas within the walls of the fort (Brickstock 2013, 121–125). The re-building of structures and extensive 4th century modifications within the fort employed recycled building materials from the abandoned extramural settlement (Birley & Blake 2007, 47). This recycling activity may well have had an impact on the distribution of some of the material culture from within the buildings being demolished for the recycling of building materials. This has to be taken into account in any discussion of the patterning of material culture on the site. It is probable that the extramural buildings closest to the west wall of the fort, and therefore readily accessible, suffered from demolition for specific reuse in the fort defences and may have been the most disturbed by these activities.

## The deposition of artefacts at Vindolanda

The pattern of use or re-cycling before being lost, discarded or purposely deposited may have differed for each artefact and varied greatly between certain artefact groups. For instance, it is unlikely that swords and beads were deposited in exactly the same way or circumstances in most contexts. Swords were more likely to have been purposely deposited or partial finds may have been the result of cast off after repairs, rather than casual loss.

Post-depositional processes (some which have already been discussed) ought to be taken into account for the deposition of artefacts, especially on a site where constant re-building was a feature of the occupation and there may have been disturbance after initial deposition had taken place. This may have been through human activities or other agencies, such as flooding, especially relevant to material which was light or buoyant and could float out of a fort ditch or wash down a street. The extramural part of the site at Vindolanda gently slopes towards the western fort wall, and as a consequence artefacts deposited on open surfaces, such as streets, or in drains, may have washed down towards the fort walls and into the western fort ditch.

The western fort ditch at Vindolanda is treated as a slightly separate area in the following discussions due to its ambiguity of use. While the ditch physically separated the fort from extramural areas it was accessible to both. Therefore the material held inside the ditch may have come from either side, intramural or extramural. This is an issue at all sites where the fort ditches directly separate the intramural and extramural spaces and in a few cases, such as at Woerden in the Netherlands, the material culture from these contexts has been associated with the fort rather than the *vicus* (Hoss 2015)

The potential within the datasets of material culture from Vindolanda to illustrate how the site was used and by whom, and the associations with use and discard sites, is best exemplified by one of Vindolanda's finest artefacts – three sherds of painted gladiator glass. All three sherds

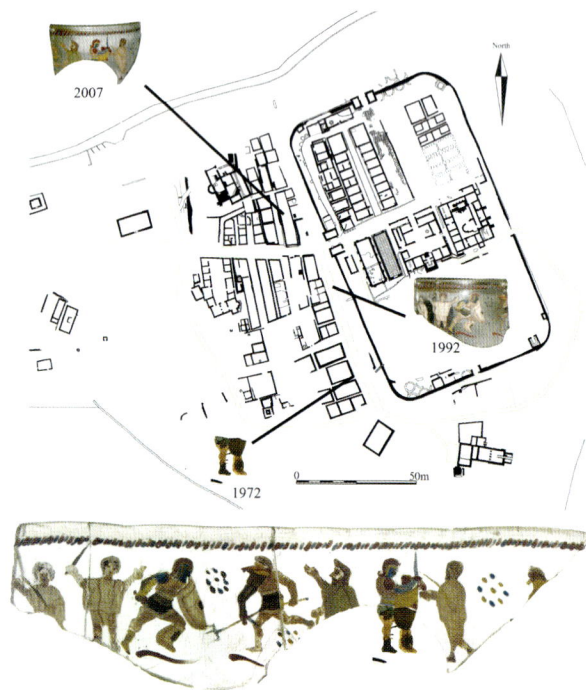

*Fig. 12.2: The Vindolanda gladiator glass spatial deposition and connections*

*Fig. 12.3: The spatial deposition of sword fragments and socketed weapons in the third and fourth centuries at Vindolanda*

came from the same vessel, and join together perfectly. These fragments of glass were recovered over a period of 35 years of excavation. Two of the sherds appeared to have been originally deposited in the western fort ditch. A large portion of the vessel sank to the west side of the ditch and remained trapped in the mud until it was recovered in 1992. The smaller sherd had floated away in antiquity and washed up in an alleyway some 60 m from the first. This was found during the excavations of 1972/3. The final sherd, recovered in 2007, had been placed within a small pit dug into the clay floor of the 3rd century extramural bar or tavern (Fig. 12.2). Each sherd, although clearly a part of the same glass vessel, showed different wear patterns caused by the variations in the depositional and post-deposition environments of the artefacts. The two sherds that were deposited into the fort ditch were duller in comparison to the sherd from the tavern pit, caused by the abrasive friction of water-borne materials moving across the surface of the glass in such a wet environment as the fort ditch.

In the case of the gladiator glass it is possible to construct a hypothesis which includes the use and the breaking of the vessel in the extramural tavern and its discard into the fort ditch. A great deal of other material within the fort ditch may well have also originated from the cleaning out the tavern, depending on how frequently this process took place. Here then, unlike Woerden (Hoss 2015), we can firmly associate material culture from stratified extramural contexts to extramural depositional patterns rather than the discard of fort rubbish in extramural ditches.

## The evidence for combatants

Weapons such as lances, spears, bolt heads and swords formed a significant part of the arsenal of the garrisons of the northern frontier of Roman Britain. Unlike the deposition of many coins, weapons and armour may have been more likely to have been deposited purposely, as ritual or grave goods, or partially as a result of repairs or discard, rather than being dropped or lost.

Many weapons were made from a variety of robust composite materials such as iron, copper-alloy and lead. As such, socketed weapons, swords and lead slingshot can survive in most archaeological environments. Despite their survival, most examples of socketed weapons and swords recovered from the 3rd and 4th century show evidence of varying degrees of decay. Many weapons are recovered in partial form: for example, the majority of swords show that they have been damaged before being deposited. Due to this, patterns of deposition and use may differ, as many weapons were obviously discarded when broken. As Bishop and Coulston pointed out:

'the vast majority of such material has quite clearly been damaged before loss. Moreover, items which appear to be undamaged may in fact have suffered what we might term "invisible attrition": a spearhead may be in immaculate condition when deposited, but it would be useless if its wooden shaft were broken'. (Bishop & Coulston 2006, 27)

The use of weapons has usually been attributed to the military presence in the context of the frontier forts and their adjacent hinterlands on the northern frontier of Roman Britain. Although it would not be unreasonable to suggest that non-combatants could have used weapons for hunting, or personal protection in the same manner as military personnel (Nicolay 2007, 10).

In provincial areas, where a large number of soldiers were recruited, such as the Batavian territories, there is a great deal of evidence to suggest that returning veterans came home with their armour and other military kit (Nicolay 2007, 12). Therefore it is possible that a similar argument may be offered as a partial explanation for the depositional pattern of military kit in extramural settlements especially in the case of veterans.

Two Roman laws on the statute books, the *Lex Iulia de vi privata* and the *Lex Iulia de vi publica*, are thought to have been put forward by Augustus to limit or control the use of weapons by citizens in the Roman Empire (Berger 1953, 554). The word *telum* (to describe a missile weapon) was often used by jurists in conjunction with the *Lex Iulia de vi publica*. An aggressor who was found guilty of using a prohibited weapon was deemed to have committed a crime of a higher degree, and therefore subject to a more severe punishment (Berger 1953, 553). Disarmament may have had more relevance in a potentially volatile frontier area, post conquest and beyond, than in other areas of the empire. The Roman army may have wished to limit access to weapons amongst the surrounding population, especially in times of unrest, in order to maintain the *pax Romana* (James 2011, 15). The extramural population, in the context of a Roman fort, is likely to have included a number of veteran soldiers and it can be assumed that they were allowed to keep their weapons which could have been regarded as personal property. Unfortunately, due to the ambiguity of Roman law and the allowance for the personal ownership of weapons for hunting and personal protection (James 2001, 83) the deposition of weapons alone may not be enough to justify the interpretation that these artefacts belonged to soldiers or reflected their presence.

To reach this conclusion the deposition of weapons must be considered beside a range of military kit.

### Socketed weapons and swords

Vindolanda has one of the largest collections of socketed weapons from a single site on Hadrian's Wall and 67 spear/lance heads are relevant to the 3rd and 4th century periods of occupation covered by this study. Of those, 29 have come from 3rd century contexts which are divided into 22 from intramural contexts and seven from extramural contexts, a ratio of 3:1 (Fig. 12.3).

What is noticeable about the patterning of the artefacts is that very few have come from obvious discard sites such as the fort ditches. Indeed the only areas where they appear to have been purposely buried are a number of small pits on the rampart mounds inside the fort. This suggests that in the 3rd century, considerable thought and effort went into the purposeful disposal of these items, rather than simply tossing them into a fort ditch.

The majority of socketed weapons were deposited within the walls of the fort, with the greatest areas of deposition coming from within the barrack rooms in the north-western quadrant. What is of interest is that many of the same barrack rooms, especially those facing the western rampart, also show the greatest concentration of evidence for non-combatants (through their material culture) inside the fort in this period. It is therefore not unusual, at Vindolanda at least, to find artefacts that can be associated with the soldiers and non-combatants side by side and within domestic contexts.

The few socketed weapons deposited in extramural contexts were mostly individual finds from domestic dwellings (Fig. 12.3), a trait they share with the intramural pattern of deposition. The exception to this is the site of the tavern which had a small concentration in the number of socketed weapons within its social front room. One might expect that such a facility so close to the west gate of the fort would have been frequently used by combatants, therefore a concentration in portable military equipment such as socketed weapons might be expected in such an area, perhaps even used as part of a themed décor within the tavern. What is perhaps more unusual is the absence of socketed weapons from areas between the tavern and fort wall. This space was utilised by metal workshops with large furnaces and high numbers of crucibles recovered from the buildings. One might have expected that the maintenance of weapons and their manufacture would have taken place in these areas, resulting in the occasional casual loss or discard from within these contexts. Cleaning regimes, or lack of cleaning may be a factor here. In the context of the workshops it is unlikely that a build-up of heather, straw and bracken (typical Vindolanda floor covering material from domestic dwellings, and the sort of material in which even a spear, knife, or blade fragment could 'disappear') would have been possible/desirable due to the fire hazard this would have represented.

There are too few examples of sword blades from this period to discern much from their deposition but it can be noted that the one intramural example came from the alleyway between two barracks and it is in an area which has one of the largest concentrations of other weapons and military kit from intramural contexts. Extramural examples were from a large courtyard building (2) which may or may not have directly served a military purpose in this period.

The 4th century spread of socketed weapons from intramural areas shows a broad continuation of the deposition practices of the earlier periods at the site, particularly with respect to domestic spaces. For the first time we see that a relatively large number of socketed weapons (given the small size of the dataset) had been deposited in public spaces such as the roadways to the north and south of the granary site, a potential market area in this period (Birley A. R. 2013b, 23). It might be tempting to simply ascribe such finds to the term 'casual loss' but in such instances it is difficult to disagree with Bishop who observed that this term has been used far too frequently to justify a lack of interpretation in the deposition of this type of artefact (Bishop 2011, 115). To avoid this trap one may therefore consider a number of potential scenarios where by such artefacts were deposited, including the possibility that the weapons in question were no-longer viewed as anything more than scrap metal at their point of loss (nearly all are in poor preservation condition and therefore their condition at point of discard is difficult to determine) and that their deposition could be seen as little more than rubbish removal or dumping. This would fit if the more open and 'social' or 'communal' spaces became general dumping grounds for other domestic material from nearby living spaces, perhaps in the same way that the fort ditches on the western side of the site between the fort at extramural settlement appeared to have been used in the 3rd century. The 4th century chalets, replacing the earlier barracks in the north-western quadrant of the fort, had weapons deposited within their rooms giving them a continued 'military' attribute to what might have been otherwise described as non-military or domestic spaces. Such terms at Vindolanda do not appear to have been mutually exclusive based on the deposition patterns of artefacts alone. The mixed use of space, from fort ramparts, *praetorium*, granaries to chalets appears to have been the norm rather than the exception here. Weapons therefore appeared to have been ever present in those environments and their use, storage and display may have been something that all members of the 4th century community were familiar with.

### *Military kit*

Crossbow brooches appear more frequently on military sites than in purely civil contexts and have been identified as being synonymous with the presence of combatants (Bayley & Butcher 2004, 199). Bayley and Butcher suggested that the large collections of crossbow brooches found at Richborough in 3rd and 3th century contexts are directly connected with the army. They cite the forerunners of this type of brooch as being common on the German *limes*, and a form of this type of brooch may have been

*Fig. 12.4: The spatial deposition of military kit at third and fourth century Vindolanda*

especially produced for the army. Other equipment that is specifically military and which may therefore be directly assigned to combatants includes shield bosses, helmet fragments, armour fragments, scabbard fittings and metal belt decorations. For the purpose of this study all of the aforementioned types of military kit have been plotted in their 3rd and 4th century contexts and it is hoped that military belt decorations will be added to future studies.

## Crossbow brooches

Crossbow brooches ('light', rather than the later developed type) constitute a small sample size with only seven examples from 3rd and 4th century contexts at the site. Of those, five are from 3rd century contexts, with three from the extramural settlement and two from inside the fort (Fig. 12.4). Two of the examples were deposited inside buildings, one in a barrack room opposite the granaries and the second in a domestic house. It is possible that the remaining three crossbow brooches were accidently thrown out with rubbish, as all three of their contexts can be associated with rubbish deposits, especially the fort ditch and adjacent roadways. Rampart mounds were also a convenient place to bury unwanted refuse with a military bearing as has been seen when discussing the deposition of socketed weapons.

The two 4th century examples of crossbow brooches came from very different contexts. The first from the floor of a granary building and the second from a small rampart pit.

## Shield bosses

Eight out of the 13 shield bosses discovered at Vindolanda were deposited in 3rd century extramural contexts. One shield boss fragment was deposited/burned in a bonfire outside the north gate of the fort. The other shield bosses were respectively deposited in a tavern (2), a workshop to the east of the tavern (1), a series of domestic dwellings (4) and a temple/tomb at the western periphery of the settlement (1). The latter may indicate an offering/grave goods associated with the burial of a combatant. The shield boss in the tavern is complemented by the deposition of socketed weapons and it is tempting to suggest that off duty combatants may have been responsible for this deposition, or that the décor of the tavern reflected either the ownership by a veteran/serving soldier or someone who had close military associations. This décor may well have been abandoned when the building ceased to function in *c* AD 270s, having being regarded as decorative rather than functional. From intramural contexts a shield boss was deposited in the barracks and the stables associated with the temple to Jupiter Dolichenus on the northern rampart mound (Birley & Birley 2012, 231–258).

Both of the 4th century shield bosses came from domestic floor material contexts, one each the north-western quadrant and the other from the north-eastern quadrant of the fort.

## Helmet fragments

Seven 3rd century examples of helmet fragments have been recovered from Vindolanda thus far with five deposited in extramural contexts. One may be considered a chance or random find deposited outside a building on the western periphery of the extramural settlement. Further helmet fragments (2) were deposited inside a domestic structure which faced the western fort wall, in a room adjacent to where a crossbow brooch was also found. More examples were recovered from the barracks inside the fort (2).

The four 4th century helmet fragments all came from the north-western quadrant of the fort and all from within buildings. From the most north westerly structure (2), a large dwelling which has shown a great concentration in both military kit and evidence for non-combatants.

## Armour

Fifteen fragments of armour have been positively identified in 3rd century contexts. Of these seven were deposited inside the walls of the fort, on the south-western rampart and the remainder within a series of barrack rooms in the north-western quadrant of the fort. In the barracks there was a notable concentration of military fitments from nearly all of the rooms apart from the centurion's apartment at the northern end of the barrack. It is interesting to observe that out of the three barracks in this area, all of which survived under almost exactly the same archaeological conditions, only one barrack produced a high concentration of military kit in comparison to the others while other aspects of material culture were more evenly spread (such as socketed weapons, beads, gaming counters). One possibility must be that the occupants of this particular barrack block were distinctly different from the others, perhaps in something as basic as their levels of cleanliness or that they may have had greater need to mend and repair their kit (or skills in doing so) than the other combatants stationed nearby. It may be that these rooms had a dual use, as both domestic spaces and workshops, although in the 3rd century there is little other evidence to support any specific industrial activities taking place within those spaces. An equally plausible alternative explanation is that some rooms may have reverted to storage spaces, perhaps even on a temporary basis.

The remaining eight armour fragments were deposited in the extramural settlement with a definite cluster of these finds in the buildings to the north and south of the main street leading to the west gate of the fort at the western edge of the settlement. The single fragment deposited immediately outside the temple/tomb at the western edge of the settlement may have been associated with the helmet fragment located inside the *cella*. One of the remaining fragments was located amongst floor material in domestic buildings close to another significant cluster of military kit, across the road from the courtyard building which produced two sword blades, helmet fragments and shield bosses. Indeed, this area has one of the most significant concentrations of military kit at the site in this period. There are several ways to interpret the deposition of these finds in floor make-up material. Perhaps the most likely is that the construction of the extramural building was undertaken by soldiers themselves rather than non-combatants. Military rubbish, including armour fragments could then find its way into the foundation material for floors. Alternatively the material could have come from recycling military spaces and the material from the floors or rooms of decommissioned military buildings.

In the 4th century, the few armour fragments that have been recovered have mainly came from within building contexts with only one found in a public space on the *via praetoria*.

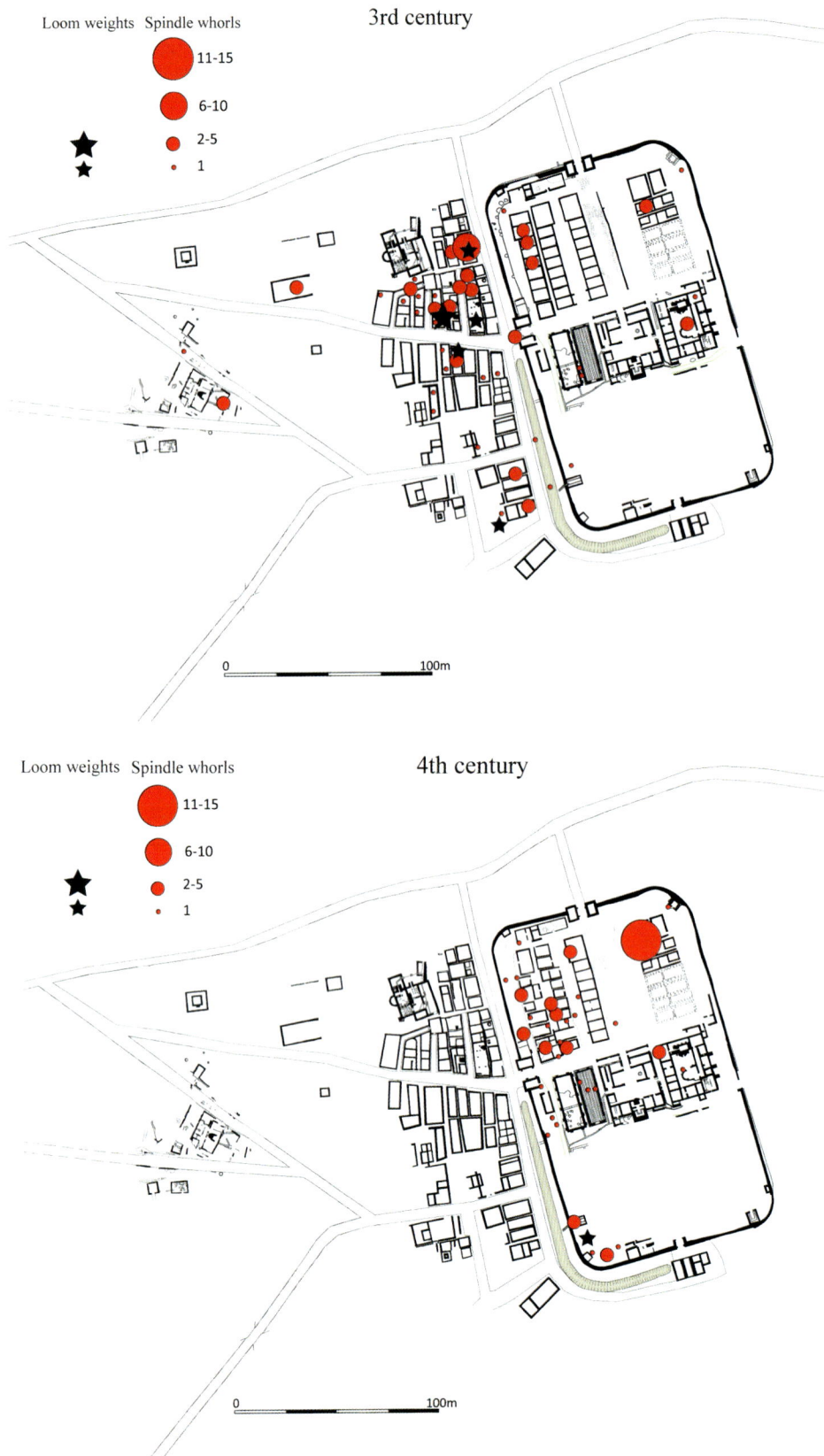

*Fig. 12.5: The spatial pattern in the deposition of third and fourth century spindle whorls and loom weights from Vindolanda*

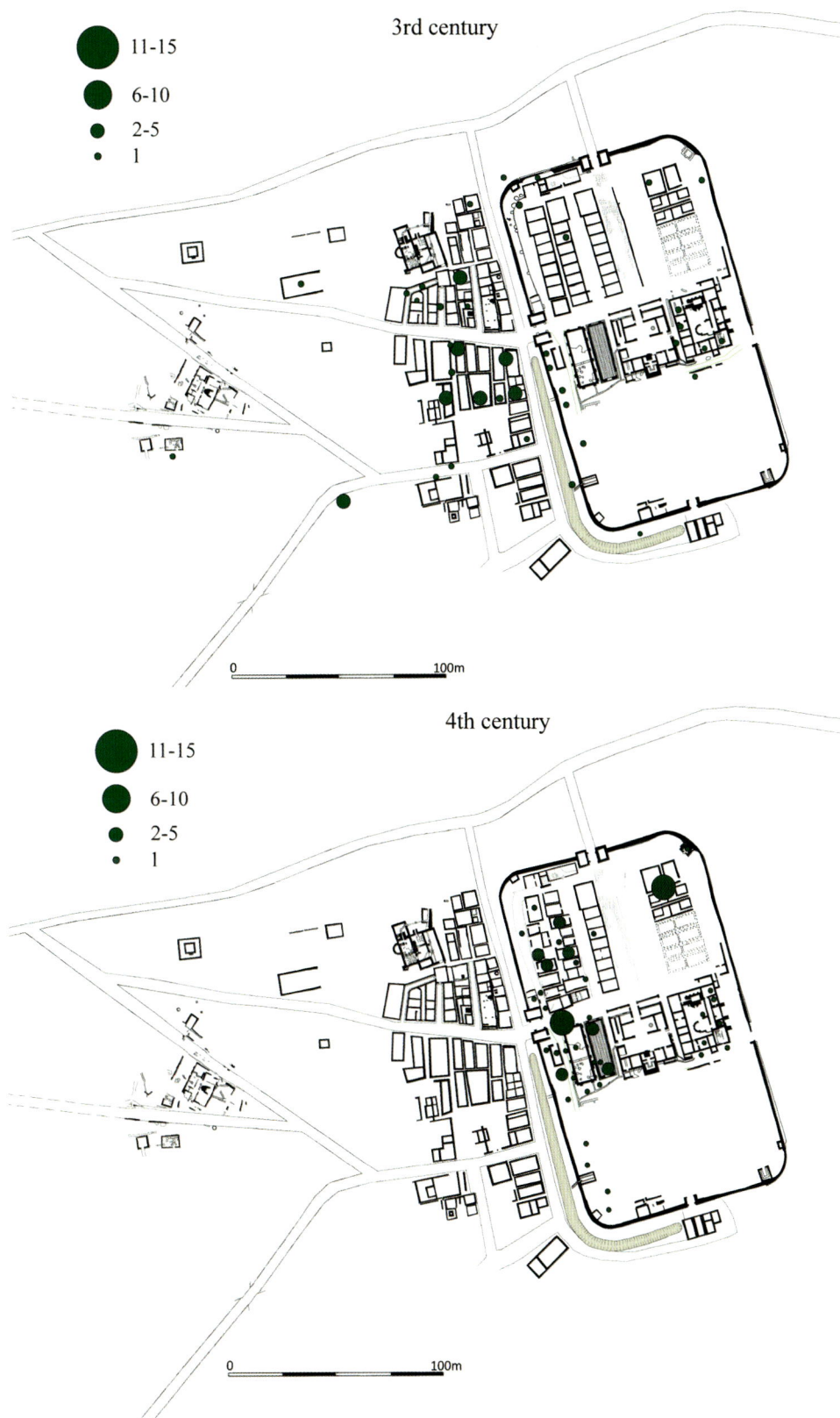

*Fig. 12.6: The spatial deposition of third and fourth century bracelets at Vindolanda*

## *Scabbard fittings*

Twenty-one scabbard fittings (for daggers and swords) were recovered from 3rd century contexts at Vindolanda. The majority of those (15) have come from extramural contexts. Almost all come from a series of domestic dwellings surrounding the 3rd century baths with a few more amongst other houses and shops on the street to the south of the main road leading to the west gate of the fort. This concentration points to a significant presence of combatants in this area of the extramural settlement, perhaps over a prolonged period of time. It raises the question whether or not soldiers resided within these structures. It is possible that some of the buildings may have been used as billets for visiting detachments, but it must be equally possible that parts of the resident garrison may have called these houses their homes. The intramural deposition of scabbard fittings is consistent with domestic deposition in extramural contexts.

The other intramural examples are from mixed contexts, find spots include the temple of Jupiter Dolichenus (1), near the north-eastern angle tower (1) and a rampart pit to the east of the *praetorium* (1). This example illustrates the careful disposal of military kit (outside of domestic spaces). It is likely that this practice can be seen to directly link with the removal of rubbish/cleaning of domestic spaces, such as barracks, from within intramural contexts. At present there is little evidence to suggest that a large proportion of the rubbish generated from buildings/occupation within the fort at Vindolanda could have been moved/disposed of outside the fort or a great distance away. This appears to have been particularly the case in the 4th century when the alleyways behind the rows of chalets in the north-western quadrant of the fort became blocked by midden material. The drains surrounding the 4th century *praetorium* were also quite literally filled to the top with discarded animal bone when excavated in 1998 (Birley *et al.* 1998, 24), suggesting that rubbish was not/no longer being removed from the fort.

## *Wider interpretation of the patterning*

Although the sample size for individual artefact categories of weapons and military kit is relatively small, when these categories are combined with the 3rd century evidence for combatants, they show some significant pattering in the deposition across many of the intramural and extramural parts of the site. Particular clusters of material culture associated with combatants can clearly be seen within the 3rd century barracks, reinforcing their military interpretation. Significant concentrations of military kit can also be see in areas surrounding the 3rd century baths, buildings on either side of the main street in the extramural settlement and in and around a large courtyard building opposite the south-western wall of the fort. All of these spaces, which combine

to cover over 70% of the extramural settlement explored to date, have as large a concentration of military kit as is found inside the 3rd century barracks.

This data reinforces the military nature of the extramural settlement as a vital extension or part of the base itself, rather than a place aside or characteristically different from the military aspects of the site. The distribution of these finds offers a direct challenge to the simplistic binary interpretations of *vicus* and fort. The baths, tavern and a series of workshops may have all been under direct or indirect military control and would have certainly been often frequented by combatants. The concentration of military kit in domestic spaces such as those surrounding the 3rd century baths suggests that this reflects areas of use rather than practices directly associated with rubbish pits or other discard sites.

This pattern of deposition continues into the 4th century with a greater proportion of military kit coming from domestic contexts or those that may be associated with domestic rubbish.

## Evidence for non-combatants as exemplified by adult women

While there is a strong argument for utilising specific artefacts to identify the presence of combatants, it can be more problematic to positively identify all of the different types or groups of non-combatants using 3rd and 4th century material culture. In earlier periods of occupation the presence of adult women and non-combatants inside fort walls has been comprehensively demonstrated by the work of van Driel-Murray through an analysis of the footwear from the 2nd century barracks at Vindolanda (1995, 18) and more recently highlighted by Greene (2013, 17–32). For the purpose of this study, where an analysis of footwear is not possible, the following artefact categories have been included as possible indicators of adult women: spindle whorls, bracelets and beads. To truly understand the complexities between intramural and extramural relationships for adult women, it is worth comparing the spatial patterning from 3rd century intramural/extramural contexts to 4th century data when the majority of occupation was concentrated inside the walls of the fort.

This approach will show that there is a great deal more evidence for adult women in intramural contexts than has previously been known. It will also highlight the significant increase in the density of this material, found also within intramural contexts, in the 4th century.

## *Spindle whorls*

Spindle whorls and loom weights are seen by many as potential representations of female activity in the Roman period (Birley A. R. 2013a, 93; Allison 2013, 96). This is well known at civil sites such as Pompeii, where there are graffiti with numerous names of female spinners attested (Moeller 1969, 566). Roman military scholars have put forward convincing arguments to suggest that this pattern of use would very likely have continued into military contexts, and that the evidence for this would be in the form of the whorls themselves (Allison *et al.* 2005, 8.3). An analysis of the spindle whorl distribution from intramural contexts could, on this basis, be used to support the theory that women were present inside the fort.

The distribution ratio of 3rd century spindle whorls at Vindolanda, between extramural and intramural areas, clearly demonstrates a considerable concentration in the extramural parts of the site (Birley A. R. 2013a, 85–105). However, when the newly acquired data from the north-western quadrant of the fort is added, the ratio of extramural to intramural almost halves from the 9:1 of the previous study to 5:1. While spindle whorls are still found more often in extramural contexts, the recent excavations suggest that these objects were more common inside the fort than previously known. The intramural distribution shows that the majority of have come from domestic spaces within the fort such as barrack rooms, as well as the *praetorium*, and there is a particular concentration from the barracks that faced the western fort wall (6). Here the barracks should perhaps be seen in context with the fort defences and the rampart mound which had eight bread ovens built into its bank. The seventh spindle whorl came from the area of the rampart with the highest concentration of ovens. When these features are combined they suggest a strong domestic composition to this part of the site and it would perhaps be no surprise to see a similar pattern from other intramural areas once they have been fully explored.

Domesticity is also a strong feature in the deposition of spindle whorls from extramural areas with nearly every spindle whorl found within buildings identified as either being partially or fully domestic in character, many complete with internal hearths and ovens. The spindle whorls located in the back rooms of the tavern are from the domestic spaces within the building, bedrooms and living quarters rather than the communal front room. If one were to remove the fort wall from the plan between the barracks and the tavern and simply view the northern and central part of the site as a single area, there is a clear concentration in the spatial deposition from this part of the site (Fig. 12.5).

Aside from the barracks, *praetorium* and other housing at Vindolanda the second greatest concentration of spindle whorls can be found in workshops, especially in the extramural settlement (the area between the bath house and fort wall and the western extremity of the extramural settlement). The spatial spread of this data from workshops, which are discussed in the communal activities section of

this paper, raises questions about the potential for either a mixed gender labour force, perhaps alluding to a family aspect to the work undertaken in those spaces. If spinning was a mainly female activity then these areas may have also been spaces where females, as well as males (perhaps soldiers), actively and perhaps directly contributed towards the economy of the settlement.

It is in extramural areas that we find the majority of loom weights (nine out of the ten) to the north of the main street in the buildings between the road and the bath house. Each loom required at least 'four loom-weights which are assumed to have hung from each corner of the loom to keep the warp spanned' (Wild 1970, 75). Regardless of how many weights looms were actually required, what is left is clearly only a fraction of the number of weights that were once employed by the people of Vindolanda. It is important to note that the presence of a single loom weight may not indicate the existence of a loom at specific locations.

As with all of the other datasets from the site, the shift from the 3rd–4th century distribution of spindle whorls is striking. By 2014, 61 spindle whorls from the 4th century fort have been found, eight more than those recovered from the 3rd century extramural settlement.

The largest increase in the deposition of spindle whorls between 3rd and 4th century deposits is in the barracks, with a particularly high concentration in the north-eastern quadrant. It is possible that this may suggest the presence of a textile workshop and was at the least a space which may have been well known at the time for this activity. However, it is in the north-western quadrant where the most interesting pattern can be seen. Here we have a multitude of smaller independent structures replacing many of the older style integrated barracks and many more of those buildings show signs of spinning taking place than in the previous century of occupation. This may show a greater diversity in the occupation of the buildings, perhaps a higher percentage of non-combatants to combatants in this period.

### Bracelets

Bracelets, made from jet, shale, bone, glass and copper-alloy, are common finds from military sites on the northern frontier of Roman Britain, making them a useful artefact for comparative purposes. Military awards of *armillae* (armlets), indicative of combatants, have not been included in this analysis. The bracelet category includes the more delicate types which may have been worn either individually or in sets or pairs, one on each arm (Birley & Greene 2006, 134). In some cases, such as the glass bracelets worn by Batavians, their use has been associated with the coming of age for women. While armlets were also worn by Celtic men (Roymans 2004, 17) the examples from Vindolanda are thinner and far less ornamental than those normally

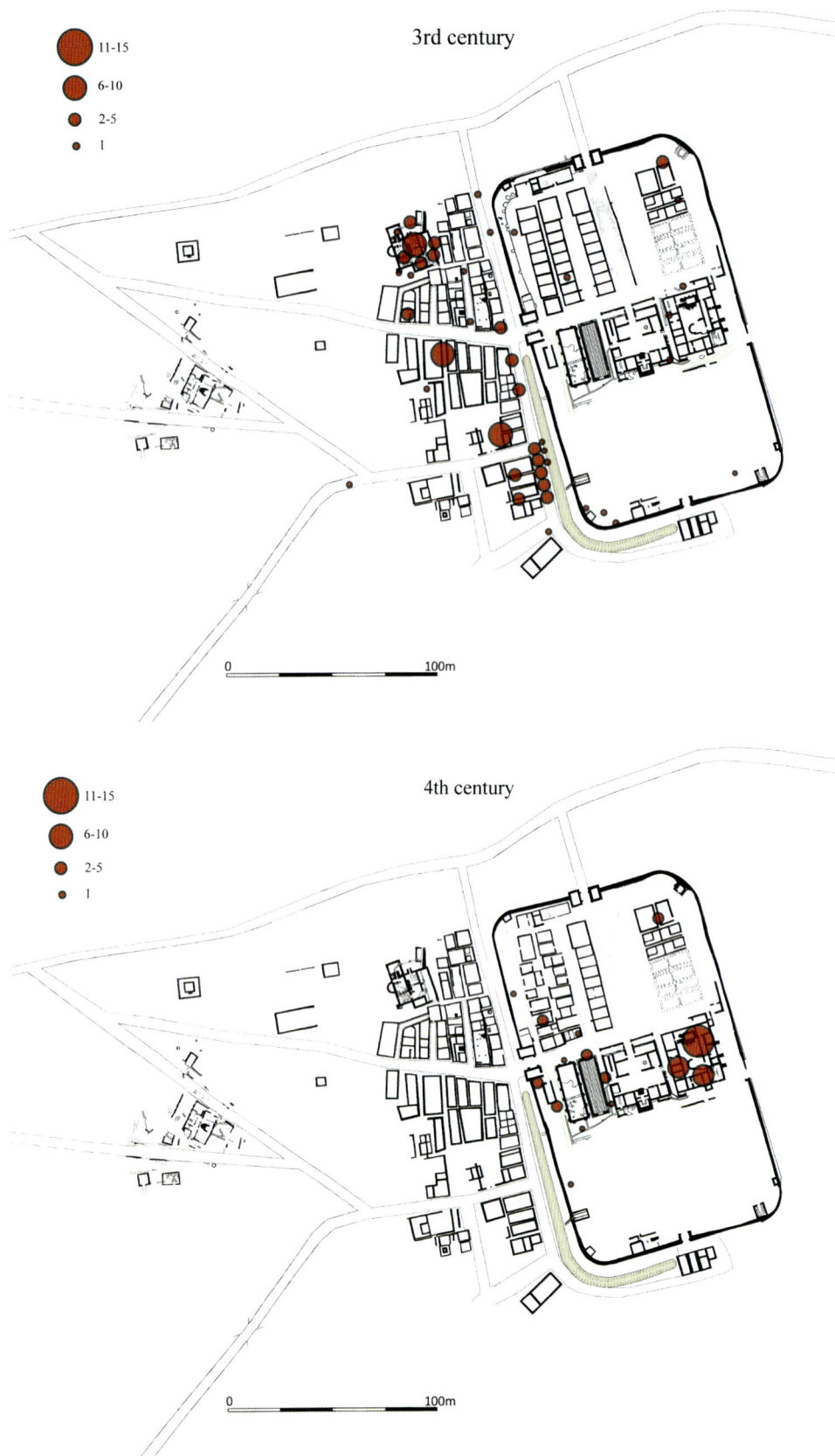

*Fig. 12.7: The depositional pattern of third and fourth century hairpins from Vindolanda*

associated with Celtic men, so bracelets can therefore be seen as *personalia*, a category of artefacts described by Gardner as dress or adornment related artefacts displayed and used by women (Gardner 2007, 131).

By the autumn of 2014 some 50 bracelets were recovered from 3rd century contexts at Vindolanda, 34 of those from extramural contexts and 16 from intramural contexts (Fig. 12.6). This gives a depositional ratio of 3.1:1 towards extramural contexts. As with the spindle whorls, the majority of bracelets from the extramural part of the site have been deposited within domestic building contexts. Others were found in more external social contexts where the process of 'appearing' may have taken place, perhaps in association with the process of 'exchanging' (Gardner 2007, 133), in other words, places where such items would have been openly exhibited by women or perhaps bought and sold. Find spots include the side street leading to the extramural baths (2) and it is interesting that they should be recovered from this area rather than from within the baths where one might expect to find items of personal adornment lost or deposited as clothes were removed for bathing. Bracelets were recovered from the south-west of the extramural settlement on a cobbled yard (2) and (1) from immediately outside a temple doorway.

Bracelets were recovered from outside the walls of the fort, (2) from between the fort wall and ditch on the southern and south-western defences and (1) example from immediately to the northwest of the north-western angle tower. All three bracelets could have been dropped from the fort wall onto the berm between the wall and ditch, rather than by the 3rd century extramural occupants, as access over the fort ditch on the south-western side may have been problematic until it became completely filled with debris by the beginning of the 4th century. Although it is possible for these bracelets to have been washed out of the fort ditch during times of flooding, no bracelets have been directly recovered from the western fort ditches in this period.

Sixteen bracelets were located in intramural contexts in the 3rd century (Fig. 12.6) and their deposition pattern is dominated by two areas, the *praetorium* and the rampart mounds. These included (1) from the centurion's quarters in the north-eastern barracks and (2) from the partially explored barrack room to the south of the *praetorium* and a barrack room in the north-western quadrant. Four of the six bracelets discovered on the western rampart mound came from contexts surrounding rampart ovens. The remaining (2) from the western rampart mound were immediately to the south of the south western guard chamber of the west gate. Single bracelets have been found on the north-eastern and north-western ramparts respectively. No bracelets were recovered from the vicinity of the 3rd century storehouse and granary, a stark

contrast to the patterning displayed in this area in the 4th century. The distribution pattern of 3rd century bracelets is almost identical to that of loom weights and spindle whorls from the same period, if slightly under-represented in barrack room contexts by comparison.

Sixty-six bracelets were recovered from 4th century contexts at Vindolanda, all of which came from the intramural settlement (significantly more than from the 3rd century extramural settlement). The rampart mounds and the *praetorium* maintain a similar distribution pattern to those from 3rd century contexts. There is a marked increase in the numbers deposited with the granaries (likely as a result of this space changing its use from being a storage facility to a market area in the 4th century), with the north-eastern and north-western quadrants accounting for the largest concentration. The pattern of deposition is entirely consistent with the data from spindle whorls from this period.

## Hairpins

Hairpins have been frequent finds from military sites across the Roman Empire and on Hadrian's Wall (Crummy 1979, 157). The sites of South Shields (Allason-Jones 1995, 28) and Vindolanda hold two of the largest collections of Roman hairpins. Hairpins were used by Roman women to hold their hair in a knot but they were also worn as jewellery (Allison 2013, 77). While it has to be acknowledged that it is possible that some hairpins could have had other utilitarian uses, such as holding together a soldier's trousers or pinning together two pieces of leather tent, one would have to ask the simple question as to why a solider would have a hairpin in the first place if it was not for the presence of women at a fort? It is perhaps unlikely that soldiers who did not require hairpins for their hair (perhaps some did) would stockpile hairpins for other uses just in case they needed them. It is therefore perhaps more likely that the hairpins recovered from military sites were used and owned by females, even if some of them may have ended up being used for other purposes along the way.

Vindolanda has an assemblage of 79 hairpins, made of bone, copper-alloy, iron, jet and occasionally silver, that are relevant to the 3rd century and which have been positively identified as having complete heads. Artefacts that have been catalogued as hairpins without their heads have been rejected, as there is little difference between copper-alloy or bone hairpin shanks and regular pins or large needles. The largest concentration in the distribution of hairpins from 3rd century contexts has come from the baths, in the drain running through the floor of the changing room. It is not surprising that so many should come from an area associated with changing clothes and preparing for a bath. It is more difficult to explain why hairpins should be found in significant numbers from the bathhouse toilet drains. A possible explanation is that the hairpins could have been washed down into the toilet drain from the changing room drains before becoming lodged in the toilet sediment. Alternatively they might have come loose when women were using the latrine or have been discarded after the daily cleaning of the baths, with the toilet drain a perhaps handy place to deposit rubbish.

Aside from the 3rd century baths, the greatest quantities of hairpins have come from the western fort ditch and berm (Fig. 12.7). Bone hairpins were especially light and buoyant, and it is possible that many may have found their way into the ditch having been washed from road surfaces or through the main extramural drains, nearly all of which emptied into the fort ditch on the western side of the fort. The five hairpins dropped onto the berm between the ditch and the fort walls and may have been either washed out of flooded ditches and deposited in the silt or dropped from the rampart mounds.

The concentration of hairpins in the north-eastern angle tower/toilet block stands out among intramural contexts, especially as the excavations of two other toilet blocks on the south-east and south-western corners of the fort did not produced any hairpins (although they were found nearby on rampart mounds). If we can accept the fact that hairpins may have been associated with women this may suggest that women living in intramural spaces may have used the north-eastern toilet block in preference to the south-western latrine. However, such a possible segregation is perhaps at odds with the evidence for the dual use of the bathhouse latrine in the same period. The *praetorium,* which was perhaps a more private facility, produced the final two intramural examples, both of which were bone.

If the hairpins recovered from the site of Vindolanda were mostly worn by women, either in their hair or as jewellery and this data was taken alone, then the distribution could be clearly presented as an indication of the dominance of female related activity in extramural contexts in this period. However, just as with spindle whorls and bracelets, several hairpins have come from rampart deposits close to ovens and a single barrack room also had a concentration of spindle whorls and bracelets.

Fifty-three hairpins have been recovered from 4th century contexts at Vindolanda, and all of those from intramural locations. The *praetorium* has by far the largest concentration of hairpins (29), followed by the streets that surrounded the former granaries (7) and the south-western rampart mound to the south of the western gates southern tower (7). It is interesting to note that here both domestic and social spaces (the area surrounding the granaries) have the greatest concentration of hairpins. The barracks/chalets in the north-eastern quadrant, unlike in the 3rd century deposits, had a smaller distribution of hairpins as did the north-western quadrant (4), three of which came from buildings close to the granary area.

## Beads

A wide variety of beads are commonly found on all Roman sites and plotting the distribution of beads on Roman military sites may reveal the presence or otherwise of female activity (Hodgson 2013, 18–28). While it is accepted that beaded necklaces were most likely worn by women or children, some types of bead, such as large melon beads with a diameter of 20–30 mm, may be more readily associated with either personal adornment by any sex or rank/affiliation and may have been used for decoration on items such as sword hilts, horse gear or other fitments (Allason-Jones 1995; 1996, 189–199; Birley & Greene 2006, 39; Allison 2013, 82). It should be noted that a context or building with a large concentration of beads deposited within, such as a bathhouse, is likely to indicate use as personal adornment rather than for other purposes (certainly not as horse gear).

The 3rd century contexts at Vindolanda have produced 269 beads (Fig. 12.8). Of these, 34 (13%) have been found in intramural contexts. Four of the beads were melon beads. This shows a heavy deposition and recovery rate of beads from extramural contexts (235 examples, 87%). This data supports the statistical evidence from the spatial deposition of hairpins, suggesting that although women were present inside the 3rd century fort, their numbers may have been fewer than in the extramural areas.

Over 80% of the structures in the 3rd century extramural settlement had beads deposited within them. Melon beads have been separated from the overall bead assemblage and given their own plots as they are recognised as having had a dual purpose, as both ornaments/jewellery for humans and in some cases for horse gear or decoration on sword hilts or other equipment, and are mainly attributed to 1st and 2nd century dates (Allison *et al.* 2005, 8.2.1.e; Allison 2013, 86; Birley & Green 2006, 39). The extramural buildings on the northern side of the east–west street running to the west gate of the fort have the heaviest concentration of beads at the site, particularly those between the bathhouse and the fort wall. One might expect a concentration of beads to be found in the baths, as the removal of clothing would have facilitated loss. It is no surprise, therefore, that the majority of beads recovered from the baths have come from the drains in the changing room and toilet block where they could have easily rolled into the drains and become lodged in silt. As the drains were fed by emptying the baths' water tanks, they would have been flushed out fairly frequently, making it likely that the beads recovered represent a small fraction of those that may have been lost in this building. Similarly, excavation of a toilet block attached to an earlier pre-Hadrianic military bath house also produced very few artefacts other than a large quantity of beads (Birley A. R. 2001, 41).

The intramural deposition of beads, especially those from barrack contexts in the north-western quadrant, is highly significant here, especially in light of the recently published paper by Hodgson who noted that evidence for the presence of women using material culture datasets such as beads from other northern frontier sites showed that 'as things stand the counter-assertion that there was widespread accommodation of [soldiers'] wives in *contubernia* lacks any substantial archaeological basis' (Hodgson 2013, 27). As with the sites used by Hodgson to support his arguments, not every barrack room had beads deposited within them, but the 11 rooms from the barracks in the north-western quadrant at Vindolanda represents a significant increase on the very low average of a few beads per barrack block that Hodgson noted from his study (2013, 24).

Outside barrack areas, and showing a similar pattern to that of the other material datasets associated with female occupation, are contexts connected with the defences of the fort such as the south-west angle tower/toilet and rampart mounds. Three beads were deposited near a series of ovens built in to the ramparts to the south-west of the granaries, and a further two were deposited on the roadway to the south of the *praetorium*. Perhaps the greatest anomaly in the data is the lack of bead deposition from within the *praetorium* itself, a location where one might expect to find beads from a mixed gender population.

As has been discussed, in the 4th century living accommodation at Vindolanda was largely confined to intramural areas, and the number of beads from those 4th century contexts is almost three times greater than those from 3rd century intramural spaces (Fig. 12.8). This shift perhaps best demonstrates the demographic changes that took place between the 3rd and 4th centuries at Vindolanda when the extramural settlement appears to have been abandoned and the population is concentrated within the walls of the fort, as well a possible change in fashion or depositional practices at the site. In simple terms, the 4th century plot of the north-western quadrant almost appears to mirror the intensity of the 3rd century extramural plot from the area between the baths and the fort wall. There are fewer buildings/rooms and spaces from this period of occupation without beads than those with beads. Based on this evidence, if one accepts that beads can be used to explore the presence of women on Roman military sites, then the evidence for women inside the 4th century fort at Vindolanda is as compelling as it was in the 3rd century, if not more so.

### Interpretation of the patterning for non-combatants

In a previous study of the spatial spread of material culture from Vindolanda it was noted that 'the low percentage of artefacts related to adult women from within the 3rd century fort may be a reasonable reflection of their presence and relative numbers' (Birley A. R. 2013a, 101–102). Based on the evidence presented in this paper this basic conclusion

must remain intact, for the moment, but an increasing volume of evidence for the presence of women inside the 3rd century fort has shown that they may have not been such a minority population within intramural contexts as previously suggested. The new datasets from Vindolanda offer a more robust case for the presence of women inside the barracks as shown by the spatial patterning of beads, spindle whorls and hairpins. This data is highly significant when considered in the context of the data presented by Hodgson (2013, 25). While it is true the Vindolanda data does not support the presence of women through material culture in every single barrack room, there is enough to suggest that they were there with the majority of the finds coming directly from occupational material rather than rubbish deposits associated with the abandonment of the buildings.

Certainly, based on the balance of the available data the presence of women in these contexts appears to have increased in the 4th century, quite considerably. Therefore the notion that the '*contubernia* may have preserved an all-male character' offered by Hodgson would seem implausible conclusion for Vindolanda, based on the updated evidence presented in this paper (Hodgson 2013, 27).

We can now suggest that for women living at Vindolanda in the 3rd century gender was not the greatest barrier to where they lived or worked. It is more likely that social status, role, family association and affiliations would have played significant roles. The same set of challenges would have undoubtedly have applied to those women who lived and worked, through self-determination or otherwise, in the extramural settlement in this period. It is just as likely that the women who lived in intramural spaces would have worked and used extramural parts of the site and the opposite may have also been true. Certainly women living inside the barracks would have used the bath house, an extramural facility, most likely contributing to the dataset of material culture from this building by depositing beads and hairpins into the bath house drains. The same would apply to the shops, taverns, workshops and communal spaces in both areas of the site.

A model which allows for the division of the spaces within the 3rd century settlement of Vindolanda along such gender specific lines would now seem an extremely tenuous proposition, once again breaking down the barrier between the simple binary categories of *vicus* and fort.

The 4th century data, from a period when there was no extramural occupation at the site shows that there can be absolutely no question about the strong presence of women inside the fort during this period, from almost every context.

### Shared activities – literacy, industry and gaming

The final category examined by this paper explores the deposition of a range of artefacts which may be seen as representative of activities undertaken by a broad

*Fig. 12.8: The pattern of deposition for third and fourth century beads at Vindolanda*

3rd century

4th century

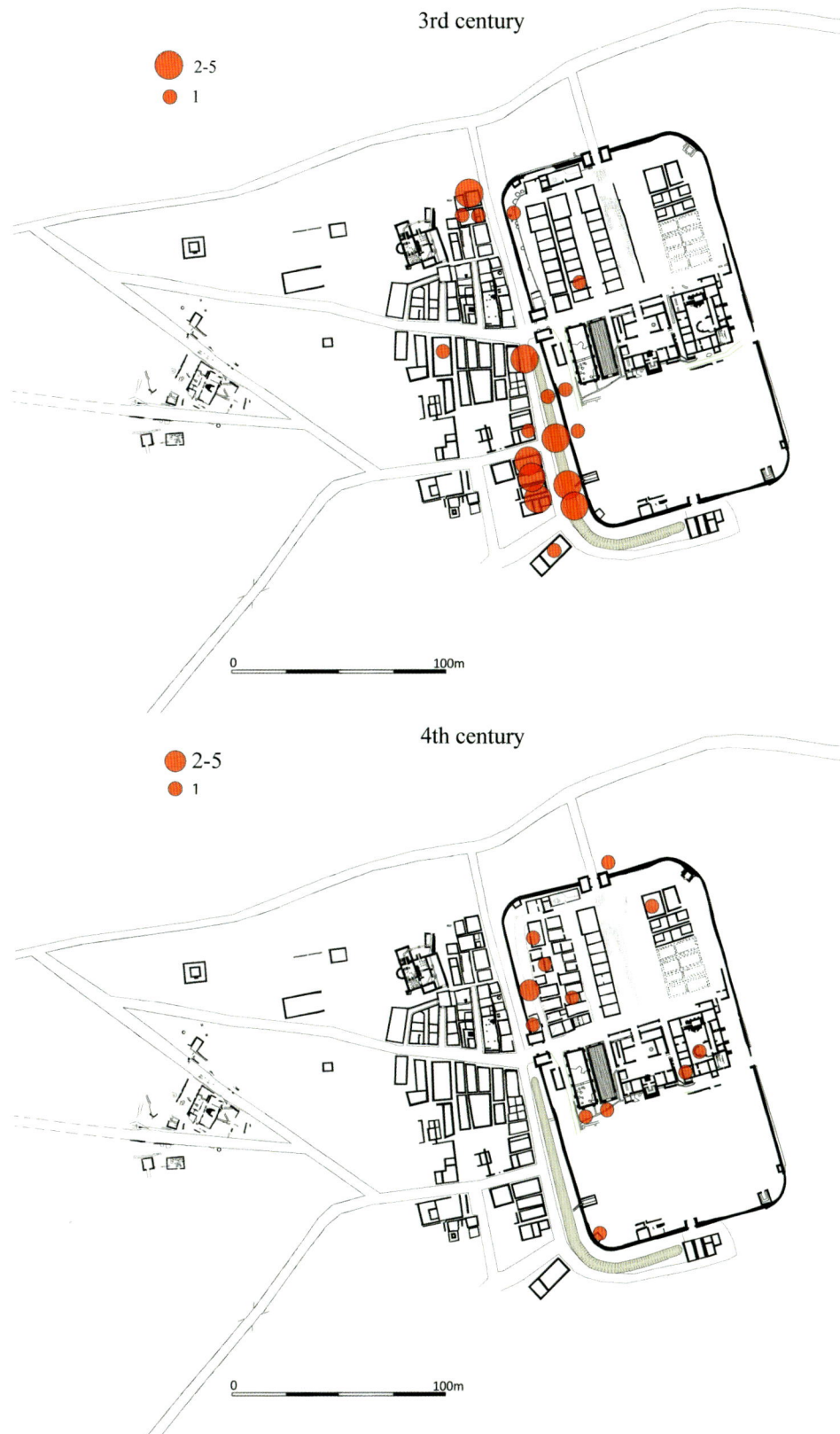

*Fig. 12.9: Styli from third and fourth century contexts at Vindolanda*

cross-section of the community. Although we have separated out artefacts that may or may not have been used by different categories of people at Vindolanda both of these potentially artificial groups were members of the same community, and combatants and non-combatants had access to many of the same materials, foods, customs and perhaps shared ideals, lives and experiences. Let us therefore examine a group of artefacts which could have crossed boundaries and defined those who lived in forts and extramural settlements as much as any other. The finds categories that have been chosen for this section include stylus pens (as potential indicators of literacy), crucibles (for industry) and gaming counters (for leisure and gambling).

Literacy was certainly an important aspect of military life (Bowman & Thomas 2003), perhaps a vital one. Therefore it is no surprise to see this category continue to be well represented through artefacts such as stylus pens into the 3rd and 4th centuries, even when the tablets themselves did not survive from those periods (Birley 1999, 7). Stylus pens were normally forged from iron, although some were of copper alloy or silver, and they varied in size and decoration to fit the hand and requirements of the owner. The pens are robust artefacts that survive even when corroded and can normally be easily identified in the archaeological record. As Hanson and Conolly noted 'these are relatively common artefacts, they offer the potential, on the basis of their context and distribution, for some assessment of the extent of literacy in Roman Britain.' (Hanson & Conolly 2002, 155).

The analysis of the spatial distribution of crucibles acknowledges the fact that the Roman army used large quantities of metal for everything from building (iron nails, t-clamps and lead) to the manufacture of utensils, tools, pens, fixtures and fittings, and the maintenance and repair of weapons and armour. The result of this was that the manufacture of goods through metalworking was likely to be a key activity on a Roman military site where the raw materials for such a process were readily available, and a large number of people would have been needed to support and maintain this industry. *Fabricae* are often identified in intramural contexts on the northern frontier of Roman Britain such as at Elginhaugh (Hanson *et al.* 2007, 86). However, not all metalworking may have been a military process, and the name 'Vindolanda' first came to prominence with the discovery of an altar to the god Vulcan, the god of smithing, set up by the *vicani Vindolandesses* (Collingwood & Wright 1965, 535 – *RIB* 1700).

Ideally, a blacksmith would have needed at least three others to support his work in keeping the fires burning and striking the metal, not to mention the labour intensive process of mining ore or the collecting of bog ore/fuel and smelting (Sim & Ridge 2002, 56–57). Each workshop could then have a support network of dozens of labourers. Despite the intensive nature of the processes involved, some

aspects of metalworking such as smithing are relatively difficult to trace in the archaeological record (Heyworth 1993, 211). This is due to the fact that smithing hearths could be set up almost anywhere and were destroyed after use to extract the metals. Often the best evidence for metalworking having taken place is either the presence of slag or crucibles from copper working (Oleson 2008, 111). A large number of crucibles were discovered outside the walls of the 3rd century fort at Vindolanda in buildings which had surviving industrial hearths. Although these buildings may have been operated by the army, and metal working and military occupation are often seen as synonymous (Bishop & Coulston 1993, 184–185), the evidence for metalworking in extramural settlements implies that non-combatants may also have been involved in this work as suggested in *RIB* 1700.

When not engaged in other activities, members of the military communities appear to have spent some of their leisure time playing games. Gaming may have been a prominent feature of life on the frontier, its scale and organisation distinguishing itself from other settlement types which were further behind the frontier zone where a wider range of leisure activities/distractions may have been accessible. Most gaming boards from northern Britain appear to have been used for one specific game and its variants, *ludus latrunculorum* (a war game), played on a board lined with squares or spaces (normally 8 × 8 or 9 × 9 spaces, but could be as many as 12 × 12 spaces). This game used gaming counters lined in rows or phalanxes called little soldiers or bandits, *latrunculi* (Bell 1979, 83). The counters were made from a variety of materials including pottery, bone and stone (and there were undoubtedly some made from wood) to professionally manufactured gaming pieces made from coloured glass and jet (Allason-Jones & Miket 1984, 56–59, Bishop & Dore 1988, 204–209).

Plotting the distribution of counters at sites can be used to reveal the locations where people may have gathered to socialise and relax, and have commercial interactions with other community members, areas which might otherwise remain hidden from our considerations of life in these settlements.

## *Stylus pens*

The spatial spread of *styli* from 3rd century Vindolanda shows a significant trend towards extramural deposition (Fig. 12.9) with the overwhelming majority of artefacts found in those areas despite significant parts of the intramural site now being excavated to a comparable level. Although the 3rd century extramural deposition is concentrated on the area immediately adjacent to the fort it does not neatly match the pattern in the distribution for either of the combatant or non-combatant sections in this paper, rather showing its own distinctive trend. For the first time we see a large number of artefacts finding their way into the fort ditch that lies between the two areas. As this is clearly a discard site, it is impossible to determine beyond doubt whether or not those pens originated from intramural/extramural areas or both, or were ritually or purposefully discarded into the ditch as has been suggested for the Walbrook site in London (Merrifield 1965). However, with the nearby concentration in the adjacent extramural buildings it is perhaps more likely that they had an extramural origin than otherwise. It is in these areas that literate and clerical activities took place in 3rd century. The question remains by whom? It is likely that the answer to this question, based on the analysis of other artefact categories may be that a wide cross-section of society engaged in expressions of literacy.

The patterning in the 4th century is far more comparable to the other datasets of the same period, with deposition of styli entirely within a number of domestic and building spaces inside the fort.

### Crucibles and industry

As with the data from the spatial deposition of stylus pens, the evidence for crucibles and industry at Vindolanda is concentrated into a central zone on the site, that which lines the edge of the fort's western defences (although there are four clear areas of industrial activity in the extramural settlement, starting from its periphery to the west). A particular concentration of crucibles matches that of the most northerly cluster of 3rd century *styli* and both of these were most likely associated with the industrial activities taking place there (Fig. 12.10). Smaller scale industrial activities, as shown by the crucibles found on the rampart mounds, can be seen having taken place inside the fort along the western ramparts. These areas undoubtedly utilised the bread oven built into the rampart mound, expanding their utilitarian function into a broader pattern of use and functionality. We have already seen that these areas show some of the greatest concentrations of evidence for non-combatants with beads, bracelets, hairpins and spindle whorls. It raises the interesting possibility of women being either directly or indirectly (through supporting roles) being engaged in industrial activities at Vindolanda.

The overall picture for industry at the site in the 3rd century is one of fairly tightly designated areas in which this activity took place, but that the majority of these processes happened in extramural contexts regardless of who was engaged in the activity itself.

Industrial activities continued in to the 4th century at Vindolanda, and we can note that these activities continued on the ramparts and that part of the granary site (Fig. 12.10) (Birley, A. R. 2013b, 36) and *praetorium* (Birley, R. *et al.* 1998) were also sacrificed for industrial purposes.

### Gaming counters

Two hundred and twenty gaming counters have been recovered from 3rd century contexts at Vindolanda to date and they are one of the most commonly found artefacts at the site (Fig. 12.11). The number represented here may only reflect, as with all of the other categories of find, a fraction of the counters that were present. Indeed, those made of bone are unlikely to have survived in as significant quantities as in earlier anaerobic levels at the site, and wood not at all from 3rd and 4th century deposits. However, the over 200 counters remain a significant dataset from the site. While they appear in many different contexts and from all areas, the plotted data clearly show that there were some parts of the site where gaming may have taken place on a larger scale than others. These include two areas of the extramural settlement; the bath house and building to its east and a roadway outside a large courtyard building on the south side of the settlement. Neither of these places was particularly hidden away from view, suggesting that gaming was a socially acceptable activity that could potentially be engaged by a large proportion of the community. Of particular note is the concentration inside the fort within the centurion's barracks in the north-eastern quadrant. Here one can perhaps see similarities between Vindolanda and the so called gambling den at the fort of Abu Sha'ar on the Red Sea coast of Egypt. This site has produced a significant number of gaming boards and counters (Mulvin & Sidebotham 2003, 602–616). At Abu Sha'ar a gaming room/den was identified inside the walls of the fort with a concentration of six boards inside a single room. Many other game boards were found across the site in both intramural and extramural contexts (Mulvin & Sidebotham 2003, 614). The concentration of game boards and counters at Abu Sha'ar, as with Vindolanda, is significant as both highlight the importance of gaming in the daily lives of members of the Roman military community, even to those who served in different centuries and at opposite ends of the Empire.

Like Abu Sha'ar, evidence for gaming at Vindolanda continued into the 4th century with evidence for intensive gaming maintained in the barracks of the north-eastern quadrant, appearing on the market street in front of the granaries, in the *praetorium* for the first time and in and around the rampart and toilet block on the south-western corner of the fort.

## The complexity of intramural and extramural relationships

There can be little doubt that when a person from Vindolanda or elsewhere referred to him/herself as a *vicanus*, they knew perfectly well the context of what they wished to express, but unfortunately we do not. This paper has attempted

3rd century industrial areas and crucibles

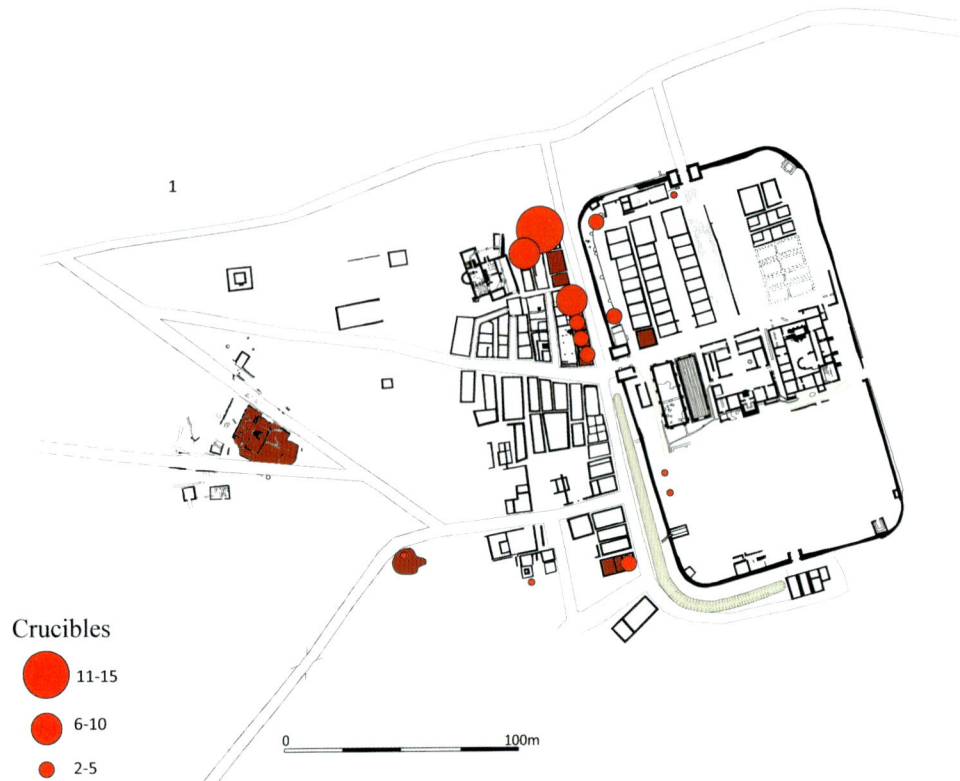

1

Crucibles

11-15

6-10

2-5

0          100m

4th century industrial areas and crucibles

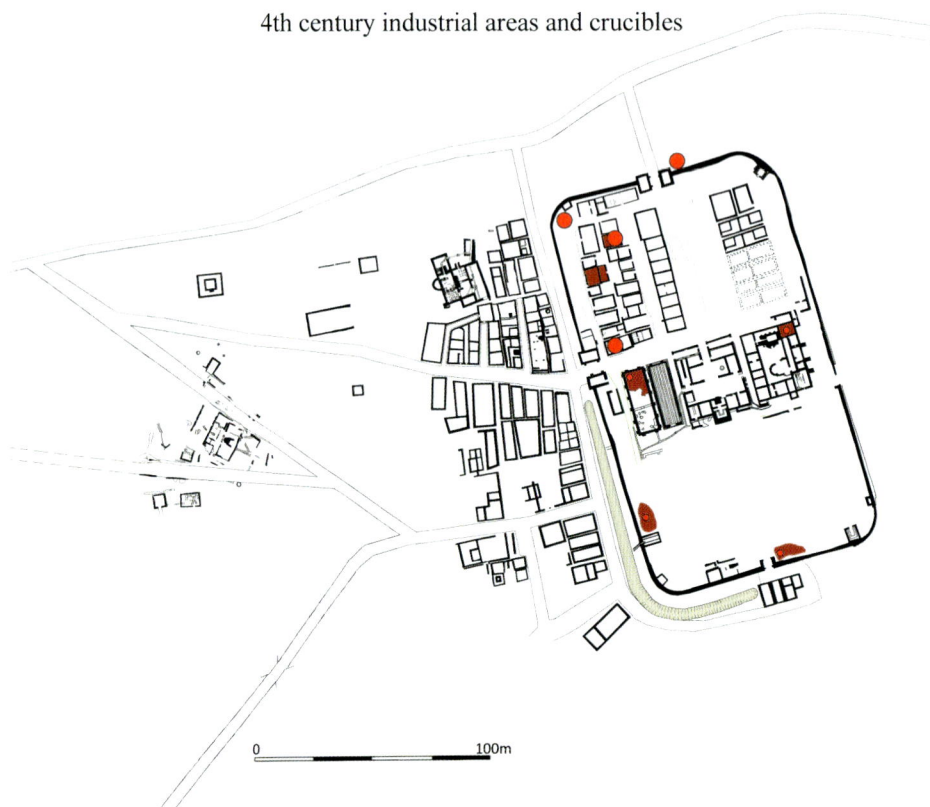

0          100m

*Fig. 12.10: The distribution of third and fourth century crucibles and workshops (marked in dark grey)*

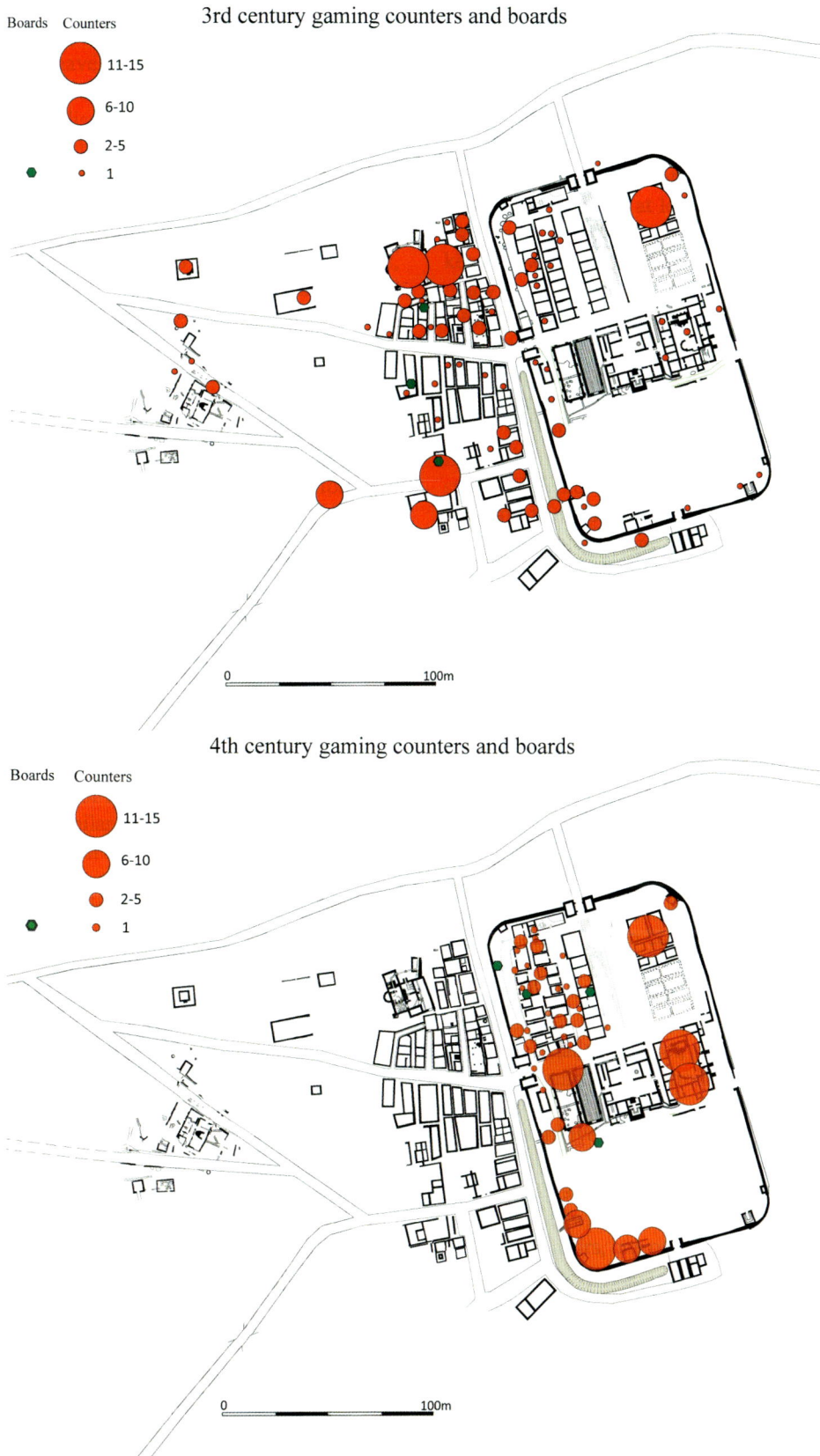

*Fig. 12.11: The third and fourth century deposition of gaming counters from the site of Vindolanda*

to highlight and then bypass the more obvious pitfalls associated with this terminology. In doing so it has turned to the every-day artefacts left behind by the people of the frontier to explore some of the many complexities of extramural and intramural relationships.

This has shown that the 'civilian' *vicus* at Vindolanda had as many military attributes as the fort itself. There were large concentrations of artefacts, in particular military kit, that can be seen to have been directly associated with combatants in extramural contexts. Particular concentrations of this material surrounded the baths, tavern and a large courtyard building in the southern part of the settlement. During the same period of occupation, the 'military' spaces within fort barracks displayed a spatial patterning which can be said to have been strongly associated with the activities of 'non-combatants' such as the deposition of beads, spindle whorls and bracelets, alluding to a far more mixed habitation than has previously been argued (Birley, A. R. 2013a, 104). This is an important consideration at a time when there is renewed scepticism on the volume of evidence for the presence of non-combatants in these areas (Hodgson 2013), a scepticism which cannot be carried to Vindolanda on the balance of evidence presented here. Was the garrison at Vindolanda then less military in its bearing than others, more bohemian? Or is it that, as shown by the example of the gladiator glass, that the site has a better rate of preservation than the others explored to date, and larger dataset from which comparisons can be made and can therefore sustain more robust conclusions.

The concentration of shared activities such as literacy, industrial work and gaming all show their own distinctive patterns, again with both intramural and extramural aspects represented. Gaming appears to have been endemic within this community, an aspect of frontier life that has parallels that stands up to evidence from other frontiers of the Roman Empire.

The image presented of Vindolanda in this period is one of fluidity rather than conformity to a strict doctrine of military rigidity, or indeed an idealised vision of what it was to be a Roman soldier living in a barrack (Hodgson 2013).

By the 4th century arguments for separation, either physically or ideologically, are difficult to maintain with the data presented here. Instead we see evidence for a diverse community living cheek by jowl within the walls of the fort. The extramural areas once occupied in the 3rd century had been abandoned with very little 4th century coinage or pottery deposited in those areas, and a similar pattern appears to have been the case at other sites on Hadrian's Wall, most notably at the nearby site of Housesteads (Allason-Jones 2013, 83). Perhaps then in this period, more than any other, the proximity of those residing within the fort walls to each other would have engaged an even stronger sense of community, ideals and goals than in earlier periods.

In the 4th century it appears that through an analysis of material culture the people of the frontier were truly 'in it together' in almost every way.

## Abbreviations

*RIB*

*JRS*

## Ancient sources

Arrianus. *Periplus Maris Euxini*. Ed. and trans. A. Liddle (2003). Bristol, Classical Press.

Arrianus. *Periplus Maris Euxini*. Ed. F. Haverfield (1911). Arrian as legate of Cappadocia. (212–233) *Essays by Henry Francis Pelham: Late President Of Trinity College, Oxford and Camden Professor of Ancient History*. Oxford, Clarendon Press.

Arrianus. *Tactical Handbook and the Expedition Against the Alans*. Trans. J. G. DeVoto (1993). Chicago, Ares Publishers.

*The Augustan History – Lives of the Later Caesars* 'Aelius Spartianus', Hadrian, 57–87. Trans. A. Birley (1976) London, Penguin Classics.

Caesar, *De bello Gallico*. trans. S. A. Handford (1982). London, Penguin Books.

Caesar, *De bello civili*. trans. J. F. Gardner (1967). London, Penguin Books.

*The Digest of Justinian, vol. 2*. Ed. A. Watson (1998). Philadelphia, University of Pennsylvania Press.

Festus, Sex. Pompeius. *De verborum significatione* (*On the meaning of words*) ed. W. M. Lindsay (1931), 93–467. Paris.

Isidorus of Seville, *Etymologiae*, ed. W. M. Lindsay (1911). Oxford, Clarendon Press.

St Patrick, *Epistola*. Hood, A. B. E. (1978). St Patrick, *His Writings and Muirchu's Life*. London, Phillimore.

Pliny the Elder, *Historia Naturalis* (*Natural History*). Ed. and trans. Rackham (1963). Loeb Classical Library. London, Heinemann.

Valerius Maximus, *Factorum ac dictorum memorabilium libri IX* (*Nine Books of Memorable Deeds and Sayings*), ed. and trans. S. Bailey (2000). Cambridge MA & London: Harvard University Press.

Varro M. Terentius, *De lingua Latina (On the Latin language)*, trans. R. Kent (1938). Loeb Classical Library. London, Heinemann.

## Bibliography

Allason-Jones, L. (1995) 'Sexing small finds.' In P. Rush (ed). *Theoretical Roman Archaeology: Second Conference Proceeding*, 21–32. Aldershot, Avebury (Worldwide Archaeology Series 14).

Allason-Jones, L. (1999) Women and the Roman army in Britain. In A. Goldsworthy & I. Haynes, (ed.) *The Roman Army As A Community*, 41–51. Journal of Roman Archaeology Supplementary Series 34. Portsmouth RI, Journal of Roman Archaeology.

Allason-Jones, L. (2001) Material culture and identity. In S. James & M. Millett (ed.) *Britons and Romans: Advancing an Archaeological Agenda*, 19–25. York, Council for British Archaeology Research Report 125.

Allason-Jones, L. (2009) The small finds. In A. Rushworth (ed.) *Housesteads Roman Fort – The Grandest Station. Vol. II. The Material Assemblages*, 430–483. Swindon, English Heritage.

Allason-Jones, L. (2013) The *vicus* at Housesteads: a case study in material culture and Roman life. In R. Collins & M. Symonds (eds) *Breaking Down Boundaries: Hadrian's Wall in the 21st century*, 71–84. Journal of Roman Archaeology Supplementary Series 93. Portsmouth RI, Journal of Roman Archaeology.

Allason-Jones, L. & Mckay, B. (1985) *Coventina's Well: A shrine on Hadrian's Wall.* Chollerford, Chesters Museum.

Allason-Jones, L. & Miket, R. F. (1984) *The Catalogue of Small Finds from South Shields Roman Fort.* Newcastle-upon-Tyne, Society of Antiquaries of Newcastle-upon-Tyne. Monograph Series 2.

Allison, P. M. (2004) *Pompeian Households: An Analysis of the Material Culture.* Los Angeles. Costen Institute of Archaeology, University of California Monograph 42.

Allison, P. M. (2006) Artefact distribution within the auxiliary fort at Ellingen: evidence for building use and for the presence of women and children. *Sonderdruck aus Bericht der Romisch-Germanischen Kommission 87*, 389–451.

Allison, P. M. (2008) Dealing with legacy data – an introduction. *Internet Archaeology* 24. (http://intarch.ac.uk). [accessed 3 June 2009]

Allison, P. M. (2013) *People and Spaces in Roman Military bases.* Cambridge, Cambridge University press.

Allison, P. M., Ellis S., Fairbairn, A., and Blackall, C. (2005) Extracting the social relevance of artefact distribution within Roman military forts. *Internet Archaeology* 17.4 (http://intarch.ac.uk). [accessed 5 November 2007]

Bayley, J. & Butcher, S. (2004) *Roman Brooches in Britain: A Technological and Typological Study based on the Richborough Collection.* London, Reports of the Research Committee of the Society of Antiquaries of London 68.

Berger, A. (1953) *Encyclopedic Dictionary of Roman Law.* Transactions of the American Philosophical Society. New Series 43(2). Philadelphia, American Philosophical Society.

Bidwell, P. (1985) *The Roman Fort of Vindolanda.* English Heritage Archaeological Report 1, London.

Bidwell, P. (1999) *Hadrian's Wall 1989–1999: A Summary of Recent Excavation and Research Prepared for the Twelfth Pilgrimage of Hadrian's Wall.* Carlisle, Cumberland & Westmorland Antiquarian Society & The Society of Antiquaries of Newcastle-Upon-Tyne.

Bidwell, P. & Hodgson, N. (2009) *The Roman Army In Northern England.* South Shields, Arbeia Society.

Bidwell, P. & Speak, S. (1994) *Excavations at South Shields Roman Fort: Volume 1.* Newcastle-upon-Tyne, Society of Antiquaries of Newcastle-upon-Tyne with Tyne and Wear Museums.

Biggins, J. A. & Taylor, D. J. A. (2004a) Geophysical survey of the vicus at Birdoswald Roman Fort, Cumbria. *Britannia* 35, 159–178.

Biggins, J. A. & Taylor, D. J. A. (2004b) A Geophysical Survey at Housesteads Roman Fort, April 2003. *Archaeologia Aeliana* 5(33), 52–60.

Biggins, J. A. & Taylor, D. J. A. (2007) The Roman Fort at Castlesteads, Cumbria: a geophysical survey of the vicus.

*Transactions of the Cumberland and Westmoreland Antiquarian and Archaeological Society* 3(7), 15–30.

Birley, A. R. (2001) *Vindolanda's Military Bath Houses: The Excavations of 1970 and 2000.* Bardon Mill, Vindolanda Trust.

Birley, A. R. (2003) *The Excavations of 2001–2002:Volume 1.* Vindolanda Research Report 2003. Bardon Mill, Vindolanda Trust.

Birley, A. R. (2010) The Nature and Significance of Extramural Settlement at Vindolanda and Other Selected Sites on the Northern frontier of Roman Britain. PhD Thesis, University of Leicester. https://lra.le.ac.uk/handle/2381/8306

Birley, A. R. (2013a) The fort wall: a great divide? In R. Collins & M. Symonds (eds) *Breaking Down Boundaries: Hadrian's Wall in the 21st Century*, 85–104. Journal of Roman Archaeology Supplementary Series 93. Portsmouth, RI, Journal of Roman Archaeology.

Birley, A. R. (2013b) *The Vindolanda Granary Excavations.* Greenhead, Roman Army Museum Publications.

Birley, A. & Birley, A. R. (2012) A new Dolichenum, inside the third-century fort at Vindolanda. In M. Blömer & E. Winter (eds) *Iuppiter Dolichenus*, 231–258. Orientalische Religionen in der Antike 8. Tübingen, Mohr Siebeck.

Birley, A. R. & Blake, J. (2005) *The Vindolanda Excavations of 2003–2004.* Bardon Mill, Vindolanda Trust.

Birley, A. R. & Blake, J. (2007) *Vindolanda Research Report 2005/6.* Bardon Mill, Vindolanda Trust.

Birley, E. B. & Keeney, G. S. (1935) Fourth report on excavations at Housesteads. *Archaeologia Aeliana* 4(12), 204–259.

Birley, E. B., Richmond, I. A. & Stanfield, J. A. (1936) Excavations at Chesterholm–Vindolanda: third report. *Archaeologia Aeliana* 4(13), 218–257.

Birley, R. E. (1977) *Vindolanda: A Roman frontier post on Hadrian's Wall.* London, Thames & Hudson.

Birley, R. E. (1994) *Vindolanda Research Reports, New Series: Volume I. The Early Wooden Forts.* Greenhead, Roman Army Museum Publications.

Birley, R. E. (2009) *Vindolanda: A Roman Frontier Fort on Hadrian's Wall.* Stroud, Amberley.

Birley, R. E., Blake, J. & Birley, A. R. (1998) *Vindolanda 1997 excavations: Praetorium Site Interim report.* Bardon Mill, Vindolanda Trust.

Bishop, M. C. (2011) Weaponry and military equipment. In L. Allison-Jones (ed.) *Artefacts in Roman Britain: Their Purpose and Use*, 114–132. Cambridge, Cambridge University Press.

Bishop, M. C. & Coulston, J. C. N. (1993) *Roman Military Equipment.* London, B. T. Batsford.

Bishop, M. C. & Coulston, J. C. N. (2006) *Roman Military Equipment: From The Punic Wars To The Fall Of Rome* (2nd edition). Oxford, Oxbow Books.

Bishop, M. C. & Dore, J. N. (1989) *Corbridge: Excavations of the Roman Fort and Town, 1947–1980.* London, Historic Buildings and Monuments Commission for England.

Blagg, T. F. C. & King, A. C (1984) *Military and Civilian in Roman Britain: Cultural Relationships in a Frontier Province.* British Archaeological Report 136. Oxford, British Archaeological Reports.

Blake, J. (2014) *The Excavations of 2007–2012 in the Vicus or Extramural Settlement ('Area B').* Greenhead, Roman Army Museum Publications.

Bowman, A. K. (1994) *Life and Letters on the Roman frontier: Vindolanda and its People.* London, British Museum.

Bowman, A. K. & Thomas, J. D. (1994) *The Vindolanda Writing-tablets: Tabulae Vindolandenses II.* London, British Museum.

Bowman, A. K. & Thomas, J. D. (2003) *The Vindolanda Writing-tablets: Tabulae Vindolandenses III.* London, British Museum.

Bowman, A. K. & Wolf, G. (1996) *Literacy and Power in the Ancient World.* Cambridge, Cambridge University Press.

Buxton, K. & Howard–Davis, C. (2000) *Bremetennacum: Excavations at Roman Ribchester 1980, 1989–1990.* Lancaster Imprints Series 9. Lancaster, Lancaster University Archaeological Unit.

Breeze, D. J. (2006) *J. Collingwood Bruce's Handbook to the Roman Wall* (4th edition) Newcastle-upon-Tyne, Society of Antiquaries of Newcastle-upon-Tyne.

Breeze, D. J. (2013) Preface. In R. Collins & M. Symonds (eds) *Breaking Down Boundaries: Hadrian's Wall in the 21st Century,* 7–8. Journal of Roman Archaeology Supplementary Series 93. Portsmouth RI, Journal of Roman Archaeology.

Breeze, D. J. & Dobson, B. (1969) Fort types on Hadrian's Wall. *Archaeologia Aeliana* 5 (29), 15–32.

Breeze, D. J. & Dobson, B. (2004) *Hadrian's Wall* (4th edition) London, Penguin History.

Brickstock, R. (2013) Vindolanda 2008: The Coins. In A. Birley, *The Vindolanda Granary Excavations,* 121–126. Greenhead, Roman Army Museum Publications.

Collingwood, R. G. & Wright, R. P. (1965) *The Roman Inscriptions of Britain* I: *Inscriptions on Stone.* Oxford, Clarendon Press.

Collingwood, R. G. & Wright, R. P (1991) *The Roman Inscriptions of Britain* II: *Instrumentum domesticum.* Oxford, Clarendon Press.

Collins, R. (2006) Late Roman frontier communities in northern Britain: A theoretical context for the 'end' of Hadrian's Wall. In B. Croxford, N. Ray, R. Roth & N. White (eds) *TRAC 2005. Proceedings of the Fifteenth Annual Theoretical Roman Archaeology Conference,* 1–11. Oxford, Oxbow Books.

Cool, H. E. M. (2002) Exploring Romano-British Finds Assemblages. *Oxford Journal of Archaeology* 21(4), 365–380.

Crummy, N. (1979) A Chronology of Romano-British Bone Pins. *Britannia* 10, 157–163.

Crummy, N. (2007) Six honest serving men: a basic methodology for the study of small finds. In R. Hingley & S. Willis (eds) *Roman Finds: Context and Theory,* 59–66. Oxford, Oxbow Books.

Frere, S. (1987) *Britannia: A History of Roman Britain* (3rd edition). London, Routledge.

Gardner, A. (2007) Artefacts, contexts and the archaeology of social practices. In R. Hingley & S. Willis (eds) *Roman Finds: Context and Theory,* 129–139. Oxford, Oxbow Books.

Hanson, W. S. & Conolly, R. (2002) Language and literacy in Roman Britain: some archaeological considerations. In A. E. Cooley (ed.) *Becoming Roman and Writing Latin?,* 151–164. Journal of Roman Archaeology Supplementary Series 48. Portsmouth RI, Journal of Roman Archaeology

Hassall, M. (1976) Aspects of the Notitia Dignitatum. In R. Goodburn & P. Bartholomew (eds) *Britain in the Notitia,* 103–118. British Archaeological Report S15. Oxford: British Archaeological Reports

Hassall, M. (1999) Homes for heroes: married quarters for soldiers and veterans. In A. Goldsworthy & I. Haynes (eds) *The Roman Army as a Community,* 35–40. Journal of Roman Archaeology Supplementary Series 34. Portsmouth RI, Journal of Roman Archaeology.

Haynes, I. (1999) Military service and cultural identity in the *auxilia.* In A. Goldsworthy & I. Haynes (eds) *The Roman Army as a Community,* 165–174. Journal of Roman Archaeology Supplementary Series 34. Portsmouth RI, Journal of Roman Archaeology.

Hayworth, M. (1993) *Excavations at Segontium (Caernarfon) Roman Fort, 1975–1979,* 211–213. Council for British Archaeology Research Report 90. York, Council for British Archaeology.

Hill, J. D. (2001) Romanisation, gender and class: recent approaches to identity in Britain and their possible consequences. In S. James & M. Millet (eds) *Britons and Romans: Advancing an Archaeological Agenda,* 12–19. Council for British Archaeology Research Report 125. York, Council for British Archaeology.

Hingley, R. & Willis, S. (2007) *Roman Finds: Context and Theory.* Oxford, Oxbow Books.

Hodgson, N. (2013) The accommodation of soldiers' wives in Roman fort barracks - on Hadrian's Wall and beyond. In R. Collins & F. McIntosh (ed.) *Life in the Limes: Studies of the peoples and objects of the Roman Frontiers,* 18–28. Oxford, Oxbow Books.

Hodgson, N. & Bidwell, P. T. (2004) Auxiliary barracks in a new light: recent discoveries on Hadrian's Wall. *Britannia* 35, 121–158.

Hoss, S. (in press). Military versus civilian and legionary versus auxiliary: the case of Germania Inferior. In *The Proceedings of the 2009 Limes Congress.* Newcastle Upon-Tyne.

James, S. J. (1999) The community of the soldiers: a major identity and centre of power in the Roman Empire. In P. Baker, C. Forcey, S. Jundi & R. Witcher (eds) *TRAC 98. Proceedings of the Eighth Annual Theoretical Roman Archaeology Conference. Leicester 1998,* 14–24. Oxford: Oxbow Books.

James, S. J. (2001) Soldiers and civilians: identity and interaction in Roman Britain. In S. J. James & M. Millett (eds) *Britons and Romans: Advancing an Archaeological Agenda,* 77–89. Council for British Archaeology Research Report 125. York, Council for British Archaeology.

James, S. J. (2011) *Rome and the Sword.* London, Thames & Hudson.

Jilek, S. & Breeze, D. (2007) The detris of life: the contribution of small finds to understanding smaller military installations. In R. Hingley & S. Willis (eds) *Roman Finds: Context and Theory,* 199–213. Oxford, Oxbow Books.

Merrifield, R. (1965) *London City of the Romans.* London, Guild Publishing.

Millett, M. (1984) Forts and the origins of towns: cause or effect? In T. F. C. Blagg & A. C. King (eds) *Military and Civilian in Roman Britain: Cultural Relationships in a Frontier Province,* 65–74. British Archaeological Report 136. Oxford, British Archaeological Reports.

Mulvin, L. & Sidebotham, S. E. (2004) Roman game boards from Abu Sha'ar (Red Sea Coast, Egypt). *Antiquity* 78(301), 602–618.

Moeller, W. (1969) The male weavers in Pompeii. *Technology and Culture* 10, 561–566.

Nicolay, J. (2007) *Armed Batavians: Use and significance of weaponry and horse gear form non-military contexts in the Rhine delta (50BC–AD 450)*. Netherlands, Amsterdam University Press.

Oleson, J. P. (2008) *The Oxford Handbook of Engineering and Technology in the Classical World*. Oxford, Oxford University Press.

Peachin, M. (2004) Review of M. Tarpin (2002) *Vici et pagi dans l'Occident romain*. Collection de l'École française de Rome 299. Rome, Ecole Francaise de Rome. *Journal of Roman Studies* 94, 271.

Peddie, J. (2005). *The Roman War Machine* (3rd edition) Stroud, Sutton.

Rivet, A. L. F. & Smith, C. (1979) *The Place Names of Roman Britain*. British Archaeological Report S781. Oxford, British Archaeological Reports.

Rivet, A. L. F. (1980) Celtic names and Roman places. *Britannia* 11, 1–20.

Rushworth, A. 2009. *Housesteads Roman Fort – The Grandest Station. Vol I. Structural Report and Discussion*. Swindon, English Heritage.

Salway, P. (1965) *The Frontier People of Roman Britain*. Cambridge, Cambridge University Press.

Sommer, C. S. (1984) *The Military Vici in Roman Britain: Aspects of their Origins, their Location and Layout, Administration, Function and End*. British Archaeological Report 129. Oxford, British Archaeological Reports

Sommer, C. S. (1988) *Kastellvicus und Kastell: Untersuchungen zum Zugmantel im Taunus und zu den Kastellvici in Obergermanien und Ratien*. Fundberichte Aus Baden-Wurttemberg. 458–705.

Sommer, C. S. (1997) Der Saalburg – *vicus*. Neue Ideen zu alten Plänen. In E. Schallmayer (ed.) *Hundert Jahre Saalburg. Vom Römischen Grenzposten zum Europäischen Museum*, 155–165. Mainz Am Rhein, Philipp von Zabern.

Sommer, C. S. (1999) The Roman army in SW Germany as an instrument of colonisation: the relationship of forts to military and civilian *vici*. In A. Goldsworthy & I. Haynes (eds) *The Roman Army as a Community*, 81–93. Journal of Roman Archaeology Supplementary Series 34. Portsmouth RI, Journal of Roman Archaeology.

Sommer, C. S. (2006) Military *vici* in Roman Britain revisited. In R. J. A. Wilson (ed.) *Romanitas: Essays on Roman Archaeology in Honour of Sheppard Frere on the Occasion of his Ninetieth Birthday*, 95–146. Oxford, Oxbow Books.

Symonds, F. A. & Mason, D. (2009) *Frontiers of Knowledge: A Research Framework for Hadrian's Wall, Part of the Frontiers of the Roman Empire World Heritage Site*. Durham, Durham University.

Tarpin, M. (2002) *Vici et pagi dans l'Occident romain*. Collection de l'École française de Rome 299. Rome, Ecole Francaise de Rome.

Tomlin R.S.O & Wright R.P. & Hassall M.W.C. 2009. *The Roman Inscriptions of Britain III*. Oxford, Oxbow Books.

van Driel Murray, C. (1993) The leatherwork. *Vindolanda: Research Reports, New Series. Volume III, The Early Wooden Forts*, 1–75. Bardon Mill, Vindolanda Trust.

van Driel Murray, C. (1999) And Did Those Feet in Ancient Time … feet and shoes as a material projection of self. In P. Baker, C. Forcey, S. Jundi & R. Witcher (ed.) *TRAC 98: Proceedings of the Eighth Annual Theoretical Roman Archaeology Conference Leicester 1998*, 131–140. Oxford, Oxbow Books.

van Driel Murray, C. (2009) Ethnic recruitment and military mobility. In A. Morillo, N. Hanel & E. Martín (eds) *Limes XX: Estudios Sobre La Frontera Romana*, II, 813–822. Madrid, Polifemo.

Wild, J. P. (1970) *Textile Manufacture in Northern Roman Provinces*. Cambridge, Cambridge University Press.

Wilson, P. R. (2002). *Cataractonium: Roman Catterick and Its Hinterland – Excavations and Research, 1958–1997, Part 1 & 2*. York, Council for British Archaeology.